IMPERIAL RUSSIA

A SOURCE BOOK, 1700–1917

EDITED BY

BASIL DMYTRYSHYN
PORTLAND STATE COLLEGE

Holt, Rinehart and Winston, Inc.
NEW YORK, CHICAGO, SAN FRANCISCO,
ATLANTA, DALLAS, MONTREAL,
TORONTO, LONDON

TO
VIRGINIA

IMPERIAL RUSSIA

A Source Book, 1700-1917

PREFACE

The purpose of *Imperial Russia* is similar to that of the companion volume *Medieval Russia*; namely, to make available to the student, the general reader, and the scholar who is not a specialist a collection of basic sources on political, social, economic, and cultural life in Russia from 1700 to 1917. It is neither a text nor a substitute for a text but an attempt to furnish what a text cannot offer—extensive, illustrative source material to amplify and enrich the text.

The selections included in this volume have been drawn from such diverse sources as official decrees, proclamations, instructions, treaties, letters, memoirs, political programs, charters, and literary classics. Many of the selections are fairly long, in order to allow an adequate acquaintance with the documents chosen. For the sake of convenience they are arranged in chronological order. Each of the selections has been provided with a brief introduction to indicate the source from which it was taken and to place it in its proper historical perspective.

In dealing with a subject as complex and controversial as the history of Imperial Russia, the task of selecting representative documents to illuminate some of the more significant aspects of the country's life and development has not been easy, and some readers may feel that their areas of interest are under-represented. The selections included, however, were chosen because they seem to be genuine sources for the understanding of Imperial Russia.

Wherever possible I have used existing translations of documents. Except where indicated in the introductions, such translations are reproduced here in their original form. Because there is no uniform way to transliterate from Cyrillic to Roman characters the selections that different scholars have translated show a diversity in the spellings of certain Russian names. ·

Many documents of this collection, however, appear here in English for the first time. In my translations I have aimed for accuracy rather than elegant rendition, and with only minor exceptions I have adhered to the system of transliteration used by the Library of Congress. Thus, all Russian proper names ending in ий have been rendered as -ii- (Speranskii); the Ю has been rendered throughout as -iu- (Iurii); and the Russian Я has been rendered as -ia- (Iaroslav). An exception to this rule is the word бояр which, because of the widely used English spelling, has been rendered as boyar. All apostrophes have been excluded and

v

plurals of nontranslatable Russian words (*boyars, gubernias*) have been anglicized.

It is a pleasant custom among scholars to thank all those who have in any way made possible the appearance of a work. I acknowledge my indebtedness to the following institutions and individuals: the Research Committee of Portland State College for financial assistance that helped to defray travel expenses for the selection of material from the Russian collection at the University of California at Berkeley; the library personnel at the University of Illinois and at Portland State College for their friendly cooperation; the publishers who kindly permitted me to reprint selections from previously translated material (individually acknowledged under each item); my colleagues at Portland State College for their sustained interest in and encouragement of this project; and Mrs. Nikki Owens and Mrs. Nancy Maurer, who volunteered their typing services.

My special thanks go to my wife, Virginia, who, now as in the past, has been my most conscientious critic as well as my best proofreader.

Basil Dmytryshyn

Portland, Oregon
June 1967

CONTENTS

1

The Revolt and Punishment
of the Streltsi in 1698:
An Eyewitness Account

During the reign of Peter the Great (1682–1725)
Russia underwent a profound transformation. The
moving force behind this change was the tsar himself, who opened the country to Western European
influence and forced many fundamental economic,
social, financial, and cultural changes. Many of his
innovations were accepted without opposition, but
others were imposed brutally, without regard for the
fate of those who objected.

The first to experience Peter's wrath were the
streltsi, a corps of musketeers of the Russian army
whom the young tsar had held in contempt since
boyhood. A rebellion of the streltsi took place in
1698 while Peter was touring western Europe. They
were dissatisfied with their conditions and when
they were denied answers to their petitions, they
mutineed. Loyal forces crushed the mutiny in a
single encounter, captured a number of the leaders,
executed some, and imprisoned others. When he
learned of the rebellion, Peter interrupted his tour,
returned to Moscow, and began reprisals against the
streltsi. Some two thousand of the streltsi were executed, many more subjected to inhuman tortures,
and the remainder dismissed from service forever.

From Johann Georg Korb, Diary of an Austrian Secretary of Legation at the
Court of Czar Peter the Great. Translated from the original Latin and edited by
Count MacDonnell (London: 1863), vol. 2, pp. 70–92, 101–114. Items in
brackets are mine. Spellings have been modernized to facilitate reading.

1

Four regiments of the *streltsi* which lay upon the frontier of Lithuania had nefariously plotted to change the sovereignty. The Theodosian Regiment abandoned Viazma, the Athanasian Regiment quit Belaia, the Ivanov left Rzhev-Vladimirov, and the Tikhonian quit Dorogobuzh, in which places they were in garrison. They drove away the loyal officers that happened to be among them, distributed military rank among themselves—the readiest for crime being held the fittest for command. At once they menaced death to all in their next neighborhood, if they would not freely join their party or should resist their design. . . .

The [loyal] regiments of the guards [in Moscow] got notice to hold themselves in readiness to march at an hour's notice, and that those who should decline to act against the sacrilegious violators of the Majesty of the Crown would be held guilty of misprision of their crime—that no ties of blood or kindred held binding when the salvation of the sovereign and the state were at stake—nay, that a son might slay his father if he rose to ruin his fatherland. General [Patrick] Gordon [1635–1699] strenuously executed this Spartan measure, and exhorted the troops entrusted to him to perform their noble task, telling them how there could be no more glorious meed than to have saved the sovereign and the state. Nor was the circumstance of this expedition against the mutineers being undertaken on the very festival of Pentecost, devoid of happy omen that the spirit of truth and justice would confound the councils of the wicked—as the event clearly showed. For there was discord between the three principal chiefs of the rebellion, which delayed their march for three days, and so gave the loyal army time to encounter the traitor *streltsi* at the monastery dedicated to the most Holy Resurrection which some call Jerusalem. For the stupendous nature of their crime brought dread, delay, and divided counsels; the concord that is sworn for crime is seldom indeed lasting. Had the rebels reached that monastery but one hour sooner, safe within its strong defenses, they might perhaps have worn out the loyal troops with such long and fruitless labor that they might have lost heart, and victory, hostile to loyalty, might have set her garland upon the brow of treason. But fortune denied to their turbulent counsels the object that they sought. A slender stream not far distant waters the rich land hereabouts. On its hither banks the tsar's troops, and on the opposite the rebel columns had begun to appear. The latter were trying the ford and if they had been really determined to pass, the tsar's force could hardly have hindered them. Fatigued with a long march, and still without sufficient force, Gordon, setting wisdom in the place of strength, strolled along to the bank to talk with the *streltsi*. He found them deliberating about crossing, and dissuaded them from their undertaking with words like these: "What did they mean to do? Whither were they going? If they were thinking of Moscow, the night was too close at hand to admit of their reaching it—there was not room for them all on the hither bank;

they would do much better to remain at the other side of the river and give the night to thinking sensibly of what they ought to do on the morrow." The seditious multitude could not resist such friendly advice; they were too much fatigued in body to have stomach for a fight where they did not expect one.

Meantime, Gordon having well examined all the advantages of the ground, occupied an advantageous height with his troops. Shein* consenting, he distributed the posts, and fortified himself, leaving nothing undone that could contribute to his own defense and security or to the detriment and damage of the enemy. With equal loyalty and resolution the imperial colonel of artillery, de Grage, bravely performed his part. He made a lodgement upon the height, placed his great guns in advantageous position, and distributed all in such excellent order that almost the whole success that attended the affair was due to the artillery. At the first dawn of day, by command of General Shein, General Gordon went again to parley with the *streltsi,* and after blaming somewhat the disobedience of the regiments, he discoursed largely of the Tsar's clemency, telling them that it was not by sedition and mobbing together that the desires of soldiers should be made known to the Tsar. Why, contrary to their usual dutiful behavior, contrary to the sanction of discipline, had they deserted the places that had been entrusted to their loyal keeping? Why should they have driven away their officers, and have broken out in designs of violence? Let them rather propose their requests peaceably, and, mindful of the loyalty they owed, return to their appointed stations, that should he see them yield to their duty, should he hear them beg for it, he would get them both satisfaction for their requests, and pardon, when they confessed it, for their shameful conduct. But Gordon's speech did not move the now hardened stubbornness of the false traitors; and they only saucily answered that they would not go back to their appointed quarters until they had been allowed to kiss their darling wives at Moscow, and had received the arrears of their pay.

Gordon related to Shein the perfectly determined wickedness of the *streltsi.* But as the latter was unwilling to despair altogether of the repentance of the criminals, Gordon did not decline to try a third time to mollify the fierce passions of the rebels with offers of payment of their arrears, and pardon for the crime they were bent upon. Not only was the advice utterly fruitless, but they were in such a state of exasperation that the negotiator was near to have paid dearly for his pains. Already they loudly upbraided and rebuked this man of grave authority, their former general; they warned him to be off forthwith, and not to waste his words to no purpose, unless he wanted a bullet to chastise his marvellous audacity; that they recognized no master, and would listen to orders from

---

* General Alexei Shein acted in Peter's absence as Commander-in-Chief of the Russian forces.—*Ed.*

nobody; that they would not go back to their quarters; that they must be admitted into Moscow; that if they were forbidden, they would open the road with force and cold steel. Their unexpected fierceness stung Gordon, and he deliberated with Shein and the other military officers present what was to be done. There was no difficulty in deciding the course that should be adopted against men that were predetermined to try the strength of their arms. Everything was made ready, consequently, for the onset and the fight, as the stubborn unanimity of the traitors forced on that last resort. Nor were the *streltsi* less busy; they drew up their array, pointed their artillery, dressed their ranks, and, as if the strife in which they were about to mingle was a struggle with a foreign foe, they preceded it with the customary prayers and invocation of God . . .

Countless signs of the cross being made on both sides, the attack began on both sides from a distance. The first reports of cannon and small arms proceeded from the lines of General Shein, by whose command none of the pieces were loaded with ball; for he entertained a secret hope that the reality of resistance might terrify them into submissive return to obedience. But the first volley passing without wound or slaughter only added courage to guilt. Vastly emboldened, they responded by a discharge, by which some were laid lifeless, and several were bloodily wounded. When death and wounds had given a sufficient lesson that stronger remedies must be applied, Colonel de Grage was no longer required to dissemble his stout will, and allowed to discharge his great guns, fraught with deadly lead and iron. Colonel de Grage had been anxiously waiting for this command, and lost no time in firing with such precision into their rebel ranks that their furious passions were checked, and the strife of resistance and skirmishing of the mutineers was changed into a piteous slaughter.

When they saw that some were stretched lifeless, courage and fierceness at once deserted the terror-stricken *streltsi*, who broke into disorder. Those that retained any presence of mind endeavored by the fire of their own artillery to check and silence that of the Tsar; but all in vain; for Colonel de Grage had anticipated that design, and directing the fire of his pieces upon the artillery of the seditious mob, whenever they would go to their guns, vomited such a perfect hurricane upon them that many fell, numbers fled away, and none remained daring enough to return to fire them. Still Colonel de Grage did not cease to thunder from the heights into the ranks of the flying. The *streltsi* saw safety nowhere; arms could not protect them; nothing was more appalling to them than the ceaseless flash and roar of the artillery showering its deadly bolts upon them from the German right. And the same men who, but an hour before, had spat upon proffered pardon, offered in consequence to surrender—so short is the interval that separates victors from vanquished. Suppliant, they fell prostrate, and begged that the artillery might cease its cruel ravages, offering to do promptly whatever they were ordered. The suppliants were directed to lay down their arms, to quit their ranks, and obey in everything that would be enjoined to them. Though they at once threw down their arms, and proceeded to the places to which they were ordered, nevertheless, for a little while, the fire of the artillery was kept up, lest with the cessation of the cause of their terror, their rash daring should return, and the mutinous strife be renewed. But when they were truly and thoroughly frightened, they were treated with contemptuous impunity. Thousands of men allowed themselves to be fettered, who, if they had but rather instead have tried their real strength, would, beyond the least doubt, have become the victors of those that vanquished them. . . .

When the ferocious arrogance with which they were swollen had been made to subside completely, in the manner we have just narrated, and all the accomplices of the mutiny had been cast into chains, General Shein instituted an inquiry, by way of torture, touching the causes, the objects, the instigators, the chiefs, and the accomplices of this perilous and impious machination. For there was a very serious suspicion that more exalted people were at the head of it. Every one of them freely confessed himself deserving of death; but to detail the particulars of the nefarious plot, to lay bare the objects of it, to betray their accomplices, was what no person could persuade any of them to do. The rack was consequently got in readiness by the executioner, as the only means left to elicit the truth. The torture that was applied was of unexampled inhumanity. Scourged most savagely with the cat, if that had not the effect of breaking their stubborn silence, fire was applied to their backs, all gory and streaming, in order that, by slowly roasting the skin and tender flesh, the sharp pangs might penetrate through the very marrow of their bones, to the utmost power of painful sensation. These tortures were applied alternately, over and over again. Horrid tragedies to witness and to hear. In the open field above thirty of these more than funeral pyres blazed at the same time, and thereat were these most wretched creatures under examination roasted amidst their horrible howlings. At another side resounded the merciless strokes of the cat, while this most savage butchery of men was being done in this very pleasant neighborhood.

After numbers had been proved by the torture, at last the obstinacy of a few was found to yield; and one of them detailed the following particulars of this most perverse plot. He said that he was not unaware how great their fault was, that all had deserved to lose their lives, and that perhaps none would be found that would shirk death. That had fortune attended their undertaking they would have decreed the same penalty against the boyars, as, now they were vanquished, they expected themselves; for that they had the intention to set on fire, sack and ruin the whole German suburb, and when all the Germans, without exception, had been got rid of by massacre, to enter Moscow by force, to murder all that would make resistance, taking the rest with them to aid in their nefarious deeds; that they meant to inflict death upon some of the *boyars,* exile upon others, and to drag them all down from their offices and dignities, in order the more easily to conciliate to themselves the sympathies of the masses. That some *popes* [Orthodox priests] were to carry an image of the Blessed Virgin, and another of St. Nicholas, before them, in order that it might appear they had been driven to take up arms by the necessity of defending the faith, and not out of malice. That when they had got possession of authority they meant to scatter papers among the public, to assure the people that the Tsar's majesty, who had gone abroad, in consequence of the pernicious advice of the Germans, had died beyond seas. But that lest the barque of the state should be buffeted at hazard by the billows to perish a wreck upon the first rock, that Princess Sophia Alexeevna [Peter's half-sister and regent from 1682 to 1689] was to be raised to the throne until the Tsarevich [Peter's son Alexei, born in 1690] should have attained his majority and the strength of manhood. That Basil Golitsyn was to have been recalled from exile to aid Sophia with prudent advice.

Now, as any one of the points of this confession was of itself weighty enough to merit death, General Shein had the sentence that was drawn up against them promulgated and executed. Numbers were condemned to be hanged and gibbeted; many laid their heads upon the fatal block and died by the axe; many were reserved to certain vengeance and laid in custody in places in the environs. It was contrary to General Gordon's and Prince Masalskii's advice that the General proceeded to execute the rebels; as in this manner the chiefs of the revolt may, without sufficient examination, have been removed by premature death from further inquest. . . .

[The news of the *streltsi* rebellion reached Peter in Vienna]; he took the quick post, as his ambassador suggested, and in four weeks' time, he had got over about three hundred [German] miles* without accident and arrived [in Moscow] on the 4th of September [1698], a monarch for the well-disposed but an avenger for the wicked. His first anxiety after his arrival was about the rebellion. In what it consisted? What the insurgents meant? Who had dared to instigate such a crime? And as nobody could answer accurately upon all points, and some pleaded their own ignorance, others the obstinacy of the *streltsi,* he began to have suspicions of everybody's loyalty, and began to cogitate about a fresh investigation. The rebels that were kept in custody, in various places in the environs, were all brought in by four regiments of the guards to a fresh investigation and fresh tortures. Prison, tribunal, and rack, for those that were brought in, was in Preobrazhenskoe [the village where Peter spent his youth].

* A German mile equals about five English miles.—*Ed.*

No day, holy or profane, were the inquisitors idle; every day was deemed
fit and lawful for torturing. As many as there were accused there were
knouts, and every inquisitor was a butcher. Prince Feodor Iurevich
Romadonovskii showed himself by so much more fitted for his inquiry,
as he surpassed the rest in cruelty. The very Grand Duke himself [Peter],
in consequence of the distrust he had conceived of his subjects, performed the office of inquisitor. He put the interrogatories, he examined
the criminals, he urged those that were not confessing, he ordered such
streltsi as were more pertinaciously silent to be subjected to more cruel
tortures; those that had already confessed about many things were
questioned about more; those who were bereft of strength and reason,
and almost of their senses, by excess of torment, were handed over to the
skill of the doctors, who were compelled to restore them to strength, in
order that they might be broken down by fresh excruciations. The whole
month of October [1698] was spent in butchering the backs of the culprits
with knout and with flames; no day were those that were left alive exempt
from scourging or scorching, or else they were broken upon the wheel, or
driven to the gibbet, or slain with the axe—the penalties which were
inflicted upon them as soon as their confessions had sufficiently revealed
the heads of the rebellion.

The Chiefs of the Rebellion

Major Karpakov was said to be as far beyond the other rebels in treason
as he was in official rank. So after being knouted, fire was applied to roast
his back to such a degree that he lost both speech and consciousness;
and then, as it was feared that death might remove him prematurely,
he was commended to the skill of the Tsar's physician, Dr. Carbonari,
that he might apply such remedies as would have the effect of restoring
his expiring strength, and as soon as he was in some degree restored, he
was subjected to the question anew, and fainted away under the sharpest
tortures.

   Vaska Girin, the insurgent ringleader, after undergoing four times the
most exquisite tortures, confessing nothing, was condemned to be hanged.
But on the very day appointed for his execution, there was led out of
prison, with the rebel *streltsi*, to the question, a certain youth of twenty
years of age, on being confronted with whom, he, of his own accord,
broke his stubborn silence, and revealed the counsels of the traitors, with
all the circumstances. Now that youth of twenty had fallen in by chance
with these rebels near the borders of Smolensk, and being forced to wait
on the principal instigators of the mutiny, they took no notice of his
listening, nor was his presence forbidden even when they used to
deliberate about the success of their nefarious enterprise. When he was
dragged along with the rebels before the tribunal, he, in order to prove

his innocence the more easily, cast himself at the judge's feet, and with the most ardent sighs implored not to be subjected to the torture—that he would confess all that he knew with the most exact truth. Vaska Girin, who was condemned to the halter, was not hanged before having made his judicial confession; for he was one of the prime rebels, and an excellent witness of what he very truly detailed. . . .

Certain *popes* that were connected with the *streltsi* became sharers in their treason. For they put up prayers to God to favor the efforts of treason, and it was they who carried the images of the Blessed Virgin and Saint Nicholas among armed men, and who had promised to draw the people to the side of the revolt, under the pretense of the marked justice of the cause, and of true piety. Hence one of them was hanged by the Tsar's buffoon, near the high church dedicated to the most Holy Trinity; another, being first beheaded with the axe, was set upon the wheel near the same place. *Dumnoi diak* [a high state official] Tikhon Moscovich (whom the Tsar calls his patriarch), was forced to be the butcher of the latter. . . .

[Sophia] was interrogated by the Tsar himself, touching these attempts, and it is still uncertain what she answered. But this much is certain— that in this act the Tsar's Majesty wept for his own lot and Sophia's. Some will have it the Tsar was on the point of sentencing her to death, and used this argument: "Mary of Scotland was led forth from prison to the block, by command of her sister Elizabeth, Queen of England—a warning to me to exercise my power over Sophia." Still once more the brother pardoned a sister's crime, and, instead of penalty, enjoined that she should be banished to a greater distance, in some monastery. . . .

The First Execution, 10th October, 1698

To this exhibition of avenging justice the Tsar's Majesty invited all the ambassadors of foreign sovereigns, as it were to assert anew on his return that sovereign prerogative of life and death which the rebels had disputed with him.

The barracks in Preobrazhenskoe end in a bare field which rises to the summit of a rather steep hill. This was the place appointed for the executions. Here were planted the gibbet stakes, on which the foul heads of these confessedly guilty wretches were to be set, to protract their ignominy beyond death. There the first scene of the tragedy lay exposed. The foreigners that had gathered to the spectacle were kept aloof from too close approach; the whole regiment of guards was drawn up in array under arms. A little further off, on a high *tumulus* in the area of the place, there was a multitude of Moscovites, crowded and crushing together in a dense circle. A German Major was then my companion; he concealed his nationality in a Moscovite dress, besides which he relied upon his military rank and the liberty that he might take in consequence of being entitled by reason of his being in the service of the Tsar to share in the privileges of the Moscovites. He mingled with the thronging crowd of Moscovites, and when he came back announced that five rebel heads had been cut off in that spot by an axe that was swung by the noblest arm of all Moscovy [*viz.*, Peter the Great]. The river Iauza flows past the barracks in Preobrazhenskoe, and divides them in two.

On the opposite side of this stream there were a hundred criminals set upon those little Moscovite carts which the natives call *vozok*, awaiting the hour of the death they had to undergo. There was a cart for every criminal, and a soldier to guard each. No priestly office was to be seen, as if the condemned were unworthy of that pious compassion. But they all bore lighted tapers in their hands, not to die without light and cross. The horrors of impending death were increased by the piteous lamentations of their women, the sobbing on every side, and the shrieks of the dying that rung upon the sad array. The mother wept for her son, the daughter deplored a parent's fate, the wife lamenting a husband's lot bemoaned along with the others, from whom the various ties of blood and kindred drew tears of sad farewell. But when the horses, urged to a sharp pace, drew them off to the place of their doom, the wail of the women rose into louder sobs and moans. As they tried to keep up with them, forms of expression like these bespoke their grief, as others explained them to me: "Why are you torn from me so soon? Why do you desert me? Is a last embrace then denied me? Why am I hindered from bidding him farewell?" With complaints like these they tried to follow their friends when they could not keep up with their rapid course. From a country seat belonging to General Shein one hundred and thirty more *streltsi* were led forth to die. At each side of all the city gates there was a gibbet erected, each of which was loaded with six rebels on that day.

When all were duly brought to the place of execution, and the half dozen were duly distributed at their several gibbets, the Tsar's Majesty, dressed in a green Polish cloak, and attended by a numerous suite of Moscovite nobles, came to the gate where, by his Majesty's command, the Imperial Lord Envoy [the envoy of the Holy Roman Emperor] had stopped in his own carriage, along with the representatives of Poland and Denmark. Next to them was Major-General de Carlowitz, who had conducted his Majesty on his way from Poland, and a great many other foreigners, among whom the Moscovites mingled round about the gate. Then the proclamation of the sentence began, the Tsar exhorting all the bystanders to mark well its tenor. As the executioner was unable to dispatch so many criminals, some military officers, by command of the Tsar, came under compulsion to aid in this butcher's task. The guilty were neither chained nor fettered; but logs were tied to their legs, which hindered them from walking fast, but still allowed them the use of their feet. They strove of their own accord to ascend the ladder, making the sign of the cross towards the four quarters of the world; they themselves covered their eyes and faces with a piece of linen (which is a national custom); very many putting their necks into the halter sprang headlong of themselves from the gallows, in order to precipitate their end. There were counted two hundred and thirty that expiated their flagitious conduct by halter and gibbet.

Second Execution, 13th October 1698

Although all those that were accomplices of the rebellion were condemned to death, yet the Tsar's Majesty would not dispense with strict investigation. The more so as the unripe years and judgment of many seemed to bespeak mercy, as they were, as one may say, rather victims of error than of deliberate crime. In such case the penalty of death was commuted into some corporal infliction—such as, for instance, the cutting off of their ears and noses, to mark them with ignominy for life—a life to be passed, not as previously, in the heart of the realm, but in various and barbarous places on the frontiers of Moscovy. To such places fifty were transported today, after being castigated in the manner prescribed.

Third Execution, 17th October, 1698

Only six were beheaded today, who had the advantage of rank over the others, if rank be a distinction of honor in executed criminals.

Fourth Execution, 21st October, 1698

To prove to all the people how holy and inviolable are those walls of the city, which the *streltsi* rashly meditated scaling in a sudden assault, beams were run out from all the embrasures in the walls near the gates, on each of which two rebels were hanged. This day beheld about two hundred and fifty die that death. There are few cities fortified with as many palisades as Moscow has given gibbets to her guardian *streltsi*.

Fifth Execution, 23rd October, 1698

This differed considerably from those that preceded. The manner of it was quite different, and hardly credible. Three hundred and thirty at a time were led out together to the fatal axe's stroke, and embrued the whole plain with native but impious blood; for all *boyars*, senators of the realm, *dumnyi diaks*, and so forth, that were present at the council constituted against the rebel *streltsi*, had been summoned by the Tsar's command to Preobrazhenskoe and enjoined to take upon themselves the hangman's office. Some struck the blow unsteadily, and with trembling hands assumed this new and unaccustomed task. The most unfortunate stroke among all the *boyars* was given by him [probably Prince Alexei Golitsyn] whose erring sword struck the back instead of the neck, and thus chopping the *strelets* almost in halves, would have roused him to desperation with pain, had not Alexei reached the unhappy wretch a surer blow of an axe on the neck.

Prince [Michael G.] Romadonovskii, under whose command previous to the mutiny these four regiments were to have watched the turbulent gatherings in Poland on the frontier, beheaded, according to order, one out of each regiment. Lastly to every *boyar* a *strelets* was led up, whom he was to behead. The Tsar, in his saddle, looked on at the whole tragedy.

Seventh Execution, 27th October, 1698

Today was assigned for the punishment of the *popes*, that is to say, of those who by carrying images to induce the serfs to side with the *streltsi*, had invoked the aid of God with the holy rites of his altars for the happy success of this impious plot. The place selected by the judge for the execution was the open space in front of the church of the most Holy Trinity, which is the high church of Moscow. The ignominious gibbet cross awaited the *popes*, by way of reward in suit with the thousands of signs of the cross they had made, and as their fee for all the benedictions they had given to the refractory troops. The court jester, in a mimic attire of a *pope*, made the halter ready, and adjusted it, as it was held to be wrong to subject a *pope* to the hands of the common hangman. A certain *dumnoi diak* struck off the head of another *pope*, and set his corpse upon the ignominious wheel. Close to the church, too, the halter and wheel proclaimed the enormity of the crime of their guilty burden to the passers by.

The Tsar's Majesty looked on from his carriage while the *popes* were hurried to execution. To the populace, who stood around in great numbers, he spoke a few words touching the perfidy of the *popes*, adding the threat, "Henceforth let no one dare to ask any *pope* to pray for such an intention." A little while before the execution of the *popes*, two rebels, brothers, having had their thighs and other members broken in front of the Castle of the Kremlin, were set alive upon the wheel; twenty others on whom the axe had done its office lay lifeless around these wheels. The two that were bound upon the wheel beheld their third brother among the dead. Nobody will easily believe how lamentable were their cries and howls, unless he has well weighed their excruciations and the greatness of their tortures. I saw their broken thighs tied to the wheel with ropes strained as tightly as possible, so that in all that deluge of torture I do believe none can have exceeded that of the utter impossibility of the least movement. Their miserable cries had struck the Tsar as he was being driven past. He went up to the wheels, and first promised speedy death, and afterward proffered them a free pardon, if they would confess sincerely. But when upon the very wheel he found them more obstinate than ever, and that they would give no other answer than that they would confess nothing, and that their penalty was nearly paid in full, the Tsar left them to the agonies of death, and hastened on to the Monastery of the Nuns, in front of which monastery there were thirty gibbets erected in a quadrangular shape, from which there hung two hundred and thirty *streltsi*. The three principal ringleaders, who presented a petition to Sophia, touching the administration of the realm, were hanged close to the windows of that princess, presenting, as it were, the petitions that were placed in their hands, so near that Sophia might with ease touch them. Perhaps this was in order to load Sophia with that remorse in every way, which I believe drove her to take the religious habit, in order to pass to a better life.

Last Execution, 31st October, 1698

Again, in front of the Kremlin Castle two others, whose thighs and extremities had been broken, and who were tied alive to the wheel, with horrid lamentations throughout the afternoon and the following night, closed their miserable existence in the utmost agony. One of them, the younger of the two, survived amidst his enduring tortures until noon the following day. The Tsar dined at his ease with the *boyar* Lev Kirilovich Naryshkin, all the representatives and the Tsar's ministers being present. The successive and earnest supplications of all present induced the monarch, who was long reluctant, to give command to that Gabriel who is so well known at his court that an end might be put with a ball to the life and pangs of the criminal that still continued breathing.

For the remainder of the rebels, who were still guarded in places round about, their respective places of confinement were also their places of execution, lest by collecting them all together this torturing and butchery in the one place of such a multitude of men, should smell of tyranny. And especially lest the minds of the citizens, already terror-stricken at so many melancholy exhibitions of their perishing fellow men should dread every kind of cruelty from their sovereign.

But considering the daily perils to which the Tsar's Majesty was hitherto exposed, without an hour's security, and hardly escaping from many snares, he was very naturally always in great apprehension of the exceeding treachery of the *streltsi*, so that he fairly concluded not to tolerate a single *strelets* in his empire—to banish all of them that remained to the farthest confines of Moscovy after having almost extirpated the very name. In the provinces, leave was given to any that preferred to renounce military service for ever, and with the consent of the *voevodas* [provincial administrators] to addict themselves to domestic services. Nor were they quite innocent; for the officers that were quartered in the camp at Azov to keep ward against the hostile inroads of the enemy told how they were never secure, and hourly expected an atrocious outbreak of treason from the *streltsi;* nor was there any doubt but that they had very ambiguous sympathies for the fortunes of the other rebels. All the wives of the *streltsi* were commanded to leave the neighborhood of Moscow, and thus experienced the consequences of the crimes of their husbands. It was forbidden by *ukaz* [an imperial decree], under penalty of death, for any person to keep any of them or afford them secret harbor, unless they would send them out of Moscow to serve upon their estates. . . .

2

Reorganization of Russia by Peter the Great

Following the punishment of the *streltsi*, Peter made a determined effort to modernize Russian society, and toward that end made many innovations. One of the earliest of these was the introduction of the Julian Calendar, in 1699, which continued in official use in Russia until February 1918. Another was the creation in 1711 of a new governing body, the Senate, which assumed many of the young tsar's

The following four items are from *Polnoe Sobranie Zakonov Russkoi Imperii* . . . (*Complete Collection of the Laws of the Russian Empire*), 1st series. "A Decree on a New Calendar" from vol. 3, no. 1736, pp. 681–682. "Decrees on the Duties of the Senate" from vol. 4, no. 2321, p. 627, and no. 2330, p. 643. "Decrees on Compulsory Education" from vol. 5, no. 2762, p. 78, and no. 2778, p. 86. "A Decree on Primogeniture" from vol. 5, no. 2789, pp. 91–94. Translation mine. Items in brackets are mine.

powers when he was absent from the country. The
Senate subsequently evolved into Russia's highest
tribunal, and remained so until the Bolshevik seizure
of power in November 1917.

For Russian society to be modern, Peter believed
that at least its upper stratum had to be educated.
He sent many young Russians to study abroad, and
opened schools at home for others. However, since
education committed the Russian nobles to life-
long state service, they chose to shun these oppor-
tunities. Early in 1714 Peter forced the reluctant
young nobles into schools and shortly thereafter,
by decreeing primogeniture, put an end to yet another way of evading service to the state. Previously,
the equal division of estates among sons had made
each son a service-exempt "breadwinner." Individuals or groups that obeyed the tsar's orders were
rewarded with rights and privileges and those who
defied him relegated to obscurity.

A Decree on a New Calendar,
December 20, 1699

The Great Sovereign has ordered it declared: the Great Sovereign knows
that many European Christian countries as well as Slavic peoples are in
complete accord with our Eastern Orthodox Church, namely: Wallach-
ians, Moldavians, Serbs, Dalmatians, Bulgars, and subjects of our Great
Sovereign, the Cherkessy [Ukrainians] and all Greeks from whom we
accepted our Orthodox faith—all these peoples number their years from
eight days after the birth of Christ, that is from January 1, and not
from the creation of the world. There is a great difference in those two
calendars. This year is 1699 since the birth of Christ, and on January 1
it will be 1700 as well as a new century. To celebrate this happy and
opportune occasion, the Great Sovereign has ordered that henceforth
all government administrative departments and fortresses in all their
official business use the new calendar beginning January 1, 1700. To
commemorate this happy beginning and the new century in the capital
city of Moscow, after a solemn prayer in churches and private dwellings,
all major streets, homes of important people, and homes of distinguished
religious and civil servants should be decorated with trees, pine, and fur
branches similar to the decoration of the Merchant Palace or the
Pharmacy Building—or as best as one knows how to decorate his place
and gates. Poor people should put up at least one tree, or a branch on
their gates or on their apartment [doors]. These decorations are to remain from January 1 to January 7, 1700. As a sign of happiness on

January 1, friends should greet each other and the New Year and the new century as follows: when the Red Square will be lighted and shooting will begin—followed by that at the homes of boyars, courtiers, and important officials of the tsar, military and merchant classes—everyone who has a musket or any other fire arm should either salute thrice or shoot several rockets or as many as he has. . . .

Decrees on the Duties of the Senate

This *ukaz* [decree] should be made known. We have decreed that during our absence administration of the country is to be [in the hands of] the Governing Senate [consisting of the following persons]: Count Musin-Pushkin, *gospodin* [Lord] Strezhnev, Prince Peter Golitsyn, Prince Michael Dolgoruky, *gospodin* Plemiannikov, Prince Gregory Volkonskii, *gospodin* Samarin, *gospodin* Vasili Opukhtin, [and] *gospodin* Melnitskii; Anisim Shchukin [is to act as] the Senate's Chief Secretary. Vasili Ershov is to administer the Moscow Gubernia [administrative unit] and to report [on it] to the Senate; the position of Prince Peter Golitsyn is to go to gospodin Kurbatov. The Military *prikaz* [department] is to be replaced by a Military Board [and is to be] attached to the above mentioned Senate.

Each *gubernia* is to send two officials to advise the Senate on judicial and legislative matters. . . .

In our absence the Senate is charged by this *ukaz* with the following:

1. To establish a just court, to deprive unjust judges of their offices and of all their property, and to administer the same treatment to all slanderers.

2. To supervise governmental expenditures throughout the country and cancel unnecessary and, above all, useless things.

3. To collect as much money as possible because money is the artery of war.

4. To recruit young noblemen for officer training, especially those who try to evade it; also to select about 1000 educated boyars for the same purpose.

5. To reform letters of exchange and keep these in one place.

6. To take inventory of goods leased to offices or *gubernias*.

7. To farm out the salt trade in an effort to receive some profit [for the state].

8. To organize a good company and assign to it the China trade.

9. To increase trade with Persia and by all possible means to attract in great numbers Armenians [to that trade]. To organize inspectors and inform them of their responsibilities.

Decrees on Compulsory Education of the Russian Nobility, January 12, and February 28, 1714

Send to every *gubernia* some persons from mathematical schools to teach the children of the nobility—except those of freeholders and government clerks—mathematics and geometry; as a penalty [for evasion] establish a rule that no one will be allowed to marry unless he learns these [subjects]. Inform all prelates to issue no marriage certificates to those who are ordered to go to schools. . . .

The Great Sovereign has decreed: in all *gubernias* children between the ages of ten and fifteen of the nobility, of government clerks, and of lesser officials, except those of freeholders, must be taught mathematics and some geometry. Toward that end, students should be sent from mathematical schools [as teachers], several into each *gubernia*, to prelates and to renowned monasteries to establish schools. During their instruction these teachers should be given food and financial remuneration of three *altyns* and two *dengas** per day from *gubernia* revenues set aside for that purpose by personal orders of His Imperial Majesty. No fees should be collected from students. When they have mastered the material, they should then be given certificates written in their own handwriting. When the students are released they ought to pay one ruble each for their training. Without these certificates they should not be allowed to marry nor receive marriage certificates.

A Decree on Primogeniture, March 23, 1714

We, Peter I, Tsar and Autocrat of All Russia, etc., issue this *ukaz* for the knowledge of all subjects of our state, regardless of their social status.

The division of estates upon the death of the father causes great harm to our state and state interests and brings ruin to subjects and the families concerned; namely:

1. *On Taxes.* A man, for instance, had 1000 households and five sons, had a fine manor, good food, and a sound relationship with the people; if after his death this property is divided among his children, each would receive 200 households; those children, remembering the fame of their father and the honor of their family, would not wish to live the life of an orphan; everyone can see that poor subjects will have to supply five instead of one table, and 200 households cannot carry the burden previously carried by 1000 (including state taxes). Does not this practice bring ruin to the people and harm to state interests? Because 200 households cannot pay as punctually to the state and to the nobleman as was possible from 1000 households, because (as noted above) one

---

* One *altyn* equalled six *dengas*, or three copecks; one *denga* equalled one-half copeck.—Ed.

lord will be satisfied with 1000 (but not with 200) and the peasants, having better conditions, will be able to pay taxes punctually both to the state and to the lord. Consequently, division of estates brings great harm to the government treasury and ruin to subject people.

2. *On Families.* And should each of those five sons have two sons, each son will receive 100 households, and should they further multiply, they will be so impoverished that they may turn into one-household owners, with the result that [the descendants of] a famous family, in place of fame, will turn into villagers, a problem which has often occurred among the Russians.

3. On top of these two harmful practices, there is yet another problem. Anyone who receives his bread gratuitously, regardless of its amount, will neither serve the state without compulsion nor try to improve his conditions: on the contrary, each will try to live in idleness, which (according to Holy Scripture) is the mother of all evil.

In contrast to Item 1 [On Taxes]: if all immovable property were to be handed down to one son and the others were to inherit only movable property, then state revenues would be sounder; the nobleman would be better off even if he should collect small amounts [from his subjects]; there will be only one manor (as stated above); and his subjects will not be ruined.

Regarding Item 2 [On Families]: families will not decline, but shall remain stable in all their glory and their manors shall remain famous and renowned.

Regarding Item 3: the remaining [members of the family] will not be idle because they will be forced to earn a living through service, teaching, trade, and so forth. And whatever they do for their own living will also benefit the state. Because this [system] is intended to bring prosperity, the following rules should be followed:

(a) All immovable property, namely hereditary, service, and purchased estates, as well as homes and stores, should neither be sold nor mortgaged but retained in the family in the following manner:

(b) Whoever has sons must will his immovable property to one who will inherit all; other children of both sexes will be rewarded by movable property which either the father or mother will divide for both sons and daughters in the amount they wish, except that the one who inherits the immovable property [will be excluded]. If an individual does not have sons, but daughters only, he should then divide [his property] in the same manner. If an individual fails to assign [his property] a government decree will assign the immovable property to the eldest son in inheritance, while movable property will be divided equally among the others; the same procedure is to apply to daughters.

(c) Whoever is childless will give his immovable property to one of the members of his family, whomever he wishes, and the movable [property] to his relatives or even to strangers. And if he fails to do this, both of these properties will then be divided by a decree among the members of the family; immovable to the nearest member of the family and the rest to all others equally. . . .

An Instruction to Russian Students Abroad Studying Navigation*

1. Learn [how to draw] plans and charts and how to use the compass and other naval indicators.

2. [Learn] how to navigate a vessel in battle as well as in a simple maneuver, and learn how to use all appropriate tools and instruments; namely, sails, ropes, and oars, and the like matters, on row boats and other vessels.

3. Discover as much as possible how to put ships to sea during a naval battle. Those who cannot succeed in this effort must diligently ascertain what action should be taken by the vessels that do and those that do not put to sea during such a situation [naval battle]. Obtain from [foreign] naval officers written statements, bearing their signatures and seals, of how adequately you [Russian students] are prepared for [naval] duties.

4. If, upon his return, anyone wishes to receive [from the Tsar] greater favors for himself, he should learn, in addition to the above enumerated instructions, how to construct those vessels aboard which he would like to demonstrate his skills.

5. Upon his return to Moscow, every [foreign-trained Russian] should bring with him at his own expense, for which he will later be reimbursed, at least two experienced masters of naval science. They [the returnees] will be assigned soldiers, one soldier per returnee, to teach them [what they have learned abroad]. And if they do not wish to accept soldiers they may teach their acquaintances or their own people. The treasury will pay for transportation and maintenance of soldiers. And if anyone other than soldiers learns [the art of navigation] the treasury will pay 100 rubles for the maintenance of every such individual. . . .

A Decree on the Right of Factories to Buy Villages, January 18, 1721†

Previous decrees have denied merchants the right to obtain villages. This prohibition was instituted because those people, outside their business, did not have any establishments that could be of any use to the state.

---

* From *Pisma i bumagi imperatora Petra Velikogo* [*Letters and Papers of Emperor Peter the Great*] St. Petersburg: 1887, vol. 1, pp. 117–118. Translation mine. Items in brackets are mine.

† The following three items are from *Polnoe Sobranie Zakonov Russkoi Imperii* . . . (*Complete Collection of the Laws of the Russian empire*), 1st series. "A Decree on the Right of Factories to Purchase Villages" from vol. 6, no. 3711, pp. 311–312. "Table of Ranks" from vol. 6, no. 3890, pp. 486–493. "A Decree on the Founding of the Academy" from vol. 7, no. 4443. Translation mine. Items in brackets are mine.

Nowadays, thanks to our decrees, as every one can see, many merchants have companies and many have succeeded in establishing new enterprises for the benefit of the state; namely: silver, copper, iron, coal and the like, as well as silk, linen, and woolen industries, many of which have begun operations. As a result, by this our *ukaz* aimed at the increase of factories, we permit the nobility as well as merchants to freely purchase villages for these factories, with the sanction of the Mining and Manufacturing College, under one condition: that these villages be always integral parts of these factories. Consequently, neither the nobility nor merchants may sell or mortgage these villages without the factories . . . and should someone decide to sell these villages with the factories because of pressing needs, it must be done with the permission of the Mining and Manufacturing College. And whoever violates this procedure will have his possessions confiscated.

And should someone try to establish a small factory for the sake of appearance in order to purchase a village, such an entrepreneur should not be allowed to purchase anything. The Mining and Manufacturing College should adhere to this rule very strictly. Should such a thing happen, those responsible for it should be deprived of all their movable and immovable property.

Table of Ranks, January 24, 1722

Military Ranks		Civilian Ranks	Grades
Naval Forces	Land Forces		
General-Admiral	Generalissimo Field Marshal	Chancelor or Active Privy Counselor	I
Admiral	General of Artillery General of Cavalry General of Infantry	Active Privy Counselor	II
Vice Admiral	Lieutenant General	Privy Counselor	III
Rear Admiral	Major General	Active State Counselor	IV
Captain-Commander	Brigadier	State Counselor	V
First Captain	Colonel	Collegial Counselor	VI
Second Captain	Lieutenant Colonel	Court Counselor	VII
Lieutenant-Captain of the Fleet	Major	Collegial Assessor	VIII
Third Captain of Artillery			
Lieutenant of the Fleet	Captain or Cavalry Captain	Titled Counselor	IX
Lieutenant-Captain of Artillery			

Military Ranks		Civilian Ranks	Grades
Naval Forces	*Land Forces*		
Lieutenant of Artillery	Staff Captain or Staff Cavalry Captain	Collegial Secretary	X
		Secretary of the Senate	XI
Midshipman	Lieutenant	Gubernia Secretary	XII
Artillery Constable	Sublieutenant	Registrar of the Senate	XIII
	Guidon Bearer	Collegial Registrar	XIV

The following rules are appended to the above Table of Ranks to inform everyone of how he should apply himself to these ranks.

1. Those princes who are related to Us by blood or those who are married to Our princesses always take precedence and rank over all other princes and high servants of the Russian state.

2. Naval and land commanding officers are to be determined in the following manner: if they both are of the same rank, the naval officer is superior at sea to the land officer; and on land, the land officer is superior to the naval officer, regardless of the length of service each may have in his respective rank.

3. Whoever shall demand respect higher than is due his rank, or shall illegally assume a higher rank, shall lose two months of his salary; if he serves without salary then he shall pay a fine equal to the salary of his rank; one third of that fine shall be given to the individual who reported on him, and the remainder will be given to a hospital fund. The observance of this rank procedure does not apply on such occasions as meetings among friends or neighbors or at social gatherings, but only to churches, the Mass, Court ceremonies, ambassadorial audiences, official banquets, official meetings, christenings, marriages, funerals, and similar public gatherings. An individual will also be fined if he should make room for a person of lower rank. Tax collectors should watch carefully [for any signs of violations of these procedures] in order to encourage service [to the state] and to honor those already in service, and [at the same time] to collect fines from impudent individuals and parasites. The above prescribed fines are applicable to male and female transgressors.

4. An identical penalty will be given to anyone who will demand a rank without having an appropriate patent for his grade.

5. Equally, no one may assume a rank that has been acquired in the service of foreign state until We approve it, an action which We shall do gladly in accordance with his service.

Vienna and then to Naples. After he was persuaded to return, Peter ordered an investigation into the motives behind his son's flight. A plot against the tsar was uncovered, which under Russian law was punishable by death, but the sentence was never carried out as Alexei died in 1718 in the Fortress of Peter and Paul.

Peter's Declaration to Alexei, October 11, 1715

tion to My Son

cannot be ignorant of what is known to all the world, to what our people groaned under the oppression of the Swedes before inning of the present war.

he usurpation of so many maritime places so necessary to our ey had cut us off from all commerce with the rest of the world, saw with regret that, besides, they had cast a thick veil before s of the clearsighted. You know what it has cost us in the begin- this war (in which God alone has led us, as it were, by the hand, guides us) to make ourselves experienced in the art of war, and a stop to those advantages which our implacable enemies ob- ver us.

ubmitted to this with a resignation to the will of God, making t but it was he who put us to that trial, till he might lead us right way, and we might render ourselves worthy to experience, same enemy who at first made others tremble, now in his turn s before us, perhaps in a much greater degree. These are the hich, next to the assistance of God, we owe to our own toil and abour of our faithful and affectionate children, our Russian sub-

t the time that I am viewing the prosperity which God has n our native country, if I cast an eye upon the posterity that is d me, my heart is much more penetrated with grief on account is to happen, than I rejoice at those blessings that are past, at you, my son, reject all means of making yourself capable of rning after me. I say your incapacity is voluntary, because you xcuse yourself with want of natural parts and strength of body, l had not given you a sufficient share of either; and though your ion is none of the strongest, yet it cannot be said that it is r weak.

ou even will not so much as hear warlike exercises mentioned; t is by them that we broke through that obscurity in which we

6. No one may be given a new rank without a release patent, unless We personally have signed that release.

7. All married women advance in ranks with their husbands, and if they should violate the order of procedure they must pay the same fines as would their husbands if they had violated it.

8. Although We allow free entry to public assemblies, wherever the Court is present, to the sons of princes, counts, barons, distinguished nobles, and high servants of the Russian state, either because of their births or because of the positions of their fathers, and although We wish to see that they are distinguished in every way from other [people], We nevertheless do not grant any rank to anyone until he performs a useful service to Us or to the state. . . .

11. All Russian or foreign-born servants who have or who have had the first eight grades have the right forever to pass these grades on to their lawful heirs and posterity; members of ancient [Russian] noble families, even though they may be of lesser status and may never before have been brought into a noble dignity by the Crown or granted a coat of arms, should be given the same merits and preferences [as other nobles]. . . .

15. Those who are not nobles but who serve in the military and who advance to an ober-officer [position], will, upon attainment of that rank, receive the status of a nobleman, as will those of their children born ex post facto. In case an individual has no children after becoming an ober-officer, but has children born earlier, he may petition the Tsar, and the status of a nobleman will be granted to one son in whose behalf the father has petitioned. Children of all other grades whose parents are not nobles, regardless of whether they serve in civil or Court positions, are not considered as nobles. . . .

A Decree on the Founding of the Academy, January 28, 1724

His Imperial Majesty decreed the establishment of an academy, wherein languages as well as other sciences and important arts could be taught, and where books could be translated. On January 22, [1724], during his stay in the Winter Palace, His Majesty approved the project for the Academy, and with his own hand signed a decree that stipulates that the Academy's budget of 24,912 rubles annually should come from revenues from custom dues and export-import license fees collected in the following cities: Narva, Dorpat, Pernov and Arensburg. . . .

Usually two kinds of institutions are used in organizing arts and sciences. One is known as a University; the other as an Academy or society of arts and sciences.

1. A University is an association of learned individuals who teach the

young people the development of such distinguished sciences as theology and jurisprudence (the legal skill), and medicine and philosophy. An Academy, on the other hand, is an association of learned and skilled people who not only know their subjects to the same degree [as their counterparts in the University] but who, in addition, improve and develop them through research and inventions. They have no obligation to teach others.

2. While the Academy consists of the same scientific disciplines and has the same members as the University, these two institutions, in other states, have no connection between themselves in training many other well-qualified people who could organize different societies. This is done to prevent interference into the activity of the Academy, whose sole task is to improve arts and sciences through theoretical research that would benefit professors as well as students of universities. Freed from the pressure of research, universities can concentrate on educating the young people.

3. Now that an institution aimed at the cultivation of arts and sciences is to be chartered in Russia, there is no need to follow the practice that is accepted in other states. It is essential to take into account the existing circumstances of this state [Russia], consider [the quality of Russian] teachers and students, and organize such an institution that would not only immediately increase the glory of this [Russian] state through the development of sciences, but would also, through teaching and dissemination [of knowledge], benefit the people [of Russia] in the future.

4. These two aims will not be realized if the Academy of Sciences alone is chartered, because while the Academy may try to promote and disseminate arts and sciences, these will not spread among the people. The establishment of a university will do even less, simply because there are no elementary schools, gymnasia or seminaries [in Russia] where young people could learn the fundamentals before studying more advanced subjects [at the University] to make themselves useful. It is therefore inconceivable that under these circumstances a university would be of some value [to Russia].

5. Consequently what is needed most [in Russia] is the establishment of an institution that would consist of the most learned people, who, in turn, would be willing: (a) to promote and perfect the sciences while at the same time, wherever possible, be willing (b) to give public instruction to young people (if they feel the latter are qualified) and (c) instruct some people individually so that they in turn could train young people [of Russia] in the fundamental principles of all sciences.

6. As a result, and with only slight modifications, one institution will perform as great a service [in Russia] as the three institutions do in other states. . . .

7. Because the organization of this Academy is similar to that of

Paris (except for this difference and advantage th. is also to do what a university and college are do that this institution can and should easily be cal plines which can be organized in this Academy three basic divisions: The first division is to cons related sciences; the second of physics; and tl history and law. . . .

3

The Problem of Imperia. Peter's Relations with H.

Peter the Great's relations with his first child, form a sad chapter of his st tsarevich, who was born in 1690, mother Eudoxia Lopukhina until 1 amorous interests led Peter to comm convent in that year, Alexei's rearing to Peter's aunts and foreign tutors. cation introduced Alexei to Western his mother and grew to dislike and Peter's limitless energy and enthusia matters, moreover, were unsympathe delicate health and deep religious co his marriage in 1711 to a German pri Wolfenbuttel, Alexei turned to heav while under the influence of alcoho cized his father's policies. Although at home, Peter nevertheless learned cisms, and in 1715, following the de in giving birth to a son, he sent Ale ing." Alexei agreed to renounce h cession. Shortly thereafter he went

From Friedrich Christian Weber, *The Present Sta* 1723), vol. 2, pp. 97–105, 190–201. Weber was D 1714 to 1720. Spellings have been modernized to f

Decla

You
degree
the be
By
state,
and w
the ey
ning o
and st
to pu
tained
We
no do
into tl
that tl
trembl
fruits
to the
jects.
But
heaped
to suc
of wh.
seeing
well-g
canno
as if G
consti
altoge
But
thoug

were involved, and that we made ourselves known to nations, whose esteem we share at present.

I do not exhort you to make war without lawful reasons; I only desire you to apply yourself to learn the art of it; for it is impossible well to govern without knowing the rules and discipline of it, was it for no other end than for the defense of the country.

I could place before your eyes many instances of what I am proposing to you. I will only mention to you the Greeks, with whom we are united by the same profession of faith. What occasioned their decay but that they neglected arms? Idleness and repose weakened them, made them submit to tyrants, and brought them to that slavery to which they are now so long since reduced. You mistake, if you think it is enough for a prince to have good generals to act under his orders. Everyone looks upon the head; they study his inclinations and conform themselves to them: all the world owns this. My brother during his reign loved magnificence in dress, and great equipages of horses. The nation were not much inclined that way, but the prince's delight soon became that of his subjects, for they are inclined to imitate him in liking a thing as well as disliking it.

If the people so easily break themselves of things which only regard pleasure, will they not forget in time, or will they not more easily give over the practice of arms, the exercise of which is the more painful to them, the less they are kept to it?

You have no inclination to learn the war, you do not apply yourself to it, and consequently you will never learn it: And how then can you command others, and judge of the reward which those deserve who do their duty, or punish others who fail of it? You will do nothing, nor judge of anything but by the eyes and help of others, like a young bird that holds up his bill to be fed.

You say that the weak state of your health will not permit you to undergo the fatigues of war: This is an excuse which is no better than the rest. I desire no fatigues, but only inclination, which even sickness itself cannot hinder. Ask those who remember the time of my brother. He was of a constitution weaker by far than yours. He was not able to manage a horse of the least mettle, nor could he hardly mount it: Yet he loved horses, hence it came, that there never was, nor perhaps is there actually now in the nation a finer stable than his was.

By this you see that good success does not always depend on pains, but on the will.

If you think there are some, whose affairs do not fail of success, though they do not go to war themselves; it is true: But if they do not go themselves, yet they have an inclination for it, and understand it.

For instance, the late King of France did not always take the field in person; but it is known to what degree he loved war, and what glorious exploits he performed in it, which made his campaigns to be called the theatre and school of the world. His inclinations were not confined solely to military affairs, he also loved mechanics, manufactures and other establishments, which rendered his kingdom more flourishing than any other whatsoever.

After having made to you all those remonstrances, I return to my former subject which regards you.

I am a man and consequently I must die. To whom shall I leave after me to finish what by the grace of God I have begun, and to preserve what I have partly recovered? To a man, who like the slothful servant hides his talent in the earth, that is to say, who neglects making the best of what God has entrusted to him?

Remember your obstinacy and ill-nature, how often I reproached you with it, and even chastised you for it, and for how many years I almost have not spoke to you; but all this has availed nothing, has effected nothing. It was but losing my time; it was striking the air. You do not make the least endeavors, and all your pleasure seems to consist in staying idle and lazy at home: Things of which you ought to be ashamed (forasmuch as they make you miserable) seem to make up your dearest delight, nor do you foresee the dangerous consequences of it for yourself and for the whole state. St. Paul has left us a great truth when he wrote: If a man know not how to rule his own house, how shall he take care of the church of God?

After having considered all those great inconveniencies and reflected upon them, and seeing I cannot bring you to good by any inducement, I have thought fit to give you in writing this act of my last will, with this resolution however to wait still a little longer before I put it in execution, to see if you will mend. If not, I will have you to know that I will deprive you of the succession, as one may cut off a useless member.

Do not fancy, that, because I have no other child but you, I only write this to terrify you. I will certainly put it in execution, if it please God; for whereas I do not spare my own life for my country and the welfare of my people, why should I spare you who do not render yourself worthy of either? I would rather choose to transmit them to a worthy stranger than to my own unworthy son.

Peter

Alexeï's Reply, October 27, 1715

Most Clement Lord and Father

I have read the paper your Majesty gave me on the 27th of October, 1715, after the funeral of my late consort.

I have nothing to reply to it, but, that if your Majesty will deprive me of the succession to the Crown of Russia by reason of my incapacity, your will be done; I even most instantly beg it of you, because I do not think myself fit for the government. My memory is very much weakened, and yet it is necessary in affairs. The strength of my mind and of my body is much decayed by the sicknesses which I have undergone, and which have rendered me incapable of governing so many nations; this requires a more vigorous man than I am.

Therefore I do not aspire after you (whom God preserve many years) to the succession of the Russian Crown, even if I had no brother as I have one at present, whom I pray God preserve. Neither will I pretend for the future to that succession, of which I take God to witness, and swear it upon my soul, in testimony whereof I write and sign this present with my own hand.

I put my children into your hands, and as for myself, I desire nothing of you but a bare maintenance during my life, leaving the whole to your consideration and to your will.

Your most humble servant and son,

Alexei

Peter's Declaration to Alexei, January 19, 1716

My last sickness having hindered me till now from explaining myself to you about the resolution I have taken upon your letter which you wrote to me in answer to my first; at present I answer that I observe you talk of nothing in it but of the succession, just as if I needed your consent to do in that affair what otherwise depends on my will. But whence comes it that in your letter you say nothing of that incapacity wherein you voluntarily put yourself, and of that aversion you have for affairs, which I touched in mine more particularly than the ill state of your health, and which you barely mention. I also remonstrated to you the dissatisfaction your conduct has given me for so many years, and you pass all that over in silence, though I strongly insisted upon it. Thence I judge that those paternal exhortations have no weight with you. I have therefore taken a resolution to write to you once more by this present which shall be the last. If you slight the advices I give you in my lifetime, how will you value them after my death?

Can one rely on your oaths, when one sees you have a hardened heart? David said: All men are liars. But supposing you have at present the will of being true to your promises, those great beards may turn you as they please, and make you break them.

Instead that at present their debauches and sloth keep them out of posts of honour, they are in hopes that one day or other their condition will mend by you who already show much inclination for them.

I do not see that you are sensible of the obligations you have to your father, to whom you owe your very being. Do you assist him in his cares and pains since you have attained the years of maturity? Certainly in nothing; all the world knows it; quite contrary you blame and abhor all the good I do, at the hazard and expence of my own health for the sake of my people and for their welfare, and I have all the reasons in the world to believe you will be the destroyer of it, if you out-live me. And so I cannot resolve to let you live on according to your own will, like an amphibious creature, neither fish nor flesh. Change therefore your conduct, and either strive to render yourself worthy of the succession, or turn monk. I cannot be easy on your account, especially now that my health begins to decay. On sight therefore of this letter, answer me upon it either in writing, or by word of mouth. If you fail to do it, I will use you as a malefactor.

Peter

Alexeï's "Confession," June 22, 1718

On the 22nd Day of June 1718. I make this answer to the articles upon which M. Tolstoy interrogated me.

1. Though I was not ignorant that it is not the practice of the world to be disobedient as I was to my father, and to be unwilling to do what pleased him, that this even is a sin and a great shame: Yet this proceeded from my living, when a child, with a governess and young women, of whom I learned nothing but amusements and to play in my chamber, and to act the bigot, to which I was naturally inclined.

The persons who were put about me after my governess was taken from me did not teach me to do better, among others Nikifore Viazmskii, Alexei Basili, and the Naryshkins.

My father taking care of my education, and being desirous that I should apply myself to what might render me worthy of being the Tsar's son, ordered me to learn the High-Dutch tongue and other sciences, to which I had a great deal of aversion. I applied myself to them but with great carelessness, only to pass away the time, nor had I ever any inclination for them.

And as my father, who then was often in the army, was far off from me, he ordered the most serene Prince [Alexander] Menshikov [1673–1729] to have an eye upon me. When I was with him, I was obliged to apply myself; but when I was out of the Prince's sight, the said Naryshkins and Viazmskii, seeing that my inclinations run solely upon bigotry, idleness, frequenting priests and monks and drinking with them, not only did not dissuade me from it, but even took delight in doing as I did: As they were persons who had been with me from my infancy, I was used to do what they told me, to fear them and to comply with them in everything; and they more and more alienated me from my father by diverting me with such sort of pleasures, and by degrees I came to abhor not only my father's military affairs and his other actions, but even his very person. This is what made me wish always to be far off from him.

When I was intrusted at Moscow with the government of the empire, seeing myself at full liberty and that I was my own master; far from considering that my father had put it into my hands in order to train me up to it, and to lead me to the succession after him, if I rendered myself capable of it: I gave myself still more up to my usual pleasures among priests and monks, and other people of that stamp. Alexander Kikin made it always his earnest business when he was with me to harden me in those disorders.

My father having compassion for me, and being desirous of rendering me worthy of that state to which I was called, sent me into foreign countries; but as I was already full grown and of a settled age, I changed none of my habits.

It is true however that the stay I made there has been useful to me in some things, but not enough so as to eradicate the bad habits which had taken so deep root in me.

2. The bad character of my wicked mind was the cause why I did not dread my father's corrections for my disobedience: I freely own it: For though I truly feared him, yet it was not with a filial awe, but such an apprehension as made me seek means how to keep away from him, that I might not perform his will. Of this I will give a plain instance.

On my return to my father, coming back from foreign parts to St. Petersburg, he received me very graciously. Among other things he asked me whether I had not forgotten what I had learned: I answered I had not. He ordered me to bring to him some drawings of my own doing: As I had learned nothing, I was afraid he might make me draw something in his presence, and fell a thinking how to disable my right hand so far as to render it unfit for working. I charged a pistol with a ball, and taking it with the left, I fired it against the palm of the right with a design of shooting it through: The ball missed the hand, but the powder burned it enough to make it sore. The ball flew into the wall of my closet where it may still be seen. My father observing that I was hurt on the hand, asked how it happened. I put some sham or other upon him, but did not tell him the truth. One may see by this, that though I feared my father, it was not with a filial awe.

3. As to my having desired the succession by other means than that of obedience, all the world may easily guess the reason of it; for being once stepped out of the good road, unwilling to imitate my father in anything, I endeavored to obtain the succession by any other method

whatsoever than what was fair. I was for having it by a foreign assistance, and if I had obtained it, and that the Emperor had put in execution what he had promised to me, *viz.* to procure the Crown of Russia to me even by armed force, I would have stuck at nothing to lay hold of the succession. For instance, if the Emperor had demanded Russian Troops against any of his enemies whomsoever, or large sums of money in return for his service, I would have done whatever he had desired, and I would also have made great presents to his ministers and generals. I would have maintained at my own expense the auxiliary forces he should have given me to put me in possession of the Crown of Russia, and in short nothing would have been too dear for me to satisfy my own will.

Official Condemnation of Alexei, June 24, 1718

By virtue of the express ordinance issued by His Tsarist Majesty, and signed with his own hand on the 13th of June last, for trying the Tsarevich Alexei Petrovich, for his transgressions and crimes against his father and his lord, the undersigned Ministers, Senators, States Military and Civil, after having been several times assembled in the Chamber of the Regency of the Senate at St. Petersburg, having more than once heard read the originals and extracts of evidences given against him, as also His Tsarist Majesty's letters of exhortation to the Tsarevich, and his answers to them written with his own hand, and the other proceedings relating to that trial; as also the Tsarevich's criminal examinations, confessions and declarations which he either wrote with his own hand, or made by word of mouth to his Lord and his father, and in presence of the undersigned persons, established by His Tsarist Majesty's authority for this present trial: They have declared and owned, that though according to the laws of the Russian Empire, it never belonged to them, who are natural subjects of His Tsarist Majesty's sovereign domination, to take cognizance of affairs of this nature, which according to their importance, solely depend on the absolute will of the sovereign, whose power depends but on God alone, and is not limited by any law: Yet submitting themselves to His Tsarist Majesty their sovereign's ordinance aforesaid, who gives them that liberty, after mature reflexion and in Christian conscience, without fear, or flattery, and without regard to the person, having nothing before their eyes but the divine laws suiting with the present case, both of the Old Testament and the New, the holy writings of the Gospel and of the Apostles, as also the Canons and Rules of the Councils, the authority of the holy fathers and doctors of the church; taking also instruction from the considerations of the Archbishops and the clergy assembled at St. Petersburg by his Tsarist Majesty's order, as above transcribed, and conforming themselves to the laws of all Russia, especially the Constitutions of this empire, to the military laws and statutes, which are conformable to the laws of many other governments, and chiefly to those of the ancient Roman and Grecian [Byzantine] emperors, and of other Christian princes: The undersigned having put it to the vote, did unanimously, without contradiction, agree and pronounce, *that the Tsarevich Alexei Petrovich deserves death* for his crimes aforesaid, and for his capital transgressions against his sovereign and his father, being his Tsarist Majesty's son and subject; so that, though his Tsarist Majesty did promise to the Tsarevich by the letter he sent to him by M. Privy-Councelor Tolstoy, and the Captain of the Guard Rumiantsev, dated Spa the 10th of July, 1717, to pardon him his evasion if he returned of his own accord and willingly, as the Tsarevich himself has owned with thanks in his answer to that letter, written from Naples on the 4th of October, 1717, saying therein that he thanks his Tsarist Majesty for the pardon that had been given to him only for his voluntary evasion; yet he has since made himself unworthy of it by opposing his father's will and by his other transgressions, which he renewed and continued, as is amply set forth in the manifesto published by his Tsarist Majesty on the 3rd of February of the present year, and because among other things he did not return of his own accord.

And though his Tsarist Majesty upon the Tsarevich's arrival at Moscow with the paper of confession containing his crimes, wherein he asked pardon for them, had commiseration of him, as is natural for a father to have for his son, and that in the audience he gave him in the hall of the castle on the said 3rd day of February, he promised him a pardon of all his transgressions: Yet his Tsarist Majesty made him that promise solely upon this express condition which he explained in the presence of all, *viz.* that the Tsarevich should declare without any restriction or reserve, all that he had committed and plotted against his Tsarist Majesty till that day, and that he should discover all the persons who advised him, his accomplices, and in general all those who knew anything of his designs and intrigues; but if he concealed any person or any thing, the pardon promised should be void and remain revoked, which the Tsarevich then agreed to and accepted, at least in outward appearance, with tears of thankfulness, and promised upon oath to declare all, without reserve. In confirmation of which he kissed the Holy Cross and the Holy Scriptures in the Cathedral Church.

His Tsarist Majesty also confirmed the same to him with his own hand the next day, in the interrogatory articles inserted above, which he caused to be given to him, having written at the top as follows:

> As you received yesterday your pardon on condition of declaring all the circumstances of your evasion and all that has any relation to it: But that if you concealed anything, you should forfeit your life; and as you have already by word of mouth made some declarations, you ought for a more

ample satisfaction, and for your own discharge, set them down in writing, according to the points set forth hereafter.

And in the conclusion there was further written with his Tsarist Majesty's own hand in the seventh article:

Declare all that has any relation to this affair, even though it be not specified here, and clear yourself as at the Holy Confession: But if you hide or conceal anything that is afterwards discovered, do not impute anything to me; for it was yesterday declared to you before everybody, that in this case, the pardon you have received, shall be revoked and void.

Notwithstanding this, the Tsarevich in his answers and confessions, spoke without any sincerity; he concealed and hid not only many persons, but also capital affairs and his transgressions, and in particular his rebellious designs against his father and his Lord, and his wicked practices which he had contrived and carried on for a long time, to attempt the usurpation of his father's throne, even in his life-time, by diverse wicked means, and under wicked pretexts, grounding his hopes and wishes for the death of his father and his Lord, on the populace's declaring in his favor, with which he flattered himself.

All this was discovered afterwards by the criminal examinations, after he had refused to declare it himself, as appeared above.

And so, it is evident from the whole conduct of the Tsarevich, and from the declarations which he made in writing and by word of mouth, and last of all from that of the 22d of June of the present year, that it was not his intention the succession to the crown should come to him after his father's death, in the manner his father would have left it to him, according to the order of equity and by the ways and means which God prescribed: But that he desired it, and had the design of getting it, even in the life-time of his father and his lord, against his Tsarist Majesty's will, and by opposing his father's intentions in everything, and not only by insurrections of rebels which he hoped for, but also by the emperor's assistance and with a foreign army which he flattered himself to have at his disposal, should even the government have been in danger of being overturned, and all have been alienated from the state, that might have been demanded of him for that assistance.

These premises therefore evidently show, that the Tsarevich, in hiding all those pernicious designs, and concealing many persons who were of intelligence with him, as he did till the last examination, and till he was fully convicted of all his machinations, had a view to keep in reserve certain means for resuming his designs afterwards when a favorable occasion should offer, and to carry on the execution of this horrid attempt against his father and his Lord, and this whole empire.

He thereby rendered himself unworthy of the clemency and of the pardon that was promised to him by his Lord and his father, which he also owned himself, as well before His Tsarist Majesty, as in the presence of all the states, ecclesiastical and secular, and publicly before the whole assembly, and he also declared by word of mouth and in writing before the undersigned judges, established by His Tsarist Majesty, that all that is above, is true and manifest by the effects that have appeared of it.

Now, seeing the foresaid laws, divine and ecclesiastical, civil and military, and especially the two latter, condemn to death without mercy, not only those whose attempts against their father and lord have been manifested by evidences, or proved by writings, but even those whose attempts have only been in the intention of rebelling, or who have simply framed designs of killing the sovereign, or to usurp the empire: Therefore such a design of rebellion, the like of which was hardly ever heard of in the world, joined to that of an horrid double parricide against his sovereign, first as father of the country, and next as his father by nature (a most clement father who caused the Tsarevich to be educated from the cradle with more than paternal care, with a tenderness and a goodness that appeared on all occasions, who endeavored to train him up to the government, and to instruct him in the art of war with incredible pains and indefatigable application, in order to render him capable and worthy of the succession to so great an empire,) how much more has such a design deserved to be punished with death?

It is with afflicted hearts and eyes full of tears, that we, being servants and subjects, pronounce this sentence, considering it does not belong to us in this quality to enter upon a judgment of so great importance, and particularly to pronounce a sentence against the son of the most sovereign and most clement Tsar our Lord. However it being his will we shall judge; we by this present declare our true opinion, and we pronounce this condemnation with a conscience as pure and as Christian, as we believe to be able to answer it before the dreadful, just, and impartial judgment of the Great God.

Submitting, as for the rest, this sentence which we give, and this condemnation which we pass, to the sovereign power, will, and clement revision of His Tsarist Majesty, our most clement Monarch.

4

Pososhkov on Poverty and Wealth

In his efforts to modernize Russia, Peter the Great
encountered many opponents but also many supporters. Among those who admired the Tsar's activity was
Ivan Tikhonovich Pososhkov (1652–1726). The self-
taught son of a peasant, Pososhkov himself through
his years of multifaceted service with the government
had become aware of numerous defects in Russian
life and of the general corruption among state officials. Unlike many of his contemporaries, he put
his impressions and plans for correcting Russia's
shortcomings into writing. The most important of
his works is A Book on Poverty and Wealth. Written
for Peter the Great (although it is not known
whether Peter actually saw it), the Book glorifies
Russian autocracy and advocates minute regulation
of every phase of the life of the tsar's subjects. It is
critical on the other hand, of the ignorance of the
Russian clergy, the abuses among officials, the laziness and illiteracy of the peasants, the corruption of
the courts, and the disrespect for the merchants.
Shortly after Peter's death Pososhkov was arrested
and imprisoned in the Fortress of Peter and Paul,
where he died in 1726. In the mid-nineteenth
century, the historian M. P. Pogodin (1800–1875)
discovered Pososhkov's work and acclaimed it as the
first major critique of mercantilism, antedating
Western European economic writings by at least
fifty years—a view that was subsequently accepted
by Soviet historians.

The Tsardom's wealth consists not of an abundance of money in the
Tsar's treasury, nor is the Tsardom wealthy when [members of] the Tsar's
Council wear gold-embroidered clothes; but the Tsardom is wealthy
when all the people are wealthy according to their own standards;

From I. T. Pososhkov, *Kniga o skudosti i bogatstve i drugie sochineniia* (A Book
on Poverty and Wealth and Other Works) (Moscow: Akademiia Nauk, 1951),
pp. 13–14, 113–114, 117–118, 120, 122–125, 134–135, 138, 166, 168, 170–172,
178–179, 182–183. Translation mine. Items in brackets mine.

wealthy in their own domestic resources and not as a result of outward appearances or the addition of ornaments. We do not enrich ourselves by ornamenting our apparel, but those states that bring these various ornaments to us do [enrich themselves]. Above material wealth we all ought to concern ourselves with immaterial wealth; that is, genuine truth. . . .

Merchants should not be reduced to insignificance, because without merchants no kingdom, be it large or small, can exist. Merchants are allies of the military; military fight and merchants aid and prepare all the necessities for them.

On account of this it is essential to give them substantial protection. Because, as a soul cannot exist without a body, so the military cannot exist without merchants; it is impossible for the military to exist without merchants and for merchants to live without the military.

The Tsardom is enlarged by the military and is enriched by the merchants. Because of this they ought to be protected from the offenders; it should also be seen that officials cause them no harm. There are many thoughtless people who hold merchants in contempt, despise them, and insult them without any cause. Yet nowhere in the world is there an occupation that has no need for a merchant.

It is worthwhile to protect merchants not only from outside offenders but also to see to it that they do not offend one another. Members of other occupations should not be allowed to join merchants and create for them great difficulties. They [the merchants] should be given free trade to enable them to enrich themselves and to increase the treasury of His Imperial Majesty.

When Russian merchants receive free trade, and neither members of other occupations nor foreigners can interfere in their business, the collection of taxes will be in better condition [than it is now]. I believe that if the present system of collection of taxes were to be employed, two or three times the amount would be collected. Today, however, more than half [of the taxes] is lost due to [the graft of] various officials. . . .

Each occupation should lead an honest life—not to sin before God and not to be indebted to the Tsar. The way a person makes a living [should determine] the kind of service he should render. If he is a soldier, let him be a soldier; those belonging to other occupations should fully protect their own. . . .

And should God will that every member of a respective occupation concern himself with his own affairs, then all occupations will flourish and merchants will prosper so much as to be beyond comparison with the present wealth. And taxes could be collected from them twice as great, and I believe even thrice or more, than are presently collected.

Because today trade is carried on by boyars, nobles, and their people, officers, soldiers, and peasants—and because they all trade without paying taxes, merchants also carry on a great deal of trade in these people's name without paying taxes. . . . And if a tax collector recognizes them and wants to collect from them, nobles then forcibly intervene in their behalf with the result that no government official dares approach them. And there are [among these people] wealthy individuals whose trade volume reaches 500 or 600 [rubles] but who pay no taxes to the Great Sovereign.

And if all this were corrected, then the merchantry would revive as if from sleep.

The merchants also adhere to an old unjust custom: they harm and cheat each other; and foreigners, as Russians, sell goods that seem outwardly to be good but really are of poor quality or of poor workmanship. Some goods, even very poor, are covered up with good ones and sold dearly. By this device they take advantage of inexperienced people; they cheat them in weight, measures, and price. . . .

Penalties should be imposed for such actions, and government officials should collect them from violators immediately upon discovery. Upon payment of the fine, their names should be entered into an appropriate register and submitted monthly to an appropriate office.

And foreigners who come to fairs without the approval of the Head of the Commerce Administration should not be allowed to trade in large or small quantities. . . .

The strange thing is that after they [foreign merchants] come to us with their trifles they set low prices for our material goods, and double prices or even more for theirs.

As if this were not enough, they even price the money of our Great Tsar, which is none of their business; they should price the money of their sovereigns because they have power over their rulers. But our great Emperor is autocrat in his state, and if he should decree that a copeck is worth a grivna, then it can be so. We, in our Tsardom, by the will of our monarch, are free to put a price on commodities they bring to us; if they do not like it they will not sell it; like it or not, we will not forcibly take anything from them. We should make one thing firm: those commodities that have not been sold, or those that are useless, should not be allowed to be stored ashore; they must be taken back or kept aboard ship.

There was a time when they were arrogant; they took every advantage over us when our monarchs were not interested in trade affairs and empowered the boyars with it. When foreigners came, they would bribe important persons with a gift, one or two hundred rubles worth, and would in return reap a profit 1000 times that because the boyars held the merchantry in contempt and were willing to sell all of merchantry for a penny. . . .

If foreigners should not trade with us because of their pride or intransigence for two or three or even five or six years, then our merchants would benefit greatly because goods that were selling in our Rus for a ruble would sell for a half or even less. Foreigners should not be allowed to buy at the lower prices because that price resulted from their intransigence.

Without any justification they placed a high price on their goods and thereby caused great hardship; for this not our but their intransigence is responsible. They found fault with our Russian money which is none of their business. When our money comes to their land, then if they do not take our copeck for even a penny, they are free to do it; it is their land and their freedom. But in our land they have no such authority; here the authority belongs to our monarch by whose will we also have some freedom. But they, having come to our land, have put a price on our money and raised prices on all of their goods. . . . A *pud* of copper formerly sold for three rubles, but now it sells for seven or eight rubles; tin sold for about three rubles, but now it sells for more than six; wax was sold for a poltina a *pud*, but now it sells for three times as high. Writing paper that sold for eight grivnas per foot now sells for two rubles. A glass jar that sold for three rubles now sells for ten. They have doubled or tripled the price on all foreign goods, and want thereby to reduce the Russian Tsardom to poverty. They take advantage over us, and instead of material goods they bring us various drinks which they praise highly: "This drink is genuine and very good." They hope that through such praise we will buy more and give them more money. And we drink their drink, and then either vomit or excrete it. They also bring to us glassware so that we would buy it, break it, and throw it away. What we ought to do is to build five or six factories and then flood all of their countries with our glassware. . . .

And if they should refuse to sell their goods at a fair price, then they should be told to take all of their commodities home. And poor quality or useless commodities should not be accepted even at half the price if we are to prevent them from thinking that we are fools and from taking undue advantage of us. . . .

For the sake of national preservation, both monks and merchants should be kept away from excessive drinking and luxurious life; they especially should be kept away from foreign drinks; not only should they not drink themselves, but also they should not bring any into an inn to someone else. I think it would not be a bad idea to extend this prohibition to all government officials, so that they would not develop a habit for foreign drinks and would not lose money easily. . . .

We do not gain anything from foreign drinks except vanity, loss of our Russian wealth, and harm to our health. For it we give them from Russian Tsardom our copper money and foreign currency, and other necessities without which they cannot exist and which make them rich. From the foreigners we get only what we drink, and which we either excrete or vomit, and which in addition endangers our health and shortens our life. . . .

It would also be desirable to introduce among merchants the idea that they should aid and not ruin one another. In case they are unable to improve themselves with their own money, they should be allowed to borrow from the Tsar's treasury or local government agencies a sum of money equal to a portion of their business so that no industrious individual would fall into poverty from a misfortune. . . .

Peasant life is poor for no other reason than of their own laziness, the disconcern of administrators, and finally, oppression by the nobility and non-protection [by the state].

If His Tsarist Majesty's taxes were levied on the land they own on the basis of the amount of land each peasant cultivates, and if these taxes were collected from them during advantageous time, and if the nobles would take nothing from the remainder and would not impose an additional burden on them, but would collect only their own dues, and require of them work for their use of land, and would look after their own peasants so that they would not waste time outside Sundays and holidays but be constantly at work, peasants would never become poor.

And peasants who become lazy should be severely punished, because any peasant who becomes dissolute will never go straight but will lean toward banditry and other thievery.

The peasant should diligently plough land during the summer and work in the forest during the winter. This will provide sufficiently for his domestic needs; and he may even obtain some profit for himself.

And if he has no useful work at his own house, then he should go to places where people work for hired wages so that he will not waste time; and if he should do this no peasant will be poor.

To protect peasant life it is essential to see to it that their homes be rebuilt to enable them to live more freely and peacefully; peasants in poor villages are often ruined because they are very crowded, and whenever one house catches on fire the whole village is burnt and not one house left standing. Through fire they lose not only homes, but food and cattle, and this reduces them to great poverty. If they were not crowded they would not suffer as much. . . .

Peasants also suffer greatly from bandits; if a village has twenty or thirty or more [peasant homes] and a small band of bandits invades the home of a peasant and begins torturing and burning him and taking his belongings openly on their wagons, his neighbors, although they see and hear all this happening, do not leave their own homes to rescue him. As a result bandits do as they wish and torture many peasants to death. Because of this it is impossible for any peasant to become rich.

To protect them from such ruin it is essential to issue in all villages and settlements a firm decree providing that in case bandits should come to someone, and neighbors in that village or settlement would not come to his rescue and would not pursue the bandits, then all those neighbors should be knouted; and whatever has been taken by the bandits because of their negligence should be restored double by his neighbors.

And if bandits should be numerous so that a given village could not handle them, neighboring villages should be notified, and grown men with arms, hooks, and clubs should go out to apprehend those bandits.

And if peasants from a village should refuse to go, they should be knouted and be forced to help restore the robbed property to the victimized village.

And should someone be tortured to death because of the peasants' unconcern, then a penalty of fifty rubles or more should be imposed on all those who failed to come to the rescue.

For if peasants were to live in harmony and were to aid and defend each other, bandits would not dare to attack them suddenly, beat them up, and set [their homes] on fire. And if peasants were to live in harmony and were not to insult each other, they all would be satisfied and would lead holy lives.

Peasants suffer greatly because there are no literate people among them. Villages that have twenty or thirty houses have not one individual that is literate. Any person can come to them with or without an imperial decree and say that he has such a decree and they believe him, and consequently suffer unnecessarily because they all are like the blind who cannot see or understand anything. As a result many individuals come to them without imperial decrees, inflict upon them great losses, and as the peasants cannot argue with them they collect from them money which ruins them.

To protect them from such unjust losses, it seems that it would not be a bad idea to force peasants to send their children ten years of age or younger to governmental clerks to learn how to read and write. I think it would be a good thing if even the smallest village had a literate person. They should be firmly told to let their children be educated, without delay, not less than three to four years. And if they do not let their children be educated, then those children who grow up illiterate should be forced to pay a penalty. For when they learn how to read and write they will be more useful not only to their nobles but to state interests as well. They will be very useful in the army, and no one will cheat them or illegally take something away from them.

I believe it would also be a good idea to issue a decree for regions of the lower [Volga] to force, if need be, the children of the Mordva people to learn how to read and write. When they learn they will like it, because, as in Russia, their villages are visited by soldiers and other government officials, sometimes with and sometimes without authorization, who do as they please because they [the natives] are illiterate and without any protection. . . .

If their children were to learn how to read and write, they would then be their spokesmen and would not allow them to be harmed as before; on the contrary, they would protect them from all illegal abuses.

Others who would learn reading and writing may learn the Christian faith and may wish to be christened, and little by little those literates could convert to Christianity other of their brethren. . . .

Nobles are not eternal but temporary masters of the peasants; for that reason they do not protect them; their direct master is the autocrat of All-Russia.

Consequently nobles should not be allowed to ruin peasants; they should be protected by a Tsar's decree stipulating that all peasants are equal because peasant prosperity is the Tsardom's prosperity.

Consequently, it seems to me, it would be desirable to issue a decree for the nobles stipulating how much corvee and other obligations they may collect from peasants, and how many days per week they are obliged to work for their nobles and perform other tasks, so that they know clearly how much taxes they must pay to the Emperor, how much to the nobleman, and how much to leave for their own needs. Judges should be instructed to see to it that nobles impose nothing in excess of what they are legally entitled to, thus bringing peasants into ruin. . . .

It seems to me that adopting the following [rule] would be very advantageous for the peasants: whenever a peasant completely fulfills his obligation to his noble, his noble cannot demand anything above the agreed amount nor oppress him in any way, but see to it only that he does not waste his time and works as hard as possible to make a living for himself. From such an arrangement those peasants who are astute could make a good living.

And if a peasant should not work on the land, and instead should waste time and not accumulate any surplus, such a peasant should be observed by nobles, government officials, and local officials, and penalized severely in order to prevent other peasants from falling on acocunt of their laziness into poverty, thievery, and drunkenness. . . .

In my judgment, not the nobles but the Tsar should protect the peasants, because the nobles control them only temporarily while the Tsar has them eternally; peasant prosperity means prosperity for the Tsardom, and peasant poverty means poverty for the Tsardom. Because of this the Tsar should concern himself not only with nobles and soldiers but with merchants and peasants as well, in order to prevent them from falling into poverty and to enable them to live in relative abundance.

5

Events Surrounding
the Assumption of Power
by Empress Anna, 1730

With no successor having been designated, Peter the Great's death in 1725 opened the way to the intrigue, coups d'état, and political uncertainty that were to plague Russia until 1762. Between 1725 and 1727 Catherine I, Peter's second wife, was technically the ruler. Power was held, however, by Alexander Menshikov (1673–1729), one of Peter's trusted lieutenants. From 1727 to 1730 the crown belonged to Peter's grandson, Peter II (born in 1715), although the aristocratic Dolgoruky family exercised great influence during this time. The early death of Peter II in 1730 created a new succession crisis, the third in five years. Let by the Golitsyn family, Russian aristocrats invited Anna, the widowed thirty-seven-year-old daughter of Ivan V (who with Peter I had been co-tsar from 1682 to 1696) to rule the empire. The invitation, however, was subject to Anna's acceptance of certain limitations on autocratic powers. Initially Anna accepted the conditions. When on her way to Moscow from her home in Livonia she was informed by representatives of the petty nobility that the terms did not meet with their approval, Anna repudiated the conditions, punished their originators, and, with the aid of her Baltic-German advisers, of whom Ernst von Biron (1690–1771) was the most influential, inaugurated one of the most unenlightened reigns in Russian history.

From Christof Herman von Manstein, *Memoirs of Russia: Historical, Political, Military from the Year 1727–1744* . . . (London: 1770), pp. 25–36. Items in brackets are mine. Certain spellings have been modernized to facilitate reading.

The young Emperor* fell sick on the 17th of January [1730] of small-pox. The ignorance of the physicians, who mistook it for merely a violent fever, and the too ungovernable vivacity of this prince were the cause of his death. He would not bear to remain quiet; he opened a window, and the small-pox, which had begun to come out, struck in again, and on the 29th of January (old style) he died in the first of the spring of his youth.

The reign of Peter II had lasted but two years and nine months, and though this Prince was so very young when he died, he was, nevertheless, regretted by the whole nation. The Russians of the old stock found in him a prince after their own heart, especially for his having quit Peters-burg, and brought back their residence to Moscow. Even at this instance all Russia pronounces this epoch the happiest that it had known for a century past. There was no compulsion to serve in the army, so that every one could stay at home quietly, enjoy his property, and even improve it. Except a few of the great, who were jealous of the power of the Dolgorukys,† all the rest of the nation were content. Universal joy appeared on every face, the treasury was replenishing, and the town of Moscow was lifting its head again out of the ruin into which Peter I had precipitated it by his taste and predilection for Petersburg. There was nothing went amiss but the marine and the army, which would have been entirely ruined if this reign had continued some years more on the same foot.

It would be difficult to define the character of Peter II on the account of his extreme youth. It is generally, however, agreed that he had a good heart, a great deal of vivacity and penetration, and an excellent memory. It was enough for him to hear any thing once to retain it; so that, if with so many naturally good qualities he could have profited of the instructions of others, it is likely he would have become a very great Prince. . . .

To the Dolgorukys it was reproached that they had contrived to hide from all the world the danger of the Emperor's sickness as long as they possibly could; and that as soon as they found there were no hopes of his recovery they had framed a will, by which Princess Catherine [Dolgoruky] who had been betrothed to the Emperor, was instituted Empress and Heiress of the Empire; which will Prince Ivan [Dolgoruky] had signed in the name of the Emperor, having been accustomed to sign the name of that Prince during his life, by his order. Accordingly, scarce had Peter II closed his eyes in death when Prince Ivan came out of the chamber with his drawn sword in his hand, flourishing it, and cried out *Long live*

---

* Peter II, grandson of Peter the Great, ruled from 1727–1730.—Ed.

† The Dolgorukys were an ancient and influential family in Russia. Their influence rose to unprecedented heights during the reign of Peter the Great and immediately following his death.—Ed.

Empress Catherine! but no one joining the cry, he saw that his project was miscarrying; upon which, putting his sword up again in his scabbard, he went home immediately and burnt the will. There are, however, many who will have it that no such will was ever made, and that it was merely an invention of the enemies of the Dolgorukys to accomplish the ruin of that family. But as this was inserted in the manifestos which were published against these princes as one of the principal articles of their guilt, I could not well avoid mentioning it; besides, as to the fact above specified of the Prince Ivan's coming out of the apartment with his sword drawn, it is perfectly true; I had it from a man of great veracity; and even from one of the family itself: it is also certain that if the Dolgorukys had not been at variance among themselves, the Princess Catherine would infallibly have mounted the throne, but the disunion that reigned among their chiefs was the destruction of all of them.

The council of state, the senate, and such of the principal generals of the army as were then at Moscow, assembled immediately after the death of Peter II and sat in close committee in a chamber of the palace of Kremlin. The high-chancellor Golovkin announced to the assembly the death of the Emperor, and as soon as he had done speaking, the Prince Dmitri Mikhailovich Golitsyn* got up and said that "since, by the demise of Peter II the whole male line of Peter I was extinct, and that Russia had suffered extremely by despotic power, to the prevalence of which the great number of foreigners brought in by Peter I had greatly contributed, it would be highly expedient to limit the supreme authority by salutary laws and not to confer the imperial crown on the new Empress that should be chosen but under certain conditions;" concluding with putting the question to the whole assembly, whether "they did not approve this proposal?" They all assented to it, without any the least opposition. Upon which the Prince Basil Lukich Dolgoruky proposed the duchess dowager of Courland; alleging, that as the crown was now falling to a female, it was but just to prefer the daughter of the Tsar Ivan V, the elder brother of Peter I to those of this emperor; that though the duchess of Mecklenburg** was the eldest, it was to be considered that she was married to a foreign Prince, whereas the Duchess of Courland was actually a widow, and not being above thirty-six years of age, might marry, and give heirs to Russia.

The true reason, however, for preferring the duchess of Courland was that she being at Mittau, the remoteness of that place would afford time for the firmer establishment of the republican system.

All the votes then united in her favor, and it was agreed that the

---

* Like the Dolgorukys, the Golitsyns were an ancient aristocratic family of Russia.—Ed.

** The Duchess of Mecklenburg had left her husband in 1719 and returned to Russia to live.—Ed.

council of state, which was at that time constituted of seven members of whom the majority were the Dolgorukys or their relations, should have the whole power, and the assembly framed the following articles:

1. That the Empress Anna was to reign only, in virtue of the resolves, upon deliberation of the privy-council.

2. That she should not declare war nor make peace on her own authority.

3. That she would not lay any new tax, or bestow any post or place of consequence.

4. That she would punish no gentleman with death unless he was duly convicted of his crime.

5. That she should not confiscate any one's property.

6. That she should not alienate or dispose of any lands belonging to the crown.

7. That she should not marry, nor choose an heir, without asking upon all these points the consent of the privy-council.

The assembly then chose three members to notify to the Empress her accession to the throne, and to propose to her the conditions under which she was to reign.

On the part of the council was deputed the Prince Basil Lukich Dolgoruky; on the part of the senate, the Prince Michael Golitsyn; and on the part of the nobility, the lieutenant-general Leontev.

In the instructions given to these deputies, it was enjoined to them to require of the Empress that she should sign the above articles, and that she should not bring her favorite with her to Moscow, Biron,* gentleman of the chamber. . . .

The council of state imagined they had sufficient precaution against the restoration of despotic government, having exacted from the whole army an oath that it would not serve the Empress but conjointly with the senate. Moreover, before the assembly broke up, they had forbidden, under pain of death, the acquainting the new Empress of any thing that had been debated and resolved. She was not to receive advice of her election and of the conditions under which she was to mount the throne but at first hand from the deputies.

Notwithstanding which the lieutenant-general Iaguzhinskii dispatched that night his aid-de-camp, Mons. Sumarokov to Mittau to apprize the Empress of every thing.

He wrote to her, and entreated her to hasten her departure from Mittau as soon as the deputies should have their audience; to submit to all the conditions that should be required of her; and for the rest, to trust to his counsels: that, in the mean while, until her arrival at Moscow, he

---

* Ernst von Biron (1690–1771), was a close associate of Empress Anna during her reign (1730–1740), and some Russian historians refer to this period as "Bironovshchina", the rule of Biron.—Ed.

would use his best endeavors to increase the party of such as were not at all pleased at this government by the council of state; that his father-in-law, the high-chancellor Golovkin, was already on her side, and that after the arrival of her Majesty everything would be terminated to her wish.

Sumarokov had a good deal of difficulty to pass, all the roads round the capital being strictly guarded. Every traveller was diligently searched for papers or letters: however, he disguised himself so well, that he got through all undiscovered. But that was not all; he had the same dangers to encounter at the advanced posts on the confines of Courland, who had orders to stop all persons that should come by the way from Moscow. The apprehension of this made him take such a large circuit that in spite of all obstacles he got safe to Mittau. It is true he had been necessarily so much retarded in his journey that he had barely time to deliver his dispatches to the Empress before the deputies arrived and demanded audience.

The Prince Dolgoruky had, I do not know by what means, discovered that a courier from Moscow had got thither before the deputies, and had had admission to the Empress. Upon this he ordered a strict search to be made for him; and finding that he was just set out on his return, he sent to pursue him, and he was accordingly brought back to Mittau. The deputies then ordered him an unmerciful bastonade; made him be put into irons and carried to Moscow, where the count Iaguzhinskii was also seized, and thrown into close prison. . . .

The Empress consented, without making any difficulty, to the signing of whatever the deputies presented to her on the part of the privy-council. She did not even oppose the leaving her favorite behind her at Mittau, and got immediately in readiness to set out for Moscow.

Her Majesty came on the 20th of February to a village called Sviatskii (or *All Saints*) situated two leagues from Moscow, where she stopped for five days. As soon as she was arrived there, the high-chancellor, at the head of the members of the privy-council, repaired thither, and presented her with the ribbon of St. Andrew, and star, in a gold basin. As soon as the Empress saw it, she said, "It is true, I had forgot to put the 'order on';" and taking it with her own hands out of the basin she made one of her attendants put it on her, without suffering any of the members of the privy-council to help her on with it; and when the high-chancellor was beginning to harangue her, she stopped him, and prevented his going on.

On the same day, she appointed the Prince Saltykov, a very near relation to the mother of the Empress, lieutenant-colonel of the guards. This was the first act of authority she took upon her since her accession to the throne. The rest of her conduct, after her arrival at Moscow gave many of the members of the council and senate reason to think that she was satisfied with the restrictions laid on despotic power. She signed anew all that the council of state required and affected to submit cheerfully to all the conditions.

Her secret conduct was very different from this her public one. Her favorite, whom, at the requisition of the council, she had left behind, was arrived at Moscow; and she took all the pains imaginable to form a strong party. She tried to engage the guards by her liberality to those who daily did duty about her person. In short, she left no arts or managements unemployed towards effectuating her purpose of creating misunderstandings among the members of the council of state. Every thing succeeded to her wish. It had been remarked to them that the family of the Dolgorukys, and its connections, would be the only persons that would be benefited by the smallness of the Empress's influence; that they had tied up her hands only to establish the more firmly the power which they had acquired under Peter II; that there were already of that family many of the members of the privy-council, and of the senate; that, little by little, the number would go on augmenting; and that they ought to reflect on the conduct of that family, after the death of the late Emperor, at which time they had aspired to transmit the imperial crown to their family, in which not having been able to succeed, they had not given up the hope of bringing it about in time, by their circumscription of the supreme power.

Neither was it omitted the instilling a mistrust into the lesser nobility, which is very numerous in Russia, by giving them to understand that none of them stood any chance of obtaining any preferment of the least consequence, while the council of state should have all the power in their hands; as each member would make a point of procuring the most considerable employments for his respective relations and creatures; and that, properly speaking, they would be the slaves of the council: whereas, if the Empress was to be declared sovereign, the least private gentleman might pretend to the first posts of the empire with the same currency as the first Princes: that there were examples of this under Peter I when the greatest regard was paid to true merit; and that if that Prince had done acts of severity, he had been obliged to it; besides, that the lesser nobility had nowise suffered by him; on the contrary, they had recovered their consequence under his reign.

Such hints thrown out with proper discretion did not fail of producing the expected effect. The guards who, even to the private soldiers, are constituted of hardly any but the nobles of the country, formed meetings. Several hundreds of country-gentlemen assembled at the houses of the Princes Trubetskoi, Bariatynskii, and Cherkasskii, as being those in whom they had the greatest confidence, and who were in the interest of the Empress. These did not fail of animating them more and more, till, on the 8th of March, they judged them ripe for the point at which they wanted them. It was then that these Princes, at the head of six hundred gentlemen, went to wait on the Empress; and having obtained an audience, entreated of her to order the council of state and the senate to assemble, for the examination of certain points touching the regency. The Empress having consented, she ordered, at the same time, count Saltykov, lieutenant-general, and lieutenant-colonel of the guards, to have all the avenues well guarded, and not to permit any one to go out of the palace. The guards were also commanded to have their pieces loaded with ball, and special care was taken to acquaint all those who came to court of the precautions which had been ordered.

While these arrangements were taking, the council of state and the senate were assembled. The Empress gave orders that both these bodies should appear before her. These princes then having repaired to the presence-chamber, or hall with the canopy, the count Matveev, advancing towards her Majesty, spoke and said that he was deputed by the whole nobility of the empire to represent to her that she had been, by the deputies of the council of state, surprised into the concessions she had made; that Russia having for so many ages been governed by sovereign monarchs, and not by council, all the nobility entreated of her to take into her own hands the reins of government; that all the nation was of the same opinion, and wished that the family of her Majesty might reign over them to the end of time.

The Empress, at this speech, affected great surprize: "How", said she, "Was it not then with the will *of the whole nation that I signed the act presented to me at Mittau?*" Upon which the whole assembly answered, "No." At this she turned toward Prince Dolgoruky, and said to him, "*How came you then, Prince Basil Lukich, to impose on me so?*" She then ordered the high-chancellor to go and bring her the writings which she had signed. This being done, she made him read them with an audible voice; and at each article she stopped him, and asked if such an article was for the good of the nation. The assembly having to all and each of them constantly answered "No;" she took the deeds out of the hands of the high-chancellor, and tore them saying, "*These writings then are not necessary.*" She declared at the same time, "That as the empire of Russia had *never been governed but by one sole monarch,*" she "claimed the same prerogatives as her ancestors had had, from whom she derived her crown by right of inheritance, and not from the election of the council of state, as they had pretended; and that whoever should oppose her sovereignty should be punished, as guilty of high-treason." This declaration was received with applause, and nothing was heard all over the town but acclamations and shouts of joy.

The Empress also gave assurance, "that though she had taken the supreme power into her own hands, she should nevertheless make it her care to govern with all imaginable mildness; that she would have nothing

more at heart than the happiness of her people; that she would constantly avail herself of the good counsels of her senate, composed of
persons of the greatest experience and the most acknowledged probity;
and that she should never have recourse to acts of rigor, unless in the
utmost extremity."

To secure her then against any enterprises of the disaffected, there were
guards posted in all the streets; the troops took afresh the oath of allegiance; and couriers were dispatched into all the provinces with the
notification of the Empress having taken on her the supreme authority.

The lesser nobility and the common people, who had dreaded the
government by a council of state, rejoiced much at this alteration of
things: but the evening after that this affair had been decided, there was
observed an Aurora Borealis, which, overspreading the whole horizon,
made it appear all in blood. This phenomenon made such an impression
on the superstitious people as to create a general terror; and in the
sequence of time the Russians pretended that this presage was but too
fatally verified by the streams of blood which Biron caused to be shed
in that country.

The consternation of the members of the council, and especially of the
Dolgorukys, was extreme, when they were summoned to appear before
the Empress. Prince Dmitri Mikhailovich Golitsyn was the only one of
them who preserved serenity of countenance, with even some disdain. He
said to some of his friends, "Well! the feast was prepared, but the
guests were not worthy of it; I know I shall be the victim of this. Be it so.
It is for my country I shall suffer. I feel the end of my career; but those
who make me now mourn will have longer cause to mourn than I. . . ."

6

Events Surrounding
the Assumption of Power
by Empress Elizabeth, 1741

Before she died, on October 17, 1740, Anna named
as her successor an infant boy, Ivan VI (born in
August 1740), the son of her sister's daughter, Anne
of Mecklenburg and Prince Anthony Ulrich von
Brunswick-Bevern-Lüneburg. She also stipulated that
until he reached the age of seventeen her close confidant Biron was to act as regent. These provisions
were made without consulting the Senate, the Holy
Synod, or any other important institutions and individuals, including the all-powerful Guard Regiments.
A conspiracy consequently developed against Biron's
regency, led by Field Marshal Burkhard Christoph
Munnich (1683–1767), commander of the Russian
armies. On November 9, 1740, Munnich arrested
Biron, making it possible for Princess Anne, mother
of Ivan VI, to proclaim herself regent of Russia with
Munnich first minister. Early in March 1741,
Munnich was replaced by Count A. I. Osterman
(1686–1747), for many years an architect of Russian
foreign policy, German in-fighting for control of the
Russian crown came to an end on December 5, 1741,
when Peter the Great's daughter Elizabeth, with the
aid of the guards, arrested the entire Brunswick
family, deposed Ivan VI, and assumed power.

The day after the decease of the Empress [Anna], the senate, the
clergy, and all who were at that time of any consequence in Petersburg,
were summoned to the summer-palace, where the Empress had passed
the last days of her life; the troops were put under arms, and the duke of

From Christof Herman von Manstein, Memoirs of Russia: Historical, Political,
Military from the Year 1727 to 1744 . . . (London: 1770), pp. 264–275, 279–
281, 308–326. Manstein took an active part in some of these events. Items in
brackets are mine. Certain spellings have been modernized to facilitate reading.

Courland [Biron] caused the act to be publicly read by which he was declared regent of the empire of Russia till the Emperor Ivan VI should have completed his seventeenth year. Every one then took the oath of allegiance to the new Emperor, and everything passed off quietly enough for the first days; but as the duke was universally detested, the murmuring soon began to break out.

The regent [Biron], who had spies everywhere, soon learnt that he was spoken of with contempt; that some officers of the guards, especially of the regiment of Semenevskii, of which Prince Anthony Ulrich was lieutenant-colonel, had said that if the Prince would undertake anything against the regent they would readily assist him. He was also informed that Princess Anne and her spouse resented their being excluded from the regency. Beginning then to be uneasy at this, he caused several officers to be taken up and carried prisoners to the citadel: Grammatin, the adjutant of the Prince, was one of them. The general Ushakov, president of the secret chancery, and the solicitor-general, Prince Trubetskoi, had orders to examine them with all imaginable severity. Some of them had the knout inflicted on them, to bring them to an impeachment of others; in short, hardly a day passed while this regency lasted without some being apprehended. . . .

[On the night of November 18, 1740, there was set in motion a palace revolution masterminded by Marshal Burkhard Munnich (1683–1767) with the assistance of his aide-de-camp, General Christof Herman von Manstein, the author of this account.]

Manstein entered the palace; and not to make too much noise, he made the detachment follow him at a distance. All the centinels suffered him to pass in without any opposition; for, as he was personally known to all the soldiers, they imagined he might be sent to the duke upon some affair of consequence, so that he crossed the guards, and got as far as the apartments, without any difficulty. . . . In the chamber he found a great bed, in which the duke [Biron] and duchess were lying buried in a profound sleep. Not even the noise he had made in forcing open the door had waked them. Manstein having got close to the bed, drew the curtains, and desired to speak with the regent. Upon this, both started up in a surprise and began to cry out loud, judging rightly enough that he was not come to bring them any good news. Manstein happening to stand on the side on which the duchess lay, the regent threw himself out of bed, on the ground, certainly with an intention to hide himself under the bed; but this officer springing quickly round to the other side, threw himself upon him, and held him fast embraced till the guards came in. The duke having at length got upon his legs again, and wanting to disengage himself from their hold, distributed blows with his double fist to the right and left, to which the soldiers made no return but with strokes from the butt-end of their muskets; and throwing him down again on the floor, they crammed a handkerchief into his mouth and bound his hands with an officer's sash; then they led him, naked as he was, to the guardroom, where they covered him with a soldier's cloak, and put him into a coach of the marshal's that was waiting for him. An officer was placed in it by the side of him, and he was carried to the winter-palace.

While the soldiers were struggling with the duke, the duchess was got out of bed in her shift, and running after him as far as into the street, when a soldier took her in his arms and asked Manstein what he should do with her. He bid him carry her back to her chamber; but the soldier not caring, it seems, to take the trouble of it, threw her down on the ground, in the midst of the snow, and there left her. The captain of the guard, finding her in this piteous condition, made her clothes be brought to her, and reconducted her to the apartments she had always occupied.

As soon as the duke was thus on the way to the winter-palace, the same colonel, Manstein, was sent to seize his younger brother Gustavus Biron, who was then at Petersburg. He was lieutenant-colonel of the Izmailov regiment of guards. But this expedition required somewhat more of precautionary measures than the first; for Gustavus Biron was beloved in his regiment, and had a guard of it in his house, consisting of a sergeant and twelve men. And, accordingly, the centinels made at first some resistance, but they soon laid hold of, and threatened with death if they made the least noise. After which Manstein went into the bedchamber of Biron and made him get up, telling him that he had an affair of great consequence to impart to him. Having then drawn him to the window, he acquainted him with his orders of arrest. Biron wanted to open the window, and began to cry out; but he was instantly let to know that the duke was seized, and under confinement, and that himself would be killed on the least resistance. The soldiers, who had waited in the adjoining room, came in directly, and satisfied him that there was nothing for him but to obey. They gave him a furred cloke, put him into a sledge, and he too was carried to the winter-palace. . . .

As soon as the duke was seized, order was sent to all the regiments that happened to be then at Petersburg to be put under arms, and to assemble round the palace. The Princess Anne then declared herself Grand-Duchess of Russia, and regent of the empire during the minority of the Emperor. She at the same time put on the collar of the order of St. Andrew, and everyone took a new oath of fidelity, in which the Grand-Duchess was mentioned by name, which had not been done in that imposed by the regent. There were none that did not make great demonstrations of joy at seeing themselves delivered from the tyranny of Biron; and from that moment every thing was quiet. Even the piquets were taken away, which the duke of Courland had posted in the streets to prevent commotions during his regency; and there were some who, at the very moment of the event, prognosticated that it would not be the last revolution; and that those who had been the most active in bringing this about would be the first that would be overset by another. Time has shown that they were not in the wrong. . . .

On the 22d of November, the Grand-Duchess bestowed several gratifications and made many promotions.

The Prince, her husband, was declared generalissimo of all the forces of Russia, as well by land as by sea;

Count Munnich had the post of prime-minister;

Count Osterman that of high-admiral, which had been many years vacant;

The Prince Cherkasskii was appointed high-chancellor, a post that had not been filled since the death of count Golovkin;

The count Golovkin, son of the high-chancellor, deceased, was made vice-chancellor.

Several others had great recompences in ready-money, or in lands. All the officers and subalterns, who had been employed in apprehending the duke, were promoted. Lieutenant-colonel Manstein had a regiment, and some fine lands, which were taken from him again when the Empress Elizabeth mounted the throne. The soldiers of the guard received their gratifications in money.

Marshal Munnich had not thus worked the duke's fall, but in order to raise himself to the highest degree of fortune; he had retained the same views as when he persuaded the duke to make himself regent; that is to say, to draw to himself the whole power, to leave to the duchess nothing but the title of regent, and himself to do all the functions of it; imagining now to himself that no one would dare to undertake any the least thing against him. He was mistaken. . . .

It has been above set forth that the duke of Courland was, on the same day that he was seized, transferred to Schlüsselburg. A commission, composed of several senators, proceeded there on his trail and condemned him to death. He had his pardon. The Princess Anne had, from the first moment of the revolution, resolved to banish him to Siberia. An engineer had been sent there to direct the building of a house, expressly designed for his prison. Marshal Munnich gave the first sketch of it with a pencil, little then imagining that it was for himself he was planning.

In the month of May [1741], the duke of Courland was, with his family, transferred from Schlüsselburg to his new habitation. . . .

The court of Petersburg had not failed to notify to the states of Courland that their duke was seized; that he had had his trial and been found guilty of high-treason; that he and all his family were sent to Siberia, where they were to pass the remainder of their lives. . . .

The Princess Elizabeth [daughter of Peter the Great], though far from satisfied during the whole reign of the Empress Anna, had remained quiet till the marriage of the Prince Anthony Ulrich with the Princess Anne was concluded. Then, indeed, she began to take some steps towards forming a party; all which, however, was transacted with such secrecy that nothing of it transpired while the Empress lived. But after her death, and the seizure of Biron, she began to think more seriously of it. . . .

At Petersburg the Princess began with gaining over some soldiers of the guards of the regiment of Preobrazhenskii. The principal of them was one Grunstein, who, from a bankrupt-merchant, had taken on to be a soldier. This man engaged many others, so that little by little there were got as far as thirty grenadiers of the guards to be of the plot. . . . [On December 4, 1741] the Grand-Duchess took the Princess Elizabeth aside, and told her that she had had several intimations concerning her conduct and that, especially, her surgeon [Lestock] had frequent conferences with the French minister [Marquess de la Chetardie], and was plotting treasonable practices against the reigning family; that hitherto, she (the Grand-Duchess) had not wished to give credit to these informations; but that, if they continued, she should be obliged to have Lestock taken up, and that means would be used to force him to confess the truth. The Princess stood out this conversation very well. She protested to the Grand-Duchess that she had never had a thought of undertaking anything against her, or against her son; that she had too much religion to break the oath she had taken; that all these informations were given by enemies, who wanted to make her unhappy; that Lestock had never set his foot in Chetardie the French ambassador's house (which was true, for there had been always a third place chosen for their interviews); that, however, the Grand-Duchess might, if she pleased, have Lestock taken up, which would but serve the more to discover her being guiltless. The Princess Elizabeth shed abundance of tears at this explanation, and succeeded so well in persuading her of her innocence, that the Grand-Duchess (who also wept much) believed her wrongfully accused. . . .

At midnight [of December 5, 1741], the Princess, accompanied by the Vorontsovs and Lestock, repaired to the barracks of the grenadiers of the regiment of Preobrazhenskii; thirty of whom were, as has been observed, personally in the plot. These assembled others, to the number of three hundred, as well subalterns, as private men. The Princess, in a few words, declared her intention to them, and asked their assistance. They all, to a man, consented to sacrifice themselves for her. Their first step of dispatch was to seize the officer of the grenadiers, who lay in the barracks, his name Grews, a Scotchman; after which they took an oath of fidelity to the Princess. She then put herself at the head of them, and marched straight to the winter-palace, and entered, with part of those that followed her, into the guard-rooms, without finding the least resistance. There she told the officers the reason of her coming. They made no show of opposition, and left her to act as she pleased. Centinels were then posted at all the doors and avenues. Lestock and Vorontsov penetrated with a detachment of grenadiers into the apartments of the Grand-Duchess, and made prisoners, her and her husband, her children, and the favorite, that was lodged near them. As soon as this was done, several detachments were sent to seize marshal Munnich, his son, lord steward of the household to the Grand-Duchess; count Osterman, count Golovkin, count Lowenwolde, grand-marshal of the court; baron de Mengden, and some others, persons of less consequence. All these prisoners were carried to the palace of the Princess. She sent Lestock to marshal Lacy, to acquaint him of what she had done; and to declare to him that he had nothing to fear; ordering him at the same time to come directly to her.

The senate, and all the greatest men of the empire that were then at Petersburg, were convened at the palace of the new Empress; and, at break of day all the troops were assembled before it, where, after the declaration to them that the Princess Elizabeth had seated herself on the throne of her father; the oath of fidelity was tendered to them, and taken without any contradiction; so that every thing was presently in as great tranquillity as before.

The same day, the Empress quit the house in which she had resided till then, and took possession of the imperial palace. . . .

On the day of the revolution, the new Empress declared, by a manifesto, that she had ascended her father's throne, in virture of her hereditary right, and that she had caused the usurpers to be seized.

Three days afterwards, another manifesto was published, which was to demonstrate her having an unquestionable title to the imperial crown. It was also therein specified that as neither the Princess Anne nor her husband had any right to the throne of Russia, they should be sent back, with their family, to Germany. They were made to leave Petersburg, with all their domestics, under an escort of the guard, commanded by general Saltykov, who had been at the head of the police in the time of the Empress Anna; they got no farther than Riga, where they were stopped from proceeding farther. At first, they were lodged in the citadel, and some months after they were transferred to the fort of Dunamund; and, at length, instead of being permitted to go to Germany, they were brought back into Russia.

They have had different places for their prisons. The Grand-Duchess died in childbed, March 1746. Her body was brought to Petersburg, and buried in the convent of St. Alexander Nevskii. . . .

There was a commission appointed, which was constituted of several senators and others of the Russian nobility, to prepare and conduct their [the prisoners'] trial. They were accused of various crimes. Among others, it was imputed to count Osterman that he had contributed, by his cabals, to the election of the Empress Anna, and that he had suppressed the will of the Empress Catherine.

Count Munnich was charged with having told the soldiers, at the time of his seizing on the duke of Courland, that it was in order to place the Princess Elizabeth on the throne.

Both of them could easily have disproved these accusations, but they were not allowed to make their defence.

The true crimes of all these prisoners were their having incurred the displeasure of the new Empress and their having too well served the Empress Anna.

Besides, the Empress had promised those who assisted her to ascend the throne that she would deliver them from the oppression of foreigners; so that she was obliged to condemn those of them who had been the highest promoted.

The tenor of the sentence was that count Osterman should be broken alive upon the wheel; that marshal Munnich should be quartered; that count Golovkin, count Lowenwolde, and the baron Mengden should be beheaded.

The Empress at once pardoned them all as to their lives; but they were banished into different parts of Siberia. Count Osterman had not his pardon till he was on the scaffold, with his head on the block.

The court caused a manifesto to be published on this occasion, in which all the crimes of which they were accused were specified.

All the fortunes of the exiled, except those that their wives had brought them, were confiscated to the profit of the court, which gratified others with them.

The permission had been indulged to these ladies of going to settle upon their own estates, and of not following their husbands; but not one of them would avail herself of the liberty.

The first care of the Empress, after her getting possession of the imperial power, was to reward those who had served her in this revolution. She began with her favorite, Razumovskii, who was declared chamberlain some months after her coronation. She raised him to the post of grandmaster of the hunt, made him a count, and gave him the blue ribbon. Shuvalov, the two Vorontsov brothers, and Balck, who had served the Princess in quality of gentlemen of the chamber, were also made chamberlains.

She declared Lestock actual privy-counsellor, first physician, and president of the college of physicians. The whole company of grenadiers of the regiment of Preobrazhenskii were ennobled and promoted. The private men of them had the rank of lieutenants, and the corporals that of majors; the armourer and quarter-master that of lieutenant-colonels; and the sergeants that of colonels of the army. It was called the company of body-guards. Her Majesty declared herself the captain of it; the Prince of Hesse-Homburg, lieutenant-captain Razumovskii, and Vorontsov, first lieutenants, with the rank of lieutenant-generals; and the Shuvalovs, lieutenants, with the rank of major-generals. Grunstein was made adjutant of this company, with the title of brigadier. . . .

This company committed all imaginable disorders for the first months that the Empress remained at Petersburg. The new noble lieutenants ran through all the dirtiest public-houses, got drunk, and wallowed in the streets. They entered into the houses of the greatest noblemen, demanding money with threats, and took away, without ceremony, whatever they liked. There was no keeping within bounds men who, having been all their lifetime used to be disciplined by drubbing, could not presently familiarise themselves to a more civil treatment. It must have been the work of time to reduce them to good manners. I do not know whether they were ever brought to correct themselves, but the most unruly of them were expelled from the corps and placed as officers in other regiments of the army, where the vacancies were many. An admirable expedient this for procuring excellent officers! . . . .

The Empress recalled from Siberia a number of the banished families, of which a great part had been sent thither in the time of the Empress Catherine [I]. All the posts were restored to them which they had occupied before their imprisonment. It was reckoned that since the commencement of the Empress Anna's reign there had been above twenty thousand sent to Siberia. There were five thousand of them of which the habitation could never be discovered, nor any the least news learnt of what was become of them. But as the Empress had recalled all that could be found, there was not a day passed but there were seen at court some new faces of persons who had passed several years successively in the most horrid prisons. . . .

7

Peter III's Charter to the Nobility, February 18, 1762

The chief beneficiaries during the era of palace revolutions were the nobles. Between 1725 and 1762 they succeeded in reducing their obligations to the state while at the same time retaining all the rights and privileges that went with that service. In 1730, for instance, Anna repealed Peter the Great's decree on primogeniture (see Chapter 2); in 1731 she established a military academy for the sons of the nobility; and in 1736 she reduced the compulsory military service of the nobles to twenty-five years. During Elizabeth's reign (1741–1761) the government established a state bank for the nobles and granted them the right to elect provincial officials with broad executive and judicial powers in local affairs. The nobility's control over their serfs was also expanded. These and other measures helped to weld the heterogeneous Russian nobility into a class-conscious social group. A significant step in that process occurred early in 1762 when the new tsar, Peter III, freed the Russian nobles from all compulsory ·service to the state. Peter's "friendly gesture," however, failed to save his life. In 1762 he was murdered by his wife's lovers.

All Europe, indeed the greater part of the world, knows what difficulties Peter the Great, wise monarch of immortal memory, Our dear sovereign grandfather and Emperor of all the Russias had encountered in his efforts to bring happiness to his country in instructing the people in military, civil, and political affairs.

From *Polnoe Sobranie Zakonov Russkoi Imperii* . . . (*Complete Collection of the Laws of the Russian Empire*), vol. 15, no. 11,444, pp. 912–915. Translation mine. Items in brackets mine.

To achieve this goal it was essential first to convince the nobles, the chief body of the state, of the great advantages enjoyed by enlightened states over those people who live in ignorance and sloth. Because circumstances then demanded extreme sacrifices from Russian nobles, he [Peter I] did not show any mercy towards them, forced them into military and civil service, induced their youth to study useful arts and sciences, sent them to European countries, and, to achieve the same goal as rapidly as possible, even established various schools in Russia itself.

It is true that in the beginning these innovations were burdensome and unendurable for the nobles, as they were deprived of peace, were forced to leave their homes, were obliged against their will to serve in the army or to perform other service, and were required to register their children [in schools]. Many nobles resented these demands, and some even tried to evade them; but they were fined. Some were even deprived of their property and accused of neglecting their own good as well as that of their children.

These demands, though burdensome in the beginning and accompanied by force, proved to be of much advantage during the reigns of Peter the Great's successors, especially during the reign of Our dear aunt, Empress Elizabeth Petrovna, of glorious memory, who followed in the footsteps of her sovereign father, who supported the knowledge of political affairs and who, by her protection, extended much useful knowledge throughout Russia. We can look with pride at everything that has occurred, and every true son of the country will agree that great advantages have resulted from all this. Manners have been improved; knowledge has replaced illiteracy; devotion and zeal for military affairs has resulted in the appearance of many experienced and brave generals; civil and political concerns have attracted many intelligent people; in a word, noble thoughts have penetrated the hearts of all true Russian patriots who have revealed towards Us their unlimited devotion, love, zeal, and fervor. Because of all these reasons We judge it to be no longer necessary to compel the nobles into service as has been the practice hitherto.

Because of these circumstances, and by virtue of the authority granted to Us by the All Mighty, We grant freedom and liberty to the entire Russian nobility, by Our High Imperial Grace, from this moment and forever, to all future generations. They may continue to perform service in Our Empire or in other European countries friendly to Our State on the basis of the following rules:

1. All nobles who are presently in our service may continue as long as they wish or as long as their health may permit them; those serving in the army should not ask for release or furlough during a campaign or three months before a campaign; they should wait for release until the end of a war; those serving in the army may request release or retirement permits from their superiors and must wait for these permits; those

serving Us in various capacities in the first eight ranks must apply for their release directly to Us; other ranks will be released by the departments for which they work.

2. At their retirement We will reward all nobles who serve Us well and faultlessly by promoting them to a higher rank, provided they have served at least one year in the rank from which they retired; those who wish to retire from military service and enter civil service, provided there is a vacancy for them, should be rewarded only if they have served three years in a given rank.

3. Those nobles who have retired or those who have terminated their military or civil service for Us, but who should express a desire to re-enter the military service, shall be admitted, provided they prove worthy to those ranks to which they belong and provided they will not be elevated to ranks higher than those of their co-servicemen who were equal in rank at the retirement; if they should be elevated in rank this should go into effect from the day they re-join the service. We issue this rule in order to give preference in promotions to those now in service over those who have retired and also to make it possible for those who have retired from one service to join other services.

4. Those nobles who will be freed from Our service and who would wish to travel to other European countries should immediately receive the necessary passports from Our Foreign College under one condition: namely, that should ever the need demand, those nobles shall return home whenever they are notified. Everyone should fulfill this request as soon as possible; those who fail to comply with it will have their property confiscated.

5. Those Russian nobles who, in addition to serving Us, serve other European sovereigns, may return to their country and enter Our service fully provided there is a vacancy; those nobles who serve foreign sovereigns in various capacities and can prove it will be accepted to Our service as vacancies develop; the same is true of the employment of lesser ranking nobles.

6. By virtue of this manifesto, no Russian nobleman will ever be forced to serve against his will; nor will any of Our administrative departments make use of them except in emergency cases and then only if We personally should summon them; this rule also applies to the nobility of the Smolensk area. An exception to this rule is St. Petersburg and Moscow, where an *ukaz* of the Sovereign Emperor Peter I stipulates that some men from among the retired nobles should be made available for various needs at the Senate and at the [Heraldic] Office; We amend this Imperial rule by decreeing that henceforth there should be selected annually thirty men to serve in the Senate and twenty to serve in the Office. These men should be chosen by the Heraldic Office from among the nobles living in gubernias and not from those still in service. No

one should be designated by name for this duty. Nobles themselves should decide who should be selected in the *gubernias* and provinces. Local officials should forward the names of those so selected to the Heraldic Office and also provide those selected with needed items.

7. Although, by this gracious manifesto we grant forever freedom to all of Our Russian nobles, except freeholders, Our fatherly concern for them as well as for their children will continue. The latter, We decree, should henceforth, whenever they reach twelve years of age, be reported to the Heraldic Office in *gubernias*, provinces, or cities or wherever is most convenient. From their parents or relatives who are bringing them up, information should be obtained about the level of the children's education up to the age of twelve and where they would like to continue their studies, whether within Our state in various institutions We have founded, in European countries, or should the means of their parents allow it, in their own homes by experienced and skillful teachers. No nobleman should keep his children uneducated under the penalty of Our anger. Those noblemen who have under 1000 serfs should report their children to Our Cadet Corps of the Nobility, where they will learn everything befitting a nobleman and where they will be educated with the utmost care. Following his education each nobleman will assume his rank in accordance with his dignity and reward, and subsequently each may enter and continue his service as indicated above.

8. Those nobles who presently are in Our military service as soldiers or lower rank officers below the rank of Ober-Officer, that is, those who have failed to attain officer rank, should not be allowed to retire unless they have served twelve years in the army.

9. We grant this gracious act to all of Our nobles for eternity as a fundamental and unalterable law; by Our Imperial word We pledge to observe it in its entirety in the most solemn and irrevocable manner. Our rightful successors should not alter it in any way whatsoever, as their adherence to this decree will serve as an indispensable support for the autocratic throne of All Russia. We hope that in return for this act Russian nobles, realizing what great concern We have shown toward them and toward their descendants, will continue to serve Us loyally and zealously and will not withdraw from Our service; on the contrary, that they will seek the service eagerly and will continue it as long as possible, and will educate their children attentively in useful knowledge; those who will not perform any service will also lead purposeless lives and will not educate their children in any useful subject. Such people, who are not concerned with the general good, We recommend that all Our faithful subjects despise and avoid. We will not allow such people any access to Our court, nor will We tolerate their presence at public assemblies and festivals.

8

Catherine II's Account of Her Accession to the Throne, 1762

When Elizabeth died in December 1761, the throne of Russia passed to Peter, the son of her sister Anna and the Duke of Holstein. Peter III, whom Elizabeth had brought to Russia in 1742 at the age of fourteen, was one of the few tsars of eighteenth-century Russia to ascend the throne legally and without the aid of a palace clique. This very factor deprived him of the support necessary to prevent his downfall. Chief among the conspirators against his rule was his wife Catherine (born Princess Sophia Augusta Frederica of Anhalt-Zerbst, on May 2, 1729), whom Elizabeth had selected to be Peter's consort. Since their marriage in 1745 the two had quarreled constantly, were unfaithful to each other, and had even disputed his responsibility for an offspring born in 1754, the future Tsar Paul (1796–1801). Peter III antagonized many Russian officers by his open admiration of Frederick the Great of Prussia, with whom the Russians were at war. With the aid of some of the officers Catherine masterminded the removal of her husband (later he was murdered) and ascended the Russian throne. She ruled the empire as Catherine II, or Catherine the Great, until her death in 1796.

[From a Letter to Poniatowski, August 2, 1762]

I am sending at once Count Keyserling as Ambassador to Poland to declare you King after the death of the present monarch and in the event of his not proving successful so far as you are concerned I want it to be Prince Adam.

Reprinted with permission of The Macmillan Company from *The Memoirs of Catherine the Great.* Edited by Dominique Maroger. With an Introduction by G. P. Gooch. Translated from the French by Moura Budberg (New York: Collier Books, 1961), pp. 271–277.

All minds here are still in a state of ferment. I beg you not to come here now, for fear of increasing it.

My advent to the throne had been planned for the last six months. Peter III lost what little intelligence he ever had. He shocked and offended everyone; he wanted to disrupt the Guards and sent them campaigning for that purpose, and would have had them replaced by his Holstein troops that were ordered to remain in town. He wanted to change his religion, marry Elizabeth Worontsov, and arrest me. On the day of the peace celebrations, after insulting me publicly at table, he ordered my arrest in the evening. My uncle, Prince George, made him withdraw the order.

From that day I kept my ears open to the offers made to me since the Empress's death. The plan was to lock him up in his room, like Princess Anne and her children. He went to Oranienbaum. We had full confidence in a great number of captains in the Guards regiments. The ins and outs of the secret were in the hands of the three brothers Orlov, the eldest of whom, according to Osten, used to follow me everywhere and committed innumerable follies. His passion for me was openly acknowledged and that is why he undertook what he did. They are all three of them very determined men and loved by most soldiers, having served in the Guards. I have great obligations in regard to them, all Petersburg is witness of it.

The Guards were all prepared and at the end there were thirty or forty officers in the secret and about ten thousand subalterns. There was not one traitor during the three weeks, because the plotters were divided into four separate sections and only the leaders met for the execution of the plan, while the real secret remained in the hands of these three brothers. Panin wanted the declaration to be made in favour of my son, but all the others were against it.

I was in Peterhof. Peter III was living and drinking at Oranienbaum. It was agreed that in case of treason we would not wait for his return but assemble the Guards and proclaim me Empress. Devotion to me acted in place of treason. On the 27th the rumour spread that I had been arrested. A soldier came to a captain called Passek, the leader of a section, and told him that this was no doubt my end. He would not allow himself to be reassured and, still greatly alarmed, went to another officer and told him the same thing. That officer was not in the secret and, horrified that another officer had listened to this soldier without arresting him, reported to the Major, who ordered Passek's arrest. The whole regiment was astir. A report of what had happened reached Oranienbaum during the night and caused alarm among our confederates. They decided to send the second of the Orlov brothers to fetch me back to town while the other two spread the news that I was arriving. The Hetman Volkonski and Panin were in the secret.

I was sleeping peacefully in Peterhof at six in the morning of the 28th. The previous day had been disturbing as I was aware of what was going on. Alexei Orlov came in very calmly and said: "All is ready for the proclamation, you must get up"; I asked for details, he said: "Passek has been arrested." I hesitated no longer, dressed promptly, without further ado, and got into the carriage in which Orlov had arrived. Another officer was acting as groom at the carriage-door, a third joined us a few miles away from Peterhof. A little further on, the eldest Orlov came to meet me with the younger Bariatinski, who gave me his seat in the coach, for my horses were exhausted. We went on to join the Ismailovski regiment, twelve men and a drummer, who started to beat the alarm. The soldiers rushed to kiss my hands, my feet, the hem of my dress, calling me their saviour. Two of them brought a priest with a cross and started to take the oath. After that I resumed my seat in the carriage, the priest with the cross walked in front, and we went on to the Semionovski regiment. They came to meet us, shouting "*Vivat!*" I alighted at the church of Kazan. Then the Preobrajenski regiment arrived, also shouting "*Vivat*" and saying: "Forgive us for being the last to come, our officers tried to arrest us, but here are four of them, whom we arrested to show you our zeal. We want what our brothers want."

The Horse Guards then came, in such a frenzy of joy as I have never seen before, weeping and shouting that the country was free at last. All this took place between the Hetman's garden and the Kazan Cathedral. The Horse Guards were led by their officers. As I knew that my uncle, to whom Peter III had given this regiment, was hated by his men, I sent word to him, begging him to stay at home, as I feared some accident to his person. But his regiment had already put him under arrest, pillaged his house, and manhandled him.

I then went to the Winter Palace where the Synod and Senate were assembled. A manifesto and the text of the oath were hastily composed. From there I walked to the troops, of which there were about 14,000 men, and was greeted with shouts of joy. Then on to the Old Winter Palace to make final arrangements. It was decided to go to Peterhof, where Peter III was to dine. I sent Admiral Talysin to Kronstadt. Chancellor Worontsov arrived loaded with reproaches. He was taken to the church to swear the oath. Then came Prince Trubetskoi and Count Shuvalov with the object of securing the regiments and killing me; they were also taken without offering resistance and made to swear the oath.

Having expedited our messengers and taken all necessary precautions, about ten in the morning I put on the Guards' uniform, having had myself proclaimed Colonel with great jubilations. I rode at the head of the troops to Peterhof and left a few men of every regiment to guard my son, who had remained in town. When we arrived at a little monastery half-way along the road, Vice-Chancellor Galitzine met us with a very flattering letter from Peter III (I forgot to say that as we left the town three soldiers from the Guards came up to me, sent from Peterhof to spread the manifesto among the people and said: "Take this, it is from Peter III but we are handing it to you and are glad to be able to join our brothers.") Then came a second letter brought by General Ismailov, who, throwing himself on his knees, asked me: "Do you consider me an honest man?" I replied that I did. "Well," he said, "it is a relief to be among intelligent people. The Emperor offers to abdicate. I will bring him to you and avoid a civil war for my country." I agreed to this and Peter III abdicated in perfect freedom at Oranienbaum, surrounded by 1,590 Holstein men and then came with Elizabeth Woronstov, Gudovich and Ismailov to Peterhof where I gave him a guard of six officers and a few soldiers.

As it was St. Peter's Day, at midday we had to have dinner. While that was being prepared, the soldiers took it into their heads that Peter III had been brought by Field-Marshal Prince Trubetskoi to try to work out a reconciliation between us. They began to whisper to anyone within earshot, including the Hetman, the Orlovs and others, that they had not seen me for three hours, that they were terrified that that old rogue Trubetskoi was pulling the wool over my eyes "by making a false peace between me and my husband and thus bringing about my ruin and theirs, too, in which case they would tear him to pieces." I went to Trubetskoi and told him to take the carriage, while I would go round the troops on foot alone. I told him what was being said. He went to town, extremely frightened, and I was received with frenzied cries, after which I sent the deposed Emperor to Ropsha, fifteen miles from Petersburg, under the command of Alexei Orlov, while respectable and comfortable rooms were being prepared for him in Schlüsselburg and also to give time to organize a relay of horses.

But God disposed differently. Fright had given him a colic that lasted three days and passed on the fourth. On that day he drank excessively— for he had everything he wanted, except liberty. The illness affected his brain, it was followed by a great weakness and in spite of all the assistance of physicians, he gave up the ghost, after asking for a Lutheran priest. I had him opened up—but his stomach showed no traces of ill-health. The cause of death was established as inflammation of the bowels and apoplexy. He had an inordinately small heart, quite withered. . . .

After he had been dispatched from Peterhof to Ropsha, I was advised to go straight to town. I foresaw that the troops might become alarmed. I spread the rumour about my departure, under the pretext of wanting to know at what time, after three days of fatigue duty, they would be ready to go. They said: "Towards ten in the evening but she must come with us." So I went with them and half-way stopped at Kurakine's estate, where I threw myself on the bed in my clothes. An officer pulled off my boots. I slept for two hours and a half and then we went on. From Catherinenhof I rode again at the head of the Preobrajenski regiment, a hussar regiment rode in front, then my escort, the Chevalier Guards, then came, immediately before me, my Court. After me came the Guards regiments in order of seniority, and three field regiments. The acclamations were frantic and I moved towards the Summer Palace where my Court, the Synod, my son, and all who attend Court were waiting. I went to church to hear the Te Deum, then came congratulations. I had neither drunk, nor eaten, nor slept from six in the morning on Friday till after dinner on Sunday, and went to bed as soon as possible and slept. At midnight a captain rushed into the room, waking me up and saying: "Our men are terribly drunk, a hussar has shouted to them: 'To arms! Thirty thousand Prussians are coming to take away our mother!' So they have taken up arms and are coming here to see how you really are. They promise to go home quietly if they find you all right. They will listen to no one, not even to the Orlovs."

So I had to get up again and, so as not to alarm my guard in the courtyard—a full battalion—I went to tell them why I was going out at this hour. Then, with two officers, I went to tackle the rioters and told them I was well, that they should go and have some sleep and leave me to have mine, that I was just about to sleep, having not slept for three nights, and that I hoped they would in future obey their officers. They replied that they had been alarmed by the rumour concerning these accursed Prussians and all wanted to die for me. I said: "Thank you, but go back to bed!" They bade me good night and good health and went home like lambs, turning back to look at me. Next day they apologized for having woken me up and said: "If we spend our time wishing to see her, we will only destroy her health and prevent her from working."

A book would not suffice to describe the officers' behaviour. The Orlovs shone by their art of leadership, their prudent daring, by the care introduced in small details, by their presence of mind and authority. They have much common sense and generous courage. Enthusiastically patriotic and honest, passionately attached to me and friends among each other, as brothers rarely are, there are five of them in all, but only three were here. Captain Passek distinguished himself by the fortitude with which he stood his twelve hours' imprisonment. The soldiers opened both windows and doors to him, but he did not wish to arouse alarm in his regiment before my arrival and was patiently waiting to be taken to Oranienbaum to be interrogated. The order came after I arrived. Princess Dashkov, younger sister of Elizabeth Worontsov, (though she wants all the honour of the execution of the plot attributed to her, simply because she knew some of the leaders) was in bad odour on account of her sister, nor did the fact that she was only nineteen years old impress anyone. Though she pretended to be the intermediary through whom everything reached me, everybody had been in touch with me for six months before she even knew their names. It is true that she is intelligent but she behaves ostentatiously and is an intriguer and disliked by our officers; only the heedless and the rash told her what they knew, which was not much more than a few details. I. Shuvalov, the lowest and meanest of men, has, I am told, written to Voltaire that a girl of nineteen has changed the face of the Empire. Please undeceive this great writer. Bariatinski, who concealed the whole matter from his beloved brother, deserves real praise. In the Horse Guards an officer called Khitrov, twenty-two years of age and a petty officer called Potemkin, displayed discernment, courage, and action.

This is in short all that happened. Everything was done, I will not conceal from you, under my own direction and finally I threw cold water on the plan because the departure to the country prevented its execution and things had been more than mature for a fortnight. The dethroned Emperor, when he learnt of the disturbance in town, was prevented by the young women in his retinue from following the advice of old Field-Marshal Munich who advised him to try Kronstadt or join the Army with a few men, and when he finally took a rowing boat to go to Kronstadt, the town was already in our hands, thanks to Admiral Talysin who disarmed General Devier, who was there on the side of the Emperor. An officer in the port threatened the poor Prince of his own accord, saying that he would riddle his boat with bullets. At last, God brought everything to the end He wished and all this is more a miracle than an organized and planned event, for so many favourable circumstances cannot be brought together without the hand of God.

I received your letter. A regular correspondence would be subject to a thousand inconveniences, I have twenty thousand precautions to take and have no time for harmful little love-letters.

I feel very embarrassed. . . . I cannot tell you what it is about, but it is true.

I will do everything for you and your family, rest assured of it.

I have thousands of proprieties and discretions to consider and also to bear the burden of government.

You must know that everything was carried out on the principle of hatred of the foreigner; Peter III himself counted as such.

Goodbye, the world is full of strange situations.

9

The Nakaz, *or* Instruction, *of Catherine II to the* *Legislative Commission of 1767–1768*

Among the enlightened despots of eighteenth-century Europe, Catherine II of Russia occupies an eminent place. She acquired this position through her associations with such prominent men of letters as Diderot, Grimm, Voltaire, and D'Alembert, through her patronage of education, and through her writings, of which the *Nakaz*, or *Instruction*, to the Legislative Commission of 1767–1768 is the most important. The *Nakaz*, which Voltaire called the finest monument of the century, represents Catherine's ambition to remodel Russia's laws in accordance with the new principles being expounded in Western Europe. Together with its two supplements, it consists of 655 articles, and took two years to prepare. About four-fifths of the articles were taken from Montesquieu's *The Spirit of Laws*, while Beccaria's *Essay on Crimes and Punishments* influenced over 100 of them. To conform with the conditions in Russia, Catherine modified and in some cases even distorted the ideas of Western writers. Although the Commission held 203 sessions, it failed to achieve anything constructive, due as much to the selfish policies of the Russian nobility as to Catherine's failure to follow her own theories in practice. In spite of this, the *Nakaz* remains an outstanding document in Russia's political, economic, and historical literature.

From *The Grand Instructions to the Commissioners Appointed to Frame a New Code of Laws for the Russian Empire: Composed by Her Imperial Majesty Catherine II* . . . Translated by Michael Tatischeff, (London: 1768), pp. 69–79, 80–82, 85–90, 95–97, 104–106, 115–118, 126–128, 132–141, 144–150, 159–166, 178–181, 185–196.

O Lord my God, hearken unto me, and instruct me; that I may administer Judgment unto thy People; as thy sacred Laws direct to judge with Righteousness!

The Instructions to the Commissioners
for Composing a New Code of Laws

1. The Christian Law teaches us to do mutual Good to one another, as much as possibly we can.

2. Laying this down as a fundamental Rule prescribed by that Religion, which has taken, or ought to take Root in the Hearts of the whole People; we cannot but suppose that every honest Man in the Community is, or will be, desirous of seeing his native Country at the very Summit of Happiness, Glory, Safety, and Tranquillity.

3. And that every Individual Citizen in particular must wish to see himself protected by Laws, which should not distress him in his Circumstances, but, on the Contrary, should defend him from all Attempts of others that are repugnant to this fundamental Rule.

4. In order therefore to proceed to a speedy Execution of what We expect from such a general Wish, We, fixing the Foundation upon the above first-mentioned Rule, ought to begin with an Inquiry into the natural Situation of this Empire.

5. For those Laws have the greatest Conformity with Nature, whose particular Regulations are best adapted to the Situation and Circumstances of the People for whom they are instituted.

This natural Situation is described in the three following Chapters.

Chapter I

6. Russia is an European State.

7. This is clearly demonstrated by the following Observations: The Alterations which *Peter the Great* undertook in Russia succeeded with the greater Ease, because the Manners, which prevailed at that Time, and had been introduced amongst us by a Mixture of different Nations, and the Conquest of foreign Territories, were quite unsuitable to the Climate. *Peter the First*, by introducing the Manners and Customs of Europe among the European People in his Dominions, found at that Time such Means as even he himself was not sanguine enough to expect.

Chapter II

8. The Possessions of the Russian Empire extend upon the terrestrial Globe to 32 Degrees of Latitude, and to 165 of Longitude.

9. The Sovereign is absolute; for there is no other authority but

that which centers in his single Person that can act with a Vigour proportionate to the Extent of such a vast Dominion.

10. The Extent of the Dominion requires an absolute Power to be vested in that Person who rules over it. It is expedient so to be that the quick Dispatch of Affairs, sent from distant Parts, might make ample Amends for the Delay occasioned by the great Distance of the Places.

11. Every other Form of Government whatsoever would not only have been prejudicial to Russia, but would even have proved its entire Ruin.

12. Another Reason is; That it is better to be subject to the Laws under one Master, than to be subservient to many.

13. What is the true End of Monarchy? Not to deprive People of their natural Liberty; but to correct their Actions, in order to attain the *supreme* Good.

14. The Form of Government, therefore, which best attains this End, and at the same Time sets less Bounds than others to natural Liberty, is that which coincides with the Views and Purposes of rational Creatures, and answers the End, upon which we ought to fix a stedfast Eye in the Regulations of civil Polity.

15. The Intention and the End of Monarchy is the Glory of the Citizens, of the State, and of the Sovereign.

16. But, from this Glory, a Sense of Liberty arises in a People governed by a Monarch; which may produce in these States as much Energy in transacting the most important Affairs, and may contribute as much to the Happiness of the Subjects, as even Liberty itself.

Chapter III

17. *Of the Safety of the Institutions of Monarchy.*

18. The intermediate Powers, subordinate to, and depending upon the supreme Power, form the essential Part of monarchical Government.

19. I have said, that the intermediate Powers, subordinate and depending, proceed from the supreme Power; as in the very Nature of the Thing the Sovereign is the Source of all imperial and civil Power.

20. The Laws, which form the Foundation of the State, send out certain Courts of Judicature, through which, as through smaller Streams, the Power of the Government is poured out, and diffused.

21. The Laws allow these Courts of Judicature to remonstrate, that such or such an Injunction is unconstitutional, and prejudicial, obscure, and impossible to be carried into Execution; and direct, beforehand, to which Injunction one ought to pay Obedience, and in what Manner one ought to conform to it. These Laws undoubtedly constitute the firm and immoveable Basis of every State.

Chapter IV

22. There must be a political Body, to whom the Care and strict Execution of these Laws ought to be confided.

23. This Care, and strict Execution of the Laws, can be no where so properly fixed as in certain Courts of Judicature, which announce to the People the newly-made Laws, and revive those which are forgotten, or obsolete.

24. And it is the Duty of these Courts of Judicature to examine carefully those Laws which they receive from the Sovereign, and to remonstrate, if they find any Thing in them repugnant to the fundamental Constitution of the State, etc., which has been already remarked above in the third Chapter, and twenty-first Article.

25. But if they find nothing in them of that Nature, they enter them in the Code of Laws already established in the State, and publish them to the whole Body of the People.

26. In Russia the Senate is the political Body, to which the Care and due Execution of the Laws is confided.

27. All other Courts of Judicature may, and ought to remonstrate with the same Propriety, to the Senate, and even to the Sovereign himself, as was already mentioned above.

28. Should any One inquire, wherein the Care and due Execution of the Laws consists? I answer That the Care and due Execution of the Laws produces particular Instructions; in consequence of which the before-mentioned Courts of Judicature, instituted to the End that, by their Care, the Will of the Sovereign might be obeyed in a Manner conformably to the fundamental Laws and Constitution of the State, are obliged to act, in the Discharge of their Duty, according to the Rules prescribed.

29. These Instructions will prevent the People from transgressing the Injunctions of the Sovereign with impunity; but, at the same Time, will protect them from the Insults and ungovernable Passions of others.

30. For, on the one Hand, they justify the Penalties prepared for those who transgress the Laws; and, on the other, they confirm the Justice of that Refusal to enter Laws repugnant to the good Order of the State, amongst those which are already approved of, or to act by those Laws in the Administration of Justice, and the general Business of the Whole Body of the People.

Chapter V

31. *Of the Situation of the People in general.*

32. It is the greatest Happiness for a Man to be so circumstanced,

that, if his Passions should prompt him to be mischievous, he should still think it more for his Interest not to give Way to them.

33. The Laws ought to be so framed as to secure the Safety of every Citizen as much as possible.

34. The Equality of the Citizens consists in this; that they should all be subject to the same Laws.

35. This Equality requires Institutions so well adapted as to prevent the Rich from oppressing those who are not so wealthy as themselves, and converting all the Charges and Employments intrusted to them as Magistrates only to their own private Emolument.

36. General or political Liberty does not consist in that licentious Notion, *That a Man may do whatever he pleases.*

37. In a State or Assemblage of People that live together in a Community, where there are Laws, Liberty can only consist *in doing that which every One ought to do, and not to be constrained to do that which One ought not to do.*

38. A Man ought to form in his own Mind an exact and clear Idea of what Liberty is. *Liberty is the Right of doing whatsoever the Laws allow:* And if any one Citizen could do what the Laws forbid, there would be no more Liberty; because others would have an equal Power of doing the same.

39. The political Liberty of a Citizen is the Peace of Mind arising from the Consciousness that every Individual enjoys his peculiar Safety; and in order that the People might attain this Liberty, the Laws ought to be so framed that no one Citizen should stand in Fear of another; but that all of them should stand in Fear of the same Laws.

Chapter VI

40. *Of Laws in general.*

41. Nothing ought to be forbidden by the Laws but what may be prejudicial, either to every Individual in particular, or to the whole Community in general.

42. All Actions which comprehend nothing of this Nature are in nowise cognizable by the Laws; which are made only with the View of procuring the greatest possible Advantage and Tranquillity to the People, who live under their Protection.

43. To preserve Laws from being violated, they ought to be so good, and so well furnished with all Expedients, tending to procure the greatest possible Good to the People; that every Individual might be fully convinced that it was his Interest, as well as Duty, to preserve those Laws inviolable.

44. And this is the most exalted Pitch of Perfection which we ought to labour to attain to.

45. Many Things rule over Mankind. Religion, the Climate, Laws, the Maxims received from Government, the Example of past Ages, Manners, and Customs. . . .

56. By what *I* have here advanced, *I* meant not, in the least, to abridge that infinite Distance which must ever subsist between Vices and Virtues. God forbid! *My* Intention was only to show that all the *political* Vices are not moral Vices; and that all the *moral* Vices are not *political* Ones. This Distinction ought to be known and carefully attended to, that in making the Laws nothing may be introduced in them which is contrary to the general Sense of a Nation.

57. The Legislation ought to adapt its Laws to the general Sense of a Nation. We do nothing so well as what we do freely and uncontrouled, and following the natural Bent of our own Inclinations.

58. In order to introduce better Laws, it is essentially necessary to prepare the Minds of the People for their Reception. But that it may never be pleaded in Excuse that it is impossible to carry even the most useful Affairs into Execution because the Minds of the People are not yet prepared for it, you must, in that Case, take the Trouble upon yourselves to prepare them; and, by these Means, you will already have done a great Part of the Work.

59. Laws are the peculiar and distinct Institutions of the Legislator; but Manners and Customs are the Institutions of the whole Body of the People.

60. Consequently, if there should be a Necessity of making great Alterations amongst the People for their greater Benefit: that must be corrected by Laws which has been instituted by Laws, and that must be amended by Custom which has been introduced by Custom; and it is extreme bad Policy to alter that by Laws which ought to be altered by Custom.

61. There are Means of preventing the Growth of Crimes, and these are the Punishments inflicted by the Laws. At the same Time there are Means for introducing an Alteration in Customs, and these are Examples.

62. Besides, the more a People have an Intercourse with one another, the more easy it is for them to introduce a Change in their Customs.

63. In a Word, every Punishment which is not inflicted through Necessity, is tyrannical. The Law has not its Source merely from Power. Things indifferent in their Nature do not come under the Cognizance of the Laws.

Chapter VII

64. *Of the Laws in particular.*

65. Laws carried to the Extremity of Right are productive of the Extremity of Evil.

66. All Laws, where the Legislation aims at the Extremity of Rigour, may be evaded. It is Moderation which rules a People, and not Excess of Severity.

67. Civil Liberty flourishes when the Laws deduce every Punishment from the peculiar Nature of every Crime. The Application of Punishment ought not to proceed from the arbitrary Will, or mere Caprice of the Legislator, but from the Nature of the Crime; and it is not the Man, who ought to do Violence to a Man, but the proper Action of the Man himself. . . .

Chapter VIII

80. *Of Punishments.*

81. The Love of our Country, Shame, and the Dread of public Censure, are Motives which restrain, and may deter Mankind from the Commission of a Number of Crimes.

82. The greatest Punishment for a bad Action, under a mild Administration, will be for the Party to be convinced of it. The civil Laws will there correct Vice with the more Ease, and will not be under a Necessity of employing more rigorous Means.

83. In these Governments, the Legislature will apply itself more to prevent Crimes than to punish them, and should take more Care to instil Good Manners into the Minds of the Citizens, by proper Regulations, than to dispirit them by the Terror of corporal and capital Punishments.

84. In a Word, whatever is termed Punishment in the Law is, in Fact, nothing but Pain and Suffering.

85. Experience teaches us that, in those Countries where Punishments are mild, they operate with the same Efficacy upon the Minds of the Citizens as the most severe in other Places.

86. If a sensible Injury should accrue to a State from some popular Commotion, a violent Administration will be at once for a sudden Remedy, and instead of recurring to the ancient Laws, will inflict some terrible Punishment, in order to crush the growing Evil on the Spot. The Imagination of the People is affected at the Time of this greater Punishment, just as it would have been affected by the least; and when the Dread of this Punishment gradually wears off, it will be compelled to introduce a severer Punishment upon all Occasions.

87. The People ought not to be driven on by violent Methods, but we ought to make Use of the Means which Nature has given us, with the utmost Care and Caution, in order to conduct them to the End we propose.

88. Examine with Attention the Cause of all Licentiousness; and you will find that it proceeds from the Neglect of punishing Crimes, not from the Mildness of Punishments. Let us follow Nature, which has

given Shame to Man for his Scourge and let the greatest Part of the Punishment consist in the Infamy which accompanies the Punishment.

89. And if a Country could be found where Infamy should not be the Consequence of Punishment; the Reason of this is to be imputed to some tyrannical Government, which inflicted the same Punishments upon the Innocent and the Guilty, without Distinction.

90. And if another Country should be known where the People are restrained by nothing but the severest Punishments; you must again be assured that this proceeds from the Violence of the Government, which has ordained those Punishments for the slightest Offences.

91. It happens frequently that a Legislator, who wants to extirpate an Evil, thinks of nothing but this Method of Cure: His Eyes are fixed on this Object only, and do not foresee the bad Consequences which attend it. When the Evil is once cured, we remark nothing but the Severity of the Legislator; but it leaves a Distemper in the State, arising from this very Severity. The Minds of the People are corrupted, for they are inured to Despotism. . . .

94. It is unjust to punish a Thief who robs on the Highway in the same Manner as another, who not only robs, but commits Murder. Every One sees clearly that some Difference ought to be made in their Punishment, for the Sake of the general Safety. . . .

96. Good Laws keep strictly a just Medium: They do not always inflict pecuniary, nor always subject Malefactors to corporal Punishment.

All Punishments by which the human Body might be maimed ought to be abolished.

Chapter IX

97. *Of the Administration of Justice in general.* . . .

119. The Laws which condemn a Man upon the Deposition of one Evidence only are destructive to Liberty. . . .

120. Two Witnesses are absolutely necessary in order to form a right Judgment: For an Accuser, who affirms, and the Party accused, who denies the Fact, make the Evidence on both Sides equal; for that Reason, a Third is required in order to convict the Defendant; unless other clear collateral Proofs should fix the Credibility of the Evidence in favour of one of them.

121. The Evidence of two Witnesses is esteemed sufficient for Conviction in every criminal Case whatsoever. The Law believes them, as if they spoke from the Mouth of Truth itself. . . .

123. The Usage of Torture is contrary to all the Dictates of Nature and Reason; even Mankind itself cries out against it, and demands loudly the total Abolition of it. We see, at this very Time, a People greatly renowned for the Excellence of their civil Polity, who reject it without any

sensible Inconveniencies. It is, therefore, by no Means necessary by its Nature. We will explain this more at large here below.

124. There are Laws which do not allow the Application of Torture, except only in those Cases where the Prisoner at the Bar refuses to plead, and will neither acknowledge himself innocent nor guilty.

125. To make an Oath too cheap by frequent Practice is to weaken the Obligation of it, and to destroy its Efficacy. The Kissing of the Cross cannot be used upon any Occasion, but when he that takes an Oath has no private Interest of his own to serve; as for Instance, the Judge and the Witnesses.

126. Those who are to be tried for capital Offences should chuse their own Judges, with the Consent of the Laws; or, at least, should have a Right of rejecting such a Number of them that those who remain in Court may seem as chosen by the Malefactors themselves.

127. It is likewise just that some of the Judges should be of the same Rank of Citizenship as the Defendant; that is, his Equals; that he might not think himself fallen into the Hands of such People as would violently over-rule the Affair to his Prejudice: Of this there are already Instances in the Martial Laws.

128. When the Defendant is condemned, it is not the Judges who inflict the Punishment upon him, but the Law.

129. The Sentence ought to be as clear and distinct as possible; even so far as to preserve the very identical Words of the Law. But if they should include the private Opinion of the Judge, the People will live in Society without knowing exactly the reciprocal Obligations they lie under to one another in that State. . . .

153. Nothing is so dangerous as this general Axiom: *The Spirit of the Law ought to be considered, and not the Letter.* This can mean nothing else but to break down the Fence which opposes the Torrent of popular Opinions. This is a self-evident Truth which is not to be controverted, how strange soever it may appear to vulgar Minds; who are more terrified by the least Irregularity which happens before their Eyes than by Consequences more remote, but infinitely more fatal, which flow from one false Principle adopted by a People. Every Man has his own particular Mode of viewing Objects presented to his Mind, different from every other. We should see the Fate of a Citizen changed, by the Removal of his Cause from one Court of Judicature to another; and his Life and Liberty depending upon Chance, either from some false Ideas, or the Perverseness of his Judge: We should see the *same* Crimes punished *differently*, at *different* Times, by the *very same* Court of Judicature; if they will not listen to the invariable Voice of the fixed, established Laws, but follow the deceitful Inconstancy of their own arbitrary Interpretations.

154. The Disorders which may possibly arise from a *strict* and *close*

Adherence to *the Letter* of *penal* Laws, are by no Means comparable to those which are produced by the *arbitrary Interpretation* of them. The Errors proceeding from the *first* are only *temporary*, and will oblige the Legislator to make, some-times, easy and necessary Corrections in such Words of the Law as are capable of a *double Meaning*. However, it will prove a Bridle to curb that *licentious* Method of *interpreting* and *deciding* at *their own Discretion*, which may prove fatal to every citizen.

155. If the Laws are not *exactly* and *clearly* defined, and understood *Word by Word;* if it be not the sole Office of a Judge to *distinguish*, and lay down *clearly*, what Action is conformable to the Laws, and what is repugnant to them: If the Rule of *just* and *unjust*, which ought to govern alike the ignorant Clown and the enlightened Scholar, be not a *simple Question* of Matter of Fact for the Judges; then the Situation of the Citizen will be exposed to strange Accidents.

156. By making the *penal* Laws always *clearly* intelligible, *Word by Word*, every one may calculate truly and know exactly the Inconveniences of a bad Action; a Knowledge which is *absolutely* necessary for restraining People from committing it; and the People may enjoy Security with respect both to their Persons and Property; which ought ever to remain so, because this is the *main Scope* and *Object* of the Laws, and without which the Community would be dissolved.

157. If the Power of *interpreting* Laws be an Evil, there is an Evil also which attends the *Obscurity* of them, and lays us under the Necessity of having Recourse to their Interpretation. This Irregularity is still greater when the Laws are written in a Language *unknown* to the People, or expressed in *uncommon* Phrases.

158. The Laws ought to be written in the *common vernacular Tongue;* and the Code, which contains all the Laws, ought to be esteemed as a Book of the utmost Use, which should be purchased at as *small* a Price as the Catechism. If the Case were otherwise, and the Citizen should be ignorant of the Consequences of his own Actions, and what concerns his Person and Liberty, he will then depend upon some few of the People who have taken upon themselves the Care of preserving and explaining them. Crimes will be less frequent in *proportion* as the Code of Laws is more *universally* read, and *comprehended* by the People. And, for this Reason, it must be ordained, That, in all the Schools, Children should be taught to read *alternately* out of the Church Books and out of *those* which contain the Laws. . . .

193. The Torture of the Rack is a Cruelty established and made use of by many Nations, and is applied to the Party accused during the Course of his Trial, either to extort from him a Confession of his Guilt, or in order to clear up some Contradictions in which he had involved himself during his Examination, or to compel him to discover his Accomplices, or

in order to discover other Crimes, of which, though he is not accused, yet he may perhaps be guilty.

194. (1) No Man ought to be looked upon as guilty before he has received his judicial Sentence; nor can the Laws deprive him of their Protection before it is proved that he has forfeited all Right to it. What Right therefore can Power give to any to inflict Punishment upon a Citizen at a Time when it is yet dubious whether he is innocent or guilty? Whether the Crime be known or unknown, it is not very difficult to gain a thorough Knowledge of the Affair by duly weighing all the Circumstances. If the Crime be known, the Criminal ought not to suffer any Punishment but what the Law ordains; consequently the Rack is quite unnecessary. If the Crime be not known, the Rack ought not to be applied to the Party accused; for this Reason, *That the Innocent ought not to be tortured;* and, in the Eye of the Law, every Person is innocent whose Crime is not yet proved. It is undoubtedly extremely necessary that no Crime, after it has been proved, should remain unpunished. The Party accused on the Rack, whilst in the Agonies of Torture, is not Master enough of himself to be able to declare the Truth. Can we give more Credit to a Man when he is light-headed in a Fever, than when he enjoys the free Use of his Reason in a State of Health? The Sensation of Pain may arise to such a Height that, after having subdued the whole Soul, it will leave her no longer the Liberty of producing any proper Act of the Will, except that of taking the shortest instantaneous Method, in the very twinkling of an Eye, as it were, of getting rid of her Torment. In such an Extremity, even an innocent Person will roar out that he is guilty, only to gain some Respite from his Tortures. Thus the very same Expedient, which is made use of to distinguish the Innocent from the Guilty, will take away the whole Difference between them; and the Judges will be as uncertain whether they have an innocent or a guilty Person before them, as they were before the Beginning of this partial Way of Examination. The Rack, therefore, is a sure Method of condemning an innocent Person of a weakly Constitution, and of acquitting a wicked Wretch, who depends upon the Robustness of his Frame.

195. (2) The Rack is likewise made use of to oblige the Party accused to clear up (as they term it) the Contradictions in which he has involved himself in the Course of his Examination; as if the Dread of Punishment, the Uncertainty and Anxiety in determining what to say, and even gross Ignorance itself, common to both Innocent and Guilty, could not lead a timorous Innocent, and a Delinquent who seeks to hide his Villanies, into Contradictions; and as if Contradictions, which are so common to Man even in a State of Ease and Tranquillity, would not increase in that Perturbation of Soul, when he is plunged entirely in Reflections of how to escape the Danger he is threatened with.

196. (3) To make use of the Rack for discovering whether the Party accused has not committed other Crimes, besides that which he has been convicted of, is a certain Expedient to screen every Crime from its proper Punishment: For a Judge will always be discovering new Ones. Finally, this Method of Proceeding will be founded upon the following Way of reasoning: Thou art guilty of one Crime, therefore, perhaps, thou hast committed an Hundred others: According to the Laws, thou wilt be tortured and tormented; not only because thou art guilty, but even because thou mayest be still more guilty.

197. (4) Besides this, the Party accused is tortured, to oblige him to discover his Accomplices. But when we have already proved that the Rack cannot be the proper Means for searching out the Truth, then how can it give any Assistance in discovering the Accomplices in a Crime? It is undoubtedly extremely easy for him, who accuses himself, to accuse others. Besides, is it just to torture one Man for the Crimes of others? Might not the Accomplices be discovered by examining the Witnesses who were produced against the Criminal, by a strict Inquiry into the Proofs alledged against him, and even by the Nature of the Fact itself, and the Circumstances which happened at the Time when the Crime was committed? In short, by all the Means which serve to prove the Delinquent guilty of the Crime he had committed? . . .

220. A Punishment ought to be immediate, analogous to the Nature of the Crime, and known to the Public.

221. The sooner the Punishment succeeds to the Commission of a Crime, the more useful and just it will be. Just; because it will spare the Malefactor the torturing and useless Anguish of Heart about the Uncertainty of his Destiny. Consequently the Decision of an Affair, in a Court of Judicature, ought to be finished in as little Time as possible. I have said before that Punishment immediately inflicted is most useful; the Reason is because the smaller the Interval of Time is which passes between the Crime and the Punishment, the more the Crime will be esteemed as a Motive to the Punishment, and the Punishment as an Effect of the Crime. Punishment must be certain and unavoidable.

222. The most certain Curb upon Crimes is not the Severity of the Punishment, but the absolute Conviction in the People that Delinquents will be inevitably punished.

223. The Certainty even of a small, but inevitable Punishment, will make a stronger Impression on the Mind than the Dread even of capital Punishment, connected with the Hopes of escaping it. As Punishments become more mild and moderate; Mercy and Pardon will be less necessary in Proportion, for the Laws themselves, at such a Time, are replete with the Spirit of Mercy.

224. However extensive a State may be, every Part of it must depend upon the Laws.

225. We must endeavour to exterminate Crimes in general, particu-

larly those which are most injurious to the Community: Consequently, the Means made use of by the Laws to deter People from the Commission of every Kind of Crimes ought to be the most powerful, in proportion as the Crimes are more destructive to the Public Good, and in proportion to the Strength of the Temptation by which weak or bad Minds may be allured to the Commission of them. Consequently, there ought to be a fixed stated Proportion between Crimes and Punishments.

226. If there be two Crimes, which injure the Community unequally, and yet receive equal Punishment; then the unequal Distribution of the Punishment will produce this strange Contradiction, very little noticed by any one, though it frequently happens, that the Laws will punish Crimes which proceed from the Laws themselves.

227. If the same Punishment should be inflicted upon a Man for killing an Animal as for killing another Man, or for Forgery, the People will soon make no Difference between those Crimes. . . .

239. (Q. 8) Which are the most efficacious Means of preventing Crimes?

240. It is better to prevent Crimes than to punish them.

241. To prevent Crimes is the Intention and the End of every good Legislation; which is nothing more than the Art of conducting People to the greatest Good, or to leave the least Evil possible amongst them, if it should prove impracticable to exterminate the whole.

242. If we forbid many Actions which are termed indifferent by the Moralists, we shall not prevent the Crimes of which they may be productive, but shall create still new Ones.

243. Would you prevent Crimes? order it so, That the Laws might rather favour every Individual, than any particular Rank of Citizens, in the Community.

244. Order it so, that the People should fear the Laws, and nothing but the Laws.

245. Would you prevent Crimes? order it so, that the Light of Knowledge may be diffused among the People.

246. A Book of good Laws is nothing but a Bar to prevent the Licentiousness of injurious Men from doing Mischief to their fellow Creatures.

247. There is yet another Expedient to prevent Crimes, which is by rewarding Virtue.

248. Finally, the most sure but, at the same Time, the most difficult Expedient to mend the Morals of the People, is a perfect System of Education. . . .

Chapter XI

250. A Society of Citizens, as well as every Thing else, requires a certain fixed Order: There ought to be some to govern, and others to obey.

251. And this is the Origin of every Kind of Subjection; which feels itself more or less alleviated, in Proportion to the Situation of the Subjects.

252. And, consequently, as the Law of Nature commands *Us* to take as much Care as lies in *Our* Power of the Prosperity of all the People; we are obliged to alleviate the Situation of the Subjects as much as sound Reason will permit.

253. And therefore, to shun all Occasions of reducing People to a State of Slavery, except that the *utmost* Necessity should *inevitably* oblige us to do it; in that Case, it ought not to be done for our own Benefit; but for the Interest of the State: Yet even that Case is extremely uncommon.

254. Of whatever Kind Subjection may be, the civil Laws ought to guard, on the one Hand, against the *Abuse* of Slavery, and, on the other, against the *Dangers* which may arise from it.

255. Unhappy is that Government which is compelled to institute *severe* Laws.

256. *Peter the Great* ordained, in the Year 1722, that Persons who were insane in Mind, and those who tortured their Vassals, should be put under the Tutelage of Guardians. This Injunction is executed with regard to the Objects of the first Part of it; the Reason why it is not put in Force with respect to the Objects of the last Part is *unknown*. . . .

260. A great Number of Slaves ought not to be infranchised all at once, nor by a general Law.

261. A Law may be productive of public Benefit, which gives some *private* Property to a Slave.

262. Let us finish all this, by repeating that *fundamental Rule;* that the government which most resembles that of Nature is that whose particular Disposition answers best to the Disposition of the People, for whom it is instituted.

263. However it is still highly necessary to prevent those Causes which so frequently incited Slaves to rebel against their masters; but till these Causes are discovered, it is impossible to prevent the like accidents by Laws; though the Tranquillity, both of the one and of the other, depends upon it.

Chapter XII

264. *Of the Propagation of the human Species in a State.*

265. Russia is not only *greatly* deficient in the *number* of her Inhabitants; but at the same Time, extends her Dominion over *immense* Tracts of Land; which are neither peopled nor improved. And therefore, in a Country so circumstanced, *too much* Encouragement can never be given to the *Propagation* of the human Species.

266. The Peasants generally have twelve, fifteen, and even twenty Children by one Marriage; but it rarely happens that one *Fourth* of these ever attains to the *Age* of Maturity. There must therefore be some Fault, either in their Nouriture, in their Way of Living, or Method of Education, which occasions this *prodigious* Loss, and disappoints the *Hopes* of the Empire. How flourishing would the State of this Empire be if we could but ward off, or *prevent* this fatal Evil by proper Regulations!

267. You must add too to *this*, that two Hundred Years are now elapsed since a *Disease* unknown to our Ancestors was imported from America, and *hurried* on the Destruction of the human Race. This Disease spreads *wide* its *mournful* and *destructive* Effects in many of our Provinces. The utmost Care ought to be taken of the Health of the Citizens. It would be highly prudent, therefore, to stop the Progress of this Disease by the Laws.

268. Those of Moses may serve here for an Example. (Leviticus, chap. xiii)

269. It seems too that the Method of exacting their Revenues, *newly* invented by the Lords, diminishes both the *Inhabitants* and the *Spirit of Agriculture* in Russia. Almost all the Villages are *heavily* taxed. The Lords, who seldom or never *reside* in their Villages, lay an Impost on every Head of one, two, and even five Rubles, without the least Regard to the *Means* by which their Peasants may be able to *raise* this Money.

270. It is highly necessary that the Law should prescribe a Rule to the Lords for a more judicious Method of raising their Revenues; and oblige them to levy *such* a Tax as *tends least* to separate the Peasant from his House and Family; this would be the Means by which Agriculture would become more extensive, and Population be more increased in the Empire.

271. Even now some Husbandmen do not see their Houses for fifteen Years together, and yet pay the Tax annually to their respective Lords; which they procure in Towns at a vast Distance from their Families, and wander over the whole Empire for that Purpose.

272. The more happily a People live under a Government, the more easily the Number of the Inhabitants increases.

273. Countries, which abound with Meadow and Pasture Lands, are generally *very thinly* peopled; the Reason is that *few* can find Employment in those Places: But arable Lands are much *more* populous; because they *furnish* Employment for a *much greater* Number of People.

274. Wherever the Inhabitants can enjoy the Conveniencies of Life, there Population will certainly increase.

275. *But a Country which is so overwhelmed with Taxes that the People, with all their Care and Industry, can with the utmost Difficulty find Means for procuring a bare Subsistence, will, in length of Time, be deserted by its Inhabitants.*

276. Where a People is poor for no other Reason but because they live under oppressive Laws, and esteem their Lands not so much a *Fund* for their Maintainance as a *Pretence* for their Oppression; in such Places, the Inhabitants cannot increase. They have not the Means of Subsistance sufficient for themselves, how then can they think of yielding a Part of it to their Offspring? They are not able to take Care of *themselves*, even in their *own* Illness; how then can they bring up, and look after *Creatures* which are in a State of *continual* Illness, that is, *Infancy?* They bury their Money in the Earth, and are afraid to let it circulate; and they fear to appear rich, because their Wealth might expose them to Persecution and Oppression.

277. The Ease of asserting, and the Incapacity for thoroughly examining an Affair, have induced many to affirm, *That the poorer the Subjects live, the more numerous their Families will be; and the heavier the Taxes are, the more readily they will find the Means of paying them.* These are two Sophisms, which ever did, and ever will bring Destruction upon Monarchies.

278. The Evil is almost incurable when the Depopulation of the Country has been of long standing, from some internal Defect in the Constitution, and a bad Administration. The People drop off there by an imperceptible and almost habitual Malady. Born in Languor and Misery, under the Oppression, or false Maxims adopted by Government, they see themselves destroyed frequently, without perceiving the Causes of their Destruction.

279. In order to re-establish a State stripped in such a Manner of its Inhabitants, it will be in vain to expect Assistance from the Children which may be born in future. This Hope is totally over: People in their Desart have neither Courage nor Industry. Lands, which might feed a whole People, can scarce yield Food for a single Family. The common People in those Parts have no *Share* even in that, which is the *Cause* of their Misery; that is, the Lands which lie *fallow* and *uncultivated*, with which the Country abounds; either some of the principal Citizens, or the Sovereign, insensibly ingross the *whole Extent* of these desert Countries. The ruined Families have *left* their Oppressors the *whole* for *Pastures*, and the laborious Man has nothing.

280. In such Circumstances, the same Method ought to be followed through the whole Extent of that Country, which the Romans practised in one Part of theirs. To *do*, in a Scarcity of Inhabitants, what they *did* in a Superfluity of them, to *divide* the Lands amongst the Families which *had none*, and to enable them to cultivate and improve them. This Division ought to be made without Loss of Time, as soon as ever one Man can be found who would undertake it on those Terms, that not a Moment might be lost before the Work is begun. . . .

Chapter XIII

293. Of handicraft Trades, and Commerce.

294. There can be neither skillful Handicraftsmen, nor a firmly-established Commerce, where Agriculture is neglected, or carried on with Supineness and Negligence.

295. Agriculture can never flourish there, where no Persons have any Property of their own.

296. This is founded upon a very simple Rule: *Every Man will take more Care of his own Property, than of that which belongs to another; and will not exert his utmost Endeavours upon that which he has Reason to fear another may deprive him of.*

297. Agriculture is the most laborious Employment a Man can undertake. The more the Climate induces a Man to shun this Trouble, the more the Laws ought to animate him to it. . . .

299. It would not be improper to give a Premium to those Husbandmen who bring their Fields into better Order than others.

300. And to the Handicraftsmen, who distinguished themselves most by their Care and Skill.

301. This Regulation will produce a Progress in the Arts, in all Parts of the Country. It was of Service, even in our own Times, in establishing very important Manufactories.

302. There are Countries where a Treatise of Agriculture, published by the Government, is lodged in every Church, from which the Peasant may be able to get the better of his Difficulties, and draw proper Advantage from the Instructions it contains.

303. There are Nations inclined to Laziness. In order to exterminate Laziness in the Inhabitants, arising from the Climate, such Laws are to be made as should deprive those who refuse to work, of the Means of Subsistance.

304. All Nations inclined to Laziness are arrogant in their Behaviour; for they who do not work esteem themselves, in some Measure, Rulers over those who labour.

305. Nations who have given themselves up to Idleness are generally proud: We might turn the Effect against the Cause from which it proceeds, and destroy Laziness by Pride itself.

306. For Government may be as strongly supported by *Ambition* as it may be endangered by *Pride*. In asserting this, we need only represent to ourselves, on the one hand, the innumerable Benefits which result from *Ambition*; such as, Industry, Arts, and Sciences, Politeness, Taste, etc., and on the other, the infinite Number of Evils arising from *Pride*, in some Nations; such as Laziness, Poverty, Disregard for every thing; the

Destruction of Nations, who accidentally fall into their Power, and afterwards the Ruin of themselves.

307. As *Pride* induces some to shun Labour, so *Ambition* impells others to excell all the rest in Workmanship.

308. View every Nation with Attention, and you will find that arrogant Pride and Laziness, most commonly, go Hand in Hand together. . . .

311. A Man is not poor because he has nothing; but because he will do no Work. He who has no Estate, but will work, may live as well as he, who has an annual Income of a Hundred Rubles, but will do no Work.

312. A Tradesman who has taught his Children his Art, has given them such an Estate as increases in proportion to their Number.

313. Agriculture is the first and principal Labour which ought to be encouraged in the People: The next is the manufacturing our own Produce.

314. Machines, which serve to shorten Labour in the mechanick Arts, are not always useful. If a Piece of Work, wrought with the Hands, can be afforded at a Price equally advantageous to the Merchant and the Manufacturer; in this Case, Machines which shorten Labour, that is, which diminish the Number of Workmen, will be greatly prejudical to a populous Country.

315. Yet, we ought to distinguish between what we manufacture for our Home-consumption, and what we manufacture for Exportation into foreign Countries.

316. Too much Use cannot be made of this Kind of Machines in our Manufactures, which we export to other Nations; who do, or may receive the same Kind of Goods, from our Neighbours or other People; especially those who are in the same Situation with ourselves.

317. Commerce flies from Places where it meets with Oppression, and settles where it meets with Protection. . . .

319. In many Countries, where all the Taxes are farmed, the *Collection* of the Royal Revenues *ruins* Commerce, not only by its Inequality, Oppression, and extreme Exactions, but also by the *Difficulties* it occasions, and the Formalities it requires.

320. In other Places, where the Duties or Customs are *collected* upon the *good Faith* of the Importers, there is a wide Difference in respect of the Conveniencies for Traffick. One Word in Writing transacts the greatest Business. The Merchant is under no Necessity of losing Time in Attendance; nor obliged to employ *Clerks*, on purpose to remove the Difficulties started by the *Financiers*, or be *compelled* to submit to them.

321. The Liberty of Trading does not consist in a Permission to Merchants of doing whatever they please; this would be rather the *Slavery* of Commerce: What *cramps* the Trader does not *cramp* the Trade. In free Countries the Merchant meets with innumerable Ob-

stacles; but in despotic Governments he is not near so much thwarted by the Laws. England prohibits the Exportation of its Wool; she has ordained Coals to be imported to the Capital by Sea; she has prohibited the Exportation of Horses fit for Stallions; she obliges Ships, which Trade from her Plantations in America into Europe, to anchor first in England. By these, and such like Prohibitions, she cramps the Merchant; but it is for the *Benefit* of Commerce.

322. Wherever there is Trade, there are Custom-houses also.

323. The Object of Trade is the Exportation and Importation of Goods, for the Advantage of the State: The Object of the Custom-houses is a certain Duty, exacted from the same Exportation and Importation of Goods, for the Advantage likewise of the State; for this Reason a State ought to preserve an exact Impartiality between the Custom-house and the Trade, and to make such proper Regulations that these two might never clash with each other: Then the People will enjoy there free Liberty of Commerce. . . .

Chapter XIV

347. *Of Education.*

348. The Rules of Education are the fundamental Institutes which train us up to be Citizens.

349. Each particular Family ought to be governed upon the Plan of the great Family; which includes all the Particulars.

350. It is impossible to give a general Education to a very numerous People, and to bring up all the Children in Houses regulated for that Purpose; and, for that Reason, it will be proper to establish some *general Rules*, which may serve *by Way of Advice* to all Parents.

351. Every Parent is obliged to teach his Children the Fear of God as the Beginning of all Wisdom, and to inculcate into them all those Duties, which God demands from us in the ten Commandments, and our orthodox Eastern Greek Religion, in its Rules and Traditions.

352. Also to inculcate into them the Love of their Country, and to enure them to pay due Respect to the established civil Laws, and to reverence the Courts of Judicature in their Country, as those who, by the Appointment of God, watch over their Happiness in this World.

353. Every Parent ought to refrain *in Presence* of his Children, not only from *Actions*, but even *Words* that *tend* to Injustice and Violence; as for Instance, *Quarrelling, Swearing, Fighting, every Sort of Cruelty, and such like Behaviour;* and not to allow those who are about his Children *to set them such bad Examples.*

354. He ought to forbid his Children, and those who are about them, the *Vice of lying,* though even *in jest;* for *Lying* is the most pernicious of *all Vices.*

355. We shall add here, for the Instruction of every Man in particular, what has been already printed, and serves as a general Rule for the Schools already founded, and which are still founding by Us, for Education, and for the whole Society.

356. Every one ought to inculcate the Fear of God into the tender Minds of Children, to encourage every laudable Inclination, and to accustom them to the fundamental Rules, suitable to their respective Situations; to incite in them a Desire for Labour, and a Dread of Idleness, as the Root of all Evil, and Error; to train them up to a proper Decorum in their Actions and Conversation, Civility, and Decency in their Behaviour; and to sympathise with the Miseries of poor unhappy Wretches; and to break them of all perverse and froward Humours; to teach them Oeconomy, and whatever is most useful in all Affairs of Life; to guard them against all Prodigality and Extravagance; and particularly to root a proper Love of Cleanliness and Neatness, as well in themselves as in those who belong to them; in a Word, to instill all those Virtues and Qualities which join to form a good Education; by which, as they grow up, they may prove real Citizens, useful Members of the Community, and Ornaments to their Country.

Chapter XV

357. Of the Nobility.

358. The Husbandmen, who cultivate the Lands to produce Food for People in every Rank of Life, live in Country Towns and Villages. *This is their Lot.*

359. The Burghers, who employ their Time in mechanick Trades, Commerce, Arts, and Sciences, *inhabit the Cities.*

360. Nobility is an Appellation of Honour, which distinguishes all those who are adorned with it from every other Person of *inferior Rank.*

361. As amongst Mankind there were *some more* virtuous *than others,* and who at the same Time distinguished themselves *more* eminently by their *merit,* the People in ancient Times agreed to dignify the *most* virtuous, and the *most* deserving, by this *honourable Appellation,* or *Title,* and determined to *invest* them with *many Privileges* which are founded upon the *Principal Rules of Virtue and Honour* above mentioned.

362. They proceeded still farther, and regulated by Law *the Means* by which *this Dignity* might *be obtained* from the Sovereign, and pointed out *those bad Actions* by which it *might be forfeited.*

363. Virtue with Merit raises People to the Rank of Nobility.

364. Virtue and Honour ought to be the Rules, which prescribe *Love* for *their Country, Zeal for its Service, Obedience and Fidelity to their*

Sovereign; and continually suggest, *never to be guilty of an infamous Action.*

365. There are few Ways which lead so directly to the Attainment of Honours as the military Service. To defend their Country, and to conquer its Enemies, is the first Duty, and Proper Employment of the Nobility.

366. But though the military Art is the most ancient Way of attaining the Rank of Nobility; and though the military Virtues are essentially necessary for the Existence and Support of the State;

367. Yet still Justice is no less required in Time of Peace than in War; and the State would be destroyed without it:

368. And from hence it proceeds, that this Dignity is not attached solely to the Nobility; but may be acquired by the *civil* Virtues, as well as by the *military.*

369. Whence it still follows, that no one can lose the Rank of Nobility, but he who forfeits it by a Conduct directly opposite to the *Rules of Virtue and Honour,* on which his Dignity was founded; and by such means renders himself unworthy of that Appellation;

370. And the Honour and Preservation of the Purity of that Dignity require that he, who by his ill Conduct has violated the *Rules* on which his Title is founded, should be excluded, after Conviction, from the Number of the Nobility, and be deprived of that Dignity.

371. The Actions which render a Man unworthy of the Appellation of *Noble* are *Treason, Robbery, Theft* of all Kinds, the *Violation of Oaths,* or his *solemn Word* given, *false Evidence,* which he either gave himself, or *suborned* others to give; *Forgery* of false Deeds, Letters, or any such Kind of Writings:

372. In a Word, *every Fraud* contrary to *Honour,* especially those *Actions* which *degrade* a Man, and bring him into Contempt.

373. And the Preservation of Honour intire, consists in the *Love of their Country,* and *Observance of all its Laws and Duties:* From whence will follow,

374. *Praise* and *Glory,* especially to *that Race* which can reckon up among *their Ancestors more* of such Persons who were *adorned* with *Virtue, Honour, Merit, Fidelity* and *Love to their Country,* and consequently *to their Sovereign.*

375. And the Prerogatives of the Nobility ought to be founded on all the above-mentioned Qualifications, which compose the very *Essence* of the Appellation of *Nobleman.*

Chapter XVI

376. *Of the middling Sort of People.*

377. *I* have mentioned in the xvth Chapter, *that those People who inhabit the Cities apply themselves to handicraft Trades, Commerce,*

Arts, and Sciences. In whatever *State* the *fundamental Qualification* for the Rank of Nobility is established, *conformably* with the Rules prescribed in the xvth Chapter, it is no less *useful* to establish the Qualification of Citizens upon *Principles* productive of *Good Manners and Industry*, by which the People we here treat of will *enjoy that Situation*.

378. This Sort of People, of whom we ought now to speak, and from whom the State expects much Benefit, are admitted into the *Middling* Rank, if their *Qualifications* are firmly *established* upon *Good Manners and Incitements to Industry*.

379. People of *this Rank* will enjoy a State of Liberty, without intermixing either with the *Nobility* or the *Husbandmen*.

380. To this Rank of People, we ought to annex all those who are neither *Gentlemen*, nor *Husbandmen;* but employ themselves in *Arts, Sciences, Navigation, Commerce,* or *handicraft Trades.*

381. Besides these, all those who are not of the *Nobility* but have been educated in *Schools* or *Colleges*, of what Denomination soever, *ecclesiastical* or *civil*, founded by *Us* and *Our* Ancestors:

382. Also the Children of People belonging to the Law. But as in that *third Species*, there are different Degrees of Privilege, therefore we shall not enter into a detail of Particulars; but only open the way for a due Consideration of it.

383. As the whole Qualification which intitles People to this *middling* Rank is founded upon good Manners and Industry; the violation of these Rules will serve, on the Contrary, for their Exclusion from it; as for Instance, *Perfidiousness* and *Breach of Promise*, especially if *caused* by *Idleness* and *Treachery*. . . .

Chapter XIX

439. *Of the Composition of Laws.* . . .

448. Each Law ought to be written in so clear a Style as to be perfectly intelligible to every one; and, at the same Time, with great Conciseness: For which Reason Explanations, or Interpretations, are undoubtedly to be added (as Occasion shall require), to enable the Judges to perceive more readily the *Force* as well as *Use* of the Law. The martial Law is full of Examples of the like Nature, which may easily be followed.

449. But the utmost Care and Caution is to be observed in adding these Explanations and Interpretations; because they may, sometimes, rather *darken* than *clear up* the Case; of which there are many Instances.

450. When Exceptions, Limitations, and Modifications are not absolutely necessary in any Law, in that Case it is better not to insert them: For *such* particular Details generally produce still *more* Details.

451. If a Legislator desires to give his Reason for making any particular Law, that Reason ought to be *good*, and *worthy* of the Law. . . .

452. Laws ought not to be filled with subtile Distinctions, to demonstrate the quick Parts of the Legislator; they are made for People of *moderate* Capacities, as well as for those of *Genius*. They are not a *Logical Art*, but the simple and plain Reasoning of a Father who takes Care of his Children and Family.

453. *Real* Candour and Sincerity ought to be *displayed in every Part* of the Laws, and as they are made for the Punishment of Crimes, they ought consequently to *include* in themselves the greatest *Virtue* and *Benevolence*.

454. The Style of the Laws ought to be simple and concise: A *plain direct* Expression will be always better understood than a *studied* one.

455. When the Style of Laws is *tumid* and *inflated*, they are looked upon only as a Work of *Vanity* and *Ostentation*. . . .

458. Laws are made for the whole Body of the People: It is the Duty of every Individual to act conformably to them; consequently, it is absolutely necessary that every Individual should understand them.

459. The *sublime*, or lofty, and elevated Expressions, are studiously to be avoided; nor should one unnecessary Word be added in the Construction of a Law; that every one, at first Sight, might readily and clearly comprehend its Meaning.

460. Due Care is likewise to be taken that amongst the Laws there should be none which do not answer the End they were made for; that is, none which abound in Words, and are deficient in Sense; which, in their Contents, are trifling, and in their Style, *bombast*.

461. Laws which prescribe *those* Actions as highly *necessary*, which partake *neither* of Vice *nor* Virtue, are subject to this pernicious Consequence, that they oblige People, at the same Time, to esteem Actions *unavoidably necessary* as *unnecessary* ones.

462. Laws for pecuniary Mulcts or Fines, which mark precisely the Sum of Money payable for particular Offences, ought at least to be re-examined every *fifty Years*; because the Payment of that Sum, which at one Time was a *sufficient* Penalty, may be *not at all* at another; for the Value of Money changes, in proportion to the Quantity of Wealth in a Nation. . . .

480. *Words*, accompanied with *Actions*, partake of the *Nature* of those Actions; therefore, a Man who goes to publick Places to excite the Subjects to Rebellion will be guilty of *High-treason*; because the *Words*, accompanied with the *Action*, partake of its *Nature*. In this Case the Laws do not punish for the *Words*, but for the *Action* committed, at the Time when the *Words* were made use of. *Words* are never imputed as a *Crime* unless they *prepare*, or *accompany*, or *follow* the *criminal Action*. He who tortures *Words* into a *Crime* worthy of Death, perverts the whole Order of Things: *Words* ought to be esteemed only the *Sign* of a Crime, worthy of capital Punishment.

481. Nothing renders the Crime of *High-treason* more dependent upon the *arbitrary* Interpretation and *Will* of another than when *indiscreet* *Words* are the *Subject* of it. The Words *spoken* in Conversation are so subject to *arbitrary* Interpretations, and *so great* a Difference subsists between *Indiscretion* and *Malice*, and so *little* between *indiscreet* and *malicious* Expressions, that the Law can by no Means subject *Words* to capital Punishment; at least, without *expressly specifying* those *particular Words* which it declares treasonable.

482. And, consequently, *Words* do not form the *Essence* of a Crime; they frequently signify *nothing* of *themselves* but by the *Tone of Voice* they are pronounced with. Frequently a Repetition of the *same Words* does not give the *same Sense*; this *Sense* depends upon the *Connexion* with what *preceded* or *followed*. Sometimes *Silence* expresses *more* than *Words*. There is nothing so *equivocal* and *uncertain* as this whole Affair about *Words*. How then can so capital a Crime as *High-treason* be made of *Words*, and punished in the *same* Manner as the very *Action* itself? I mean not to lessen the Indignation which every one ought to have for *those* who try to *tarnish* the Glory of their Sovereign; but will say this, that simple corrective Punishment will *suit better*, on these Occasions, than the *Charge of High-treason*, which is always terrible even to *Innocence* itself.

483. *Writings* contain Things which are more durable than *Words*; but if they do not *lead* to the Crime of *High-treason*, they cannot, of *themselves*, constitute the *Essence* of High-treason.

484. Satirical Writings are prohibited in Monarchies; but they make them a *Misdemeanor* subject to the *Police* of the Town, and not a *Crime:* And great Care ought to be taken, in the *Examination* of *these Libels*, how we *extend it farther*; representing to ourselves that Danger of *debasing* the human Mind by *Restraint* and *Oppression*; which can be productive of nothing but *Ignorance*, and must *cramp* and *depress* the *rising Efforts* of Genius, and destroy the very *Will* for Writing.

485. Slanderers ought to be punished. . . .

493. (c) *Rules necessary, and of great Importance.*

494. In such a State as *Ours*, which extends its Sovereignty over so many different Nations, to forbid, or not to allow them to profess *different Modes* of Religion, would greatly indanger the Peace and Security of its Citizens.

495. And the most certain Means of bringing back these wandering Sheep to the true Flock of the Faithful is a *prudent Toleration* of other Religions, not repugnant to our orthodox Religion and Polity.

496. The human Mind is irritated by Persecution, but the Permission to *believe* according to *one's Opinion* softens even the most *obdurate* Hearts, and draws them gradually from their *inveterate* Obstinacy, by

stifling their Disputes; which are detrimental to the *Tranquillity* of the State, and the *Union* of the Citizens.

497. We ought to be extremely cautious in the Examination of Persons accused of *Witchcraft* and *Heresy*. Accusations of these two Crimes may break terribly in upon the Tranquillity, Liberty, and Welfare of the Citizens; and prove the Source of innumerable Acts of Tyranny, unless *Bounds* are set to them by the Laws. For as this Kind of Accusation does not directly strike at the Actions of a Citizen, but the imaginary Idea which People form of his Character, it becomes highly dangerous, in proportion to their *Ignorance*; and, in that Case, a Citizen will always find himself in Danger; because neither the *most* exemplary Behaviour in Life, nor the *most* conscientious Discharge of every moral Duty, can protect him against the Effects of Suspicions of these Crimes. . . .

501. (d) *How can we know, when a State approaches to its Fall, and entire Dissolution?*

502. The Corruption of every Government generally begins by the *Corruption of its fundamental Principles.*

503. The fundamental Principles of a Government are not only corrupted, when they extinguish that Idea of the State ingrafted in the Minds of the People by the Law, which may be termed the *Equality prescribed by the Laws;* but even then, when this *Idea of Equality* shall take root in the People, and grow to such a Pitch of Licentiousness, that every one aims at being equal to him, who is ordained by the Laws to rule over him.

504. If they do not shew Respect to the *Sovereign,* to the *Courts of Judicature,* and to *Governors;* and if they do not respect the *Ancient,* neither will they respect *Fathers,* nor *Mothers,* nor *Masters;* and the State insensibly will run to ruin.

505. When the fundamental Principles of Government are corrupted, then the *Regulations* introduced in it are termed *Hardships,* or *Severities.* The established *Rules* are termed *Restraints;* what was *Caution* before, is now termed *Fear.* The *Property* of particular Persons constituted, in former Times, the *Wealth of the People;* but now the *Wealth of the People* becomes the *Inheritance of particular Persons,* and the Love of their Country vanishes.

506. In order to preserve the *fundamental Principles* of a well-regulated Government inviolate, the State ought to be supported in its present Grandeur; and this State will fall to Decay if its fundamental Principles should be *altered.*

507. There are two Kinds of Corruption; the first is, when *the Laws are not observed;* the second when *the Laws are so bad that they corrupt themselves;* and the Evil then is *incurable;* because the *Remedy* of the Evil is to be found only in *itself.*

508. A State may change also two different Ways; either because the

Constitution of it *mends,* or because the *same* Constitution *corrupts.* If the *fundamental* Principles in a State are preserved, the Constitution of it *mends;* but if the fundamental Principles of it are destroyed, the Constitution *changes,* and then it *corrupts.*

509. The *more* capital Punishments increase, the *more* a State is in Danger of Destruction; for capital Punishments *increase* in Proportion to the *Corruption* of Manners, and Corruption of Manners produces the *Ruin* of a State. . . .

511. A Monarchy is destroyed when the Sovereign imagines that he displays his Power more by *changing* the Order of Things, than by adhering to it, and when he is more fond of *his own Imaginations* than of *his Will,* from which the Laws proceed, and have proceeded.

512. It is true, there are Cases, where Power ought and can exert its full Influence without any Danger to the State. But there are Cases also where it ought to act according to the *Limits* prescribed by itself.

513. The supreme Art of governing a State consists in the *precise* Knowledge of *that* Degree of Power, whether *great* or *small,* which ought to be exerted according to the *different* Exigences of Affairs: For, in a Monarchy, the Prosperity of the State depends, in Part, on a mild and condescending Government.

514. In the best constructed Machines, Art employs the *least Moment, Force,* and fewest Wheels possible. This Rule holds *equally good* in the Administration of Government; the most *simple Expedients* are often the *very best,* and the *most intricate* the *very worst.*

515. There is a certain Facility in the Method of governing: It is better for the Sovereign to *encourage,* and for the Laws to *threaten.*

516. That Minister is ill qualified for his Office who shall always tell you, "That the Sovereign is displeased; that he is unexpectedly prevented; that he will act as he pleases."

517. It would be a grievous Misfortune to a State if no one should dare to represent the Danger of some future Accident; nor excuse his bad Success, proceeding from ill Fortune; nor presume to speak his Mind freely.

518. But if any one should inquire, *When* a Sovereign ought to punish, and *when* to pardon? this is a Point which can be more easily *felt* than *prescribed to.* When *Lenity* is dangerous, the *Dangers* arising from it are extremely *obvious.* It is easy to distinguish *Lenity* from that *Weakness,* which brings the Sovereign into an Aversion for punishing, and into such a Situation, that he cannot himself *decide whom he ought to punish.*

519. It is certain that a *high* Opinion of the *Glory* and *Power* of the Sovereign would *increase* the *Strength* of his Administration; but a *good* Opinion of his *Love of Justice* will *increase it* at least as much.

520. All this will never please those Flatterers, who are daily instilling this pernicious Maxim into all the Sovereigns on Earth, *That their People*

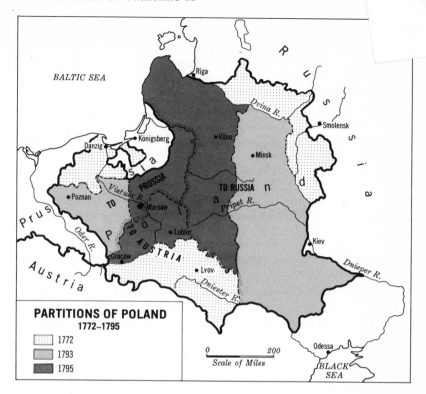

PARTITIONS OF POLAND
1772–1795

- [ ] 1772
- 1793
- 1795

are created for them only. But We think, and esteem it Our Glory to declare, "That We are created for Our 'People' "; and, for this Reason, We are obliged to Speak of Things just as they ought to be. For God forbid! that, after this Legislation is finished, any Nation on Earth should be more just; and, consequently, should flourish more than Russia; otherwise the Intention of Our Laws would be totally frustrated; an Unhappiness which I do not wish to survive.

521. All the Examples and Customs of different Nations, which are introduced in this Work, ought to produce no other Effect than to cooperate in the Choice of those Means, which may render the People of Russia, humanly speaking, the most happy in themselves of any People upon Earth.

522. Nothing more remains now for the Commission to do but to compare every Part of the Laws with the Rules of these Instructions.

Conclusion

523. Perhaps some Persons may object, after perusing these Instructions, that they will not be intelligible to every one. To this it may be

answered: It is true, they will not be readily understood by every Person after one slight Perusal only; but every Person may comprehend these Instructions, if he reads them with Care and Attention, and selects occasionally such Articles as may serve to direct him, as a Rule, in whatever he undertakes. These Instructions ought to be frequently perused, to render them more familiar: And every one may be firmly assured that they will certainly be understood; because,

524. Assiduity and Care will conquer every Difficulty; as, on the Contrary, Indolence and Carelessness will deter from every laudable Attempt.

525. To render this difficult Affair more easy; these Instructions are to be read over once, at the Beginning of every Month, in the Commission for composing the New Code of Laws, and in all the subordinate Committees, which depend upon it; particularly the respective Chapters and Articles intrusted to their Care, till the Conclusion of the Commission.

526. But as no perfect Work was ever yet composed by Man; therefore, if the Commissioners should discover, as they proceed, that any Rule for some particular Regulations has been omitted, they have Leave, in such a Case, to report it to Us, and to ask for a Supplement.

The Original signed with Her Imperial Majesty's own Hand, thus,

Moscow, July 30 1767. Catherine

10

The Pugachev Rebellion

When Peter III released Russian nobles from compulsory service to the state in 1762 (see Chapter 7), unfounded rumors began to circulate among the peasants that their own emancipation from the nobility would follow. Peasant expectations were shattered first by the murder of Peter III and then

From William Tooke, *The Life of Catherine II, Empress of All the Russians* (Dublin: 1800), vol. 2, pp. 345–346. Spellings have been modernized to facilitate reading.

by the increased rigors of serfdom that followed
Catherine II's accession to the throne, among them
her dissolution of the Legislative Commission and
her issuance in August 1767 of a decree prohibiting
all complaints by serfs against their masters. The
closing of this only avenue of redress increased
peasant restlessness and precipitated the peasant revolt of 1773–1774. The leader of this war was an
obscure Cossack, Emelian Pugachev (1730–1775),
who posed as Emperor Peter III. His forces seized
control of vast areas in the Volga Basin, terrorized
many nobles, and promised freedom to the lower
strata of Russian society. Catherine II tried to calm
the panic-stricken nobility through patriotic appeals
and through the dispatch of strong military forma-
tions against Pugachev. Late in 1774 the tide turned
in favor of the government forces and Pugachev was
captured, tried, and executed.

Catherine II's Manifesto against Pugachev, December 23, 1773

By the Grace of God, We, Catherine II, Empress and Autocratrix of All
the Russias, etc.

Make known to all Our faithful subjects that We have learnt, with the
utmost indignation and extreme affliction, that a certain Cossack, a
deserter and fugitive from the Don, named Emelian Pugachev, after
having traversed Poland, has been collecting, for some time past, in the
districts that border on the river Ural, in the government of Orenburg,
a troop of vagabonds like himself; that he continues to commit in those
parts all kinds of excesses, by inhumanly depriving the inhabitants of
their possessions, and even of their lives; and that in order to attract to
his party, hitherto composed of robbers, such persons as he meets, and
especially the unhappy patriots, on whose credulity he imposes, he has
had the insolence to arrogate to himself the name of the late Emperor
Peter III. It would be superfluous here to prove the absurdity of such
an imposture, which cannot even put on a shadow of probability in the
eyes of sensible persons: for, thanks to the Divine Goodness, those ages
are past in which the Russian Empire was plunged in ignorance and
barbarism when Gregory Otrepiev, with his adherents and several other
traitors to their country, made use of impostures as gross and detestable
to arm brother against brother, and citizen against citizen.

Since those times, which it is grievous to recollect, all true patriots have enjoyed the fruits of public tranquillity, and shudder with horror at the very remembrance of former troubles. In a word, there is not a man deserving of the Russian name, who does not hold in abomination the odious and insolent lie by which Pugachev fancies himself able to seduce and to deceive persons of a simple and credulous disposition, by promising to free them from the bonds of submission, and obedience to their sovereign, as if the Creator of the universe had established human societies in such a manner as that they can subsist without an intermediate authority between the sovereign and the people.

Nevertheless, as the insolence of this vile refuse of the human race is attended with consequences pernicious to the provinces adjacent to that district; as the report of the flagrant enormities which he has committed may affright those persons who are accustomed to imagine the misfortunes of others as ready to fall upon them, and as We watch with indefatigable care over the tranquillity of Our faithful subjects, We inform them by the present manifesto that We have taken, without delay, such measures as are the best adapted to stifle the sedition: and in order to annihilate totally the ambitious designs of Pugachev, and to exterminate a band of robbers, who have been audacious enough to attack the small military detachments dispersed about those countries, and to massacre the officers who were taken prisoners, We have dispatched thither, with a competent number of troops, General Alexander Bibikov [1727–1774], general in chief of Our armies, and major of Our regiment of life guards.

Accordingly We have no doubt of the happy success of these measures, and We cherish the hope that the public tranquillity will soon be restored, and that the profligates who are spreading devastation over a part of the government of Orenburg will shortly be dispersed. We are moreover persuaded that Our faithful subjects will justly abhor the imposture of the rebel Pugachev, as destitute of all probability, and will repel the artifices of the ill-disposed, who seek and find their advantage in the seduction of the weak and credulous, and who cannot assuage their avidity but by ravaging their country, and by shedding of innocent blood.

We trust, with equal confidence, that every true son of the country will unremittedly fulfil his duty of the contributing to the maintenance of good order and of public tranquillity, by preserving himself from the snares of seduction, and by duly discharging his obedience to his lawful sovereign. All Our faithful subjects therefore may dispel their alarms and live in perfect security, since We employ Our utmost care, and make it Our peculiar glory, to preserve their property, and to extend the general felicity.

Given at St. Petersburg, December 23, 1773.

Pugachev's "Emancipation Decree," July 31, 1774

We, Peter III, by the Grace of God Emperor and Autocrat of All-Russia, etc.

This is given for nationwide information.

By this personal decree, with our monarchial and fatherly love, we grant [freedom] to everyone who formerly was in serfdom or in any other obligation to the nobility; and we transfer these to be faithful personal subjects of our crown; [to the Old Believers] we grant the right to use the ancient sign of the Cross, and to pray, and to wear beards; while to the Cossacks [we restore] for eternity their freedoms and liberties; we [hereby] terminate the recruiting system, cancel personal and other monetary taxes, abolish without compensation the ownership of land, forest, pastures, fisheries and salt deposits; and [finally] we free everyone from all taxes and obligations which the thievish nobles and extortionist city judges have imposed on the peasantry and the rest of the population. We pray for the salvation of your souls and wish you a happy and peaceful life here [on earth] where we have suffered and experienced much from the above-mentioned thievish nobles. Now since our name, thanks to the hand of Providence, flourishes throughout Russia, we make hereby known by this personal decree the following: all nobles who have owned either *pomesties*, [estates granted by the state] or *votchinas* [inherited estates], who have opposed our rule, who have rebelled against the empire, and who have ruined the peasantry should be seized, arrested, and hanged; that is, treated in the same manner as these unchristians have treated you, the peasantry. After the extermination of these opponents and thievish nobles everyone will live in a peace and happiness that shall continue to eternity.

Given July 31, 1774   Peter

<hr>

From *Pugachevshchina: Iz arkhiva Pugacheva. Manifesty, ukazy i perepiska* (*The Pugachev Upheaval: From the Pugachev Archive. Manifestos, Decrees and Correspondence*), (Moscow-Leningrad: Tsentrarkhiv, 1926), vol. 1, pp. 40–41. Translation mine. Items in brackets are mine.

11

Catherine II's Charter to the Nobility, April 21, 1785

On April 21, 1785, Catherine II granted the Russian nobles a charter of rights and privileges. In part an expression of Catherine's thanks for the support they had given her, the charter also represented the last stage in the general improvement of the nobility's position since the death of Peter I. Under the new charter, the nobles in each gubernia or administrative district, became a privileged class with broad powers of self-government and great administrative influence. Each noble was exempted from state service, the payment of taxes, and army conscription. He possessed absolute right of ownership over his land and peasants and was at liberty to pursue trade or industry. The Russian nobles called Catherine's reign their "golden age."

. . . As a result of new gains and the expansion of our Empire, when we everywhere enjoy every kind of internal and external peace, we direct our great deed more and more toward an uninterrupted occupation with delivering to our faithful subjects in all vital branches of internal state administration durable and lasting decrees aimed at the increase of happiness and order for future times; toward that aim we find it appropriate to extend our solicitude to our loyal Russian *dvorianstvo* [nobility], in view of the services, zeal, attention, and undeviating faith to All-Russian autocrats—to ourselves as well as to our throne—which it [the nobility] has shown during troublesome times, in war as well as peace. And following God's examples of justice, mercy, and grace, which have beautified the Russian throne and glorified our ancestors, and being moved by our own motherly love and distinct gratitude to the Russian nobility, our imperial judiciousness and will orders, decrees, announces, and approves

From *Polnoe Sobranie Zakonov Russkoi Imperii* . . . (*Complete Collection of the Laws of the Russian Empire*), 1st Series, vol. 22, no. 16,187, pp. 346–351. Translation mine. Items in brackets are mine.

undeviatingly for eternity, for the benefit of Russian nobility, in our and imperial service, the following articles:

1. The title of the nobility is hereditary and stems from the quality and virtue of leading men of antiquity who distinguished themselves by their service—which they turned into merit and acquired for their posterity the title of the nobility.

2. It is to the advantage of both the Empire and the Crown, as it is also just, that the respectful title of the nobility be maintained and approved firmly and inviolably; and therefore, as formerly, now and in the future the title of the nobility is irrevocable, hereditary, and belongs to those honorable families who use it; and accordingly:

3. A nobleman transmits his noble title to his wife;

4. A nobleman transmits his noble title to his children hereditarily;

5. Neither a nobleman nor a noblewoman can be deprived of the title of the nobility unless they forfeit it themselves by an act contrary to the standards of noble dignity.

6. The following acts are contrary to the standards of noble dignity and can deprive one of the title: (a) violation of an oath; (b) treason; (c) robbery; (d) thefts of all sorts; (e) deceitful acts; (f) violations which call for either corporal punishment or a deprivation of honor; (g) incitement of others to commit violations—if this be established.

7. But since the title of the nobility cannot be revoked except as a result of violation, and marriage is an honest [institution] set up by divine law, when a noblewoman marries a non-noble man she does not forfeit her title; but she cannot pass on her nobility to her husband or her children.

8. A nobleman cannot be deprived of his title without due process of law.

9. A nobleman cannot be deprived of his honor without due process of law.

10. A nobleman cannot be deprived of his life without due process of law.

11. A nobleman cannot be deprived of his property without due process of law.

12. A nobleman can be judged by his peers only.

13. A nobleman who has committed a crime and is legally liable to be deprived either of his title, honor, or life, cannot be punished without his case being presented before the Senate and then approved by his Imperial Majesty.

14. All criminal acts of a nobleman which for ten years went either unnoticed or had no action taken on them we decree be henceforth forgotten forever. . . .

15. A nobleman cannot be subjected to corporal punishment.

16. Noblemen who serve as junior officers in our armed forces should be punished according to regulations applicable to senior officers.

17. We confirm freedom and liberty to the Russian nobility on an hereditary basis for eternity.

18. We confirm the right of the nobles now in service to continue their service or to ask freedom from service on the basis of the regulations established for that purpose.

19. We confirm the right of the nobles to enter the service of other European countries friendly to us and to travel abroad.

20. Since the title and privileges of the nobility in the past, present, and future are acquired by service and work useful to the Empire and the throne, and since the very existence of Russian nobility depends on the security of the country and the throne, whenever Russian autocracy needs the service of the nobility for the general well being, every nobleman is then obligated, the moment the autocratic government calls him, to perform fully his duty and sacrifice his life, if need be, to government service.

21. A nobleman has the right to sign his name not only as lord of his *pomestie* estate, granted to him by the state, but also as owner of his *votchina* estate, inherited from his ancestors or granted through grace.

22. A nobleman has the power and the authority to give away to whomever he wishes the property which he acquired legally as first owner, to bequeath this property in his will, to confer it as dowry, or to sell or give it away for his livelihood. He may, however, dispose of inherited property only in conformity with the provisions of the law.

23. The inheritable property of a nobleman who may be convicted of a serious crime should pass on to his legal heirs.

24. No one should attempt to seize or damage arbitrarily a nobleman's property without due process of law or the legal judgment of the appropriate court of justice.

25. If a nobleman has a claim against another nobleman he should bring it before the appropriate court of justice.

26. The nobles have the right to purchase villages.

27. The nobles have the right to sell wholesale whatever their villages grow or their handicrafts produce.

28. The nobles may have factories and mills in their villages.

29. The nobles may build small towns on their estates on which they may organize trade and annual fairs. [This activity must not be] contrary to state laws, must be done with the full knowledge of governor generals and *gubernia* administrations, and must be arranged in such a way as not to conflict with fairs of other local cities.

30. The nobles have the right to have, to build, or to buy homes in cities and to have handicrafts there.

31. In case a nobleman prefers to make use of the municipal code of civil rights, he may subordinate himself to it.

32. The nobles are hereby permitted to sell abroad wholesale the products harvested or made on their property, or to have them exported from the designated harbors.

33. The nobles have the right granted to them by the gracious ukaz of June 28, 1782 to ownership of not only the fruits of the land belonging to them, but also all resources found beneath the surface and in waters, and all of their products, as is fully stated in that ukaz.

34. The nobles have the right of ownership of forests which grow on their property and of their free utilization as is fully explained in the gracious ukaz of September 22, 1782.

35. The homes of the nobility in villages are to be free from quartering of soldiers.

36. A nobleman is personally freed from the soul tax. . . .

37. We grant our faithful nobles the permission to assemble in the gubernias where they live, to organize in every *namestnichestvo* [district] an Association of Nobles, and to enjoy the rights, privileges, distinctions, and preferences stated below.

38. Nobles may assemble in the *gubernia* by and with the permission of the governor-general or governor every three years during the winter for the purpose of electing noble representatives as well as to hear proposals of the governor-general or the governor.

39. The meeting of nobles in the *namestnichestvo* has permission to elect a *gubernia* marshal of the nobility; this election will occur every three years at which time the names of two marshals of the *uezd* nobility will be submitted to the imperial representative or administrator. The governor-general or the governor will then designate which will be *gubernia* marshal of the nobility for that *gubernia*.

40. By virtue of articles 64 and 211 of the statutes, the *uezd* marshal of the nobility is elected by the nobility of the *uezd* through secret ballot every three years. . . .

47. The Association of Nobles has permission to present its needs and interests to the governor-general or the governor.

48. The Association of Nobles has permission to petition, through its deputies, both the Senate and the Imperial Majesty in accordance with the law. . . .

62. The Association of Nobles cannot elect a nobleman whose annual income from his village is below 100 rubles, or who is under twenty years of age, to perform functions of an elective representative of the nobility.

63. A nobleman who either has no village or is under twenty years of age can participate in the Association of Nobles but cannot have an elective voice.

nobleman who never performed any service or who served but
ttain officer rank (even though officer rank was given to him at
ıt may be a member of the Association of Nobles; but he cannot sit in deliberation with the worthy ones or have the right to elect
or be elected. . . .

12

*Radishchev's Journey
from St. Petersburg to Moscow*

In 1790, Alexander N. Radishchev (1749–1802), a
Leipzig-educated Russian revolutionary, published
A Journey From St. Petersburg to Moscow. In it, this
first great disciple of European enlightenment in
Russia crusaded for a humane government, the rule
of law, and freedom of speech and press. He cham-
pioned the downtrodden and the rights of individual
citizens, indicted the autocratic state machine and
its two basic pillars—the nobles and the clergy—and
expressed abhorrence for militarism and colonial conquest. The book contained such rich descriptions of
peasant field work, the transportation system, an
auction sale of serfs, the recruiting system, forced
marriages, and other aspects of eighteenth-century
Russia that its reprinting was barred in Russia for
over a hundred years. Although Radishchev was
tried and sentenced to death, Catherine II commuted the sentence to exile in Siberia. He returned to
Russia after her death in 1796. Below are reproduced two passages from this remarkable book:
"An Ode on Liberty," wherein Radishchev indicts

Reprinted by permission of the publishers from Aleksandr Nikolaevich Radish-
chev, *A Journey From St. Petersburg to Moscow.* Translation by Leo Wiener.
Edited with an Introduction and Notes by Roderick Page Thaler (Cambridge,
Mass.: Harvard University Press, 1958, by the President and Fellows of Harvard
College), pp. 194–212.

the Russian political system through the words of
his "travelling companion," and a description of the
recruiting system in Russia in the 1780s.

1

O blessed gift of the heavens, source of all great deeds, O Liberty,
Liberty, priceless gift! Permit a slave to sing of you. Fill my heart with
your fire; with the stroke of your mighty arms, transform serfdom's night
into light. Let Brutus and Tell wake once more, and let kings enthroned
in [tyrannous] might be dismayed at your voice.

"This stanza was condemned for two reasons: first, because the verse
'transform serfdom's night into light' is very stiff and hard to pronounce
on account of the frequent repetition of the letter 'T' and the piling up
of too many consonants. In 'serfdom's night' there are ten consonants
to three vowels, whereas it is possible to write as melodiously in Russian
as in Italian–. Agreed—although some thought this verse successful,
finding in the roughness of the verse an onomatopoetic expression of the
very laboriousness of the action–. The second objection: 'Let kings be
dismayed at your voice.' To wish a king dismay is to wish him evil, consequently–. But I do not want to tire you with all the remarks made
about my verses. Many of them, I must confess, were justified. Let me
read it to you.

2

I came into the world and you with me. . . .

We shall omit this stanza. Its theme is: man is free in all things from
birth–.

3

But what stands in the way of my freedom? Everywhere I behold a
barrier to my yearnings; a communal power has arisen in the people, the
source of power everywhere. Society obeys it in everything, and is everywhere of one accord with it. No limits are set to the general welfare. In
the power of all I see my lot: in doing the will of all, I do my own: this
is what law in society means.

4

Amidst a fertile dale, amidst fields heavy with grain, where tender lilies
bloom, in the shade of peaceful olive trees, whiter than Parian marble,
brighter than the rays of the brightest day, stands a temple open to every
view. There no false sacrifice swirls up in smoke, there the fiery inscription
may be seen: 'Have done with the miseries of the innocent!'

5

Crowned with an olive branch, seated upon a hard stone, dispassionate and cold, a deaf divinity. . . .

And so forth. Law is represented in the form of a divinity within a temple whose guards are Truth and Justice.

6

He lifts up his stern countenance, and spreads joy and terror around him; he looks with equanimity upon all persons, neither hating nor loving. He ignores flattery, subservience, high descent, eminence, wealth; and despises mortal offerings; he knows neither ties of blood nor of friendship, and distributes rewards and punishments impartially: he is the image of God on earth.

7

Behold a horrible monster, hydra-like, with a hundred heads! It looks mild and its eyes are ever full of tears, but its jaws are full of venom. It tramples upon the earthly powers, and stretches its head up toward Heaven, which it claims as its native home. It sows false phantoms and darkness everywhere, and commands all to believe blindly.

8

It has enshrouded reason in darkness, and everywhere it spreads its creeping poison; . . .

The portrayal of religious superstition, robbing man of sensitiveness, enticing him into the yoke of slavery, and clothing him in the armor of error:

It commands him to fear the truth. . . .

[Tyrannous] power calls this monster Revelation; reason calls it Deceit.

9

Let us look into the vast regions where the tarnished throne of slavery stands;
In peace and quiet, religious and political superstition, each supporting the other,
join to oppress society. The one tries to fetter reason, the other strives to destroy the will: "For the common good," they say.

10

In the shadow of slavish peace no golden fruit can grow; where everything hinders the spirit's striving, nothing great can thrive.

And all the evil consequences of slavery, such as recklessness, idleness, trickery, hunger, and so forth.

11

Raising his haughty brow and grasping his iron scepter, the king seats himself augustly on the throne of terror and sees his people only as base creatures. Holding life and death in his hands, he says: "At will I can spare the evildoer or delegate my power. When I laugh, all laugh; if I frown threateningly, all are confounded. You live only so long as I permit you to live."

12

And we look on calmly . . .

as the ravenous dragon, reviling all, poisons their days of joy and happiness. But though all stand before your throne with bended knees, tremble, for, lo, the avenger comes, proclaiming liberty. . . .

13

Everywhere martial hosts will arise, hope will arm all; everyone hastens to wash off his shame in the blood of the crowned tormentor. Everywhere I see the flash of the sharp sword; death, flying about in various forms, hovers over the proud head. Rejoice, fettered peoples! The avenging law of nature has brought the king to the block.

14

Having rent the curtain of deceptive night with a mighty thunderbolt, having overthrown the enormous idol of haughty and stubborn power, having fettered the hundred-armed giant, it drags him to the throne, where the people now sit. "Violator of the power I granted you! Speak, villain whom I crowned, how dared you rise against me?

15

"I clad you in the purple that you might preserve equality in society, watch over the widow and orphan, save innocence from calamity and be its loving father, but an implacable enemy of vice, the lie, and calumny; that you might reward merit with honor, forestall evil through order, and maintain purity of morals.

16

"I have covered the sea with ships. . . .

I have provided means for achieving wealth and well-being. I desired that the peasant should not be a captive in his field, and that he should bless you. . . .

17

"Ruthlessly, out of my own blood, I raised up a mighty host; I cast the brazen cannon with which to punish your external enemies. I commanded them to obey you and with you to strive for glory. For the common good, all things are permitted me. I tear up the bowels of the earth and extract the glittering metal for your adornment.

18

"But you, forgetting the oath you swore to me, forgetting that I had chosen you, came to think that you had been crowned for your own pleasure, and that you were the master, not I. With the sword you destroyed my laws; you silenced all rights; you made truth blush with shame. You have opened the door to all abominations, you have begun to appeal not to me, but to God, and you thought you could scorn me.

19

"Garnering with bloody sweat the fruit I planted for sustenance, dividing my crumbs with you, I did not spare my strength. But to you all treasures are insufficient! Tell me, what did you lack, to justify your tearing the rags off my back? To reward a sycophantic courtier or a woman lost to honor! Or have you made gold your god?

20

"You gave to the arrogant the token of distinction established to reward the deserving; you brandished against the innocent my sword, sharpened against evildoers. The hosts brought together for the defense of the homeland—are you leading them into glorious battle to avenge suffering humanity? You fight in bloody fields so that tipsy Athenians, yawning, may call you a hero.

21

"O evildoer, worst of all evildoers . . .

You have combined all crimes in yourself and have directed your sting against me. . . .

Die, then, die a hundred deaths."

So spake the people. . . .

22

O great man full of perfidy, hypocrite, flatterer, blasphemer! You alone might have given the world a great example of benevolence. I consider you, Cromwell, a criminal, because, having power in your hands, you destroyed the citadel of freedom. But you have taught generation after generation how nations can avenge themselves; you had Charles executed by due process of law.

23

The voice of freedom resounds on all sides. . . .

The whole nation streams to the assembly; it destroys the iron throne, and, as Samson did of yore, it pulls down the perfidious palace. It builds the citadel of nature on the foundation of the law. Thou art great, aye great indeed, Spirit of Liberty; creative as God Himself!

24

The next eleven stanzas consist of an account of the kingdom of Liberty and its achievements, that is, security, peace, well-being, greatness. . . .

34

But the passions that goad men to madness . . .

turn the civil peace into disaster. . . .

stir the father up against the son, tear asunder the bonds of marriage,

and bring all the dread consequences of boundless lust for power. . . .

35, 36, 37

Description of the ruinous consequences of luxury. Civil discord. Civil war. Marius, Sulla, Augustus. . . .

He put troublesome freedom to sleep, and wound flowers around the iron scepter. . . .

Thence came slavery. . . .

38, 39

This is the law of nature: from tyranny, freedom is born; from freedom, slavery. . . .

40

Why marvel at this, for man, too, is born to die. . . . The following eight stanzas contain prophecies about the future fate of our country, which will fall into separate parts—all the sooner, the greater it grows. But the time for that has not yet come. When it comes, then

The heavy fetters of night will break.

Even in its death throes, stubborn Power will set up a guard against
free speech, and gather all its strength for its expiring effort to crush
rising freedom. . . .

49

But humanity will roar in its fetters, and, moved by the hope of freedom and the indestructible law of nature, will push on. . . . And tyranny
will be dismayed. Then the united force of all despotism, of all oppressive power

> Will in a moment be dispersed. O chosen day of days!

50

> Even now I hear the voice of nature, the primal voice, the voice of
> the Godhead.

The dark citadel totters, and liberty shines forth with a glorious radiance.
"That's the end," the newfangled poet said. I was very glad of it, and
wanted to say something to him, perhaps raise an unpleasant objection
to his verses, but the bell reminded me that in traveling it is better to
make reasonable haste with post nags than to climb on Pegasus when he
is mettlesome.

Gorodnya

As I drove into this village, my ears were assailed not by the melody of
verse, but by a heart-rending lament of women, children, and old men.
Getting out of my carriage, I sent it on to the post station, for I was
curious to learn the cause of the disturbance I had noticed in the street.

Going up to one group of people, I learned that a levy of recruits was
the cause of the sobs and tears of the people crowded together there.
From many villages, both crown and manorial, those who were to be
drafted into the army had come together here.

In one group an old woman fifty years of age, holding the head of a
lad of twenty, was sobbing. "My dear child, to whose care are you committing me? To whom will you entrust the home of your parents? Our
fields will be overgrown with grass, our hut with moss. I, your poor old
mother, will have to wander about begging. Who will warm my decrepit
body when it is cold, who will protect it from the heat? Who will give
me food and drink? But all that does not weigh so heavily upon my heart
as this: who will close my eyes when I die? Who will receive my maternal
blessing? Who will return my body to our common mother, the moist
earth? Who will come to remember me at my grave? Your warm tears
will not fall upon it; I shall not have that consolation."

Near the old woman stood a grown-up girl. She, too, was sobbing. "Farewell, friend of my heart; farewell, my shining sun. I, your betrothed, will never know comfort or joy again. My friends will not envy me. The sun will not rise for me in joy. You are leaving me to pine away, neither a widow nor a wedded wife. If our inhuman village elders had only let us get married, if you, my darling, could have slept but one short night on my white breast. Perhaps God would have taken pity on me and given me a little son to comfort me."

The lad said to them: "Stop weeping, stop rending my heart. Our Sovereign calls us to service. The lot fell on me. It is the will of God. Those not fated to die will live. Perhaps I will come home to you with the regiment. I may even win rank and honors. Dear Mother, do not grieve. Take care of my Praskov'yushka." This recruit was drafted from an Economic village.*

From another standing nearby I heard altogether different words. Amidst them I saw a man of about thirty, of medium size, standing erect and looking happily at the people around him.

"The Lord has heard my prayers," he said. "The tears of an unfortunate man have reached the Comforter of all men. Now I shall at least know that my lot may depend on my own good or bad behavior. Heretofore it depended on the arbitrary whims of a woman. I am consoled by the thought that hereafter I shall not be flogged without a fair trial!"

Having gathered from what he said that he was a manorial serf, I was curious to learn the cause of his unusual joy. To my question he replied: "Dear sir, if a gallows were placed on one side of you and a deep river ran on the other, and you, standing between these two perils, could not possibly escape going either to the right or to the left, into the noose or into the water, which would you choose? Which would sense and impulse make you prefer? I think everyone would rather jump into the river, in the hope of escaping from peril by swimming to the other shore. No one would willingly investigate the strength of the noose by putting his neck into it. This was my situation. A soldier's life is a hard one, but better than the noose. Even that would be all right, if that were the end, but to die a lingering death under the cudgel, under the cat-o'nine-tails, in chains, in a dungeon, naked, barefooted, hungry, thirsty, under constant abuse—my lord, although you look upon your peasants as your property, often less regarded than cattle, yet, unfortunately, they are not without feeling. You appear to be surprised to hear such words from the lips of a peasant; but why, when you hear them, are you not surprised at the cruelty of your brothers, the noblemen?"

And in very truth I had not expected such words from a man dressed

---

* A village of serfs, formerly belonging to a monastery, but after the secularization of monastic lands by the Emperor Peter III in 1762, belonging to the government and administered by the Economic College.

in a gray caftan and with his head shaven. But wishing to satisfy my curiosity, I asked him to tell me how, being of such a low estate, he had arrived at ideas which are frequently lacking in men improperly said to be nobly born.

"If it will not tire you to hear my story, I will tell you: I was born in slavery, the son of my master's former valet. How happy I am to think that they will never again call me Van'ka or any other offensive name, that they will never again call be like a dog by whistling. My old master, a kindhearted, reasonable, and virtuous man, who often lamented the fate of his slaves, wanted, on account of my father's long service, to do something special for me; so he gave me the same education as his son. There was hardly any difference between us, except that the cloth of his coat was perhaps better. Whatever they taught the young master, they taught me, too; our instruction was exactly the same, and I can say without boasting that in many things I did better than my young master.

" 'Vanyuasha,' the old master said to me, 'your happiness depends entirely on you. You have more of an inclination for learning and morality than my son. He will be rich by inheritance and will know no want, while you have known it from birth. So try to be worthy of the pains I have taken for you.' When my young master was in his seventeenth year, he and I were sent to travel abroad with a tutor, who was told to look upon me as a traveling companion, not a servant. As he sent me away, my old master said to me: 'I hope that you will return to give me and your parents joy. You are a slave within the borders of this country, but beyond them you are free. When you return, you will not find fetters imposed upon you because of your birth.' We were away for five years and then returned to Russia, my young master happy at the thought of seeing his father, and I, I must confess, flattering myself that I would obtain what I had been promised. My heart was atremble as I again entered the borders of my country. And indeed my foreboding was not false. In Riga my young master received the news of his father's death. He was deeply moved by it; I was thrown into despair. For all my efforts to win his friendship and confidence had been in vain. Not only did he not love me, but—perhaps from envy, as is characteristic of small souls—he hated me.

"Observing the anxiety produced in me by the death of his father, he told me he would not forget the promise that had been made to me, if I would be worthy of it. It was the first time he had ventured to tell me so, for, having received control of his property through the death of his father, he had dismissed his tutor in Riga, paying him liberally for his labors. I must do justice to my former master: he has many good qualities, but timidity of spirit and thoughtlessness obscure them.

"A week after our arrival in Moscow, my master fell in love with a pretty girl, but one who with her bodily beauty combined a very ugly soul and a hard and cruel heart. Brought up in the conceit of her station, she respected only external show, rank, and wealth. In two months she became my master's wife, and I became her slave. Until then I had not experienced any change in my condition and had lived in my master's house as his companion. Although he never gave me any orders, I generally anticipated his wishes, as I was aware of his power and of my position. Scarcely had the young mistress crossed the threshold of the house, in which she was determined to rule, before I was made aware of my hard lot. On the first evening after the wedding and all next day, when I was introduced to her by her husband as his companion, she was occupied with the usual cares of a bride; but in the evening, when a fairly large company came to the table and sat down to the first supper with the newly married pair, and I sat down in my usual place at the lower end of the table, the new mistress said to her husband in a fairly loud voice that if he wished her to sit at the table with the guests, he must not permit any serfs to sit there. He looked at me and, at her instance, sent word to me that I should leave the table and eat supper in my room. Imagine how deely this humiliation hurt me! I suppressed the tears that came to my eyes, and withdrew. I did not dare to make my appearance the next day. They brought me my dinner and supper without saying anything to me. And so it went on succeeding days. One afternoon, a week after the wedding, the new mistress inspected the house, and, after apportioning the duties and living quarters to all the servants, entered my rooms also. They had been furnished for me by my old master. I was not at home. I will not repeat what she said there, to ridicule me, but when I returned home they gave me her order, whereby I was sent down to a corner on the ground floor with the unmarried servants, where my bed and my trunk, with my clothes and linens, had already been placed; all my other things she had left in my former rooms, in which she installed her serving maids.

"What took place in my soul when I heard this is easier to feel, if you can, than to describe. But so as not to detain you with superfluous details: my mistress, after taking control of the house and finding that I had no aptitude for service, made me a lackey and decked me out in livery. The least, imaginary remissness in my duties led to my ears being boxed, beatings, and the cat-o'-nine-tails. O, my lord, it would have been better if I had never been born! How many times did I complain against my dead benefactor for having fostered a responsive soul in me. It would have been better for me if I had grown up in ignorance and had never learned that I am a man, equal to all others. Long, long ago I would have freed myself from my hateful life, if I had not been held back by the prohibition of our Supreme Judge. I determined to bear my lot patiently. And I endured not only bodily wounds, but also those which she inflicted upon my soul. But I almost broke my vow and cut short the miserable remains of my woeful life as a result of a new blow to my soul.

"A nephew of my mistress, a youngster of eighteen years, a sergeant of the Guards, educated in the fashon of Moscow dandies, became enamored of a chambermaid of his aunt's, and, having quickly won her ready favors, made her a mother. Although he was usually quite unconcerned in his amours, in this case he was somewhat embarrassed. For his aunt, having learned about the affair, forbade the chambermaid her presence, and gently scolded her nephew. She intended, after the fashion of benevolent mistresses, to punish the one whom she had formerly favored by marrying her off to one of the stable boys. But since they were all married already, and since, for the honor of the house, there had to be a husband for the pregnant woman, she selected me as the worst of all the servants. In the presence of her husband, my mistress informed me of this as though it were a special favor. I could not stand this abuse any longer. 'Inhuman woman!' I cried. 'You have the power to torment me and to wound my body; you say the laws give you the right to do this. I hardly believe it, but I know full well that no one can be forced to marry.' She listened to my words in ominous silence. Then I turned to her husband and said: 'Ungrateful son of a generous father, you have forgotten his last will and testament, you have forgotten your own promise; but do not drive to despair a soul nobler than yours! Beware!' I could say no more, because, by command of my mistress, I was taken to the stable and whipped mercilessly with the cat-o'-nine-tails. The next day I could hardly get up out of bed from the beating; but I was brought before my mistress again. 'I will forgive you your impudence of yesterday,' she said; 'marry my Mavrushka; she begs you to, and I want to do this for her, because I love her even in her transgression.' 'You heard my answer yesterday,' I said; 'I have no other. I will only add that I will complain to the authorities against you for compelling me to do what you have no right to.' 'Then it's time for you to become a soldier!' my mistress screamed in fury. —A traveler who has lost his way in a terrible desert will rejoice less when he finds it again than I did when I heard these words. 'Take him to be a soldier!' she repeated, and the next day it was done. Fool! She thought that being made a soldier would be a punishment for me, as it is for the peasants. For me it was a joy, and as soon as they had shaved my forehead, I felt like a new man. My strength was restored. My mind and spirit began to revive. O hope, sweet solace of the unfortunate, remain with me!" A heavy tear, but not a tear of grief and despair, fell from his eyes. I pressed him to my heart. His countenance was radiant with new joy. "All is not yet lost," he said; "you arm my soul against sorrow by making me feel that my misery is not endless."

From this unfortunate man I went to a group in which I saw three men fettered in the strongest irons. "It is amazing," I said to myself as I looked at these prisoners, "now they are downcast, weary, timid, and they not only do not want to become soldiers, but the greatest severity is required to force them into that status; but as soon as they become accustomed to the execution of their hard duty, they grow alert and spirited, and even look with scorn upon their former condition." I asked one of the bystanders who, to judge from his uniform, was a government clerk: "No doubt you have put them in such heavy fetters because you are afraid they will run away?"

"You guessed it. They belonged to a landed proprietor who needed money for a new carriage and got it by selling them to crown peasants, to be levied into the army."

I. –"My friend, you are mistaken. Crown peasants can't purchase their brothers."

He. –"It isn't done in the form of a sale. Having by agreement received the money, the master sets these unfortunates free; they are presumed to be 'voluntarily' registered as crown peasants of the commune which paid the money for them; and the commune, by common consent, sends them to be soldiers. They are now being taken with their emacipation papers to be registered in our commune."

Free men, who have committed no crime, are fettered, and sold like cattle! O laws! Your wisdom frequently resides only in your style! Is this not an open mockery? And, what is worse, a mockery of the sacred name of liberty. Oh, if the slaves weighed down with fetters, raging in their despair, would, with the iron that bars their freedom, crush our heads, the heads of their inhuman masters, and redden their fields with our blood! What would the country lose by that? Soon great men would arise from among them, to take the place of the murdered generation; but they would be of another mind and without the right to oppress others. This is no dream; my vision penetrates the dense curtain of time that veils the future from our eyes. I look through the space of a whole century. I left the crowd in disgust.

But the fettered prisoners are free now. If they had any fortitude, they could put to naught the oppressive intentions of their tyrants. Let us go back to them. –"My friends," I said to the captives, these prisoners of war in their own country, "do you know that if you do not freely wish to enter the army, no one can now compel you to do so?" "Stop making fun of poor wretches, sir. Even without your jesting, it was hard enough for us to part, one from his poor old father, another from his little sisters, a third from his young wife. We know that our master sold us as recruits for a thousand rubles."

"If you did not know it before, you must know now that it is against the law to sell men as recruits, that peasants cannot legally buy men, that your master has set you free, and that the purchasers intend to register you in their commune, as though of your own free will."

"O, sir, if that is really so, we do thank you. When they line us up for muster, we will all say that we do not want to become soldiers and that we are free men."

"Add to it that your master sold you at a time when such a sale was not legal, and that they are delivering you up as recruits in violation of the law."* One can easily imagine the joy that lighted up the faces of these unfortunates. Leaping up from their places and vigorously shaking their fetters, they seemed to be testing their strength, as though they would shake them off. But this conversation could have gotten me into serious trouble, for the recruiting officers, having heard what I said, rushed toward me in violent anger, and said, "Sir, don't meddle with other people's business, and get away while the getting's good!" When I resisted, they pushed me so violently that I was forced to leave this crowd as fast as I could.

As I approached the post station, I found another gathering of peasants, surrounding a man in a torn coat. He seemed to be somewhat drunk. He was making faces at the people, who laughed till the tears came, watching him. "What is it all about?" I asked a boy. "What are you laughing at?"

"Well, the recruit is a foreigner and can't speak a word of Russian." From the few words he spoke, I gathered that he was a Frenchman. That made me still more curious; I wanted to find out how a foreigner could be offered as a recruit by the peasants. I asked him in his native tongue: "My friend, by what fate did you get here?"

Frenchman. —"Fate wanted it so. Where things go well, there one should stay."

I. —"How did you become a recruit?"

Frenchman.—"I love a soldier's life. I've known it before, and I wanted it."

I. —"But how does it happen that you are sent from a village? Usually they take only peasants, and Russians at that, as soldiers from the villages; but I see that you are neither a peasant nor a Russian."

Frenchman. —"It happened this way. As a child I was apprenticed to a hairdresser in Paris. I left for Russia with a gentleman whose hair I dressed for a whole year in Petersburg. He had no money to pay me; so I left him and almost starved to death, looking for a job. Luckily I got a berth as a sailor, on a ship flying the Russian flag. Before putting to sea, I had to take an oath as a Russian subject; then we set off for Lübeck. On the way the bosun often beat me with a rope's end for being lazy. Through my carelessness I fell from the rigging to the deck and broke three fingers, which ruined me for ever dressing hair again. When we got to Lübeck I fell in with Prussian recruiting officers and served in various regiments. They often took the stick to me for being lazy or

---

* During the time of a levying of recruits, it is against the law to make any contract for the sale of serfs.

drunk. When I was stationed in the garrison at Memel, I got drunk one day and stabbed a fellow; so I had to get out of there in a hurry. Remembering that I had taken my oath in Russia and that I was a faithful son of the fatherland, I started out for Riga, with two thalers in my pocket. On the way I lived on charity. In Riga my good luck and skill served me in good stead. I won some twenty rubles in a tavern, bought myself a good overcoat for ten, and went off with a Kazan' merchant as his lackey. As we were going along a street in Moscow, I met two of my countrymen, who advised me to leave my master and look for a teaching job in Moscow. I told them I could hardly read, but they said, 'You talk French—that's enough.' My master did not see me leaving him on the street, and kept on his way, while I stayed in Moscow. My countrymen soon found me a teaching job paying a hundred and fifty rubles a year, plus a pood of sugar, a pood of coffee, ten pounds of tea, my board, a servant, and carriage. But I had to live in the country. So much the better. There they didn't find out for a whole year that I couldn't write. But some one of my master's in-laws, who was living at the same place, gave my secret away to him, and they took me back to Moscow. I couldn't find such another fool, I couldn't dress hair with my broken fingers, and I was afraid I'd starve to death; so I sold myself for two hundred rubles. They registered me as a peasant, and now they're sending me as a recruit. I hope," he said with an important air, "that as soon as a war comes along, I'll get to be a general; and if there isn't any war, I'll stuff my pockets (if possible), and, crowned with laurel, return to my country for a well-earned rest."

More than once I shrugged my shoulders as I listened to this rogue, and with a heavy heart I lay down in my carriage and continued on my journey.

13

Conditions of Peasants
in the 18th Century

In contrast to the improvement in the position of
Russian nobles during the eighteenth century (see
Chapters 7 and 11), the condition of Russian peasants deteriorated steadily. So unbearable was their
lot that many left their native villages in search of
improvement elsewhere, even abroad. These flights,
which often involved whole villages, hurt the interests of the state, and both Peter the Great and
Anna issued decrees aimed at halting them. When
this avenue of escape was closed, the peasants rose
in the violent rebellion led by Pugachev (see Chapter 10.) It was not until the end of the eighteenth
century that the government formally relaxed obligations of peasants to their masters. It was also
at the end of the eighteenth century that newspaper
advertisements for the sale of peasants began to appear in Russia.

Peter I's Decree Against Peasant Flights,
April 5, 1707

Last year, 1706, fugitives and peasants appeared in Moscow and other
cities; on settlements, crown villages and on the estates of the patriarch,
bishops, monasteries, church and other clergy; these fugitives and
peasants, with their wives, children, and belongings, should be returned
to their previous *pomeshchiks* and *votchinniks* from whom they fled
within half a year from the date of this *ukaz*. Whoever retains these
fugitives and peasants beyond that date and will not return them to
their rightful owners will lose half of his estate to the Great Sovereign,

---

The following four items are from *Polnoe Sobranie Zakonov Russkoi Imperii* . . .
(*Complete Collection of the Laws of the Russian Empire*), 1st Series. "Peter I's
Decree Against Peasant Flights" from vol. 4, no. 2147, pp. 378–379. "Anna's
Decree Against Peasant Flights" from vol. 9, no. 6951, pp. 809–810. "Catherine
II's Decree on Deportation of Serfs" from vol. 17, no. 12,311, p. 10. Paul's
Decree on Reduction of Work Days for Serfs" from vol. 24, no. 17,909, p. 587.
Translation mine. Items in brackets are mine.

the other half going to those to whom the fugitives or peasants belong. And should those fugitives and peasants who were sent to their original places be unable to reach them because of interference by other nobles, stewards, elders, or peasants who would like to have them for themselves, should this be established beyond doubt, then . . . this will be contrary to the sovereign's ukaz. The great sovereign was informed this year, 1707, that many nobles have lost the fear of God, have overlooked the ukaz of the Great Sovereign, and have kept the fugitives and peasants and sent other people away from their estates, but not to the original places; while some nobles do not allow them [the fugitives] to reach their destination by taking them in. The Great Sovereign, Peter Alekseevich, Tsar and Grand Prince, autocrat of all Great, Little and White Russia, by this personal ukaz orders that these nobles, stewards and elders who keep the old fugitives and peasants, or who take on new ones, or do not return them to their rightful destination . . . will be punished without delay. Voevodas [administrative leaders] should go into villages and collect information from nobles, stewards, and elders as to whether they have fulfilled their duties or not; and in each small village they should collect from five to six, and in large [villages] from ten to fifteen, good respectable men, testimony sworn on the penalty of death about the above mentioned fugitive peasants. Copies of this ukaz of the Great Sovereign should be posted on all gates, and be distributed in cities and offices for everyone to remember.

Anna's Decree Against Peasant Flights, May 6, 1736

According to an ukaz of February 23, 1721, issued by Emperor Peter the Great, Our uncle of blessed and eternal memory, anyone who [without fulfilling his obligations] flees and then is caught is to be punished severely by a public whipping, in order to discourage others from doing the same. But while this ukaz calls for a severe punishment of all those who flee—as the crime is the same—there is nevertheless a great difference.

1. Anyone who flees, committing beforehand a robbery or a murder, or fled a long time ago and during his absence let his taxes be paid by other peasants, should be subjected to the most severe punishment.

2. Anyone who flees on account of hunger or because of rumors he did not understand, and then having realized his mistake returns shortly thereafter, and no one as a consequence is forced to pay his taxes, such individuals—unlike the first—according to the rules of natural law should be punished less severely.

Consequently We decree that throughout Our state this ukaz be made known so that all those who have fled be punished by knout, whip, lash, or stick upon their apprehension. Administrators of the crown, church, bishopric, and monastery lands should determine which punishment should be applied to their peasants; [on the estates of the nobility] the nobles or their stewards should determine their cases.

Catherine II's Decree on Deportation of Serfs to Hard Labor, January 17, 1765

We herewith make it publicly known:

Following Her Imperial Majesty's confirmation, which on January 17, [1765] was presented to the Senate, it was decreed that in case any landowner wants to deliver for better disciplining in hard labor his serfs who, because of very impudent behavior, deserve a just punishment, the Board of Admiralty will take charge of them and use them for heavy work as long as the landlord concerned desires it. During this whole period these people, together with convicts, will be provided with food and clothing from the treasury. When the landlord shall want them back, they [serfs] are to be returned without question, but under one condition: the clothes and shoes of the people, if they are not completely worn out, are to be collected again for the treasury.

Paul's Decree in Reduction of Work Days for Serfs, April 5, 1797

We make known to all Our faithful subjects:

God's law, as it is given to us in the form of the Ten Commandments, teaches us that we offer the seventh day to Him; in this day, the holy day of Christianity and the day in which We decided to accept the holy anointment and the coronation on Our dynastic throne, We feel that it is Our duty before the Creator and the Giver of all blessings to emphasize that throughout Our empire this law be adhered to exactly and infallibly. I am hereby instructing everyone to observe [this law] and [am informing everyone] not to force under any pretext whatsoever the peasants to work on Sundays. For agricultural works there are six days in the week. These should be divided equally, [three] for the peasants [to work on their own land, and three] to work for the nobleman. [If this division] is properly organized it will be sufficient to fulfill all agricultural needs.

*Newspaper Advertisements for the Sale of Serfs, 1797**

1

For sale well behaved menial craftsmen: two tailors, a shoemaker, a watchmaker, a cook, a coach maker, a wheeler, an engraver, a night work-

---

* From A. K. Dzhivelegov, S. P. Melgunov and V. I. Picheta, eds. *Velikaia Reforma: Russkoe obshchestvo i krestianskii vopros v proshlom i nastoiashchem* (*The Great Reform: Russian Society and the Peasant Problem in the Past and at Present*) (Moscow: 1911), vol. 1, p. 258. Translation and items in brackets mine.

man and two coachmen. They may be seen and the price [for them] may be ascertained from their own *pomeshchik* [landlord] in the Third Part, Fourth Quarter, No. 51. There, too, are available for sale three young racing horses, one stallion, two geldings, and a herd of hunting dogs, about fifty, which will be one year old in January or February.

2

There is for sale, in the Fifteenth Part, Second Quarter, No. 183, in the parish of Adrian and Natalia, in the Second Meshchanskaia Street near the Church, a menial man. He is 25 years old, a trained woman's shoe maker who knows his profession exceptionally well; in addition he performs all domestic, coachman's, and footman's tasks, as well as waiting at the table. He has a pregnant wife 22 years old who sews, irons, starches, waits on the lady of the house, and cooks. They have a 3 year old daughter.

3

For sale a 35 year old peasant, with his wife about the same age, and three young children. Those who wish to purchase may learn the price from their owner at the Tenth Part, in Nicholas parish, on Bolvanovka, No. 529.

4

In Part Twelve, an officer has for sale a 16 year old girl, formerly belonging to a poor house, who knows how to knit, sew, iron, starch, and dress a lady; she has a nice figure and pretty face.

14

Czartoryski's Account
of the Events
Surrounding the Assassination
of Paul, 1801

One of the most tragic rulers of eighteenth-century Russia was Tsar Paul (1796–1801). Though he was her first son, Catherine II never showed any love for him, viewed him as hopelessly incapable, and even allowed her numerous favorites to insult him. Paul resented this treatment and blamed Catherine for the death of Peter III. The antipathy between mother and son became so intense that when Paul ascended the throne in 1796 he sought to undo most of Catherine's work. He dismissed many of her favorites and rehabilitated her enemies, including Radishchev. He introduced a strict new law on imperial succession and even sought to improve the condition of the serfs. By these actions Paul, who was inexperienced in the art of government, alienated important groups and caused a great deal of confusion, irritation, and uncertainty. Early in 1801 a conspiracy developed against him. It was masterminded by Count Nikita P. Panin, a vice chancellor; Joseph Ribas, a Spanish soldier of fortune and an admiral in the Russian navy; and Count Peter Pahlen, military governor of St. Petersburg. Paul was murdered and was succeeded by his son, Alexander I (1801–1825), who had been Catherine's choice in the first place.

From Memoirs of Prince Adam Czartoryski and His Correspondence with Alexander I. Edited by Adam Gielgud (London: Remington and Co., 1888), vol. 1, pp. 227–248, 251–255. Prince Adam Czartoryski (1770–1861) was for a number of years one of Alexander's closest associates.

. . . Then he [Alexander I] spoke to me of his father's death with inexpressible grief and remorse. We often returned to this subject, and Alexander gave me full details of it, which I shall repeat below, together with information communicated to me by other actors in the tragedy. . . .

Alexander told me that the first man who spoke to him about the plans of the conspirators was Count Panin, and he never forgave him. This personage seemed destined more than anyone else to play an important part in the affairs of the Empire, and he had all that was wanted for such an undertaking; a celebrated name, uncommon talents, and much ambition. . . . As will be seen further on, Panin was one of the chief leaders of the conspiracy which brought about Paul's death, though he did not actually take part in it. . . .

The two Counts Panin and Pahlen were at that time the strongest heads of the Empire. They saw further and more clearly than the other members of Paul's Council, to which both of them belonged; and they agreed to initiate Alexander into their plans. It would not have been prudent to attempt anything without being assured of the consent of the heir to the crown. Devoted fanatics or enthusiasts might no doubt have acted otherwise. By not implicating the son in the dethronement of his father, by exposing themselves to a certain death, they would have better served both Russia and the prince who was to be called upon to govern her; but such a course would have been almost impracticable, and it would have demanded an audacity and antique virtue which in these days very few men possess. Pahlen, as Governor of St. Petersburg, had easy means of access to the Grand-Duke, and obtained from him a secret audience for Panin; their first interview took place in a bath. Panin represented to Alexander the evils from which Russia was suffering and would continue to suffer if Paul continued to reign. He said that Alexander's most sacred duty was to his country, and that he must not sacrifice millions of people to the extravagant caprices and follies of a single man, even if that man was his father; that the life, or at least the liberty, of his mother, of himself, and of the whole of the Imperial family was threatened by Paul's inconceivable aversion for his wife, from whom he was entirely separated; that this aversion increased from day to day, and might prompt him to the most outrageous acts; and that it was therefore necessary to save Russia, whose fate was in Alexander's hands, by deposing Paul, which would be the only means of preventing him from inflicting greater calamities on his country and his family, and securing to him a quieter and more happy life. This speech produced a great impression on Alexander but it did not convince him. It required more than six months to enable his tempters to obtain his consent to their plans. Pahlen had at first left all the speaking to Panin, who was an adept at specious arguments; but when the latter was sent to Moscow, Pahlen completed the work of his colleague by hints and allusions, intelligible

only to Alexander himself, which were so skilfully introduced with a
military frankness which he made almost as effective as eloquence, that
Alexander became more and more persuaded that the aims of the conspiracy were just and good.

It was a thousand pities that a prince so anxious and so well qualified
to be a benefactor to his country did not hold entirely aloof from a
conspiracy which resulted almost inevitably in his father's assassination.
Russia certainly suffered much under the almost maniacal Government
of Paul, and there are no means in that country of restraining or con-
fining a mad sovereign; but Alexander felt and exaggerated in his own
mind all his life the sombre reflection of the crime committed on his
father, which had fallen on himself, and which he thought he could
never wipe out. This ineffaceable stain, although it was brought about
solely by his inexperience and his total and innocent ignorance of Russian affairs and the Russian people, settled like a vulture on his conscience, paralysed his best faculties at the commencement of his reign,
and plunged him into a mysticism sometimes degenerating into superstition at its close.

At the same time it must be admitted that the Emperor Paul was pre-
cipitating his country into incalculable disasters and into a complete
disorganisation and deterioration of the Government machine. Paul governed intermittently, without troubling himself about the consequences,
like a man who acts without reflection according to the impulse of the
moment. The higher classes, the principal officials, the generals and other
officers of rank—all, in a word, who thought and acted in Russia—were
more or less convinced that the Emperor had fits of mental alienation.
His reign became a rule of terror. He was hated even for his good qualities, for at bottom he desired justice, and this impulse sometimes led
him to do a just thing in his outburst of rage; but his feeling of justice
was blind, and struck at all without discrimination of circumstances;
always passionate, often capricious and cruel, his decrees were constantly
suspended over the heads of the military and civil officers, and made
them detest the man who thus filled their lives with uncertainty and
terror. The conspiracy had the sympathy of all, for it promised to put
an end to a regime which had become intolerable. A sovereign may commit grave mistakes, bring evils on his country, cause its wealth or its
power to decline, without exposing himself to death as a punishment for
his misdeeds. But when the sovereign authority weighs at every moment
on each individual in the State, and continually disturbs like a fever the
peace of families in the ordinary relations of life, passions are excited
which are much more formidable than those produced by evils which,
though affecting the entire community, are little felt by individuals. This
was the real motive of Paul's assassination. I utterly disbelieve the story
that English money contributed to this event. For even supposing—and

I am sincerely convinced there is no foundation for such a belief—that the English Government of that day was devoid of all feelings of morality, such an expenditure would have been totally unnecessary. The deposition, if not the murder, of Paul had become inevitable in the natural course of events. Even before my departure from St. Petersburg it was the fashion among the young men of the Court to talk freely on this subject, to make satirical epigrams on Paul's eccentricities, and to suggest all kinds of absurd plans for getting rid of him. The universal aversion to his rule was shown, often without any attempt at concealment, on every possible occasion; it was a State secret which was confided to all, and which no one betrayed, though the people lived under the most redoubted and the most suspicious of sovereigns, who encouraged espionage, and spared no means of obtaining exact information not only of the actions, but of the thoughts and intentions of his subjects. The wish to get rid of the Emperor Paul showed itself more strongly the nearer one approached the Court and the capital, but it did not really become active until almost at the moment of its execution. Notwithstanding the extreme favour with which the conspiracy was regarded in the most distinguished society of the Empire, it could not have attained its objects, and would probably have been discovered, if the appointment of Governor-General of St. Petersburg, which placed at his disposal the garrison and the police, had not been in the hands of the chief promoter of the enterprise.

One day the Emperor said, with a scrutinizing glance at Pahlen: "I hear a conspiracy is being formed against me." "Such a thing is impossible, Sire," replied the General with his frank and good-natured smile; "it cannot be formed unless I belong to it." This reassured Paul, though it is said that his suspicions were aroused by anonymous letters, and that on the eve of his death he had sent for General Araktcheyeff to give him the place of Governor-General of St. Petersburg, after dismissing Pahlen. If Araktcheyeff had come in time St. Petersburg would have been the scene of many tragic events; he was a man imbued with a strong sentiment of order and with an energy which sometimes grew into ferocity. His return would probably have been followed by that of Count Rostopchin, and Paul might then have been saved. . . .

Although everybody sympathised with the conspiracy, nothing was done until Alexander had given his consent to his father's deposition. The men who undertook to carry out the plan were Pahlen and the two Zuboffs, whom Paul had recalled from exile and loaded with favours, thinking he had nothing to fear from them now he was in his new castle. Their first step was to induce a number of Generals and other officers of rank who were their friends to come under various pretexts to St. Petersburg; and this was rendered more easy by the fact that Paul himself had invited many high functionaries and Generals to be present at the fêtes he was about to give on the marriage of one of his daughters. Pahlen and the Zuboffs took steps to enlist the services of some of the more eminent of the Generals, without stating positively what they intended to do. But it was necessary to act at once, for the slightest imprudence or revelation might place the Emperor in possession of their secret, and he was already so suspicious that he might at any moment take some step which would be their ruin. It was not known whether he had already sent for Araktcheyeff and Rostopchin. The former lived at twenty-four hours' journey from St. Petersburg and might come at any moment. Doubtless he and Rostopchin would endeavour to moderate the Emperor's excesses, but their influence would probably not be sufficient to put a stop to the severities he wished to exercise with regard to several members of the Imperial family. It was evident that any further delay or vacillation would be most dangerous, and might be the cause of incalculable calamities; and the conspirators accordingly decided to strike the blow on the 3rd of March, 1801.

On that evening Plato Zuboff gave a grand supper, to which were invited all the Generals and other officers of rank who were supposed to approve of the objects of the conspiracy. These were only now clearly explained to them, as the only way to secure the enterprise against accidents was for two or three leaders to prepare it, and not to announce it to the others who were to take part in it until the moment for its execution should arrive.

Zuboff represented to his guests the deplorable condition in which Russia was placed by the insanity of her sovereign, the dangers to which both the State and each individual citizen were exposed, and the probability that new and more outrageous excesses might at any moment be expected. He pointed out that the insane act of a rupture with England was contrary to the essential interests of the Russian nation, dried up the sources of its wealth, and exposed the Baltic ports, and the capital itself, to the gravest disasters; and that none of those whom he addressed could be sure of their fate on the morrow. He enlarged on the virtues of the Grand-Duke Alexander, and on the brilliant destinies of Russia under the sceptre of a young Prince of such promise, whom the Empress Catherine, of glorious memory, had regarded as her successor, and had intended, if she had not been prevented by her death, to place on the throne. He concluded by declaring that Alexander, rendered desperate by the misfortunes of his country, had decided to save it; and that all that was now necessary was to depose the Emperor Paul, to oblige him to sign a deed of abdication, and, by proclaiming Alexander Emperor, to prevent his father from ruining both himself and his Empire. Pahlen and both the Zuboffs repeated to the assembled guests the assurance that the Grand-Duke Alexander approved of their plan. They were careful not to say how much time it took them to persuade him, and with what extreme difficulty and with how many restrictions and modifications his consent was finally obtained. The last point was left vague, and everyone probably explained it after his own fashion.

When the company had been made to understand that Alexander's consent had been given there was no further hesitation. Meanwhile champagne was drunk freely and there was general excitement. Pahlen, who had gone away for a short time on business connected with his functions as Governor-General, came back from the Court and announced that the Emperor did not seem to suspect anything, and had said goodnight to the Empress and the Grand-Dukes as usual. Those who had been at supper in the palace afterwards said they recollected that Alexander, when he took leave of his father, did not change countenance or show that he was conscious of the scene which was preparing. Probably they did not look at him, for he has often told me how agitated he was, and certainly the risks he ran not only for himself, but for his mother, his family, and many others were enough to make him sad and anxious. The Grand-Dukes were always obliged to maintain an attitude of strict reserve before their father, and this constant habit of concealing their emotions and thoughts may explain why at this grave and supreme moment no one perceived in Alexander's countenance what was passing in his mind.

At the Zuboffs' house the guests had become so convivial that time went fast. At midnight the conspirators set out for the Emperor's palace. The leaders had drunk but moderately, wishing to keep their heads clear, but the majority of those who followed them were more or less intoxicated; some could hardly even keep their legs. They were divided into two bands, each composed of some sixty Generals and other officers. The two Zuboffs and General Bennigsen were at the head of the first band, which was to go to the palace direct; the second was to enter through the garden, and was under the command of Pahlen. The aide-decamp in waiting, who knew all the doors and passages of the palace, as he was daily on duty there, guided the first band with a dark lantern to the entrance of the Emperor's dressing-room, which adjoined his bedroom. A young valet who was on duty stopped the conspirators and cried out that rebels were coming to murder the Emperor. He was wounded in the struggle which ensued, and rendered incapable of further resistance. His cries waked the Emperor, who got out of bed and ran to a door which communicated with the Empress's apartments and was hidden by a large curtain. Unfortunately, in one of his fits of dislike for his wife, he had ordered the door to be locked; and the key was not in the lock, either because Paul had ordered it to be taken away or because his favourites, who were opposed to the Empress, had done so, fearing lest he should some day have a fancy to return to her. Meanwhile the conspirators were confused and terrified at the cries of Paul's faithful defender, the only one he had at a moment of supreme danger when he believed in his omnipotence more than ever and was surrounded by a triple line of walls and guards. Zuboff, the chief of the band, lost heart and proposed to retire at once, but General Bennigsen (from whom I obtained some of these details) seized him by the arm and protested against such a dangerous step. "What?" he said, "You have brought us so far, and now you want to withdraw? We are too far advanced to follow your advice, which would ruin us all. The wine is drawn, it must be drunk. Let us march on."

It was this Hanoverian that decided the Emperor's fate; he was one of those who had only that evening been informed of the conspiracy. He placed himself at the head of the band, and those who had most courage, or most hatred for Paul, were the first to follow him. They entered the Emperor's bedroom, went straight to his bed, and were much alarmed at not finding him there. They searched the room with a light, and at last discovered the unfortunate Paul hiding behind the folds of the curtain. They dragged him out in his shirt more dead than alive; the terror he had inspired was now repaid to him with usury. Fear had paralysed his senses and had deprived him of speech; his whole body shivered. He was placed on a chair before a desk. The long, thin, pale, and angular form of General Bennigsen, with his hat on his head and a drawn sword in his hand, must have seemed to him a terrible spectre. "Sire," said the General, "you are my prisoner, and have ceased to reign; you will now at once write and sign a deed of abdication in favour of the Grand-Duke Alexander." Paul was still unable to speak, and a pen was put in his hand. Trembling and almost unconscious, he was about to obey when more cries were heard. General Bennigsen then left the room, as he has often assured me, to ascertain what these cries meant, and to take steps for securing the safety of the palace and of the Imperial family. He had only just gone out the door when a terrible scene began. The unfortunate Paul remained alone with men who were maddened by a furious hatred of him, owing to the numerous acts of persecution and injustice they had suffered at his hands, and it appears that several of them had decided to assassinate him, perhaps without the knowledge of the leaders or at least without their formal consent. The catastrophe, which in such a case was, in a country like Russia, almost inevitable, was doubtless hastened by the cries above referred to, which alarmed the conspirators for their own safety. Count Nicholas Zuboff, a man of herculean proportions, was said to be the first that placed his hand on his sovereign, and thereby broke the spell of imperial authority which still surrounded him. The others now saw in Paul nothing but a monster, a tyrant, an implacable enemy—and his abject submission, instead of disarming them, rendered him despicable and ridiculous as well as odious in their eyes.

One of the conspirators took off his official scarf and tied it round the Emperor's throat. Paul struggled, the approach of death restoring him to strength and speech. He set free one of his hands and thrust it between the scarf and his throat, crying out for air. Just then he perceived a red uniform, which was at that time worn by the officers of the cavalry guard, and thinking that one of the assassins was his son Constantine, who was a colonel of that regiment, he exclaimed: "Mercy, your Highness, mercy! Some air, for God's sake!" But the conspirators seized the hand with which he was striving to prolong his life, and furiously tugged at both ends of the scarf. The unhappy Emperor had already breathed his last, and yet they tightened the knot and dragged along the dead body, striking it with their hands and feet. The cowards who until then had held aloof surpassed in atrocity those who had done the deed. Just at that time General Bennigsen returned. I do not know whether he was sincerely grieved at what had happened in his absence; all he did was to stop the further desecration of the Emperor's body.

Meanwhile the cry "Paul is dead!" was heard by the other conspirators, and filled them with a joy that deprived them of all sentiment of decency and dignity. They wandered tumultuously about the corridors and rooms of the palace, boasting to each other of their prowess; many of them found means of adding to the intoxication of the supper by breaking into the wine cellars and drinking to the Emperor's death.

Pahlen, who seems to have lost his way in the garden, came to the palace with his band immediately after the deed had been consummated. It is said that he had delayed his arrival on purpose, so as to be able to profess to have come to the Emperor's assistance in case his colleagues should have failed. Be this as it may, he was extremely active directly he arrived, giving the necessary orders during the rest of the night, and omitting nothing which could give him a claim to reward as the prime mover and commander of the enterprise.

It will be seen from the above narrative how easy it would have been for the undertaking to have been foiled by an accident, notwithstanding the precautions which had been taken to ensure its success. The conspiracy had the sympathies of the higher classes and most of the officers; but not of the lower ranks of the army. The persons who suffered from Paul's insane fits of rage and severity were usually the higher military and civil officials; his caprices very seldom affected men of the lower ranks, who, moreover, were continually receiving extra pay and rations of bread, wine, and brandy when they were on drill or on a parade. The punishments to which the officers were exposed did not therefore produce any unpleasant impression on the common soldier; on the contrary, they were a sort of satisfaction to him for the blows and ill-treatment he constantly had to endure. Moreover, his pride was flattered by the great importance attached to his calling, for to Paul nothing could be more important than a foot raised too soon on the march, or a coat badly buttoned on parade. It amused and pleased the soldiers to see their Emperor dispensing endless punishments and severities among the officers while he took every opportunity to afford to the men ample compensation for the work and trouble that was required of them. The soldiers of the Guard, many of whom were married, lived with their families almost in opulence, and both they and those of the other regiments were satisfied with and attached to their Emperor. General Talyzin, one of the principal conspirators, who was very popular among the soldiers, had undertaken to bring to the palace one of the battalions of the first regiment of the Guard which was under his command. He assembled the men after leaving Zuboff's supper, and began to tell them that their fatigues were about to cease, and that they would now have an indulgent and kind sovereign who would not impose upon them the rigorous duties they had hitherto had to perform. He soon perceived, however, that his words were not listened to with favour; the soldiers preserved a gloomy silence, their faces had a sombre expression, and some murmurs were heard. The General cut short his speech, uttered in a sharp tone of command the words "Right wheel—march," and the battalion, which had now again become a machine, marched to the palace, all the outlets from which it occupied.

Count Valerian Zuboff, having lost a leg in the Polish War, could not belong to either of the bands of the conspirators. He entered the palace soon after the death of the Emperor became known, and then went to the guard-room to sound the opinions of the soldiers. He congratulated them on having a new and a young Emperor; but this compliment was ill received, and he was obliged to leave the room hastily to avoid disagreeable manifestations. All this shows how easy it would have been for Paul to crush the conspirators if he had been able to escape them for a moment and to show himself to the guards in the courtyard. It also shows how illusory and impracticable was Alexander's plan of keeping his father in confinement. If Paul's life had been saved, blood would have flowed on the scaffold, Siberia would have been crowded with exiles, and his vengeance would probably have extended to his sons.

I will now describe what happened during this terrible night in the part of the palace which was inhabited by the Imperial family. The Grand-Duke Alexander knew that his father would in a few hours be called upon to abdicate, and without undressing he threw himself on his bed full of anxiety and doubt. About one o'clock he heard a knock at his door, and saw Count Nicholas Zuboff, his dress in disorder, and his face flushed with wine and the excitement of the murder which had just been committed. He came up to Alexander, who was sitting on his bed, and said in a hoarse voice: "All is over." "What is over?" asked Alexander in consternation. He was somewhat deaf, and perhaps he feared to misunderstand what was being said to him, while Zuboff on his side feared to state exactly what had been done. This somewhat prolonged the conversation; Alexander had not the least idea that his father was dead, and did not therefore admit the possibility of such a thing. At length he perceived that Zuboff, without clearly explaining himself, repeatedly addressed him as "Sire" and "Your Majesty," while Alexander thought he was merely Regent. This led to further questioning, and he then learnt the truth. Alexander was prostrated with grief and despair. This was not surprising, for even ambitious men cannot commit a crime or believe themselves the cause of one without repulsion, while Alexander was not at all ambitious. The idea of having caused the death of his father filled him with horror, and he felt that his reputation had received a stain which could never be effaced. As for the Empress, directly the news reached her she dressed hastily and rushed out of her apartments with cries of despair and rage. Perceiving some grenadiers, she said to them repeatedly: "As your Emperor has died a victim to treason, I am your Empress, I alone am your legitimate sovereign; follow me and protect me." General Bennigsen and Count Pahlen, who had just brought a detachment of men whom they could trust to the palace to restore order, strove to calm her and forced her with difficulty to return to her room. She had scarcely entered it, however, than she wished to go out again, although guards had been placed at her door. At first she seemed determined at all risks to seize the reins of government and avenge her husband's murder. But though she was generally respected, she was not capable of inspiring those feelings of enthusiastic devotion which cause men to act impulsively and without weighing the consequences. Her appeals to the soldiers (which were perhaps rendered somewhat ridiculous by her German accent) produced no effect, and she retired in confusion, vexed at having uselessly disclosed her ambitious views.

I never heard any details of the first interview between the Empress and her son after Paul's assassination. Subsequently they came to an understanding with each other; but during the first terrible moments Alexander was so absorbed by his remorse that he seemed incapable of saying a word or thinking of anybody. His mother, on the other hand, was in a passion of grief and animosity; the only member of the Imperial family that retained her presence of mind was the young Empress. She did her utmost to console Alexander and give him courage and self-reliance. She did not leave him during the whole of the night, except when she went for a few moments to calm her mother-in-law and persuade her to stop in her room and not expose herself to the fury of the conspirators. While in this night of trouble and horror some were intoxicated with triumph and others plunged in grief and despair, the Empress Elizabeth alone exercised a mediatory influence between her husband, her mother-in-law, and the conspirators.

During the first years of his reign, Alexander's position with regard to his father's murderers was an extremely difficult and painful one. For a few months he believed himself to be at their mercy, but it was chiefly his conscience and a feeling of natural equity which prevented him from giving up to justice the most guilty of the conspirators. He knew that there was a general sympathy for the objects of the conspiracy, and that those who had personally taken part in their realisation had only decided to do so when they were assured of his consent. It would have been difficult under these circumstances to distinguish between degrees of guilt; every member of the society of St. Petersburg was more or less an accomplice in the fatal deed, for those who wished Paul to be deposed must have known that his deposition, if resisted, might have involved his death. If the assassins alone had been brought to trial, they would certainly have accused the other conspirators and have referred to Alexander's consent in justification of their action, though the crime had been committed against his express wish. Moreover, he did not for many years know who they were, as all the conspirators were interested in keeping the secret. The assassins all perished miserably, including Count Nicholas Zuboff, who, not daring to show himself at Court, died in retirement, consumed by illness, by remorse, and by disappointed ambition. . . .

The views of the Zuboffs as to the conspiracy were communicated to me by Count Valerian Zuboff a few days after my return to St. Petersburg. He complained that the Emperor did not declare himself for his true friends, who had placed him on the throne and had not feared any danger they had incurred in his service. The Empress Catherine had acted otherwise; she had always supported those who had helped her, and had not hesitated to maintain them in power. By this wise and sagacious conduct, said Zuboff, she had been able always to reckon on their devotion. No one hesitated to make a sacrifice for her, as such sacrifices were always rewarded; but Alexander was exposing himself by his vacillating conduct to the most serious consequences, and was discouraging his best friends. Zuboff added that the Empress Catherine had expressly enjoined him and his brother to look upon Alexander as their only legitimate sovereign, and to serve him alone with unshaken zeal and fidelity. This they had done, and what was their reward? He said this to exculpate his brother and himself in the eyes of the young Emperor with regard to the assassination of his father, and to prove to him that their conduct was the necessary result of the engagements Catherine had demanded of them as to her grandson. But they did not know that Alexander, and even his brother Constantine, by no means regarded their grandmother's memory with veneration or attachment. During this conversation, which lasted more than an hour, I several times interrupted the Count to explain the young Emperor's conduct. It was evident that the Zuboffs wished me to communicate their views to the Emperor, and though I did not promise, I considered it my duty to do so. Their statements produced but little impression on Alexander, but they showed that the conspirators were still very proud of their achievement, and that they felt convinced they had done a great service to Russia, had a right to Alexander's gratitude and confidence, and were necessary to the security and prosperity of the new reign. They even hinted that their discontent might be dangerous to him. Alexander, however, was deaf both to their arguments and their threats. He could not look with favour on his father's murderers, or give himself up into their hands. Moreover, he had already dismissed Pahlen, who was perhaps the only one of the conspirators who by his ability, his connections, his boldness, and his ambition, could inspire serious fear or become really dangerous. Alexander also dismissed other leaders of the conspiracy who were not dangerous, but the sight of whom was odious and disagreeable to him. The only leader who remained at St. Petersburg was Count Valerian Zuboff, who was a member of the Imperial Council. His amiability and frankness pleased Alexander and inspired him with confidence; and this feeling was confirmed by the attachment which the Count professed (I think sincerely) to have for the Emperor personally, and also by his indolence, his unwillingness to take appointments to which onerous duties were attached, and especially by his amours, which occupied nearly the whole of his time.

The punishment of Pahlen and the other leaders of the conspiracy was the most painful that could have been inflicted on them, and Alexander punished himself with more severity than the others. His grief and the remorse which he was continually reviving in his heart were inexpressibly deep and touching. In the midst of the pomp and the festivals of the coronation, the young Emperor was reminded of the similar ceremonies which had been passed through by his father, and he saw in imagination Paul's mutilated and blood-stained body on the steps of the throne which he was now himself to ascend. This brilliant display of supreme power, instead of rousing his ambition or flattering his vanity, increased his mental tortures, and he was never, I think, more unhappy. He remained alone for hours, sitting in silence with fixed and haggard looks.

With me, as the confidant of his secret thoughts and troubles, he was most at his ease, and I sometimes entered his room when he had been too long under the painful influence of these fits of despair and remorse. I tried to recall him to his duties; he acknowledged that a painful task was before him, but the severity of his condemnation of his own conduct deprived him of all energy. He replied to all my exhortations and words of encouragement and hope: "No, it is impossible, there is no remedy. I must suffer. How can I cease to suffer? This cannot change."

Those who approached him often feared that his mind would be affected, and as I was then the only person who could speak to him freely I was constantly urged to do so. I think I was of some use in preventing Alexander from succumbing under the weight of the terrible thought that pursued him. Some years later, the great events in which he took a leading and glorious part gave him some consolation and for a time, perhaps, absorbed all his faculties; but I am certain that towards the end of his life it was the same terrible thought that so depressed him, filling him with a disgust of life and a piety which was perhaps exaggerated, but which is the sole possible and real support in the most poignant grief. When we returned to this sad topic, Alexander often repeated to me the details of the plan he had formed to establish his father in the Palace of St. Michael and afterwards to enable him as much as possible to reside in the Imperial Palaces in the country. "The Palace of St. Michael," he said, "was his favourite residence, and he would have been happy there. He would have had the whole of the winter garden to walk and ride in." Alexander intended to attach a riding-school and a theatre to the palace, so as to bring together within its precincts everything that could have amused the Emperor Paul and made his life happy. He judged of his father by himself. There was always in his noble character a feminine element, with its strength and weakness. He often used to make plans which could not be realised, and on this idealistic foundation he raised complete structures which he made as perfect as possible. Nothing was more impracticable—especially in Russia—than the romantic means which Alexander had devised of rendering his father happy, while depriving him of his crown and of the possibility of tormenting and ruining the country. Alexander was not only young and inexperienced; he had almost the blind and confiding inexperience of childhood, and this characteristic remained with him for some years until it was destroyed by the realities of life.

I have not concealed anything in regard to the catastrophe which inaugurated his reign, for this was the best way of doing him justice. The complete truth, without any restriction, exculpates him up to a certain point from an odious accusation, and explains how he was led into an action which he abhorred and why he seemed not to have punished the assassins with sufficient rigour. I have shown how inexperienced and unambitious he was, and what were the plausible and even honourable motives by which he was actuated. We may pity Alexander, but we must hesitate to condemn him.

15

Alexander I's Decree
on Free Agriculturists,
February 20, 1803

Tsar Alexander I surrounded himself with a number
of personal friends whose ideas coincided with his
own, among them Czartoryski, Stroganov, Novosilt-
sev, and Kochubey. With their aid he reorganized
Russia's administrative structure and brought a number of important educational reforms. Alexander
sought to alleviate the conditions of serfs. In 1801
he prohibited the advertising of serfs for sale without land. He later discontinued the practice of
making gifts to favorites of land populated by state
peasants (who thereby became serfs), and in February 1803 he approved a decree aimed at creating
a new social group called "free agriculturists." Under
the terms of this decree, published on the initiative
of Count S. P. Rumiantsev, Russian nobles were
given the right to reach an agreement with their
serfs regarding the terms of their freedom, to provide them with land, and to turn them into free,
taxpaying citizens. This measure, which aimed at a
voluntary abolishment of serfdom, was disappoint-
ing. It has been estimated that during the reign of
Alexander I only some 37,000 male serfs were freed
under the terms of the decree while during the reign
of Nicholas I (1825–1855) some 67,000 were freed.
Both figures represented a mere fraction of the
servile population.

Count [S. P.] Rumiantsev, Active Privy Counsellor, has given to some
of his serfs upon their emancipation an opportunity to obtain as their
own property those parts of the lands they have used, either through

From *Polnoe Sobranie Zakonov Russkoi Imperii* . . . (*Complete Collection of
the Laws of the Russian Empire*), 1st series, vol. 27, no. 20, 620, pp. 462–463.
Translation mine. Items in brackets are mine.

purchase or through other free arrangements. He has requested that similar arrangements, freely entered into, be given the same legal sanction and force as those of serf obligations; and peasants freed in this manner could be placed in the category of free agriculturists, with a pledge not to pursue any other form of livelihood.

Finding that, on the one hand, on the basis of the existing laws, namely the manifesto of 1775 and an ukaz of 1801, the freeing of peasants and their owning of land is allowed; and on the other, that such an approval of land ownership may in many instances benefit noblemen and be beneficial for the improvement of agriculture and other branches of the national economy, We feel that it is both proper and useful for Count Rumiantsev, as well as any nobleman who wishes to follow his example, to allow such a regulation. For such a regulation to have legal force We decree the following:

1. Should any nobleman wish to free his acquired or hereditary serfs, singly or in whole villages, and, at the same time, will them a grant of land or an entire homestead; then, having made mutually acceptable arrangements with them, he must present these in his application through the *gubernia* representative of the nobility to the Ministry of Internal Affairs for Our examination and approval; and if We approve it, these conditions are then to be presented in the *Grazhdanskaia Palata* [State Court] where they will be registered in the Department of Serf Affairs upon the payment of legal dues.

2. These conditions, made between the nobleman and his serfs and registered with the Department of Serf Affairs, must be viewed as serf obligations and must be strictly and undeviatingly fulfilled. Upon the death of the nobleman, his legal heir or heirs enter into all obligations and rights stipulated in these conditions.

3. In case of a breach of these conditions by either party, the courts will investigate complaints and pass judgments on the basis of regulations dealing with contracts and serfdom, and will be guided by the following rule: if a peasant or a whole village fails to fulfill its obligations, the nobleman will then get back his land and all the families will return under the nobleman's rule as before.

4. Should peasants and villages freed by the nobles with land under such stipulations decide not to enter into other conditions, they may remain on their own land as agriculturists and will thus form a special social layer of free agriculturists.

5. Household people and peasants who until now have been freed individually, with the obligation of selecting their means of livelihood, may under the terms of this law enter into the status of free agriculturists, provided they acquire some land for themselves. This rule is also applicable to those who already have other professions but who may wish to turn to agriculture, assuming of course all obligations of such a change.

6. Peasants who have been freed by the nobility, and who own land, are subject to state soul tax on a par with the nobles and must fulfill their recruiting obligations in kind; moreover, since they fulfill their land obligation on a par with other state peasants, they do not pay any quit rent to the treasury.

7. They have the same courts and administration in the same places as the state peasants; their right to their land, as owners of an immovable property, is determined by a recorded document.

8. As soon as they fulfill their obligations, those peasants who have land as their property have the right to sell it, lease it, or pass it on to their heirs, without dividing it into parts of less than eight *desiatinas*; likewise they have the right to purchase new lands, and move from one *gubernia* to another. These changes must be done with the full knowledge of the *Kazennaia Palata* [*Gubernia*'s Tax Office] in order to adjust their personal tax and recruiting obligations.

9. Since these peasants have immovable property, they may enter into any obligation; hence the *ukazes* of 1761 and 1765, which prohibit the peasants to enter into contracts without the consent of their superiors, are inapplicable here. . . .

10. In case peasants who were freed by the nobleman with lands are indebted to the state or to a private individual, they may, with state permission or the permission of the private creditor, assume a new debt . . .

On the basis of this decree the Governing Senate will issue appropriate regulations.

16

Speranskii's Proposed Brief Outline of State Organization, 1809

Alexander I's achievements as tsar can be traced to
the influence of three associates. At the beginning
of his reign most of his ideas were stimulated by his
Swiss tutor, Frédéric C. La Harpe (1754–1838). Between 1806 and 1812 Alexander's dreams were
inspired by Michael M. Speranskii (1772–1839).
After 1812 General Aleksei Arakcheev (1769–1834)
influenced many of his actions. While each left a
distinct imprint on Alexander I's reign, of the three
men the influence of Speranskii is perhaps the most
interesting. The son of a village priest, Speranskii
was a self-made man. He developed a familiarity
with contemporary political and economic theories
and had been exposed to the harsh realities of Russian life. With this rare combination of the theoretical and the practical Speranskii was invaluable to
Alexander I, who selected him as his chief adviser
from 1806 to 1812. In this capacity Speranskii prepared a plan for the reorganization of the empire.
Had Alexander accepted the plan, Russia might have
evolved into a constitutional monarchy, but such
was not the case. Soon after the proposal was presented, Alexander, frightened by the excesses of the
French Revolution and influenced by the opponents
of change, dismissed Speranskii and sent him to
Siberia.

Basic Components

State power is represented in three branches—legislative, judicial, and
executive.

The [State] Council coordinates all activity and passes it on to the
sovereign.

From M. M. Speranskii, *Proekty i zapiski* (*Projects and Notes*), Edited by A. I.
Kopanev, M. V. Kukushkina and C. N. Valka (Moscow-Leningrad: Akademiia
Nauk, 1961), pp. 222–231. Translation mine. Items in brackets are mine.

The State Duma is entrusted with lawmaking.
The Senate is entrusted with courts.
Ministries are entrusted with administration.

Organization of the [State] Council

Departments within the Council	Competence
I. Legal	Review of laws, statutes, and proposals presented by commissions and ministries.
II. Military Affairs	Affairs pertaining to the Ministries of War and Navy.
III. State Economy	Internal affairs, land and water communication system. Finance and Treasury. Ministry of Enlightenment.
IV. Civil and Religious Affairs	Police, Justice, and Religious Departments.
Institutions within the Council	
State Chancellery	General central execution of all affairs that come before the State Council.
Legislative Commission	Preparation of state laws.
Commission on Petitions	Review of petitions addressed to the sovereign.

Main Components

The [State] Council consists of members appointed by the sovereign. Ministers are members of the Council in accordance with rank. Every department has a chairman appointed every six months. All matters enter departments through ministries. Important matters from departments are brought before a general meeting. In the general meeting the chairman is appointed annually. Nothing emanates from the Council without the approval of the sovereign.

Organization of the State Duma

Composition	Competence
The State Duma consists of deputies elected from all free classes at the *gubernia* dumas.	Proposed laws are presented by the government, are considered by the Duma, and are approved by the sovereign.
Chairman of the Duma is chosen from among three candidates after the Duma is elected. The Duma has a Chancellor who supervises its rules,	The Duma receives ministerial reports; in case of an open violation of the State Constitution, the Duma has the right to demand a reply from

Composition	Competence
archives, and the conduct of its affairs.	ministries and to present its view to the sovereign.

Main Components

No new law can be issued without being considered by the Duma. Imposition of new taxes, duties, and obligations is considered by the Duma.

A law that has been considered in the Duma is presented for the sovereign's approval. A legislative measure that has been rejected by a majority of votes [in the Duma] is considered invalid.

For a detailed review of a legislative project the Duma selects temporary committees from among its members.

Organization of the Senate

Composition	Competence
The Senate consists of elected senators who will gradually replace the current members.	All court matters are entrusted to the Senate.
[The Senate] is divided into departments. Within the Senate there is organized a High Criminal Court in which members of the [State] Council, the Duma, and the Senate participate.	This High Court has jurisdiction over ministries, members of the [State] Council, senators and governor-generals.
In the Senate there is established the position of a Chancellor of Justice.	He supervises publications and documents of the Senate. He is Minister of Justice in the High Criminal Court.
Minister of Justice	He supervises legal forms and legal procedures both within the Senate and in other courts.

Organization of Ministries

Ministries	Ministers	Competence
Foreign Affairs	Minister of Foreign Affairs	Foreign Relations
Military	Minister of War	Land Forces
Naval	Minister of Navy	Naval Forces
Internal Affairs	Minister of Internal Affairs	Agriculture, Industry, Domestic Trade, Posts
	Chief Director of Communication	Communication
	Minister or Chief Director of Schools	Administration of schools

Ministries	Ministers	Competence
Finances	Minister of Finances	Revenues: collection of taxes and dues; administration of mines, forests, customs, etc.
	Minister of the Treasury	Circulation of capital and credit. Administration of currency, banks, etc.
	Minister or Chief Director of Accounting	Control of all accounts
Justice	Minister of Justice Ober-Procurator of the	Supervision and protection of courts
Religious Affairs		Department of Religious Affairs
	Synod	
Police	Minister of Police	Protection of internal security. State Police

Main Components

Every Ministry has as many departments as there are chief parts. Every department has a director. These directors comprise the Council of the Ministry.

All ministers have a general instruction that determines the picture of their activity, their relation to the Council, and degrees of their power and responsibility.

Matters that require a general meeting of ministers are introduced to the Committee of Ministers.

Organization of the Legislative Order in *Gubernias*

Composition	Competence
Volost dumas are organized in volosts from all owners of immovable property and from officials of state volosts.	To elect deputies to the okrug duma. To elect judges to volost courts. To elect members of the Council attached to volost administration. To elect a certain number of more distinguished citizens to organize a census in the volost. To account volost expenses and to redistribute new tax obligations. To present needs of the volost.
Okrug dumas composed of a determined number of deputies elected by the volost dumas.	To elect deputies to the *gubernia* dumas, to the okrug court, to the council attached to the okrug administration; to elect a definite num-

Competence	Composition
	ber of more distinguished citizens from volost rosters to give an account of okrug taxes and to distribute same, and to present needs of the okrug.
Gubernia dumas	Election of deputies to the State Duma, to gubernia courts, to councils attached to the gubernia administration, etc.

Main Components

The volost dumas represent the first, so to speak, element of legislative order, which, emerging in the volost gradually rises as a result of elections of deputies, every three years, and forms the State Duma.

All dumas have chairmen.

The lists of all gubernia dumas are to be submitted to the Chancellor of the [State] Duma. From these lists then is prepared a state list, from which are recruited officials, approved by public opinion, for the performance of certain administrative tasks.

Organization of the Executive Administration in Gubernias

Composition	Competence
The gubernia administration	
The chief official in the gubernia is the governor (wherever no governor-general exists). Gubernia administration branches are divided into offices: each office has its own chief. Chiefs of these branches under the chairmanship of the governor form the gubernia administration.	All matters of police, treasury collections, and taxes and general well being, are subjects of the gubernia administration.
Important matters are decided at a general meeting; current [matters] in the offices. The governor has an instruction determining the degree of his authority and responsibility. At the gubernia administration is located a Council of Deputies of the gubernia duma for the distribution of annual obligations, for accounting and for presenting needs [of the gubernia]. It meets once a year.	

The Okrug Administration

The chief of the okrug is the vice-governor; the government is divided into offices similar to those in the *gubernia* administration. Chiefs of the expeditions under chairmanship of the vice-governor comprise an okrug administration. Attached to it is an okrug council, consisting of deputies of the okrug duma. Local *uezd* police stations, city mayors, and district police officers are part of the okrug administration. Through them the okrug administration reaches *uezds*.

The same problems as in the *gubernia* administration, except that they are smaller in scope.

The Volost Administration

It is organized along the same lines as the okrug administration, with smaller competence.

The same problems, except smaller in scope.

17

Alexander I's Proclamations During the War of 1812

The most eventful episode in the reign of Alexander I (1801–1825) was Napoleon's invasion of Russia in 1812. Napoleon decided to undertake the campaign after Alexander's official withdrawal from the Continental System in December 1810. If successful, the undertaking would have eliminated the

From General Sir Robert Wilson, *Narrative of Events During the Invasion of Russia by Napoleon Bonaparte and the Retreat of the French Army, 1812.* Edited by Herbert Randolf. 2d ed. (London: 1860), pp. 46–48, 368–369.

last obstacle in Napoleon's attempt to control Europe. His past record seemed to assure quick success, and to make his victory certain Napoleon assembled a force of over 600,000 men and led them into Russia in June 1812. But the Russian strategies of retreat and scorched earth upset Napoleon's plans, making it impossible for him to defeat the enemy or even to provision his own armies. The only engagement, the battle of Borodino, was costly and indecisive, as the Russians retreated in orderly fashion toward Moscow, which Napoleon's forces occupied in September 1812. Late in October, to avoid wintering his overextended forces in Moscow, Napoleon ordered the retreat, which has remained a classic military horror. The Grand Army lost some 400,000 men to battle casualties, exposure, and starvation, and about 100,000 were imprisoned. The Russian success was due in large measure to favorable natural circumstances, the strategy of Marshal M. I. Kutuzov, and the aroused patriotism which the tsar helped to stimulate by appealing to his subjects to defend the country, the Orthodox religion, and "liberty."

Alexander's Proclamation to the Nation, July 18, 1812

The enemy has passed the frontiers and carried his arms into the interior of Russia. Since perfidy cannot destroy an empire which has existed with a dignity always increasing for so many generations, he has determined to attack it by violence, and to assault the empire of the Czars with the forces of the continent of Europe.

With treason in the heart and loyalty on the lips, he flatters the ears of the credulous and enchains their arms; and if the captive perceives fetters under the flowers, the spirit of domination discovers itself, and he calls forth war to assure the work of treason! But Russia has penetrated his views. The path of loyalty is open to her: she has invoked the protection of God; she opposes to the plots of her enemy an army strong in courage, and eager to drive from her territory this race of locusts who consume the earth, and whom the earth will reject, finding them too heavy a burden to sustain.

We call out sufficient armies to annihilate the enemy. Our soldiers who are under arms are like lions who dart on their prey; but we do not disguise from our faithful subjects that the intrepid courage of our warriors actually under arms needs to be supported by an interior line of troops. The means ought to be proportioned to the object; and the

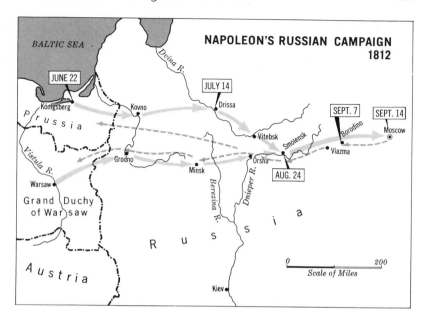

NAPOLEON'S RUSSIAN CAMPAIGN 1812

object placed before you is to overthrow the tyrant who wishes to over-throw all the earth.

We have called on our ancient city of Moscow, the first capital of our empire, to make final efforts, and she is accustomed to make them, by sending her sons to the succour of the empire. After her, we call on all our subjects of Europe and Asia to unite themselves for the cause of humanity! We call on all our civil and religious communities to co-op-erate with us by a general rising against the universal tyrant.

Wherever in this empire he turns his steps he will be assured of find-ing our native subjects laughing at his frauds, scorning his flattery and his falsehoods, trampling on his gold with the indignation of offended virtue, and paralyzing, by the feeling of true honour, his legions of slaves. In every noble Russian he will find a Pojarskoi, in every ecclesiastic a Palitsyn, in every peasant a Minin.

Nobles! You have been in all ages the defenders of our country! Holy Synod! And you members of our Church! You have in all circumstances by your intercession called down upon our empire the Divine protection! Russian people! Intrepid posterity of Sclavonians! It is not the first time that you have plucked out the teeth from the head of the lion, who sprung on you as upon a prey, and met his own destruction! Unite your-selves! Carry the cross in your hearts and the sword in your hands, and human force never can prevail against you.

I have delegated the organization of the new levies to the nobles of every province; and I have charged with the care of assembling the brave patriots who will present themselves of their own accord for the defence of the country the gentlemen amongst whom the officers will be chosen. The number of those who will be assembled ought to be sent to Moscow, where they will be made acquainted with the commander-in-chief.

Given at our camp of Polotzk, the 18th of July, 1812.

Alexander

Alexander's Victory Proclamation to the Army, January 13, 1813

Merecz, 13th January 1813

Soldiers,

The year has ended—a year forever memorable and glorious—one in which you have trampled in the dust the pride of the insolent aggressor.

The year has passed, but your heroic deeds survive.

Time will not efface their trace. They are present to your contemporaries—they will live with their posterity.

You have purchased at the price of your blood the deliverance of your country from the hostile powers leagued against its independence.

You have acquired rights to the gratitude of Russia, and to the admiration of mankind. You have proved by your fidelity, your valour, and your perseverance, that when hearts are filled with the love of God, and devotion of their Sovereign, the efforts of the most formidable enemies resemble the furious waves of the ocean, which break in impotent lashings against indestructible rocks, and leave behind only confused sounds.

Soldiers! Desirous of distinguishing all those who have participated in these immortal exploits, I have ordered medals of silver to be struck, which have been blessed by our holy Church. They bear the date of the memorable year 1812: suspended to a blue ribbon, they will decorate the warrior breasts which have served as bucklers of the country.

Each individual of the Russian army is worthy to bear this honourable recompense of valour and constancy.

You have all shared the same fatigues and dangers; you have had but one heart, one mind; you will all be proud to wear the same distinction; it will proclaim every where that you are the faithful children of Russia —children on whom God the Father will pour His benedictions.

Your enemies will tremble on seeing these decorations: they will know that under these medals hearts are beating, animated with unconquerable valour, and imperishable, because it is not based upon ambition or impiety, but on the immutable foundation of patriotism and religion.

Alexander

18

Polish Freedoms under the Constitution of 1815

The three partitions of Poland by Russia, Austria, and Prussia (1772, 1793, and 1795) terminated the independent existence of that monarchy, but it also aroused Polish patriotism. At first the Poles attempted to defend themselves, but when this failed thousands of Poles joined the revolutionary armies of Napoleon and took an active part in his reorganization of Europe. To keep Polish hopes alive, and at the same time to call forth even greater sacrifices, Napoleon created a duchy of Warsaw in 1806. It collapsed, however, with Napoleon's defeat in 1812–1814.

The disunity among the victors (Russia, Austria, and England) over what should be done with Napoleonic Europe moved the Polish question again to the forefront of international issues. After much deliberation the Congress of Vienna assigned Napoleon's Grand Duchy of Warsaw to Russia as a constitutional kingdom with Alexander I as its constitutional monarch. By this arrangement on November 27, 1815 Alexander granted the new kingdom a constitution. The document was based largely on the Charter of the Grand Duchy of Warsaw of July 22, 1807 and on Speranskii's ill-fated reform project of 1809. It provided for an elected bicameral legislature to meet every two years, made Polish the official language of the area, guaranteed freedom of press and person, allowed Poland to have its own army of 40,000 men, and stipulated that all administrative posts be held by Polish subjects. Considering the time and circumstances, the Polish constitution of 1815 was a liberal and enlightened document, and for a time it appeared that Alexander I might even

From Le Comte D'Angeberg [Chodzko], *Recueil des traites, conventions et actes diplomatiques concernant la Pologne 1762–1862* (A Collection of Treaties, Conventions and Diplomatic Papers Concerning Poland, 1762–1862) (Paris: 1862), pp. 707–724. Translation mine.

grant a similar one to his own country. However this proved to be an illusion, as Alexander turned to extreme conservatism soon after 1815.

Article 1

The kingdom of Poland is united in perpetuity to the Russian Empire. . . .

Article 3

The crown of the kingdom of Poland is hereditary in Our person and in those of Our descendants, heirs and successors, on the basis of the order of succession established for the imperial throne of Russia.

Article 4

The constitutional charter establishes the mode and the principles of sovereignty.

Article 5

The king, in his absence, shall nominate a lieutenant who shall reside in the kingdom. The lieutenant is revocable at will. . . .

Article 8

Foreign policy relations of Our empire are the same as those of the kingdom of Poland.

Article 9

The sovereign alone shall have the right to decide whether the kingdom of Poland shall take part in the wars of Russia, as well as in the treaties of peace or of commerce that that power may conclude.

Article 10

In case Russian troops should be brought to Poland or Polish troops to Russia, or in case of transit of those troops through a province of the two states, their maintenance and cost of transportation will be borne by the state to which they belong. The army of Poland shall never be employed outside Europe.

Article 11

The Roman Catholic religion, professed by the majority of the inhabitants of the kingdom of Poland, shall receive the most careful attention from the government, without in any way diminishing the freedom of other sects, which without exception shall be allowed to worship freely and publicly, and shall enjoy the protection of the government. Whatever distinction there may be between Christian sects, there shall be no distinction in the enjoyment of civil and political rights. . . .

Article 16

Freedom of the press is guaranteed. The law shall regulate the ways and shall repress abuses.

Article 17

The law shall protect equally all citizens without regard to their class or their status . . .

Article 19

No person shall be arrested otherwise than according to procedures established by the law. . . .

Article 24

Every Pole is free to move his person and his property in accordance with procedures established by the law.

Article 25

All convicts shall be punished for their crimes in the kingdom; no person shall be deported except when banishment is provided by the law.

Article 26

All property, regardless of its nature, . . . is declared sacred and inviolable. . . .

Article 28

All administrative, judicial, and military public business, without any exception, shall be conducted in the Polish language.

Article 29

Public offices, civil and military, may be occupied only by Poles. The positions of presidents of courts of first instance, presidents of palatinal commissions and of courts of appeal, members of palatinal councils, the offices of nuncios and deputies of the Diet, and those of senators, may be given only to landowners. . . .

Article 31

The Polish nation shall have in perpetuity a national representative body: the latter will consist of a Diet composed of the king and two houses. The Senate will be the first house; Chamber of Nuncios and Deputies of the Communes will form the second house. . . .

Article 33

Any foreigner who shall have acquired property, become naturalized, and shall have learned the Polish language shall be eligible to hold public office after five years residence, if his conduct be irreproachable.

Article 34

Nevertheless, the king may at his pleasure, or upon request of the Council of State, admit foreigners distinguished for their abilities to any public office except those designated in Article 90.

Article 35

The government is inherent in the person of the king. He exercises in all their fullness the functions of the executive power. All executive or administrative authority can emanate only from him.

Article 36

The person of the king is sacred and inviolable.

Article 37

Official acts of tribunals, courts, and of all magistrates are made in the name of the king. . . .

Article 38

The king has the exclusive right to direct the armed forces in peace and in war and to appoint commanders and officers.

Article 39

The king disposes of the revenues of the state in conformity with the budget he prepares and approves.

Article 40

The right to declare war and to conclude all treaties and conventions whatsoever is reserved to the king.

Article 41

The king nominates senators, ministers, state councilors, *les maîtres des requêtes*, presidents of local commissions, presidents and judges of various courts, diplomatic and commercial agents, and all other administrative officials who are subordinate to him or to authorities to whom he had delegated the power.

Article 42

The king nominates archbishops and bishops of different cults, suffragan bishops, and prelates.

Article 43

The right to pardon is reserved exclusively to the king. He alone has the power to commute punishment.

Article 44

The sovereign enjoys the right to issue statutes and to publish civil and military orders. . . .

Article 46

The right to grant titles of nobility, to naturalize and to distribute honorary titles, belongs exclusively to the king. . . .

Article 63

The Council of State, presided over by the king, or his lieutenant, is composed of the ministers, councillors of state, *maîtres des requêtes*, and such persons as it shall please the king to summon especially to attend.

Article 64

The lieutenant and the Council of State administer in the king's absence, and in his name, the public affairs of the kingdom.

Article 65

The Council of State includes the Administrative Council and the General Assembly.

Article 66

The Administrative Council shall be composed of the lieutenant, the principal ministers of the five governmental departments, and other persons especially summoned by the king.

Article 67

The members of the Administrative Council shall have the right to express their opinions. The opinion of the lieutenant alone shall be decisive. . . .

Article 73

The General Assembly of the Council of State shall be composed of all the members designated in Article 63. It will be presided over by the king or his lieutenant, and in their absence by the first members of the council as stipulated in Articles 62 and 63.

Its functions are: (a) To discuss and draw up all projected laws and regulations for the general administration of the country; (b) To order the trial of any administrative officers appointed by the king for breach of trust in the exercise of their duties, except all those who are under the jurisdiction of the National Supreme Court; (c) To decide in cases of conflict of jurisdiction; (d) To examine annually the accounts rendered by each of the principal administrative departments; (e) To consider abuses or anything that may derogate from the Constitutional Charter, and to draw up a general report thereon, which it shall address to the sovereign, who shall decide what instructions are to be sent to the Senate or to the Diet. . . .

Article 76

The execution of the laws shall be entrusted to the various departments of public administration, namely: (a) The Ministry of Sects and of Public Instruction; (b) The Ministry of Justice, chosen from among the members of the Supreme Court; (c) The Ministry of Interior and of Police; (d) The Ministry of War; (e) The Ministry of Finance and of the Treasury.

A minister shall be nominated to preside over each of these ministries.

Article 77

There shall be created a minister to act as Secretary of State, who shall be in constant attendance on the person of the king.

Article 78

There shall be a Court of Accounts charged with the final revision of accounts and the discharge of responsible officers. It shall be responsible to the king. . . .

Article 86

The legislative power rests in the person of the king and in the two legislative chambers in conformity with the provisions of Article 31.

Article 87

The Diet shall meet every two years in Warsaw at a time stated in the summons issued by the king. The sessions shall last for thirty days. The king alone may prorogue, adjourn, or dissolve it.

Article 88

The king may convoke an extraordinary Diet if he sees a need for it.

Article 89

A member of the Diet, so long as he shall be a member, may not be arrested nor judged by a criminal court, save by vote of the Chamber to which he belongs.

Article 90

The Diet shall decide on all projects of civil, criminal, or administrative laws that are to be sent to it by the king or the Council of State. It shall act on all plans which the king may send it relating to proposed changes or modifications of the functions of offices or of constitutional powers such as those of the Diet, Council of State, the judicial organization, or the governmental departments.

Article 91

The Diet shall decide, in accordance with the message of the sovereign, on the increase or reduction of taxes, contributions, or public levies of any kind; on any changes which these may necessitate; on the best and the most equitable distribution; on the framing of the budget, both as to receipts and as to expenditures; on the regulation of the monetary system; on the raising of recruits; as well as on any other matter referred to it by the sovereign.

Article 92

The Diet shall decide further on any matters referred to it by the king as a result of the general report which the Assembly of the Council of State is charged by Article 73 to render. Finally, the Diet, after having decided all these matters, shall give attention to communications, requests, representations, or claims made to it by the nuncios and by the deputies of the communes to promote the welfare and interests of their constituents. It shall transmit them to the Council of State, which shall submit them to the sovereign. When they shall have been sent back to the Diet through the medium of the Council of State, it shall decide on such laws as are proposed in consequence of these claims. . . .

Article 94

The Diet can concern itself only with the matters included in these functions or in the act of convocation.

Article 95

The two chambers shall hold public sessions. They may, however, resolve themselves into a committee of the whole at the desire of one tenth of those members present.

Article 96

Legislative acts which originate in the Council of State are sent to the Diet on order of the king by members of the said Council.

Article 97

The king decides whether proposed laws shall be sent first to the Senate or to the Chamber of Nuncios. Proposed financial laws are an exception; they must go first to the Chamber of Nuncios. . . .

Article 101

Members of the Council of State have the right to sit in the two chambers and to speak when government measures are being discussed. They have the right to vote only in case they are themselves senators, nuncios or deputies.

Article 102

Proposals shall be decided by majority vote. Votes shall be given orally. A proposed law, thus adopted in one chamber by a majority vote, shall go to the other chamber, which shall discuss it and decide on it in the same manner. In case of a tie, the proposal shall be considered carried.

Article 103

A proposed law by one chamber may not be modified by the other; it must be adopted or rejected as it stands.

Article 104

A proposal adopted by both chambers is submitted for the approval of the king.

Article 105

If the king gives his assent, the proposal shall become a law. The king orders the publication of the new law in a prescribed manner. If the king refuses to give his assent, the proposal shall be dropped. . . .

Article 108

The Senate is composed of: Princes of the blood imperial and royal; Bishops; Palatines; Castellans.

Article 109

The number of senators shall not exceed half the number of the nuncios and of the deputies. . . .

Article 118

The Chamber of Nuncios is composed of: (a) One hundred nuncios nominated by the districts or assemblies of the nobility, one nuncio to a district; (b) Sixty-seven deputies of the communes. A marshal chosen from among its members and nominated by the king shall preside over the chamber. . . .

Article 120

Members of the Chamber of Nuncios are elected for a period of six years. . . . Members have the privilege of being re-elected many times. . . .

Article 124

The king has the right to dissolve the Chamber of Nuncios; if the king uses this right he must order a new election of the nuncios and of the deputies within two months.

Article 125

Landowning nobles in each district, meeting in the Dietine, shall choose one nuncio, two members of the Council of the Palatinate, and shall draw up a list of candidates for offices in the government departments.

Article 126

The Dietines shall meet only when the king shall summon them, setting the day, the length of the session, and the business to be decided. . . .

Article 129

The Dietines are presided over by a marshal nominated by the king.

Article 130

A communal assembly shall be held in each district of the commune; it shall elect a deputy to the Diet and a member of the Council of the Palatinate, and shall draw up a list of candidates for offices in the government departments.

Article 131

To the communal assemblies shall be admitted: (a) All non-noble citizen-proprietors who pay taxes on landed property; (b) All manufacturers and foremen; all merchants who own a business or shop valued at 10,000 Polish florins; (c) All curés and vicars; (d) Professors, instructors, and other persons in charge of public instruction; (e) Every artist distinguished for his talent, his knowledge, or for his services rendered to his profession or to the arts. . . .

Article 138

The judicial system is constitutionally independent. . . .

Article 140

The courts consist of judges nominated by the king and of judges selected in conformity with the organic statute.

Article 141

Judges nominated by the king are irremovable for life; judges selected are equally irremovable for the duration of their functions. . . .

Article 159

The penalty of confiscation is abolished and shall never, in any case, be re-established. . . .

Article 165

All laws and former regulations which are contrary to the present charter are abolished. . . .

19

The Question
of Imperial Succession

One of the most tragic problems in the history of Imperial Russia is the question of succession. A major concern of Peter the Great (see Chapter 3), it was also of importance in the reigns of Anna (see Chapter 5), Elizabeth (see Chapter 6), and Catherine II (see Chapter 8). To prevent palace revolutions or unlawful usurpations of power, Tsar Paul, soon after his ascension, issued a new law of succession by which the throne of Russia was to pass from the father to the eldest son and, if there were no sons, to the next eldest brother of the tsar. Paul's death in 1801 (see Chapter 14) placed his eldest son Alexander I on the throne.

Because Alexander I had no sons to succeed him, under the 1797 law the throne was to pass at his death to his brother Constantine (1779–1831). Early in 1822, however, Constantine, who lived in Warsaw with his morganatic wife, renounced his right to succession in favor of his younger brother, Nicholas (1796–1855). The arrangement was made with such secrecy that when Alexander died late in 1825 there followed a strange comedy of errors that helped to precipitate the Decembrist Revolution.

Constantine's Renunciation
of His Right to the Throne
January 26, 1822

Sire!

Encouraged by all the proofs of the infinitely sympathetic disposition of Your Imperial Majesty toward me, I am once more laying at your feet, Sire, a most humble prayer.

The following three items are from Paul Lacroix, *Histoire de la vie et du regne de Nicholas Ier Empereur de Russie* (*History of the Life and of the Reign of Nicholas I, Emperor of Russia*) (Paris: 1864), vol. 1, pp. 238–239, 244–247, 395–399. Translation mine.

Not finding in myself either the genius, or the talents, or the force necessary to be elevated to the sovereign dignity to which I have the right by virtue of my birth, I beg Your Imperial Majesty to transfer this right to whomever follows after me, and thus to assure forever the security of the empire. As for myself, I will add by this renunciation a new guarantee and a new force to the engagement which I have voluntarily and solemnly contracted on the occasion of my divorce from my first wife.

All the circumstances of my own situation, bearing more and more upon this measure, prove to the Empire and to the entire world the sincerity of my views.

Sire, accept with good will my prayer; help me secure the consent of our Imperial Mother to this plan and sanction it with your Imperial assent.

In the sphere of private life, I shall pledge myself always to serve as an example to your faithful subjects, and to all those who are animated by a love for our dear country.

I am with profound respect for your Majesty, your most faithful subject and brother,

St. Petersburg, 26 January, 1822   Tsarevich Constantine

Alexander I's Manifesto on the Succession, August 28, 1823

By the grace of God, We, Alexander I, Emperor and Autocrat of all the Russians, etc., hereby make known to all Our faithful subjects:

From the moment of Our coming to the throne of all the Russias, We have constantly felt that it was Our duty toward All Mighty God not only to guarantee and increase during Our life the happiness of Our beloved country and Our people, but also to prepare and assure their security and their well being after Us by a clear and precise designation of Our successor in accordance with the laws of Our Imperial House and the interests of the Empire. We were unable to designate him immediately, as Our predecessors had done, because We waited in the hope that it would perhaps please Divine Providence to give Us an heir to the throne in a direct line. But as the years have passed, it has more and more seemed to Us Our duty to place Our throne in such a position that it will not remain vacant even for a moment.

While We bear this anxiety in Our heart Our well beloved brother, Tsarevich and Grand Duke Constantine, following the dictates of his own conscience, has addressed to Us the request that We transfer his right to the sovereign dignity, a position to which he would one day be elevated by virtue of his birth, to a person who might possess this right after him. He revealed at the same time his intention to give new force to the additional act relative to the succession to the throne which We promulgated in 1820, an act freely and solemnly recognized by him insofar as that act concerned him.

We are profoundly moved by the sacrifice which Our beloved brother has felt that he should make in his own interests for the consolidation of the fundamental laws of Our Imperial House, and the unshakable peace of the Empire of all the Russias.

Having invoked the aid of God, having seriously reflected upon a subject as dear to Our heart as it is vital for the Empire, and finding that the statutes which exist on the order of succession to the throne do not deprive those who have the right of the power to renounce it, and because in this special circumstance it does not present any difficulty in the order of hereditary succession to the throne, with the consent of Our noble Mother, who is the supreme head of the Imperial family to which We belong, and by the absolute power which We possess from God Himself, We ordered and shall order:

First, the voluntary act by which Our younger brother, Tsarevich and Grand Duke Constantine, renounces his rights to the throne of all the Russias shall be irrevocable. The said act of renunciation shall be, in order to insure knowledge of its existence, preserved in the Cathedral of the Assumption in Moscow and in the three high Courts of Our empire; in the Holy Synod, in the Council of the Empire, and in the Governing Senate. Secondly, on the basis of the strict provision of the statute on succession to the throne, be it known that Our successor shall be Our second brother, Grand Duke Nicholas.

As a result, We have the well founded hope that on the day it shall please the King of Kings to recall Us, following the common law of all mortals, from Our temporal reign to eternity, the properly constituted authorities of the Empire, to whom We have made known Our irrevocable wish in this matter, will hasten to swear submission and allegiance to the emperor whom We have just designated as heir to the indivisible crown of the Empire of all the Russias, of the Kingdom of Poland, and of the Grand Duchy of Finland. As for Ourselves, We ask that all Our faithful subjects, with the same feeling of love with which We have considered Our first responsibility on earth to be the care given to their constant prosperity, address fervent prayers to Our Lord Jesus Christ, that He might deign, in His infinite sympathy, to receive Our souls into His eternal kingdom.

Given at Tsarskoe-Selo, August 28, year of Grace 1823, and of Our reign the 23rd.

Alexander

Nicholas I's Manifesto upon Ascending the Throne, December 24, 1825

By the grace of God, We, Nicholas, Emperor and Autocrat of all the Russias, etc., make known to all Our faithful subjects:

In the sorrow of Our heart, in the midst of the general sadness which surrounds Us, We, Our Imperial house, and Our dear country, humble Ourselves before the unalterable decrees of the All-Mighty, and seek from Him alone Our strength and Our consolations. He has just called to Him Emperor Alexander I, of glorious memory, and We have all lost a father and a sovereign, who, for twenty-five years, has worked for the well-being of Russia and of Us.

When, on December 9, We learned the news of this sad event, We took pains, even in this moment of sadness and tears, to perform a sacred duty and follow only the impulse of Our heart, and We took the oath of allegiance to Our beloved brother Tsarevich Grand Duke Constantine as the legitimate heir to the throne of Russia by the right of primogeniture.

We had just discharged this sacred obligation when We were notified by the Council of Empire that on October 15, 1823, there had been placed in their hands a packet, sealed with the sign of the Emperor, on which there had been written in the hand of His Imperial Majesty himself: "To hold in the Council of Empire until I order otherwise; and in the case of my death to be opened at an extraordinary session, before proceeding to any other act." This sovereign order had been executed by the Council and the following items had been found in the said packet: (1) A letter of Tsarevich Grand Duke Constantine, dated January 26, 1822, addressed to the Emperor, by which his Imperial Highness renounced his succession to the throne which belonged to him by the right of primogeniture; (2) a manifesto of August 28, 1823, signed by his Imperial Majesty's own hand, by which, after having expressed his agreement to the renunciation of Tsarevich and Grand Duke Constantine, it is stated that, being next in age after him, We are, by virtue of the fundamental law, the proper heir to the throne. We were informed at the outset that identical documents had been deposited with the Holy Synod and in the Cathedral of the Assumption in Moscow.

The above mentioned facts did in no way change the determination which We had made. We recognize the acts of renunciation made by His Imperial Highness during the life of the Emperor and confirmed by the assent of His Imperial Majesty; but We have neither the wish nor the right to consider this renunciation as irrevocable since it has neither been published nor transformed into law. We wish thus to show Our respect for the first fundamental law of Our country on the unchanging order of succession to the throne; and faithful to the oath which We have taken, We insist that the entire Empire follow Our example. In this grave circumstance Our desire is not to contest the validity of the resolutions expressed by His Imperial Highness. He has again besought Us not to oppose the wishes of the late Emperor, Our father and common benefactor, wishes which We shall always hold sacred; We seek only to guarantee the letter of the law which rules the order of succession to the throne, to reveal fully the loyalty of Our intentions, and to preserve Our dear country in a moment of uncertainty over the person of the legitimate sovereign. This determination, conceived in the purity of Our conscience before God who reads the depths of Our hearts, was blessed by Her Imperial Majesty Marie, Our beloved Mother.

However, the sad news of the death of His Majesty, the Emperor, was taken directly from Taganrog to Warsaw on December 7, two days sooner than it was received here. Immovable in his resolution, Tsarevich and Grand Duke Constantine confirmed it on the following day by two acts, dated December 8, which he entrusted Our beloved brother Grand Duke Michael to bring to Us. These acts consist: first, of a letter addressed to her Imperial Majesty, Our beloved mother, a letter in which—renewing his earlier decision and resting upon a rescript of the late Emperor, dated February 14, 1822, which served as a response to his act of renunciation of which there was a copy attached—His Imperial Highness renounced definitively and solemnly all his rights to the throne, and on the basis of the order established by fundamental law, made them known to Us as well as to Our heirs; second, a letter addressed to Us, in which His Imperial Highness reiterates the first expression of his determination, gives to Us the title of Imperial Majesty, reserving only for himself that of Tsarevich which he bore formerly, and calls himself the most faithful of Our subjects.

Regardless of how decisive these acts may have been, and regardless of their certainty up to that time, the evidence was clear that the decision of His Imperial Highness was absolute and irrevocable and the nature of the problem and Our feelings in the matter caused Us to defer the publication of the said acts until such time as His Imperial Highness had manifested his desires relative to the oath which We rendered to him as well as to that of the entire Empire. . . .

As a result of all these acts, and by virtue of the fundamental law of the Empire on the order of succession, with a heart full of respect for the unalterable decrees of Providence which guides Us, We ascend the throne of Our ancestors, the throne of the empire of all the Russias, and those of the kingdom of Poland and the Grand Duchy of Finland, which are inseparable, and We order:

1. That the oath of allegiance be taken to Us and to Our heir, His Imperial Highness Grand Duke Alexander, Our well beloved son;

2. That the time of Our accession to the throne be dated from December 1, 1825.

Finally We ask all Our faithful subjects to raise with Us their fervent prayers toward the All-Mighty that He grant Us the power of His support for the burden which Divine Providence has imposed upon Us, that He sustain Us in Our firm intentions to live only for Our beloved country and to follow in the footsteps of the monarch who preceded Us. Then Our reign will be only a continuation of his, and We shall be able to accomplish all the wishes which he conceived for the well being of Russia, he whose sacred memory nourishes in Us the desire and hope to merit the blessings of heaven and the love of Our people!

Given in Our imperial residence at St. Petersburg, December 24, in the year of grace, 1825, and of Our reign the first.

Nicholas

20

The Decembrist Movement

After the victorious campaigns against Napoleon, many Russian officers returned home with boxes crammed with books and heads full of ideas for improving their country. Small secret groups were organized, of which the most important was the Union of Salvation. In 1818 this group, composed of a southern and a northern branch, changed its name to the Union of Welfare. The southern branch, led by Colonel Paul I. Pestel (1793–1826), advocated, in the Jacobin tradition, drastic changes in Russia's social, economic, and political structure. The northern branch, headed by such men as Prince Sergei P. Trubetskoi (1790–1860) and Nikita M. Muraviev (1795–1826), proposed a more moderate plan. The

From I. Ia. Shchipanov, ed. *Izbrannye sotsialno-politicheskie i filosofskie proizvedeniia dekabristov* (*Selected Socio-Political and Philosophical Works of the Decembrists* (Moscow: Gospolitizdat, 1951), vol. 1, pp. 241–250, 299–319. Translation mine. Items in brackets are mine.

first Russian revolution began on December 26,
1825, at the height of confusion within the imperial
family over the succession following the death of
Alexander I. The revolt proved a dismal failure, for
many reasons. Many of the more resolute leaders
were arrested and the others failed to act decisively;
the expected popular uprising failed to materialize;
and, finally, the armed forces remained loyal to the
regime. The attempts of the Decembrists, as this
group is commonly called, became an ideal of self-
sacrificing struggle against autocracy for later generations of Russian revolutionaries.

Statute of the Union of Welfare

Book 1. Aims of the Union of Welfare

1. Convinced that good morals represent the firm foundation of national welfare and valor, and that all the efforts of the government to
attain them will fail unless the governed take active part in realizing these
well-intentioned aims, the Union of Welfare believes that it is its sacred
obligation to disseminate the true rules of morality and enlightenment
among fellow citizens, and to assist the government in elevating Russia
to the level of greatness and welfare to which the Creator has predestined it.

2. Because its aim is the *welfare of the country*, the Union does not
conceal it [its aim] from well-meaning citizens, but in order to avoid the
censure of malice and jealousy its activity must be conducted in secrecy.

3. Because in all of its actions it will strive to observe strictly the
rules of justice and virtue, the Union will not try to expose those wounds
which it cannot remedy immediately, inasmuch as it is guided neither
by lust for glory nor similar motives, but by a desire for the common
welfare.

4. The Union hopes to receive benevolent support from the government; this hope is based on the following statements of the *Nakaz* by
the late Empress Catherine II: "If their minds are inadequately prepared
for them (the laws), then assume the responsibility of preparing them
and you will accomplish thereby a great deal." And in another place:
"That policy is bad which corrects through law what should have been
corrected through manners."

5. The following four basic fields constitute the aim of the Union:
(1) philanthropy; (2) education; (3) justice; and (4) national economy.

6. *First Field: Philanthropy* The Union supervises all philanthropic
institutions in the state, such as hospitals, orphanages, etc., and also those

places where mankind is suffering; namely, dungeons, prisons, etc. With zeal that befits its noble aim, the Union will seek to survey, and if possible to improve, the above mentioned institutions and to establish new ones. It will bring to the attention of the government all inadequacies and abuses that have been detected in those institutions. [The Union] is fully convinced that it [the government] is genuinely sympathetic with all of this, and that it is ready to extend a helping hand to all those who suffer. The Union also is concerned that invalids be cared for in appropriate places.

7. *Second Field: Section 1: Dissemination of moral principles* The Union will attentively disseminate among all estates of the population genuine principles of virtue and will remind and explain to all their obligations toward faith, neighbors, the country, and existing authorities. It will point out the unbreakable tie that exists between the people's virtue, that is, good morals, and its welfare, and will use every means to eradicate the vices that have entered our hearts, especially preference for personal rather than public gains, baseness, vile passions, hypocrisy, extortion, and cruelty toward subordinates. In short, by enlightening all about their duties, it [the Union] will try to reconcile and to persuade all classes, ranks, and races in the state, and to encourage them to strive unanimously toward the government's aim: The *common good*, so that a general public opinion will emerge as a true tribunal of morality whose beneficent influence will complete the formation of good habits and thereby will place on a firm and indestructible foundation the welfare and virtue of the Russian people.

The Union will achieve this end through publication of periodical works consonant with the educational level of each class, [and] writing and translation of books pertaining to man's obligations. Personal examples and words [of members] will also contribute to this aim. Clergymen, belonging to the Union, are especially obligated to enlighten their parishioners, without exception, about their duties. Those clergymen who are not members of the Union should be encouraged to do the same.

8. *Section 2: Education of youth* The education of youth represents also a permanent aim of the Union of Welfare. Under its supervision should be placed without exception all national educational institutions. The Union should inspect them, improve them, and establish new ones. As far as the education of youth is concerned, special effort must be made to arouse in it a love for everything virtuous, useful, and elegant, and contempt for everything that is imperfect and low, in order to stop the strong impulse of the passions by the firm but just reminder of an enlightened reason and conscience.

With respect to private education, the Union should try subtly to persuade the parents to instill the principles of virtue in their children and to support all deserving educators; those, however, who under the guise [of educators] creep into households to sow dissension and debauchery the Union will try not only to expel, but will try to deprive them, as corrupters of youth's morals, from earning their daily bread in this profession. The Union will especially supervise foreigners who, in addition to sowing dissension and corruption in households, instill in the children contempt for [everything that is] native and an attachment to [things that are foreign. The Union will seek to dissuade parents from educating their children in foreign countries. The education of the female sex, as a source of virtue in private education, is also of concern to the Union.

The Union will use the following means to attain this end: its own example, the spoken word, and periodical publications, which, among others, should include methods of education, names of recognized good educators, and books useful for that purpose.

9. *Section 3: Dissemination of knowledge* By all available means the Union will fight ignorance and will seek to instill genuine enlightenment by directing the minds to useful occupations and especially toward a knowledge of the fatherland. To this end it will write and translate books —good textbooks as well as those that will aid useful learning. It will try to disseminate education among the common people. It will use satire to divert people away from books that are contrary to the aims of the Union, or those that have no impact. Only the truly elegant will be allowed in literature and everything that is either bad or mediocre will be eliminated.

10. *Third Field: Justice* Next to good morals, justice is, without doubt, one of the main aspects of national welfare and is therefore an integral part of the aim of the Union. The Union will supervise the execution of governmental measures; will encourage civil and religious officials to fulfill their duties; will keep informed of all pending cases, and will seek to direct everything to the path of justice; will support poor but honest and trusted officials; will compensate for losses incurred in the cause of justice; will promote genuinely deserving individuals; will try to direct the dishonest and depraved into a proper path, and, in case of a failure, will try to deprive them of the opportunity to do harm. The Union will also try to limit and eradicate the lust for power and disregard for human rights which we acquired during our up-bringing, and will try to convince everyone of the truth that *the general prosperity of the people is infallibly based on private [prosperity] and that every individual, regardless of his estate, has the right to use it.*

11. *Fourth Field: National economy* National economy as the foundation of national wealth should be the aim of the Union—because through trade and industry it unites not only all estates but all vast areas of the state, and because transfer of wealth from one hand to another equalizes fortunes and thereby provides everyone with the hope that through industriousness he can enjoy that part of prosperity he has envied in others.

The Union will pay particular attention to agriculture and to all forms of cultivation of the soil in order to develop useful produce; it will support every useful industry in the state; it will supervise foreign and domestic trade and will seek to develop it, and through it to vitalize the unproductive regions of the country; it will support and call to the attention of the government that it [should] reward those merchants and industrialists who distinguish themselves in trying to do things for the general good; it will single out honest merchants, and will try to turn dishonest [ones] to their duties; and in general it will seek that more honesty be introduced in trade. The Public Treasury is also an object of interest of the Union.

Book Two. General Laws of the Union of Welfare

1. *Qualifications of the candidates* Having as its aim the *general welfare*, the Union of Welfare invites to membership all those who, by their honest life, have earned for themselves a good name in society, and who, feeling the nobility of the aim of the Union, are prepared to endure all the hardships that are associated with its attainment.

2. The Union does not consider differences in occupation and estates: all Russian citizens—nobles, clergy, merchants, townsmen, and free men —who agree with the above, who profess the Christian faith, and who are at least eighteen years old, are eligible for membership in the Union of Welfare.

Note: The Union considers to be Russian citizens those who were born in Russia and who speak Russian. Foreigners who left their country to serve a foreign state [Russia] do not deserve confidence by this act, and consequently cannot be considered Russian citizens. The Union considers worthy of this honor only those foreigners who have rendered important services to our country and who are passionately attached to it.

3. Women will not be admitted to the Union. Efforts should be made, however, to bring them subtly to organize philanthropic and *private societies*, whose aims are similar to those of the Union.

4. Anyone known to be a dishonest individual, and who has not improved his reputation, cannot be admitted to the Union of Welfare. In general all those who are depraved, vicious, and subject to vile passions, are precluded from participating in the Union.

5. *Duties of the members* Every member, upon joining the Union, is required, depending on his qualifications, to enroll in one of the fields listed in the aims [of the Union] and contribute as much as possible to [the success of] its work.

6. Every member is unquestionably required to obey all lawful orders of the Union authorities, diligently execute all of their assignments, and

cheerfully submit to all the reprimands which these authorities may impose for failure to carry out obligations.

7. Members of the Union not only should not avoid public obligations, but as true sons of the Fatherland should accept them with pleasure and execute them with zeal; and by their faultless conduct, justice, and nobility, elevate the prestige of their position in the eyes of others.

8. In every occupation, in every position, a member of the Union is obligated to aid others, to show respect for virtuous and distinguished people and to try to establish contact with them, keeping the Union informed about it. He must oppose the evil and the depraved by all means, without violating public order.

9. Members of the Union should aid one another in public life; members of the nobility are obligated to aid members from among the merchants, townsmen, and husbandmen, while members from these classes must act in a similar manner among themselves and towards nobles. Members of the civil service must defend those in the military and the military must speak for the civilians. All this, however, should not be contrary to truth or to the benefit of vice or crime. In general, every [member] must disseminate this truth: that every class and service is useful to the state, must be equally respected by true sons of the Fatherland, and that only those persons who deviate from their obligations and prefer vice to virtue deserve contempt.

10. Every member, under the penalty of punishment, is obligated to report to the authorities of the Union all illegal and shameful acts of his fellow members.

11. Other obligations of the Union members stem naturally from the aims of the Union. To the extent of his abilities, every member is obligated to accelerate the attainment of these aims. By his own example and word he must encourage everyone to virtue, disseminate ideas consonant with the aims of the Union, and speak the truth and defend it fearlessly; in short, he must strive to build a moral wall that will protect the present as well as future generations from all misfortunes of vice, and thereby erect an everlasting and unshakable foundation for the greatness and welfare of the Russian people.

12. Every member, upon joining the Union, must contribute annually one *twenty-fifth* of his income to the common treasury. In this matter the Union depends completely on the honesty of every member, because no other feeling than virtue induces everyone to contribute to the common good.

13. *Rights of the members* The difference in civil positions and ranks is abolished in the Union and is replaced by submission to the authorities of the Union. This, however, should not preclude normal respect for officials: a member of the Union must always and everywhere fulfill zealously his public obligations.

14. Every member has the right as well as the duty to participate within the legal framework in administration and legislation of the Union. He also has the right to submit in writing his views on any problem to lower as well as to higher authorities of the Union.

15. No member [of the Union] may be accused on grounds of suspicion alone; he may not be punished until sufficient evidence against him has been presented.

16. Every member has the right to organize or be a member of any society approved by the government, but he must inform the Union of everything that transpires in them and should subtly direct them to the aims of the Union. Members are prohibited from joining societies that are not approved by the government, because the Union, acting for the good of Russia, and for the aims of the government, does not wish to arouse the latter's suspicion.

17. No one may speak with outsiders about the work and affairs of the Union without specific permission; no one has the right, without special permission, to expound his thought in writing either against or in behalf of the Union; on the contrary, every member is obligated to refrain from revealing to non-members any disagreement within the Union; if there is a need he must defend the Union and its members with appropriate dignity.

18. If it should happen that some people, even those who have some virtue, and who have become fully acquainted with the aims and the permanent procedures of the Union, decide to leave it . . . the Union allows them to withdraw on condition that they keep secret everything they know.

Project for a Constitution
by Nikita M. Muraviev: Second Draft

Chapter I. The Russian People and Government

1. The Russian people are free and independent, and consequently are not, and cannot be, the property of any individual or family.

2. The source of *supreme power* is the people, who have the exclusive right to make *fundamental laws* for themselves.

Chapter II. Citizens

3. *Citizenship* is the right to participate, in accordance with the rules set forth in this Constitution, in the government—either *indirectly*, that is, through the election of officials or electors, or *directly*, that is, through being elected to any public office of the *legislative, executive* or *judicial* branches.

4. *Citizens* are those inhabitants of the Russian Empire who enjoy the above-mentioned rights.

5. To be a citizen a person must meet the following qualifications:
   (a) Be twenty-one years old.
   (b) Have a known and permanent residence.
   (c) Possess a healthy mind.
   (d) Have personal freedom.
   (e) Pay public obligations on time.
   (f) Be unimpeached before the law.

6. An alien who was not born in Russia, but who has resided there continuously for seven years, has the right to petition *the court* for Russian citizenship, provided he has renounced under oath his association with the government whose subject he previously had been.

7. An alien who has not been granted Russian citizenship cannot perform any public or military duty in Russia, has no right to serve as a soldier in the Russian army, and cannot acquire lands.

8. Twenty years after the promulgation of this Constitution of the Russian Empire no person who has not become literate in the Russian language may be recognized as a citizen.

9. The right of citizenship can be lost *temporarily* through:
   (a) Court declaration of insanity.
   (b) Court-imposed prison sentence.
   (c) *Temporary deprivation* of rights by a court.
   (d) Declaration of bankruptcy.
   (e) Embezzlement of public funds.
   (f) Personal servitude.
   (g) Lack of permanent home, occupation, and means of livelihood.
   [The right of citizenship may be lost] *forever* through:
   (a) Entering the service of another state.
   (b) Accepting service or obligation in a foreign country without the consent of his [the Russian] government.
   (c) Decision of a court for dishonorable punishment, which carries *the loss* of the citizenship rights.
   (d) Acceptance without the approval of the parliament, of a gift, pension, a sign of distinction, [or a] title, whether honorary or one which brings him gain, from a foreign government, sovereign, or people.

Chapter III. Status, Personal Rights, and Obligations of Russians

10. All Russians are equal before the law.

11. All native inhabitants of Russia, and Russian-born children of foreigners who are of age, are considered to be Russians until they announce that they do not wish to enjoy this privilege.

12. Everyone must fulfill his public obligations, obey the laws and au-

thorities of the Fatherland, and come to the defense of the country whenever the law should require it.

13. Serfdom and slavery are abolished; any slave who reaches Russian soil becomes free. No distinction is recognized between noblemen and commoners, because this is contrary to our faith, according to which all men are *brothers*, all *well-born* by divine will, all born *for the good*, and all simply men: because all are weak and imperfect.

14. Everyone has the right to express freely his thoughts and feelings and communicate them through print to his countrymen. Books, similarly as all other acts, may be brought before the court by other citizens and must be tried before a *jury*.

15. All the existing merchant and craft *guilds* are abolished.

16. Everyone has the right to engage in any occupation he feels will benefit him most: *agriculture, cattle raising, hunting, fishing, handicrafts, industry, trade*, etc.

17. Every litigation involving property exceeding the value of one pound of pure silver (twenty-five silver rubles), goes before a jury court.

18. Every criminal case is tried by a jury.

19. Anyone suspected of a crime may be detained by lawfully constituted authorities in accordance with established procedure; however, within twenty-four hours (those responsible for his detention) must inform him in writing of the reason for his detention; otherwise he is set free immediately.

20. Unless he is arrested for a criminal offense, a prisoner is to be set free immediately if *bail* is posted for him.

21. No one may be punished except under terms of a law that had been properly introduced and duly promulgated *before the crime was committed*.

22. This Constitution will outline what officials, and under what circumstances, have the right to issue written orders *to detain* a citizen, *search his home, seize his papers*, and *open his letters*. Equally, it will outline the responsibility for committing such offenses.

23. The right to property, especially movable property, is sacred and inviolable.

24. The land belongs to landowners. The houses of villagers and their gardens, together with all of their agricultural implements and cattle belonging to them, is their property.

25. Economic and appanage peasants will be called *common owners*, as are *free agriculturists*, because the land on which they now live will be given to them in *common possession* and recognized as their property. The Appanage Administration is abolished.

26. Subsequent legislation will determine how these lands will be transferred from a *common* to *private ownership* of each of the villagers,

and the rules that will determine the *division* of common land among them.

27. Villagers living on leased estates are also *freed*, but the land remains in the possession of the lessees for the duration of the lease.

28. *Military colonies* are abolished forthwith. Members of settled battalions and squadrons, and their families, join the class of common *owners*.

29. The division of men into fourteen classes is terminated. Civil ranks that were borrowed from the Germans, and which differ very little among themselves, are abolished in conformity with the ancient customs of the Russian people. Such titles and classes as freeholders, merchants, nobles, and *eminent citizens* are replaced by *citizen* or *Russian*.

30. The clergy will continue to receive their salaries. They are, however, freed from quartering and carting duties.

31. Nomadic tribes do not enjoy the rights of citizens. They have, however, the right to take part in the election of a *volost elderman*.

32. Citizens have the right to organize different societies and associations without requesting permission or authorization from anyone, provided their actions are not illegal.

33. Each of such societies has the right to make its own bylaws, provided the latter are not contrary to this Constitution or to public laws.

34. No foreign-based society can have a subordinate branch or a subsidiary in Russia.

35. No violation of the law may be excused by reference to orders from superiors. The *violator* of the law is punished first, then whoever authorized the illegal act.

36. Citizens have the right to address their complaints or petitions to the National Assembly, the Emperor, and the governing bodies of the states [of the Empire].

37. Underground dungeons and casements, and in general all the so-called state prisons, are abolished. No one may be imprisoned except in public prisons, designated for this purpose.

38. *Accused* should not be imprisoned in the same place together with *convicts*, nor should those imprisoned for debts or minor offenses be put together with criminals and villains.

39. Citizens should elect prison officials from among people of good conscience, who would be accountable for every illegal and inhuman act against prisoners.

40. The present police officials are released from duty and are to be replaced by officials elected by the inhabitants.

41. Any citizen who would violate free election of *national representatives*, by violence or bribery, will be brought before the court.

42. No one may be prevented from the exercise of his religion accord-

ing to his conscience and feelings, as long as he does not violate the laws of nature and morality.

Chapter IV. On Russia

43. For legislative and executive purposes Russia is divided into thirteen states, two regions, and 569 districts or parishes . . .

State	Capital
I. State of Bothnia	Helsingfors
II. State of Volkhov	City of St. Peter
III. Baltic State	Riga
IV. Western State	Vilno
V. State of the Dnieper [River]	Smolensk
VI. Black Sea State	Kiev
VII. Caucasian State	Tiflis
VIII. Ukrainian State	Kharkov
IX. Trans-Volga State	Iaroslavl
X. State of the Kama [River]	Kazan
XI. State of the Lower Steppe	Saratov
XII. State of the Ob [River]	Tobolsk
XIII. State of the Lena [River]	Irkutsk
Moscow Region	Moscow
Don Region	Cherkassk . . . .

Chapter VI. National Assembly

59. The National Assembly, consisting of the Supreme Duma and the Chamber of People's Representatives, is invested with all legislative power.

Chapter VII. The Chamber of Representatives, Number, and Election of Representatives

60. The Chamber of Representatives consists of members elected for two years by the citizens of the States.
61. At the time of his election a representative must reside in the state that elects him.
62. Until they have fulfilled them, individuals who have public works contracts cannot serve as representatives. . . .

Chapter VIII. The Supreme Duma

73. The Supreme Duma consists of three citizens from every state, two from the Moscow Region, and one from the Don Region, a total of forty-two members. Members of the Supreme Duma are elected by the

governing institutions of the states and regions; *i.e.*, by *State Dumas* and the *Chambers of Electors* at joint sessions.

74. Immediately upon arrival in the capital, members of the Supreme Duma are divided into three equal groups. Members of the first group will terminate their position in the Duma in two years; members of the second group after four years; and members of the third group after six years. Thus, one-third of the membership of the Duma will be elected every two years . . .

75. Criteria indispensable for membership in the Supreme Duma are: thirty years of age; nine years of Russian citizenship for a [naturalized] foreigner; residence in the state that elects him; immovable property worth 1500 pounds of pure silver, or movable property worth 3000 pounds of pure silver. . . .

77. Within the competence of the Supreme Duma belongs the impeachment of ministers, supreme court justices, and all other officials of the Empire who have been accused by people's representatives. No one can be sentenced except by the judgment of two-thirds of the members present. The Duma has no authority to impose any other sentence except to declare that *the accused is guilty and to deprive him of the seat and position he occupies*. . . .

Jointly with the Emperor, the Duma participates in the conclusion of peace, in the appointment of judges to superior courts, commanders-in-chief of land and naval forces, corps commanders, chiefs of squadrons, and chief keeper of the order. Consent by two-thirds of the members of the Duma are required for this.

Chapter IX. Power and Prerogatives of the National Assembly, and the Law-making Process

78. The National Assembly meets at least once a year. . . .

79. Each Chamber decides on the rights and credentials of its members . . .

80. Each Chamber has the right to censure its members for unbecoming conduct or in case of crime, *but never for expressing an opinion*; it may expel a member by a *decision* of two-thirds of the members.

81. The sessions of both Chambers are public. At the Emperor's request, however, both Chambers may deliberate behind closed doors, having removed [from the premises] all unauthorized persons. . . . Women and minors under 17 years of age are not admitted to the sessions of either Chamber.

82. Each Chamber keeps minutes of its daily proceedings and publishes them periodically, except those that they decide to keep secret. . . .

83. Members of the Supreme Duma and representatives are remunerated from the State Treasury for each day of their service. . . .

84. In no instance, except *treason*, or transgressions or violations of public order, may members of the National Assembly be arrested during the session, or during their trip to the capital, or during their return home. Never should they be threatened for what they have said in their Chambers, and no one has the right to demand that they explain their speeches. A member accused of transgression is suspended by his Chamber until a court verdict.

85. No official in public service may be a member of either Chamber as long as he retains his official position.

86. No member of the Duma or a Representative may be appointed to any government office during the entire term for which he has been elected. . . .

89. To attain force of *law*, each bill passed by the Duma and the Chamber of Representatives must be submitted to the Emperor. If the Emperor approves the bill, he signs it; if he disapproves, he sends it back with his comments to the Chamber where it was initiated; the Chamber enters into its minutes all of the Emperor's comments against the bill and reopens debate on it. If, after this second debate on a bill, two-thirds of the members favor it, then the bill goes with all of the Emperor's comments to the other Chamber where it is debated anew, and if a *majority* approves it, then the bill becomes *law*. . . .

92. The National Assembly has the power to make and annul laws dealing with the judiciary and the executive; that is:

(a) Issue a civil, criminal, commercial, and military code for Russia . . .

(b) Declare through a law, in case of invasion or rebellion, that a given region is on a war footing and under *martial law*.

(c) Make public the law of *amnesty* . . .

(d) Declare war.

(e) [Supervise] taxes, loans, auditing of expenditures, pensions, grants, all revenues and expenditures; in short, [have control over] all financial matters. But it cannot approve a budget for more than two years.

(f) [Concern itself with] all governmental measures pertaining to industry, national wealth, postal service, maintenance of old and creation of new land and water ways, and establishment of banks.

(g) Protect sciences and useful arts, and grant authors and inventors exclusive right to derive benefits from their works and inventions for a specific number of years. . . .

(h) Receive reports from ministers in case of physical or mental illness of the Emperor, and on his death or abdication declare a regency or proclaim the heir Emperor.

(i) Elect governors of states.

93. The National Assembly has no power to make new *constitutional*

laws, or annul the existing ones; it has no right to issue measures on any matter not listed as belonging within its competence.

94. The *National Assembly,* composed of men elected by the Russian people and representing them, assumes the character of their majesty. . . .

98. The National Assembly does not have authority to establish or to prohibit any denomination or sect. Faith, conscience, and views of citizens, so long as they do not violate any law, are not within the competence of the National Assembly. . . . The National Assembly has no authority to infringe freedom of speech or press. . . .

100. . . . Powers which this Constitution does not delegate to any of the herein designated assemblies or officials belong to the entire Russian people.

Chapter X. The Supreme Executive Power

101. The Emperor is the Supreme official of the Russian government. His rights and privileges are as follows:

(a) His power is hereditary in direct line from father to son, but from the father-in-law it passes to the son-in-law.

(b) In his person he concentrates the entire executive power.

(c) He has the right to halt the action of the legislative branch and to compel it to review the law.

(d) He is commander-in-chief of land and naval forces.

(e) He is the supreme chief of any branch of militia on active duty for the Empire.

(f) He may demand a written statement from chief officials of any executive department on any matter related to their duties.

(g) He negotiates and concludes peace treaties with foreign states with the advice and consent of two-thirds of the voting members of the Supreme Duma. A treaty concluded in this manner becomes a supreme law.

(h) He appoints ambassadors, ministers, and consuls, and represents Russia in all of her relations with foreign states. He appoints all officials not listed in this Constitution.

(i) He may not include in treaties any article that would violate rights and property of citizens within the Fatherland. Equally, without the consent of the National Assembly he may not include any provision to attack a country or to relinquish any territory belonging to Russia.

(j) He appoints judges to Supreme Court vacancies with the advice and consent of the Supreme Duma. . . .

(k) During the session of both chambers, he must present before the National Assembly a report on the state of Russia, and recommend to it adoption of measures which in his view are either indispensable or desirable.

(1) He has the right to call both Chambers into session, and [to convene] the Supreme Duma in case of treaty negotiations or impeachment.

(m) He may not use military forces inside Russia, in case of rebellion, without submitting a request concerning it to the National Assembly, which must satisfy itself through an immediate inquiry of the need for a state of siege. . . .

(n) He receives ambassadors and plenipotentiaries of foreign governments.

(o) He supervises the strict execution of public laws.

(p) He grants titles to all officials of the Empire.

(q) He is entitled His Imperial Majesty; no other title is permitted. . . .

(r) At his assumption of the reign, the Emperor takes the following oath in the National Assembly:

> I solemnly swear that I will faithfully execute the duties of Russian Emperor, and with all my might shall preserve and defend this Constitution of Russia.

(s) Members of the Imperial family are not distinguished from other individuals; they are subject to the same rules and the same acts of the government as all other [citizens], and enjoy no special rights or privileges. . . .

105. The ruler of the Empire cannot be absent from it without creating serious difficulties. . . .

106. The Emperor's departure from Russia is considered tantamount to his abandoning it and abdicating his imperial title; in such cases the National Assembly immediately proclaims the heir Emperor.

Excerpts from Pestel's Testimony

Until the age of twelve I was brought up in the home of my parents. In 1805, with my brother who is now Colonel in the Regiment of the Cavalier Guard, I went to Hamburg, and from there to Dresden, from where I returned in 1809 to my parents' home. During our absence from the fatherland, our education was guided by a certain Seidel, who, upon entering Russian service, was on the staff of General [Nicholas] Miloradovich in 1820. In 1810 I was assigned to the Corps of Pages,

From I. Ia. Shchipanov. ed. *Izbrannye sotsialno-politicheskie i filosofskie proizvedeniia dekabristov (Selected Socio-Political and Philosophical Works of the Decembrists)* (Moscow: Gospolitizdat, 1951), vol. 2, pp. 163–169, 187–188. Translation mine. Items in brackets are mine.

from which I graduated in 1811 as a lieutenant of the Lithuanian Life Guard [Regiment], which now is called the Moscow Life Guard Regiment. Until I began preparing for entrance to the Corps of Pages I had not the slightest conception of political sciences, whose understanding was required for admission to the upper class. I studied them then under Professor and Academician [Karl F.] Hermann [1767–1838], who at that time taught these sciences in the Corps of Pages.

After I left the Corps of Pages, military and political sciences interested me most, but I was fascinated primarily by political and then by military [matters].

During the winter of 1816–1817 I attended a course in political science [offered] by Professor and Academician Hermann in his quarters on Vasilevskii Island. I learned from him then very little that was new, because in his lectures he presented almost the same material that I already had heard from him at the Corps of Pages. The format of his lectures was different, but the subject matter was the same.

I cannot name any single individual who was responsible for imbuing me with free thinking and liberal ideas. Nor can I state definitely the time when these began to emerge, because this did not happen suddenly but little by little and in the beginning without making any great impression on me. I have the honor now to tell the [Investigating] Committee honestly and with complete frankness [how it all occurred]. After I received the fundamentals of political science I became infatuated. I had a burning desire and with all my heart I wished to do good. I saw that prosperity and disaster of kingdoms and peoples depends to a great extent on governments, and this belief directed me increasingly to those studies that discuss these problems and show the way to them. But in the beginning I was preoccupied with these studies as well as with the reading of political works in a good natured manner and without any freethinking, and with but just one aim: to be sometimes, at an appropriate time and place, a useful servant of the sovereign and of the fatherland.

This activity later induced me to think whether in the structure of the Russian government the rules of political science were observed or not. I did not question yet the supreme power, but thought only of ministers, of local government, of individual officials, and similar problems. I then discovered that there were many contradictions within the rules of political science, as I understood them, and I began to study various problems in depth; namely, what kind of decrees could change, supplement, or improve them. I also directed my thoughts and attention to the condition of the people, and serfdom affected me always very strongly, similarly as did the privileges enjoyed by the aristocracy. I considered the latter as a kind of wall between the monarch and the people— a wall which, for the sake of its own advantages, tried to hide from the monarch the true condition of the people. With time I began to develop thoughts on diverse topics and doctrines: namely, privileges of the annexed provinces; rumors about military colonies; the decline of trade, industry and general prosperity; lack of justice, and corruption of the courts and other departments; the burden of military service for soldiers; and many similar topics which, in my judgement, could contribute to individual dissatisfaction; and when I put these [problems] together I saw the whole picture of national poverty. Then a grumbling against the government began to emerge within me.

I believe that the turning point in my political views, understanding, and thinking, was the restoration of the House of Bourbon on the French throne. As I reflected on this development I began to realize that a majority of the basic propositions introduced by the revolution were not only retained at the restoration but were even acknowledged as useful; this in spite of the fact that everybody, including myself, had always been opposed to revolution. This led me to conclude that a revolution is really not as bad as they say, and that it can even be quite valuable. This thought led me, in turn, to another proposition; namely, that those states that did not have any revolution were deprived of similar privileges and institutions. These thoughts began then to merge with those noted earlier, and simultaneously they gave birth to constitutional and revolutionary thoughts. The constitutional [thoughts] were fully monarchial, while the revolutionary [thoughts] were rather weak and unclear. Slowly the former became fixed and clear, while the latter became strong. The reading of political books strengthened and developed within me all those thoughts, views, and understanding. The horrible consequences that occurred in France during the revolution forced me to seek means to prevent their occurrence [in Russia], and this led me to develop the idea of a provisional government as a necessary means to prevent civil war.

I moved from monarchial-constitutional to republican thinking as a result of the following facts and reflections: The work of Destute de Tracy [1754–1836], in French, exerted a powerful influence on me. He shows that every government wherein one person is the head of state, especially if it is hereditary, will inevitably end in despotism. All newspapers and political works so strongly applauded the growth of prosperity in the United States of America, Attributing it to the governmental structure, that it appeared to me as a clear indication that the republican form of government was superior [to all other forms].

[M. I.] Novikov [1777–1822] spoke to me about his republican constitution for Russia, but at the time I still favored monarchy; subsequently I began to recall his views and agreed with them. I recalled the glorious time of Greece when it was a republic and its pitiful condition thereafter. I compared the mighty glory of Republican Rome with its lamentable fate under the rule of emperors. The history of Great Novgorod likewise strengthened in me republican ideas. I discovered that in France and England, constitutions are only covers that in no way prevent English ministers or French kings from doing what they want. Because of this I preferred autocracy to such constitutions, for I thought that under the autocratic form of government the unlimited power [of the ruler] is open for everyone to see. In constitutional monarchies, on the other hand, there also exists limitless power, but it acts slowly, and as a result cannot quickly correct a mistake. As for the two chambers, they exist only as mere covers.

It seemed to me that the main trend of our times was the struggle between popular masses and all kinds of aristocracies, whether based on wealth or on hereditary rights. I thought that these aristocracies would ultimately emerge stronger than any monarch, as was true in England, that they represented the main obstacle to the prosperity of the state, and that they could be removed only by a republican form of government. Developments in Naples, Spain and Portugal then exerted a profound influence on me. I found in them the irrefutable proof of the instability of monarchial constitutions, and sufficient causes for distrusting the sincerity of the monarchs who accepted them. The latter considerations greatly strengthened my republican and revolutionary thinking.

From all that has been said, the Committee will note that I was influenced in developing my views by reading of books, by thinking of various developments, and also by exchanging my ideas with those of other members of the Society. All this led me to become a convinced republican, and I could not visualize any greater prosperity or higher aspiration for Russia than a republican form of government. When I discussed this problem with other members of the Society who asked my thoughts, visualizing the whole picture of happiness which Russia, in our judgment, would then enjoy, we all were excited to the point of ecstasy, and I and the other members were willing not only to agree to try everything but to do everything possible to strengthen and realize our system. We were very cautious to remove or to prevent every form of political chaos, disorder, or civil war, which I always considered to be an implacable enemy.

Having openly and candidly presented the development of my liberal and freethinking ideas, it is appropriate now to add that during the entire year 1825 my ideas became weak and I began to view things somewhat differently. It was, however, too late to turn back. I could not write the *Russkaia Pravda* [Russian Justice] as easily as before. They demanded that I finish it. I tried, but the work produced no results and I did not write anything during the entire year, but only corrected here and there what had already been written before. I was very frightened of civil war and internal chaos, and this problem cooled me off as it did also our aim. In our conversations I still would get excited, but only for a short time; everything was different than it formerly was. Finally, the fear that our Society had been discovered by the government brought me back

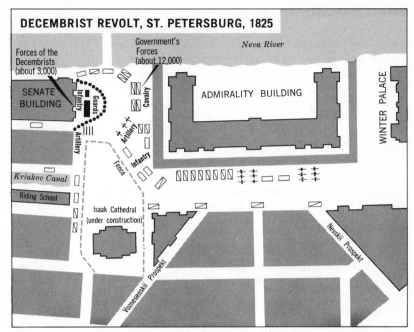

DECEMBRIST REVOLT, ST. PETERSBURG, 1825

into the movement. I did nothing serious, however, and remained with the regiment in complete inactivity until my arrest [on December 25, 1825]. . . .

In 1816 or 1817—I do not recall exactly where—during a discussion about the [Welfare] Society with me and Nikita Muraviev, [M. S.] Lunin spoke of executing a regicide on the road to Tsarskoe Selo, to be carried out by a group of masked members when the time should arrive to start the action. Whether Lunin or Nikita Muraviev informed anyone else about this I truly do not know. During meetings of the Society itself, Lunin's suggestion was never mentioned while I was present. I paid no attention to this suggestion at the moment because I thought that the time to begin a revolution was quite distant, and because I believed that it was first essential to prepare a constitution, and then write various decrees and regulations so that simultaneously with the outbreak of the revolution the new order could be fully introduced. I did not yet entertain any idea of a provisional government. On account of my beliefs, Lunin facetiously suggested that I planned to write an encyclopedia first and then start a revolution.

I was preoccupied with the elaboration of my constitution, more than with the realization of a revolution itself, though I frequently gave thoughts to that problem as well.

In conclusion I would like to state before the Committee that all the inadequacies that the Committee has noticed or may notice [in my testimony] are exclusively my own. They stem either from my perplexity or from lack of memory. They are not by-products of dishonesty, because with all my fortitude I have always tried to present all the facts very frankly and am now undeniably prepared to reveal everything that pertains to me. The proof that I always did everything candidly has never been more strongly demonstrated than now.

A Manifesto of Prince Trubetskoi

Lord save Thy people and give [them] Thy blessing.
    A Manifesto of the Senate makes hereby known that:
    1. The old government has been overthrown.
    2. A Provisional Government has assumed authority pending elections and formation of a new government.
    3. Freedom of the press [is hereby established] and accordingly censorship is abolished.
    4. Freedom of religious worship is extended to all religious faiths.
    5. Slavery is [hereby] abolished.
    6. Equality before the law of all social strata [is hereby established], and accordingly military courts and all kinds of judicial commissions whose decisions are brought before civil courts are hereby abolished.
    7. Every citizen has the right to make such a living as he wants, and therefore a nobleman, a merchant, city inhabitant and a peasant have the right to serve in the army, civil service, clergy, and engage in wholesale or retail trade upon payment of established sales taxes. [Everyone] has the right to acquire property such as land and homes in cities as well as villages. [Everyone] has the right to enter into relations with another and bring him [in case of a violation] before the court of justice.
    8. Collection of soul taxes is hereby discontinued.
    9. Monopolies on salt and hard liquor are hereby abolished, and accordingly free distilling and salt extraction is established with a tax on the amount of salt and of vodka produced.
    10. Recruiting systems and military colonies are hereby abolished.
    11. Reduction of the military service for lower social ranks is hereby established. The exact amount of military service will be set following the equalization of military obligation among all social strata.
    12. Everyone without exception who has served 15 years will be released from the military service.
    3. *Volost, uezd, gubernia* and *oblast* administrations are to replace all officials appointed by previous administration.
    14. Open courts are hereby established.

From *Vosstanie dekabristov. Materialy* (The Decembrist Uprising. Sources) (Moscow-Leningrad: Gosizdat, 1925), vol. 1, pp. 107–108. Translation mine. Items in brackets are mine.

15. Introduction of jurors in criminal and civil courts is hereby established.

A Provisional Government of two or three persons is established. To this government all branches of the central government—all Ministries, the Council, the Committee of Ministers, Army, and Fleet—are to be subordinated; that is, the entire executive but not the judicial or the legislative branches. The judicial branch will have its own ministry, subject to the Provisional Government, but cases not decided by lower courts will be handled by civil and criminal departments of the Senate which will pass final judgments. Members of these departments, until the new elected government shall take control, will be the same as they are now.

The Provisional Government is charged with solution of the following problems:

1. Equalization of the rights of all layers of society.

2. Organization of local *volost, uezd, gubernia* and *oblast* administrations.

3. Organization of domestic militia.

4. Organization of the judicial branch of the government with jurors.

5. Equalization of recruiting obligations among all social strata.

6. Abolition of the permanent army.

7. Devising of a system of election for the legislative branch, whose members will decide on the composition of the government and the nature of the fundamental law.

21

Nicholas I's Manifesto on Peasant Unrest, May 2, 1826

Although the Decembrist upheaval was primarily the work of young nobles, it stimulated activity among the Russian peasants, as they believed that if the revolution succeeded they would be freed from paying state taxes and from performing obligations to their masters. Nicholas I tried to deal with peasant unrest just as severely as with dissatisfaction among his officers. He was not very successful, in repressing it, however, for during his reign (1825–1855) Russia witnessed over 700 peasant uprisings, half of them serious enough to require military action. In fairness to Nicholas, it must be said that he paid more attention to the peasant problem than any previous tsar, and that his administration introduced a series of reforms, supervised by Count Paul D. Kiselev (1788–1872), aimed at improving the condition of state peasants.

Governors have called to Our attention that in some settlements peasants of the state and of the nobility, misled by malicious rumors and evil talk, digress from normal order and think that the former, that is, state peasants, will be freed from tax payments, while the latter, that is, peasants of the nobility, [will be freed] from their obligations to their masters.

Feeling sorry about the misleading of these villagers, and wishing to direct them to the truth by means of the kindness natural to Our fatherly mercy, I am ordering announced everywhere:

1. That all talk about freedom of state peasants from the payment of taxes and of the nobility peasants and household people from obligations

---

From *Polnoe Sobranie Zakonov Russkoi Imperii* . . . (Complete Collection of the Laws of the Russian Empire) 2nd series, vol. 1, no. 330, p. 455. Translation mine. Items in brackets are mine.

to their masters is a malicious rumor conceived and spread by ill-intended people for a profit motive, that is, to enrich themselves at peasant expense.

2. All social strata within the state, including state and nobility peasants and household people, should fulfill all of their obligations according to the law and obey their appointed superiors submissively.

3. After this declaration has been published, should there occur among state or nobility peasants or household people some disturbance based on a false rumor about freedom from payment of taxes or legal authority of the nobility, the guilty ones will invite Our anger and will be punished immediately to the fullest severity of the law.

4. Governors are hereby authorized to keep continuous vigilance and to bring the spreaders of such rumors or talk before the court without delay and deal with them likewise to the fullest severity of the law.

5. And inasmuch as We have received weekly petitions from peasants written on the basis of the above mentioned rumors and talk, to terminate this evil and to preserve safety and order, We decree that the composers or writers of such petitions be brought before the court as disturbers of general peace and punished to the fullest severity of the law.

The Governing Senate will make an appropriate regulation for the publication of Our order for universal knowledge, causing it to be read in churches on Sundays and Holy Days, at fairs and markets for a period of six months from the day this manifesto is received in the gubernia. Governors are, in addition, instructed to keep continuous vigilance in execution of Our order, as they will be personally responsible for any disorder that may occur.

Nicholas

22

Belinskii's Letter to Gogol, July 15, 1847

The period of uncompromising reaction, as the reign of Nicholas I is commonly known, witnessed great literary creativeness and a deep philosophical search for answers to questions of Russia's future. In literature the giant was Nikolai V. Gogol (1809–1852), author of *Dead Souls* and *Inspector General* —masterly portrayals of social, economic, and bureaucratic ills of Russian life. In criticism the leader was Vissarion G. Belinskii (1810–1848), Russia's greatest literary critic. Initially one of Gogol's warmest admirers, Belinskii introduced him to the Russian reading public as a realist who was clearly in touch with Russia's social and political conditions. However, when in 1847 Gogol published a collection of moralizing sermons entitled *Selected Passages from a Correspondence with Friends* advocating a return to conservative virtues and defending such Russian institutions as serfdom and autocracy, Belinskii broke with Gogol and denounced him bitterly. Belinskii's death in 1848 saved him from official persecution, but his letter to Gogol circulated widely and the Russian reading public came to know it by heart.

You are only partly right in regarding my article as that of an angered man: that epithet is too mild and inadequate to express the state to which I was reduced on reading your book. And you are entirely wrong in ascribing that state to your indeed none too flattering references to the admirers of your talent. No, there was a more important reason for this. One could suffer an outraged sense of self-esteem, and I would have had sense enough to let the matter pass in silence were that the whole gist of the matter; but one cannot suffer an outraged sense of truth and

---

Reprinted from V. G. Belinsky, *Selected Philosophical Works* (Moscow: Foreign Languages Publishing House, 1948), pp. 503–512.

human dignity; one cannot keep silent when lies and immorality are preached as truth and virtue under the guise of religion and the protection of the knout.

Yes, I loved you with all the passion with which a man, bound by ties of blood to his native country, can love its hope, its honour, its glory, one of the great leaders on its path of consciousness, development and progress. And you had sound reason for at least momentarily losing your equanimity when you forfeited that love. I say that not because I believe my love to be an adequate reward for a great talent, but because I do not represent a single person in this respect but a multitude of men, most of whom neither you nor I have ever set eyes on, and who, in their turn, have never set eyes on you. I find myself at a loss to give you an adequate idea of the indignation which your book has aroused in all noble hearts, and of the wild shouts of joy which were set up on its appearance by all your enemies—both the non-literary—the Chichikovs, the Nozdrevs and the mayors . . . and by the literary, whose names are well known to you. You see yourself that even those people who are of one mind with your book have disowned it. Even if it had been written as a result of deep and sincere conviction it could not have created any other impression on the public than the one it did. And it is nobody's fault but your own if everyone (except the few who must be seen and known in order not to derive pleasure from their approval) received it as an ingenious but all too unceremonious artifice for achieving a sheerly earthly aim by celestial means. Nor is that in any way surprising; what is surprising is that you find it surprising. I believe that is so because your profound knowledge of Russia is that of an artist but not of a thinker, whose role you have so ineffectually tried to play in your fantastic book. Not that you are not a thinker, but that you have been accustomed for so many years to look at Russia from your *beautiful far-away*; and who does not know that there is nothing easier than seeing things from a distance the way we want to see them; for in that *beautiful far-away* you live a life that is entirely alien to it, you live in and within yourself or within a circle of the same mentality as your own which is powerless to resist your influence on it. Therefore you failed to realize that Russia sees her salvation not in mysticism, nor asceticism, nor pietism, but in the successes of civilization, enlightenment and humanity. What she needs is not sermons (she has heard enough of them!) or prayers (she has repeated them too often!), but the awakening in the people of a sense of their human dignity lost for so many centuries amid the dirt and refuse; she needs rights and laws conforming not with the preaching of the church but with common sense and justice, and their strictest possible observance. Instead of which she presents the dire spectacle of a country where men traffic in men, without even having the excuse so insidiously exploited by the American plantation owners who claim that the Negro is not a

man: a country where people call themselves not by names but by
sobriquets, such as Vanka, Vaska, Steshka, Palashka; a country where
there are not only no guarantees for individuality, honour and property,
but even no police order, and where there is nothing but vast corpora-
tions of official thieves and robbers of various descriptions! The most
vital national problems in Russia today are the abolition of serfdom and
corporal punishments and the strictest possible observance of at least
those laws which already exist. This is even realized by the government
itself (which is well aware of how the landowners treat their peasants
and how many of the former are annually done away with by the latter),
as is proven by its timid and abortive half-measures for the relief of the
white Negroes and the comical substitution of the single-lash knout by
a cat-o'-three tails.

Such are the problems which prey on the mind of Russia in her
apathetic slumber! And at such a time a great writer, whose beautifully
artistic and deeply truthful works have so powerfully contributed towards
Russia's awareness of herself, enabling her as they did to take a look at
herself as though in a mirror—comes out with a book in which he teaches
the barbarian landowner in the name of Christ and Church to make still
greater profits out of the peasants and to abuse them still more. . . .
And you would expect me not to become indignant? . . . Why, if you
had made an attempt on my life I could not have hated you more than
I do for these disgraceful lines. . . . And after this, you expect people
to believe the sincerity of your book's intent! No! Had you really been
inspired by the truth of Christ and not by the teaching of the Devil
you would certainly have written something entirely different in your
new book. You would have told the landowner that since his peasants
are his brethren in Christ, and since a brother cannot be a slave to his
brother, he should either give them their freedom, or, at least, allow
them to enjoy the fruits of their own labour to their greatest possible
benefit, realizing as he does, in the depths of his own conscience the
false relationship in which he stands towards them.

And the expression: "*Oh, you unwashed snout, you!*" From what
Nozdrev and Sobakevich did you overhear this, to give to the world as a
great discovery for the edification and benefit of the muzhiks, whose only
reason for not washing is that they have let themselves be persuaded by
their masters that they are not human beings? And your conception of
the national Russian system of trial and punishment, whose ideal you
have found in the foolish saying that both the guilty and innocent should
be flogged alike? That, indeed, is often the case with us, though more
often than not it is the man who is in the right who takes the punishment, unless he can ransom himself, and for such occasions another
proverb says: *guiltlessly guilty!* And such a book is supposed to have been
the result of an arduous inner process, a lofty spiritual enlightenment!

Impossible! Either you are ill—and you must hasten to take a cure, or
. . . I am afraid to put my thought into words! . . .

Proponent of the knout, apostle of ignorance, champion of obscurant-
ism and Stygian darkness, panegyrist of Tatar morals—what are you
about! Look beneath your feet—you are standing on the brink of an
abyss! . . . That you base such teaching on the Orthodox Church I can
understand: it has always served as the prop of the knout and the servant
of despotism; but why have you mixed Christ up in this? What in common have you found between Him and any church, least of all the
Orthodox Church? He was the first to bring to people the teaching of
freedom, equality, and brotherhood and set the seal of truth to that
teaching by martyrdom. And this teaching was men's *salvation* only until
it became organized in the Church and took the principle of Orthodoxy
for its foundation. The Church, on the other hand, was a hierarchy consequently a champion of inequality, a flatterer of authority, an enemy
and persecutor of brotherhood among men—and so it has remained to
this day. But the meaning of Christ's message has been revealed by the
philosophical movement of the preceding century. And that is why a man
like Voltaire who stamped out the fires of fanaticism and ignorance in
Europe by ridicule, is, of course, more the son of Christ, flesh of his
flesh and bone of his bone, than all your priests, bishops, metropolitans
and patriarchs! Do you mean to say you do not know it! It is not even
a novelty now to a schoolboy. . . . Hence, can it be that you, the author of *Inspector General* and *Dead Souls,* have in all sincerity, from the
bottom of your heart, sung a hymn to the nefarious Russian clergy which
you rank immeasurably higher than the Catholic clergy? Let us assume
that you do not know that the latter had once been something, while
the former had never been anything but a servant and slave of the secular
powers; but do you really mean to say you do not know that our clergy
is held in universal contempt by Russian society and the Russian people?
Of whom do the Russian people relate obscene stories? Of the priest, the
priest's wife, the priest's daughter and the priest's farm hand. Does not
the priest in Russia represent for all Russians the embodiment of glut-
tony, avarice, servility and shamelessness? Do you mean to say that you
do not know all this? Strange! According to you the Russian people is
the most religious in the world. That is a lie! The basis of religiousness
is pietism, reverence, fear of God. Whereas the Russian man utters the
name of the Lord while scratching himself somewhere. He says of the
icon: *if it isn't good for praying it's good for covering the pots.*

Take a closer look and you will see that it is by nature a profoundly
atheistic people. It still retains a good deal of superstition, but not a
trace of religiousness. Superstition passes with the advances of civilization, but religiousness often keeps company with them too; we have a
living example of this in France, where even today there are many sin-

cere Catholics among enlightened and educated men, and where many people who have rejected Christianity still cling stubbornly to some sort of god. The Russian people is different; mystic exaltation is not in its nature; it has too much common sense, a too lucid and positive mind, and therein, perhaps, lies the vast scope of its historic destinies in the future. Religiousness with it has not even taken root among the clergy, since a few isolated and exclusive personalities distinguished for such cold ascetic reflectiveness prove nothing. The majority of our clergy has always been distinguished for their fat bellies, scholastic pedantry and savage ignorance. It is a shame to accuse it of religious intolerance and fanaticism; rather could it be praised for an exemplary indifference in matters of faith. Religiousness with us appeared only among the Schismatic sects who formed such a contrast in spirit to the mass of the people and were so insignificant before it numerically.

I shall not dilate on your panegyric to the affectionate relations existing between the Russian people and its lords and masters. I shall say point-blank: that panegyric has met sympathy nowhere and has lowered you even in the eyes of people who in other respects stand very close to you in outlook. As far as I am concerned, I leave it to your conscience to admire the divine beauty of the autocracy (it is both safe and profitable), but continue to admire it judiciously from your *beautiful far-away*: at close quarters it is not so attractive, and not so safe. . . . I would remark but this: when a European, especially a Catholic, is seized with a religious ardour he becomes a denouncer of iniquitous authority, similar to the Hebrew prophets who denounced the iniquities of the great ones of the earth. With us on the contrary: no sooner is a person (even a reputable person) afflicted with the malady which is known to psychiatrists as *religiosa mania* then he begins to burn more incense to the earthly god than the heavenly one, and so overshoots the mark in doing so that the former would fain reward him for his slavish zeal did he not perceive that he would thereby be compromising himself in society's eyes. . . . What a rogue our fellow the Russian is! . . .

Another thing I remember you saying in your book, claiming it to be a great and incontrovertible truth, that literacy is not merely useless but positively harmful to the common people. What can I say to this? May your Byzantine God forgive you that Byzantine thought, unless, in committing it to paper, you knew not what you were saying. . . . But perhaps you will say: "Assuming that I have erred and that all my ideas are false, why should I be denied the right to err and why should people doubt the sincerity of my errors?" Because, I would say in reply, such a tendency has long ceased to be a novelty in Russia. Not so very long ago it was drained to the lees by Burachok and his fraternity. Of course, your book shows a good deal more intellect and talent (though neither of these elements is very richly represented) than their works; but then they have developed your common doctrine with greater energy and greater consistence, they have boldly reached its ultimate conclusions, have rendered full meed to the Byzantine God and left nothing for Satan, whereas you, wanting to light a taper to each of them, have fallen into contradiction, upholding for example, Pushkin, literature and the theatre, all of which, in your opinion, if you were only conscientious enough to be consistent, can in no way serve the salvation of the soul but can do a lot towards its damnation. . . . Whose head could have digested the idea of Gogol's identity with Burachok? You have placed yourself too high in the regard of the Russian public for it to be able to believe you sincere in such convictions. What seems natural in fools cannot seem so in a man of genius. Some people have been inclined to regard your book as the result of mental derangement verging on sheer madness. But they soon rejected such a supposition, for clearly that book was not written in a single day, or week, or month, but very likely in one, two or three years; it shows coherence; through its careless exposition one glimpses premeditation, and the hymn to the powers that be nicely arranges the earthly affairs of the devout author. That is why a rumour has been current in St. Petersburg to the effect that you have written this book with the aim of securing a position as tutor to the son of the heir-apparent. Before that, your letter to Uvarov became known in St. Petersburg, wherein you say that you are grieved to find that your works about Russia are misinterpreted; then you evince dissatisfaction with your previous works and declare that you will be pleased with your own works only when the tsar is pleased with them. Now judge for yourself, is it to be wondered at that your book has lowered you in the eyes of the public both as a writer and still more as a man? . . .

You, as far as I can see, do not properly understand the Russian public. Its character is determined by the condition of Russian society, in which fresh forces are seething and struggling for expression but, weighed down by heavy oppression and finding no outlet, they induce merely dejection, weariness and apathy. Only literature, despite the Tatar censorship, shows signs of life and progressive movement. That is why the title of writer is held in such esteem among us, that is why literary success is easy among us even for a writer of small talent. The title of poet and writer has long since eclipsed the tinsel of epaulettes and gaudy uniforms. And that especially explains why every so-called liberal tendency, however poor in talent, is rewarded by universal notice, and why the popularity of great talents which sincerely or insincerely give themselves to the service of orthodoxy, autocracy, and nationality declines so quickly. A striking example is Pushkin who had merely to write two or three verses in a loyal strain and don the *kamer-junker's* livery to suddenly forfeit the popular affection! And you are greatly mistaken if you believe in all earnest that your book has come to grief not because of its bad trend, but because of

the harsh truths alleged to have been expressed by you about all and
everybody. Assuming you could think that of the writing fraternity, but
then how do you account for the public? Did you tell it less bitter home
truths less harshly and with less truth and talent in *Inspector General*
and *Dead Souls?* Indeed the old school was worked up to a furious pitch
of anger against you, but *Inspector General* and *Dead Souls* were not
affected by it, whereas your latest book has been an utter and disgraceful
failure. And here the public is right, for it looks upon Russian writers as
its only leaders, defenders, and saviours against Russian autocracy, orthodoxy, and nationality; and therefore, while always prepared to forgive a
writer a bad book, will never forgive him a pernicious book. This shows
how much fresh and healthy intuition, albeit still in embryo, is latent in
our society, and this likewise proves that it has a future. If you love
Russia rejoice with me at the failure of your book! . . .

I would tell you, not without a certain feeling of self-satisfaction, that
I believe I know the Russian public a little. Your book alarmed me by
the possibility of its exercising a bad influence on the government and
the censorship, but not on the public. When it was rumoured in St.
Petersburg that the government intended to publish your book in many
thousands of copies, and to sell it at an extremely low price, my friends
grew despondent; but I told them there and then that the book, despite
everything, would have no success and would soon be forgotten. In fact
it is now better remembered for the articles which have been written
about it than for the book itself. Yes, the Russian has a deep, though
still undeveloped instinct for truth.

Your conversion may conceivably have been sincere, but your idea of
bringing it to the notice of the public was a most unhappy one. The days
of naive piety have long since passed, even in our society. It already
understands that it makes no difference where one prays, and that the
only people who seek Christ and Jerusalem are those who have never
carried Him in their breasts or who have lost Him. He who is capable of
suffering at the sight of other people's sufferings and who is pained at
the sight of other people's oppression, bears Christ within his bosom and
has no need to make a pilgrimage to Jerusalem. The humility which you
preach is, first of all, not novel, and, secondly, savours on the one hand
of prodigious pride, and on the other of the most shameful degradation
of one's human dignity. The idea of becoming a sort of abstract perfection, of rising above everyone else in humility, is the fruit of either pride
or imbecility, and in either case leads inevitably to hypocrisy, sancti-
moniousness and Chinaism. Moreover, in your book you have taken the
liberty of expressing yourself with gross cynicism not only of other people
(that would be merely impolite) but of yourself—and that is vile, for
if a man who strikes his neighbour on the cheek evokes indignation, the
sight of a man striking himself on the cheek evokes contempt. No, you
are not illuminated, you are simply beclouded; you have failed to grasp

either the spirit or the form of Christianity of our time. Your book breathes not the true Christian teaching but the morbid fear of death, of the devil, and of hell!

And what language, what phrases? "Every man hath now become trash and a rag"—do you really believe that in saying *hath* instead of *has* you are expressing yourself biblically? How eminently true it is that when a man gives himself wholly up to lies, intelligence and talent desert him. Did not this book bear your name, who would have thought that this turgid and squalid bombast was the work of the author of *Inspector General* and *Dead Souls*?

As far as it concerns myself, I repeat: you are mistaken in taking my article to be an expression of vexation at your comment on me as one of your critics. Were this the only thing to make me angry I would have reacted with annoyance to this alone and would have dealt with all the rest with unruffled impartiality. But it is true that your criticism of your admirers is doubly bad. I understand the necessity of sometimes having to rap a silly man whose praises and ecstasies make the object of his worship look ridiculous, but even this is a painful necessity, since, humanly speaking, it is somehow awkward to reward even false affection with enmity. But you had in view men who, though not brilliantly clever, are not quite fools. These people, in their admiration of your works, have probably uttered more ejaculations than talked sense about them; still, their enthusiastic attitude toward you springs from such a pure and noble source that you ought not to have betrayed them neck and crop to both your common enemies and accused them into the bargain of wanting to misinterpret your works. You, of course, did that while carried away by the main idea of your book and through indiscretion, while Vyazemsky, that prince in aristocracy and helot in literature, developed your idea and printed a personal denunciation against your admirers (and consequently mostly against me). He probably did this to show his gratitude to you for having exalted him, the poetaster, to the rank of great poet, if I remember rightly for his "pithless, dragging verse." That is all very bad. That you were merely biding your time in order to give the admirers of your talent their due as well (after having given it with proud humility to your enemies)—I was not aware; I could not, and, I must confess, did not want to know it. It was your book that lay before me and not your intentions: I read and reread it a hundred times, but I found nothing in it that was not there, and what was there deeply offended and incensed my soul.

Were I to give free rein to my feelings this letter would probably grow into a voluminous notebook. I never thought of writing you on this subject though I longed to do so and though you gave all and sundry printed permission to write you without ceremony with an eye to the truth alone. Were I in Russia I would not be able to do it, for the local "Shpekins" open other people's letters not merely for their own pleasure but as a matter of official duty, for the sake of informing. This summer incipient consumption has driven me abroad, [and Nekrasov has forwarded me your letter to Salzbrunn which I am leaving today with Annenkov for Paris via Frankfort-on-Main]. The unexpected receipt of your letter has enabled me to unburden my soul of what has accumulated there against you on account of your book. I cannot express myself by halves, I cannot prevaricate; it is not in my nature. Let you or time itself prove to me that I am mistaken in my conclusions. I shall be the first to rejoice in it, but I shall not repent what I have told you. This is not a question of your or my personality, it concerns a matter which is of greater importance than myself or even you; it is a matter which concerns the truth, Russian society, and Russia. And this is my last concluding word: If you have had the misfortune of disowning with proud humility your truly great works, you should now disown with sincere humility your last book, and atone for the dire sin of its publication by new creations which would be reminiscent of your old ones.

Salzbrunn, July 15, 1847.

23

Program of the Society of Sts. Cyril and Methodius

While the government of Nicholas I officially pursued "autocracy, orthodoxy and nationality," the educated public unofficially debated three divergent currents of thought: *Westernism,* whose advocates followed with keen interest the social, economic, and political, as well as the artistic, literary, and revolutionary developments of Western Europe; *Slavophilism,* whose followers, inspired by romantic nationalism, extolled the imaginary virtues of a truly

The following text of the program of the Society of Sts. Cyril and Methodius and two of its appeals are from *Byloe (The Past),* no. 2 (February 1906), pp. 66–68. Translation mine. Items in brackets are mine.

Russian national way; and *Pan-Slav Federalism*, whose adherents advocated cultural and political freedom for all Slavic peoples within a Slavic federation. The Westerners and Slavophiles were predominantly Russian nationals who advocated their ideas quite openly. The Pan-Slav Federalists, with a mixed membership of Russians and Ukrainians, operated secretly. In 1846 the Pan-Slav Federalists organized a society or brotherhood of Sts. Cyril and Methodius. As its name indicates, its ideas of Slavic solidarity were strongly based on religious grounds. In 1847 authorities arrested the leaders of the society and, because of his outspoken criticism of serfdom and autocracy, singled out for especially harsh treatment Taras Shevchenko (1814–1861), a liberated serf and the greatest Ukrainian poet.

Statute and Rules of the Cyril-Methodius Society

Main Ideas

1. We believe that spiritual and political unity of Slavs is their true destiny toward which they all should strive.

2. We believe that after the unification each Slavic nation should have its own independence. We recognize the following [Slavic] nations: South Russians, North Russians and Belorussians, Poles, Czechs and Slovaks; Lusatians, Illirian Serbs and Croats, and Bulgars.

3. We believe that every nation should have its own national government and should subscribe to complete equality of citizens regardless of their birth, religious belief, or social status.

4. We believe that governments, laws, right of private property, and education of all the Slavs should be based on the teachings of the Holy religion of Our Lord Jesus Christ.

5. We believe that under such equality both education and moral standards should serve as a basis for participation in the affairs of government.

6. We believe that there should exist a general Slavic Assembly consisting of representatives of all [Slavic] nations.

Basic Rules of the Society

1. We are organizing a society whose basic aim is to disseminate the above stated ideas, primarily through the education of youth, through literature, and through the increase of membership of the society. The

society selects as its patrons the saintly educators Cyril and Methodius, and accepts as its symbol a chain link and an icon with the name or image of these saints.

2. Upon joining the society every member will take an oath pledging gifts, work, fortune, and public contacts to attain the aims of the society; and should he undergo persecution or even torture for ideas advocated by the society, after taking the oath, no member is allowed to compromise other members who are his brothers.

3. In case a member falls into enemy hands and leaves behind a needy family the society will help it.

4. Every member who joins the society can opt a new member without revealing to him the names of other members of the society.

5. Slavs of all nations and occupations are eligible to become members of the society.

6. Absolute equality must prevail among members of the society.

7. Because Slavic nations currently profess diverse religious faiths and have national prejudices against each other, the society will strive to remove all national and religious animosities among them and will disseminate among them the idea that differences among Christian churches may possibly be accommodated.

8. The society will strive to eliminate at the earliest possible moment serfdom and all other forms of discrimination against lower classes, and at the same time will seek to spread literacy everywhere.

9. The society as a whole and every member individually should base their activity on Christian principles of love, kindness and suffering. The society considers godless the maxim that the end justifies the means.

10. Those members of the society who live in a given area may hold their own meetings and adopt their own rules to guide their activity. These rules, however, should not contradict the basic ideas and rules of the society.

11. No members shall reveal the existence and composition of the society to those who are neither joining it nor have expressed any desire of joining it.

Appeals of the Society

Brother Ukrainians!

We present for your consideration the following statements. Consider whether these points are beneficial:

1. We believe that all Slavs should unite.

2. But [at the same time we believe that] every nation should be an independent republic and should govern itself independently; that every nation should use its own language and its literature; and that it should

have its own political system. We recognize the following nations [in the future Pan-Slav Union]: Great Russians, Ukrainians, Poles, Czechs, Lusatians, Croats, Illirian Serbs and Bulgars.

3. There should be organized a parliament or a Slavic Assembly where deputies would come from all Slavic republics and would deliberate and decide on matters that affect the entire Slavic Union.

4. Every republic should have its own administrator elected for a specified period of time. The union as a whole should have a similar administrator also elected for a specified period of time.

5. Universal equality and freedom should prevail in every republic and classes should be abolished everywhere.

6. Elected representatives and other officials [in every republic] should be chosen by the people not on the basis of birth or property qualification but by virtue of their intelligence and education.

7. Christian belief should be the foundation for legislation and public order in the Union as a whole as well as in every republic.

Here, brother Ukrainians, inhabitants of the Ukraine on both sides of the Dnieper [River], we offer you this for your consideration. Read it carefully and let each individual decide how best to accomplish all this or even to improve it. There is a proverb that says where there are many heads there is also much wisdom. Think seriously about all this, and when the time comes for you to express yourself God will endow you with reason and understanding.

Great Russian and Polish Brothers!

This appeal to you comes from the Ukraine, your younger sister whom you have crucified and divided, but who not only wants to forget this evil but who actually sympathizes with your misfortunes and is ready to shed the blood of her children for your freedom. Read this brotherly appeal, consider the vital matter of your own salvation, and awake from your dream and drowsiness. Eliminate in your hearts the foolish hatred toward one another, as this hatred was implanted there by the Tsars and masters in order to eliminate our freedom. Become ashamed of the yoke which you carry on your shoulders, become ashamed of your corruption. Place a curse on the sacrilegious name of the earthly tsar and the landlord. Abandon the spirit of distrust which you have acquired from German and Latin nations. Abandon the spirit of stubbornness which the Tartars have implanted in you. Adopt Slavic natural love toward mankind, and remember also your brothers who are still oppressed either in the silk chains of the Germans or under the rule of the Turks. Let the following be the aim of life of every one of you: Slavic Union, universal equality, brotherhood, peace and love of Our Lord Jesus Christ. Amen.

24

Herzen's Letter to Michelet, September 22, 1851

Nineteenth-century Russian society produced a galaxy of dedicated revolutionaries and profound revolutionary thinkers. The most honored and respected among the latter is Alexander I. Herzen (1812–1870). The son of a wealthy nobleman, Herzen attended the University of Moscow where he actively participated in student debates and where he emerged as a forceful spokesman for the Russian Westernizers. Herzen's early radical views were variously influenced by the ideas of the French enlightenment, French utopian socialism, and German idealistic philosophy. To escape persecution Herzen went into voluntary exile in 1847, first to Paris, then to Italy, London, Geneva, and again to Paris, where he died on January 21, 1870. His writings exerted a strong influence on Russian political thought, and it has been reported that Alexander II himself (1855–1881) read Herzen's newspaper, *Kolokol* (The Bell), which was published in London. While in exile Herzen became acquainted with many of the leading European revolutionaries, debated various issues with them and, under the impact of the experience, evolved his own theory of Russian socialism based on the peasant commune. This theory laid the ideological foundation for the revolutionary populism which, until 1917, inspired much of the activity of the Russian radical intelligentsia.

Dear Sir,

You are held in such high esteem by all thinking men, and every word which comes from your noble pen is received by European democracy with such complete and merited confidence that I cannot remain silent

From Alexander Herzen, *Selected Philosophical Works* (Moscow: Foreign Languages Publishing House, 1956), pp. 470–501.

in a matter that concerns my deepest convictions. I cannot leave un-answered the description of the Russian people which you have given in your legend of Kosciuszko.

I deem this answer necessary also for another reason. The time has come to show Europe that they cannot speak about Russia as of some-thing mute, absent, and defenceless.

We, who have left Russia for the sole purpose of bringing free Russian speech to the ears of Europe at last, are on the spot and consider it our duty to raise our voice when a man with so great and deserved an au-thority affirms that "Russia does not exist," that "Russians are not human, that they lack any moral sense."

If by this you mean to disparage official Russia, the tsardom façade, the Byzantine-German Government, you are welcome to do so. We agree beforehand with everything you tell us—we do not feel called upon to take up arms in its defence. The Russian Government has so many agents in the press that it will never lack eloquent apologies for its actions.

But it is not official society alone that is treated in your work; you go deeper into the question: you speak of the people itself.

Poor Russian people! There is no one to raise a voice in its defence! Judge whether I can under the circumstances remain silent.

The Russian people, my dear sir, exists: strong, vigorous, and not old—indeed, very young. Men happen to die even in their youth, but it is not the usual thing.

The past of the Russian people is obscure, its present is frightful, but it has claims on the future. It does not *believe* in the immutability of its present state. It has the boldness to expect much from the future, having received so little in the past.

The period which has been the hardest for the Russian people is drawing to its close. A terrible conflict awaits them; their enemies are making ready.

The great question, "to be or not to be," will soon be decided for Russia. But we have no right to despair of success before the fight has begun.

The Russian question is assuming enormous and disquieting propor-tions; it becomes a matter of grave concern to all parties; I think, how-ever, that too much attention is being paid to imperial Russia, to official Russia, and too little to the voiceless Russia of the people.

Even considering Russia solely from the point of view of the govern-ment, do you not think it worthwhile to become better acquainted with such a troublesome neighbour who makes himself felt in every corner of Europe, in one place with bayonets, in another with spies? The Russian Government has spread out to the Mediterranean by protecting the Ottoman Empire, to the Rhine by protecting its German uncles and relatives-in-law, and to the Atlantic by maintaining *order* in France.

It would not be amiss, I repeat, to appraise this universal protector at its true value, to enquire whether this strange state is destined to play no other part than that assumed by the Petersburg Government—the ignoble part of a barrier continually blocking the path of human progress.

Europe is approaching a terrible cataclysm. The medieval world is crumbling into ruins. The end of the feudal world is drawing near. Political and religious revolutions are flagging under the weight of their own impotence; they have accomplished great things, but have not proved equal to their tasks. They have stripped the throne and the altar of their prestige, but have not realized the ideal of freedom; they have kindled in men's hearts desires which they are incapable of satisfying. Parliamentarism, Protestantism, are but stopgaps, temporary harbours, untenable bulwarks against death and resurrection. Their day is over. Since 1849, it has become evident that neither Roman law, nor subtle casuistry, nor threadbare philosophic deism, nor sterile religious rationalism, can retard the fulfilment of social destiny.

The storm is approaching, there is no denying it. Revolutionaries and reactionaries are at one about that. Everyone's mind is perturbed; the difficult, vital question oppresses the hearts of all. With growing uneasiness people ask themselves whether old Europe, that decrepit Proteus, that decaying organism, still has a chance to survive. The answer is awaited with misgivings and the suspense is terrible.

It is, indeed, a fearful question! Will old Europe have the strength to infuse new blood into its veins and fling itself headlong into the boundless future, to which it is being precipitously borne by an irresistible force over the ruins of its ancestral home, the fragments of past civilizations, and the trampled treasures of modern culture?

The full gravity of the moment has been fully appreciated by both sides; Europe is plunged in that stifling gloom which precedes the decisive conflict. It is not life, but an oppressive, agonizing suspense. There is no regard for law, no justice, not a ghost of freedom; everywhere the sway of the secular inquisition is supreme; instead of legality, there is a state of siege, all are governed by a single feeling—fear, and there is plenty of it. Every question is overshadowed by the interests of reaction. Governments, apparently most hostile, are united into a single world-wide police. The Russian Emperor rewards the Prefect of the Paris police without concealing his hatred for the French; the King of Naples bestows a decoration on the President of the Republic. The Prussian King dons the Russian uniform and hastens to Warsaw to embrace his foe, the Emperor of Austria, with the benediction of Nikolai; while the latter, that schismatic of the one church of salvation, proffers his aid to the Pope of Rome. In the midst of these saturnalia, this Sabbath of reaction, nothing can safeguard freedom from the caprices of tyranny. Even the guarantees which exist in the less developed societies—in China or Persia, for instance, are no longer respected in the capitals of the so-called civilized world.

One can hardly believe one's eyes. Can this be the Europe which we once knew and loved?

Indeed, if it were not for free and proud England, "this precious stone set in the silver sea," if Switzerland were to renounce its principles like Peter, in fear of Caesar, and if, finally Piedmont, that only free branch still left of Italy, the last refuge of freedom hounded beyond the Alps and unable to cross the Apennines, were to be led astray by the example of her neighbours and infected by the deleterious spirit being blown from Paris and Vienna, the conservatives might be thought to have succeeded in bringing the old world to its final disintegration and the days of barbarism to have returned to France and Germany.

In the midst of this chaos, of these agonies of death and throes of birth, in the midst of a world falling into dust at the foot of the cradle of the future, men's eyes involuntarily turn to the East.

Yonder a hostile, menacing empire looms up through the mists like a dark mountain; at times it seems as though it is advancing on Europe like an avalanche, and that like an impatient heir it is ready to hasten her tardy death.

This empire, absolutely unknown two-hundred years ago, has suddenly made its appearance, and, uninvited, uncalled-for, has peremptorily raised its voice in the council of European powers, demanding a share in the booty won without its assistance.

No one has dared to contest its claims to interference in the affairs of Europe. Once Charles XII tried to do so, but his sword, hitherto invincible, was broken: Frederick II attempted to resist the claims of the Petersburg Court; Königsberg and Berlin became the prey of his northern foe. Napoleon who at the head of an army half a million strong, penetrated to the very heart of the giant, had to flee alone in the first peasant sledge he came upon. Europe gazed with astonishment at Napoleon's flight, at the swarms of Cossacks racing in pursuit of him, at the Russian troops marching on to Paris, incidentally presenting the Germans with their national independence on their way there. Vampire-like, Russia has since been lying in wait to catch the mistakes of the people and the kings. Yesterday she almost crushed Austria assisting her against Hungary; tomorrow she will proclaim Brandenburg a Russian province to conciliate the Prussian King.

Is it credible that on the very eve of the great conflict nothing should be known of this combatant? There he stands fully armed and menacing, prepared to cross the frontier at the first summons of reaction, yet people scarcely know his weapons, or the colour of his flag, and are satisfied with his official speeches and the vague, contradictory tales that are told of him.

Some tell us only of the omnipotence of the Tsar, the insolence of his arbitrary government, and the slavishness of his subjects; others assert that, on the contrary, the imperialism of Petersburg has nothing in common with the people, which, oppressed by the double despotism of the government and the landowners, is not resigned to the yoke it bears and is not crushed, but only unfortunate. They also declare that this very people cements the colossus of tsardom which crushes it. Some add that the Russian people is a *rabble of knaves and drunkards*, while others maintain that Russia is inhabited by an industrious and richly gifted race. It seems to me that there is something tragic in the senile heedlessness with which the old world mixes up the different accounts it hears of its antagonist. This medley of contradictory opinions contains so much senseless repetition, distressing superficiality, and tenacious prejudice, that a comparison with the days of the fall of Rome invariably suggests itself. . . .

You have performed a great service: you were the first in France to speak of the people of Russia, and you have, unawares, touched on the very heart, the very source of life. The truth would have stood revealed to you immediately if you had not, in a moment of anger, pulled back your outstretched hand and turned away from the source because its waters were troubled.

It hurt and saddened me to read your bitter words. It is in vain that I tried to discover in them the historian, the philosopher, and, above all, the tender-hearted man whom we all know and love. I hasten to add that I fully realize the cause of your indignation: sympathy for unhappy Poland prompted your words. We, too, feel deeply with our Polish brothers, and our feeling is not merely one of compassion, but of shame and remorse. Love for Poland! We all love her—but must one absolutely combine that feeling with hatred for another people equally unhappy, a people forced to aid with its fettered hands the crimes of its atrocious government? Let us be just! Let us not forget that the nation benefited by all the trophies of the recent revolution has acquiesced in the establishment of *order* in Rome. And today? Take a look and see what is going on around you. Yet we do not say that the French *have ceased to be human*, do we?

It is time to forget this unhappy conflict between brethren. Neither side was victorious. Poland and Russia have succumed to a common foe. Even the victims and the martyrs turn their backs upon the past, which is equally sorrowful for them as it is for us. Let me cite, as you do, your friend, the great poet Mickiewicz.

Do not say of the Polish bard's opinions that they are "due to mercifulness, to a sacred delusion." No; they are the fruits of long and conscientious meditation and a profound understanding of the destinies of the Slav world. It is beautiful to forgive one's enemies but there is something even more beautiful and humane: to understand one's enemies, for understanding is at one and the same time forgiveness, justification, and reconciliation.

The Slav world is striving towards unity. That tendency became apparent immediately after the Napoleonic period. The idea of Slavonic federation had already taken shape in the revolutionary plans of Pestel and Muravyov. Many Poles had a hand in the Russian conspiracy of December 1825.

When the Revolution of 1830 broke out in Warsaw, the Russian people displayed not the slightest animosity against the rebellious subjects of their Tsar. The sympathy of our youth was most heartfelt. I remember with what impatience we awaited tidings from Warsaw; we cried like children at the news of the memorial services held in the capital of Poland for our Petersburg martyrs. Sympathy for the Poles exposed us to the risk of cruel punishment so that we were forced to conceal it in our hearts and remain silent.

I admit that during the war of 1830 a feeling of exclusive nationalism and quite natural hostility probably prevailed in Poland. But since those days the influence of Mickiewicz, the historical and philological studies of many Slav scholars, a closer knowledge of other European nations, purchased at the hard price of exile, has given a very different turn to Polish thought. The Poles have come to realize that the real issue lies not between the Russian people and themselves: they have learned that henceforth the only way to fight is to fight *for their freedom and ours,* as the inscription on their revolutionary banner reads.

Konarski, who was tortured and shot by Nicholas at Vilna, called upon Russians and Poles, regardless of their nationality, to rise in revolt. Russia showed her gratitude by one of those tragedies which hardly ever come to light and by which every heroic action of ours ends under the German jackboot.

Karavayev, an army officer, resolved to save Konarski. His turn to be on duty was not far off and everything was prepared for the escape, but the treachery of one of the Polish martyr's comrades brought his plans to nought. The young man was arrested and sent to Siberia, and nothing has been heard of him since.

I spent five years in exile in the remote provinces of the empire. There I met many Polish exiles. Almost in every uyezd town there is either a whole group, or at least one of the luckless champions of independence. I would gladly appeal to their evidence; certainly they cannot complain of lack of sympathy on the part of the people around them. Of course, I do not include the police or members of the higher military hierarchy among them. They are nowhere conspicuous for their love of freedom, and least of all in Russia. I might appeal to the Polish students sent annually to Russian universities to remove them from the influence of their native land; let them describe the way they were received by their Russian comrades. They parted from us with tears in their eyes.

You remember that when in 1847 the Polish emigrants in Paris celebrated the anniversary of their revolution, a Russian mounted the platform to plead for their friendship and ask forgiveness for the past. That was our unhappy friend Bakunin. But not to quote my fellow-countrymen, I will, for evidence on this subject, choose one of those who is counted among our enemies, a man whom you have yourself mentioned in your legend of Kosciuszko. I mean one of the veterans of the Polish democracy, Biernacki, a minister of revolutionary Poland. I boldly appeal to him, though long years of grief might well have embittered him against everything Russian. I am convinced that he will confirm all that I have said.

There is no denying the solidarity binding Russia and Poland to each other and to the whole Slav world—it is so obvious. There is, indeed, no future for the Slav world apart from Russia. Without Russia it will not develop, it will fall to pieces and be absorbed by the German element; it will become Austrian and lose its independence. But that in our opinion is not what it is destined for.

Following the gradual development of your idea, I must confess that I cannot agree with your view of Europe as a single individual in which every nationality plays the part of an essential organ.

It seems to me that all the German-Latin nationalities are essential to the European world because they exist in it by virtue of some necessity. Aristotle long ago drew a distinction between pre-existent necessity and subsequent necessity; nature accepts the inevitability of the accomplished fact, though the range of various possibilities is very great. By the same token the Slav world can lay its claim to unity, especially since it is composed of one race.

Centralization is alien to the Slav spirit—federation is far more natural to it. Only when grouped in a league of free and independent peoples will the Slav world at last enter upon its genuine historical existence. Its past can be regarded as a mere period of growth, of preparation and purification. The political forms in which the Slavs have lived do not correspond to their national aspirations, though vague and instinctive, yet displaying an extraordinary vitality and rich promise. Throughout their history the Slavs have always displayed a strange unconcern for their destiny, an amazing pliability. Thus Russia passed over from paganism to Christianity without a shock or revolt, simply in passive obedience to the Grand Duke Vladimir, and in imitation of Kiev. Without regret the Slavs flung their old idols into the Volkhov and accepted the new god as a new idol.

Eight hundred years later, part of Russia accepted a civilization imported from abroad in precisely the same way.

The Slav world is like a woman who has never loved, and for this very reason apparently takes no interest in what is going on about her. She is unwanted and a stranger to everybody. However, there is no telling: she is still young, and already a strange yearning has taken possession of her heart and sets it beating faster.

As for the richness of the national spirit, we need only point to the Poles, the only Slavonic nation which was once both free and powerful.

The Slav world is not essentially made up of nationalities so different in kind. Its people are physiologically and ethnographically identical whether they live under the outer crust of chivalrous, liberal and Catholic Poland or of imperial enslaved Byzantine Russia, or under the democratic rule of the Serbian Voivod, or under the bureaucratic yoke with which Austria oppresses Illyria, Dalmatia, and the Banat, or under the patriarchal authority of the Osmanli and with the blessing of the Archbishop of Montenegro.

The greater number of the Slav nations have never been enslaved by conquest. The dependence in which they so often found themselves for the most part consisted only in the recognition of a foreign potentate and the payment of tribute. Such, for instance, was the character of the Mongol rule in Russia. Thus the Slavs have through long centuries preserved their nationality, their customs, and their language.

Are we then not entitled to look upon Russia as the centre of this crystallization, the centre towards which the Slav world is gravitating in its striving toward unity, especially as Russia is so far the only nation of the great race organized into a powerful and independent state?

The answer to this question would be perfectly clear if the Petersburg Government had the faintest idea of its national destiny, if that dull-witted, deadly despotism could reconcile itself to any human idea. But things being as they are, what honest man will bring himself to suggest to the Western Slavs a union between them and an empire which is in a perpetual state of siege, and where the sceptre has been turned into a bludgeon that beats men to death?

The imperial Pan-Slavism, eulogized from time to time by men who have been suborned, or who are labouring under some delusion, has, of course, nothing in common with a union resting on the principles of freedom.

At this point logic inevitably confronts us with a question of primary importance. Assuming that the Slav world can hope for a fuller development in the future, which of the elements now in an embryonic state warrants such a hope? If the Slavs believe that their time has come, this element must be in harmony with the revolutionary idea in Europe.

You indicated that element—you mentioned it, in passing, but it escaped you, because a generous feeling of compassion for Poland diverted your attention away from it.

You say that "the fundamental basis of the life of the Russian people is *communism*," and maintain that "their strength lies in their agrarian law, in the perpetual redivision of the land."

What a terrible *mene tekel* has dropped from your lips! . . . Communism is the fundamental basis! Strength depending on redivision of the land! Weren't you horrified at your own words?

Ought we not to pause here to reflect, to look more deeply into the question, and not to drop it before making certain whether it is the truth or a mere illusion?

Is there in the nineteenth century an interest of any importance which does not involve the question of communism, the question of the redivision of the land?

Carried away by your indignation you go on: "They (the Russians) lack the true attribute of humanity: a moral sense, the sense of good and evil. Truth and justice have no meaning for them; if you speak of those things—they answer nothing, they smile and know not what the words signify." Who may those Russians be to whom you have spoken? What conceptions of *truth* and *justice* were beyond their comprehension? This is not a superfluous question. In our profoundly revolutionary age the words "truth and justice" have lost their absolute meaning, identical for all men.

The *truth* and *justice* of old Europe are *falsehood* and *injustice* to the nascent Europe. Nations are products of nature, history is the progressive continuation of animal development. Applying our moral standards to nature will not get us very far. She cares nought for our censure or our praise. Our verdicts and the Montyon prizes for virtue do not exist for her. The ethical categories created by our individual caprice are not applicable to her. I think that a nation cannot be called either bad or good. The life of a people is always true to its type and cannot be false. Nature produces only what is feasible under the given conditions: all that exists is drawn onwards by her creative ferment, her insatiable thirst for self-realization, that thirst common to all living things.

There are peoples who lived a prehistoric life, others are living a life outside the pale of history; but once they enter the broad stream of history, one and indivisible, they belong to *humanity*, and, on the other hand, all the past of humanity belongs to them. In history—that is, in the life of the active and progressive part of humanity—the aristocracy of facial angle, of complexion, and other distinctions is gradually effaced. That which has not become human cannot be history; on the other hand, no nation which has become part of history can be reckoned a herd of beasts, just as there is no nation which deserves to be called an assembly of the elect.

There is no man bold enough, or ungrateful enough, to deny the importance of France in the destinies of the European world; but you must allow me the frank confession that I cannot share your view that the participation of France is the *sine qua non* of historical progress.

Nature never stakes all her fortune on one card. Rome, the eternal city—which had no less right to the hegemony of the world—tottered, fell into ruins, and vanished, while pitiless humanity strode on over its grave.

On the other hand, unless one regards nature as madness incarnate, it is hard to label as an outcast race, as a vast deception, as a casual rabble, human only through its vices, a people that has grown and spread out for ten centuries, has obstinately preserved its nationality, formed itself into an immense empire, and has intervened in history far more perhaps than it should have.

What makes such a view all the more difficult to accept is the fact that this people, even according to its enemies, is far from being in a stagnant condition. It is not a race that has attained social forms approximately corresponding to its desires and has sunk into slumber in them, like the Chinese; still less is it a people that has outlived its prime and is wasting away in senile impotence, like the people of India. On the contrary, Russia is quite a new state—an unfinished structure in which everything smells of fresh plaster, in which everything is at work and being worked out, in which nothing has yet attained its object, and in which everything is changing, often for the worse, but changing nonetheless. In brief, this is the people whose fundamental principle, to quote your opinion, is communism, and whose strength lies in the redivision of the land. . . .

With what crime, after all, do you charge the Russian people? What does your accusation rest on?

"The Russian," you say, "is a liar and a thief; he is perpetually stealing, lying—quite innocently, too, because this is in his nature."

Disregarding the sweeping character of your verdict, let me ask you a simple question: who is it that the Russian deceives, from whom does he steal? Obviously the landowner, the government official, the steward, the police officer, in fact the sworn foes of the peasant, whom he looks upon as ungodly strangers, as apostates, as half-Germans? Deprived of every means of defence, the peasant resorts to cunning in dealing with his oppressors; he deceives them, and he is perfectly justified in doing so.

Cunning, dear sir, is, in the words of the great thinker, the irony of brute force.

Through his aversion for private landowning so correctly noted by you, through his heedless and indolent temperament, the Russian peasant has gradually and imperceptibly been enmeshed by German bureaucracy and the landowner's power. He has submitted to this degrading yoke with a passivity born of despair, but he never recognized the rights of the landlords, or of the law-courts, or the equity of the executive power. For nearly two hundred years the peasant has lived in mute opposition to the existing scheme of things. He submits to coercion, and suffers in silence, but evinces no concern for anything that goes on outside the village commune.

The name of the Tsar stirs a superstitious feeling in the people. It is not, however, to Tsar Nicholas that the peasant does homage, but to the abstract idea, the myth: in the popular imagination the Tsar stands for a menacing avenger, an incarnation of truth, an earthly providence.

Only the clergy could, after the Tsar, possibly have an influence on Orthodox Russia. They alone represent old Russia in governing spheres; the clergy do not shave their beards, and by observing that ancient custom have remained true to the people. Common people believe in the monks. But the monks and the higher clergy, preoccupied solely with the afterlife, care nought for the people, while the village priests have lost all their influence through their greed, drunkenness, and close relations with the police. In their case, too, the peasants respect the idea but not the person.

As for the dissenters, they hate both person and idea, both Tsar and priest.

Apart from the Tsar and the clergy every element of government and society is utterly alien and essentially antagonistic to the people. The peasant is literally an outlaw. The law-court affords him no protection; his share in the existing order of things is entirely confined to the two-fold tribute that lies heavy upon him, and is paid in his toil and his blood. A veritable outcast, he has instinctively realized that the whole system is built up not for his benefit, but to his detriment, and that the aim of the government and the landowners is to wring out of him as much labour, money, and recruits as possible. Since he understands this and is gifted with a flexible and resourceful mind, he deceives them wherever and whenever he can. It could not be otherwise; if he spoke the truth he would thereby be recognizing their authority over him; if he did not steal from them (mark you that to conceal part of the produce of his own labour is considered theft in a peasant) he would thereby be recognizing the lawfulness of their demands, the rights of the landowners, and the justice of the law-courts.

To fully appreciate the Russian peasant's position, you should see him in the law-courts; look at his hopeless face, his frightened, searching glance, and you will understand that he is a prisoner of war before the court-martial, a traveller facing a gang of brigands. A single glance shows plainly that the victim has not the slightest faith in the hostile, pitiless, insatiable robbers who are questioning him, tormenting him, and fleecing him. He knows that if he has money he will be acquitted; if not, he will be found guilty.

The Russian people speak their own old language, the judges and the attorneys write in a new bureaucratic jargon hideous and barely intelligible; they fill whole folios with forensic mummery, and gabble it off to the peasant. Let him understand it if he can and find his way out of the muddle if he knows how. The peasant sees through them and is on his guard. He will not say one word too much, and stands silent, concealing his uneasiness and pretending to be a fool.

The peasant who has been acquitted by the court trudges home, no more elated than if he had been condemned. In either case the decision seems to him arbitrary or accidental.

In the same way, when summoned as a witness he stubbornly pleads ignorance, even if confronted with incontestable evidence. Being found guilty by a law-court does not disgrace a man in the eyes of the Russian peasant. He regards exiles and convicts as merely *unfortunate* people. The life of the Russian peasantry has hitherto been confined to the village commune. It is only in relation to the commune and its members that the peasant recognizes that he has rights and duties. Outside the commune everything seems to him based upon violence. What is fatal is his submission to that violence, and not his refusal in his own way to recognize it and his attempt to protect himself by guile. Lying to a judge set over him by unlawful authority is far more straightforward than a hypocritical show of respect for the verdict of a jury tampered with by a corrupt prefect. The peasant respects only those institutions which coincide with his innate conception of law and right.

There is a fact which no one who has been in close contact with the Russian peasantry can doubt. The peasants rarely cheat each other. Their trust in each other is almost boundless; they know nothing of contracts and written agreements.

The problems connected with the surveying of their fields are necessarily complicated owing to the perpetual redivision of the land in accordance with the number of taxpayers in the family; yet the work is carried through without complaint or resort to the law-courts. The landowners and the government eagerly seek an opportunity for interference, but in vain. Petty disputes are submitted to the judgment of the elders of the commune on the commune assembly, and the decision is unconditionally accepted by all. The same is true of the *artels*. The *artels* are often made up of several hundred workmen, who form a cooperative for a definite period—for instance, for a year. At the expiration of the year the workmen divide their earnings by common agreement, in accordance with the work done by each. The police never get the satisfaction of meddling in their accounts. As a rule, the *artel* makes itself responsible for every one of its members.

The bonds between the peasants of the commune are even closer when the peasants are not orthodox but dissenters. From time to time the government makes a savage raid on some dissenting village. Peasants are put into prison and sent into exile, all of which is done without rhyme or reason, without any need or provocation, solely to satisfy the clergy and keep the police busy. It is during these hunts for heretics that the character of the Russian peasants, the solidarity existing among them, is displayed. At such times it is worth seeing them tricking the police, saving their comrades, and concealing their holy books and vessels; they endure the most awful tortures without uttering a word. I challenge any one to bring forward a single case in which a dissenting commune has been betrayed by a peasant, even by an orthodox one.

The peculiarity of the Russian character makes police enquiries exceedingly difficult. I can only heartily rejoice at the fact. The Russian peasant has no morality except that which naturally, instinctively derives from his communism. This morality is deeply rooted in the people; the little they know of the Gospel supports it; the flagrant injustice of the landowner binds the peasant still more closely to his principles and to the communal system.

The commune has saved the Russian people from Mongol barbarism and imperial civilization, from the Europeanized landlords and the German bureaucracy. The communal system, though shattered, has withstood the interference of the authorities; it has successfully survived *to see the development of socialism in Europe.*

This circumstance is of infinite importance to Russia.

The Russian autocracy is now entering upon a new phase. Engendered as it was by an anti-national revolution, it has accomplished its mission. It has created an immense empire, a formidable army, and a centralized government. Without real roots, without tradition, it is doomed to stagnation. True, it undertook a new task—that of introducing Western civilization into Russia, and was to some extent successful in doing that while it played the part of an enlightened government.

That part it has now abandoned.

The government, which parted ways with the people in the name of civilization, has lost no time in renouncing enlightenment in the name of absolutism.

It did so as soon as it found the tricoloured phantom of liberalism showing through its tendencies. Then it tried to veer round to the nation at large, to the people. That was impossible—the people and the government had no longer anything in common: the former had grown away from the latter, while the government seemed to discern a new still more terrible ghost lurking deep in the masses—the Red Cock. Liberalism was certainly less dangerous than a new Pugachovism, but the terror and aversion for new ideas had grown so strong that the government was no longer capable of reconciling itself to civilization.

Since then the sole aim of tsarism has been tsarism. It rules in order to rule, its immense powers are employed to destroy each other and thus preserve an artificial peace. But autocracy for autocracy's sake finally becomes impossible: it is too absurd and too sterile.

It has realized this and has turned to look for some occupation in Europe. The activities of Russian diplomacy are inexhaustible: notes, threats, promises, counsels are showered everywhere; its spies and agents are to be found everywhere.

The Russian Emperor regards himself as the natural protector of the German Princes; he meddles in all the petty intrigues of the petty German courts; he settles all their disputes, scolding one, rewarding another with the hand of a Grand Duchess. But this is not a sufficient outlet for his energy. The mainstay of every reaction, every persecution, he undertakes the duty of chief gendarme of the universe. He aspires to represent the monarchical principle in Europe and assumes the *airs* and *graces* of the aristocracy, as though he were a Bourbon, or a Plantagenet, and his courtiers Gloucesters and Montmorencys.

Unfortunately, feudal monarchism with its fixed moral principle, its past, and its social and religious ideas, has nothing in common with the Napoleonic despotism of the Petersburg Tsar with no moral principle whatever behind it; indeed, nothing but a deplorable historic necessity, a transitory usefulness.

The Winter Palace, like a mountain summit in later autumn, is more and more thickly covered with snow and ice. The vital sap artificially raised to these governmental heights is gradually freezing; sheer material power remains, and the hardness of the rock, which can still stand up against the battering waves of revolution.

Surrounded by his generals, his ministers, and his bureaucrats, Nicholas tries to forget his isolation, but grows gloomier, more morose and uneasy with every passing hour. He sees that he is not loved; the silence that reigns near him seems all the more deadly because of the distant murmur of the impending tempest. The Tsar seeks to forget himself, and has openly proclaimed that his aim is the aggrandizement of the imperial power.

That avowal is nothing new: for the last twenty years he has been steadily labouring for that sole object. It is for the sake of it that he has neither pitied the tears nor spared the blood of his subjects.

He has succeeded in everything: he has crushed national aspirations in Poland and suppressed liberalism in Russia.

What more does he want? Why is he so gloomy?

The Emperor feels that Poland is not yet dead. In place of the liberalism which he persecuted with such savagery—which was quite superfluous, for that exotic flower cannot take root in Russian soil—another problem, as menacing as a thundercloud, is looming up.

The peasantry is beginning to chafe against the yoke of the landowners;

local insurrections keep breaking out—you yourself quote a terrible instance of this.

The party of progress demands the emancipation of the peasants; it is ready to sacrifice its own privileges. The Tsar hesitates—he desires emancipation yet holds it back. He realizes that freeing the peasants involves freeing the land; that this, in turn, means the beginning of a social revolution, the proclamation of rural communism. To evade the question of emancipation is impossible. To defer its solution to the next reign is, of course, easier, but it is a faint-hearted resource. It is merely a respite—like a few hours' wait for horses at a wretched posting station.

From all this you can appreciate how fortunate it is for Russia that the village commune has not perished and personal ownership has not split up the property of the commune; how fortunate it is for the Russian people to have remained outside all political movements, outside European civilization, which would undoubtedly have undermined the commune, and which has today reached in socialism the negation of itself.

Europe, as I have said in another place, has not solved the antimony between the individual and the state, though she has set herself that task. Russia has not found the solution either. This is what we have in common.

At the first step toward social revolution Europe encounters a people which offers a system, though half-savage and unorganized, but still a system—of perpetual redivision of the land among its tillers. Note that this great example is set not by educated Russia, but by the people at large, by the actual everyday life of the people. We Russians who have been schooled by European civilization are no more than a means, a leaven, mediators between the Russian people and revolutionary Europe. In Russia the future belongs to the peasant, just as in France it belongs to the workman.

But if this is so, has not the Russian people some claim on your indulgence, sir?

Poor peasants! Every possible injustice is hurled at them: the Emperor decimates their ranks by recruiting, the landowner robs them of their labour, the official mulcts them out of their last ruble. The peasant endures everything in silence but does not despair: he still has his commune. If a member is wrested away from it, the commune reacts by serrying its ranks. The peasant's lot should have aroused compassion, yet it touches no one. Instead of defending him, people upbraid him.

You do not leave him even the last refuge, in which he can still feel himself human, in which he can love and be free from fear. "His commune is not a commune," you say. "His family is not a family, his wife is not a wife; she belongs to the landowner rather than to him; his children are not his children—who knows who is their father?"

So you expose this luckless people not to analysis but to the contempt of other nations, who read your legends so trustingly.

I regard myself in duty bound to say a few words on this subject.

Family life among all the Slavs is very highly developed; it may be, indeed, the one conservative element of their character, the point at which their destructive negativism stops.

The peasants are very reluctant to split up the family; not uncommonly three or four generations go on living under the same roof centered around the grandfather, who enjoys a patriarchal authority. The woman, commonly oppressed, as is always the case in the agricultural class, is treated with respect and consideration when she is the widow of the eldest son, and the whole family is often ruled by a grey-haired grandmother. Can it be said that the family does not exist in Russia?

Let us pass to the landowner's relation to the family of his serf. For the sake of clearness, we will distinguish the lawful practice from its abuses, in other words, what is done legally from what is done in violation of the law.

Jus primae noctis has never existed in Russia.

The landowner cannot legally demand a breach of conjugal fidelity. If the law were carried out in Russia, the violation of a serf-woman would be punished exactly as though she were free; namely, by penal servitude or exile to Siberia with deprivation of all civil rights. Such is the law. Now let us turn to the facts.

I do not pretend to deny that, with the power given by the government to the landowners, it is very easy for them to violate the wives and daughters of their serfs. By means of hardships and punishment the landowner can always bring his serfs to a pass in which some will offer him their wives and daughters, just like that worthy French nobleman who, in the eighteenth century, asked as a special favour that his daughter should be installed in the Parc-aux-Cerfs.

It is no wonder that honourable fathers and husbands can find no redress against the landowners thanks to the excellent judicial system of Russia. For the most part, they find themselves in the position of Monsieur Tiercelin, whose daughter of eleven was stolen by Berryer, at the instigation of Louis XV. All these filthy abuses are possible; one has but to think of the coarse and depraved manners of a section of the Russian nobility to be certain of it. But as far as the peasants are concerned they by no means endure their masters' debauchery patiently.

Allow me to give you a proof of it.

Half of the landowners murdered by their serfs (the statistics give the number as sixty to seventy a year) lose their lives for their amorous misdemeanors. Legal proceedings on such grounds are rare: the peasant knows that the judges would show little respect for his complaints. He has, however, his axe; he is a master hand at it, and knows that he is.

I will say no more about the peasants, but beg you to listen to a few more words about educated Russia.

Your view of the intellectual movement in Russia is no more indulgent than your opinion of the popular character; with one stroke of the pen you strike off all the work hitherto done by our fettered hands!

One of Shakespeare's characters, wishing to show his utmost contempt for a despised opponent, says to him: "I even doubt of your existence!" You have gone further, for it is not a matter of doubt to you that Russian literature does not exist. I shall quote your own words:

"We are not going to attach importance to the attempts of those few clever people who have taken to exercising themselves in the Russian language and amusing Europe with a pale phantom of an allegedly Russian literature. If it were not for my deep respect for Mickiewicz and his saintly aberrations, I should really censure him for the indulgence, one might even say charity, with which he speaks of this trifling."

I search in vain, sir, for the grounds for the contempt with which you regard the first cry of anguish uttered by a people that has awakened in its prison-house, that groan stifled by the gaoler.

Why did you refuse to listen to the haunting notes of our mournful poetry, to our chants throbbing with sobs? What has made you blind to our mirthless laughter and perpetual irony behind which the deeply tortured heart seeks refuge, and which is, after all, the confession of our helplessness? I wish I could make for you a worthy translation of some poems of Pushkin and Lermontov, some songs of Koltsov! Then you would hold out to us a friendly hand at once, and be the first to beg us to forget your words!

Next to the communism of the peasants, nothing is so deeply characteristic of Russia, nothing is such an earnest of her great future, as her literary movement.

Between the peasantry and literature towers the monster of official Russia—"Russia the deception, Russia the pestilence," as you call it. This Russia begins with the Emperor and extends from gendarme to gendarme, from official to official, down to the lowest policeman in the remotest corner of the Empire. With every step, the ladder, as *bolgia* in Dante, gains a new power for evil, a new degree of corruption and tyranny. This living pyramid of crimes, abuses, and bribery, of police scoundrels, heartless German officials who are ever greedy, ignorant judges who are ever drunk, aristocrats who are ever base: all this is held together by a community of interest in plunder and gain, and rests on six hundred thousand animated machines with bayonets. The peasant is never defiled by contact with this cynical world of government; he endures its existence—and that is all he is to blame for.

The camp hostile to official Russia consists of a handful of men, ready to face anything, who protest against it, fight against it, denounce and

undermine it. These isolated champions are from time to time thrown
into dungeons, tortured and sent to Siberia, but their place is not long
vacant—fresh champions arise. It is our tradition, our inalienable inheritance. The terrible consequences of the human word in Russia inevitably lend it a peculiar force. The voice of freedom is listened to with
love and reverence, because only those who have something to say raise
it. One does not so easily put one's thoughts into print when every page
seems to conjure up a vision of a gendarme, a troika, and some Tobolsk
or Irkutsk in immediate prospect.

In my last pamphlet I have said enough about Russian literature. Here
I will confine myself to a few general observations.

Melancholy, scepticism, irony, those are the three chief strings of the
Russian lyre.

Pushkin begins one of his finest poems with these terrible words:

> All say—there is no justice upon earth—
> But there is no justice up above us either!
> To me that is as clear as a piano scale,—

Do they not grip your heart, do you not divine, under the mask of com-
posure, the broken life of a man who has long suffered? Lermontov,
profoundly disgusted with the society surrounding him, turns in 1838
to his contemporaries with his terrible.

> With mournful heart I watch our generation
> Tragic or trivial must its future be.

I only know one contemporary poet who can stir the sombre strings
of man's soul with the same power. He, too, was a poet born in slavery
and died before the revival of his country; I mean the signer of death, the
celebrated Leopardi, to whom the world appeared as a vast league of
criminals ruthlessly persecuting a handful of righteous madmen.

Russia has only one painter who has won general recognition, Bryullov.
What is the subject of his finest work which won him fame in Italy?

Glance at this strange painting.

Groups of terrified figures are crowded in confusion on an immense
canvas. They seek in vain for safety. They will be buried by an earthquake, a volcanic eruption, by a veritable tempest of cataclysms. They
will be overwhelmed by savage, senseless, ruthless force, to which all
resistance is futile. Such are the images inspired by the Petersburg
atmosphere.

The Russian novel is constantly concerned with the sphere of pa-
thology, with the evil that is consuming us; an evil that is relentless,
pitiless, and so peculiar to us. You will not hear voices from heaven,
promising Faust forgiveness for sinful Margaret—here the only voices

raised are those of doubt and damnation. Yet if there is salvation for Russia, it lies only in this profound awareness of our position, in the truthfulness with which she lays bare her plight before the sight of all. He who boldly recognizes his failings feels that there is in him something that has been kept intact in the midst of downfalls and failures; he knows that he can expiate his past, and not only lift up his head, but change from "Sardanapalus the profligate into Sardanapalus the hero."

"The Russian peasantry does not read." But, as you know, Voltaire and Dante were not read by villagers either, but by the nobility and a section of the middle class. In Russia the educated section of the middle class forms part of the nobility, which consists of all that has ceased to be the common people. There is even a proletarian nobility which merges into the common people, and free peasants who rise up to the nobility. This fluctuation, this continual renewal, imparts to the Russian nobility a character which you do not find in the privileged classes of the backward countries of Europe. In brief, the whole history of Russia, from the time of Peter the Great, is merely the history of the nobility and of the influence of enlightenment upon it. I will add that the Russian nobility numerically equals the electorate of France under the law of the 31st of May.

In the course of the eighteenth century, the new Russian literature fashioned that rich, sonorous language which we now possess: supple and powerful, it is capable of expressing both the most abstract ideas of German metaphysics and the light sparkling play of French wit. This literature, called into being by the genius of Peter the Great, bore, it is true, the impress of the government—but in those days the banner of the government was progress, almost revolution.

Up to 1789 the imperial throne complacently draped itself in the majestic vestments of enlightenment and philosophy. Catherine II deserved to be deceived with cardboard villages and palaces of painted boards. . . . No one could dazzle spectators by a gorgeous stage effect as she could. In the Hermitage there was continual talk about Voltaire, Montesquieu, Beccaria. You, sir, know the reverse side of the medal.

Yet in the midst of the triumphal chorus of the courtiers' songs of praise, a strange, unexpected note was already sounding. That was the sceptical, fiercely satirical strain, which soon silenced all the other artificial chants.

The true character of Russian thought, poetical and speculative, developed in its full force after the accession of Nicholas to the throne. Its distinguishing feature was a tragic emancipation of conscience, a pitiless negation, a bitter irony, an agonizing self-analysis. Sometimes these were broken by fits of laughter, but there was no gaiety in it.

Cast into oppressive surroundings, and endowed with a clear eye and incorruptible logic, the Russian has quickly freed himself from the faith and ways of his fathers.

The thinking Russian is the most independent man in the world. What is there to stop him? Respect for the past? But what serves as a starting-point of the modern history of Russia, if not the denial of nationality and tradition?

Or can it be the tradition of the Petersburg period? That tradition lays no obligation on us; on the contrary, that "fifth act of the bloody drama staged in a brothel" completely frees us from all obligation.

On the other hand, the past of the Western European peoples serves us as a subject of study and nothing more; we do not regard ourselves as the executors of their historic testaments.

We share your doubts, but your faith does not cheer us. We share your hatred, but we do not understand your devotion to what your forefathers have bequeathed you. We are too downtrodden, too unhappy, to be satisfied with half-freedom. You are restrained by moral considerations or held back by afterthoughts. We have neither afterthoughts nor moral considerations; all we lack is strength. This is the source of our irony, of the anguish which gnaws us, makes us frantic and urges us on till we reach Siberia, exile, hardships, premature death. We sacrifice ourselves with no hope—from sheer spite, or boredom. There is, indeed, something erratic in our lives, but there is nothing commonplace, nothing stagnant, nothing philistine.

Do not accuse us of immorality because we do not respect the same things you do. Can you reproach a foundling for not respecting his parents? We are independent because we are starting life anew. We have no law but our nature, our national character; it is our essence, our flesh and blood, but by no means a binding authority. We are independent because we possess nothing. We have hardly anything to love. All our memories are filled with bitterness and resentment. Education, learning, were inculcated in us with the knout.

What do we care for your sacred duties, we younger brothers robbed of our heritage? And can we be honestly content with your threadbare morality, unchristian and inhuman, existing only in rhetorical exercises and speeches for the prosecution? What respect can be inspired in us by your Roman-barbaric law, that hollow clumsy edifice without light or air, repaired in the Middle Ages and whitewashed by the newly enfranchised middle classes? I admit that the daily brigandage in the Russian law-courts is even worse, but it does not follow from that that your laws or your courts are just.

The distinction between your laws and our imperial decrees is confined to the formula with which they begin. Our imperial decrees begin with a crushing truth: "The Tsar has been pleased to command"; your laws begin with a revolting falsehood, the ironical abuse of the name of the French people, and the words Liberty, Equality, and Fraternity. The code of Nicholas is drawn up for the benefit of the autocracy and to the detriment of his subjects. The Napoleonic code has absolutely the same character. We are fettered with too many chains to fasten fresh ones about us of our own free will. In this respect we stand precisely on a level with our peasants. We submit to brute force. We are slaves because we have no possibility of being free; but we accept nothing from our enemies.

Russia will never be a Protestant country.

Russia will never be *juste-milieu*.

Russia will never make a revolution with the object of getting rid of Tsar Nicholas, and replacing him by other tsars—parliamentary representatives, judges, and police officials. We perhaps ask for too much and shall get nothing. That may be so, but yet we do not despair; before the year 1848 Russia could not, and should not, have entered the arena of revolution: she had to learn her lesson. Now she has learnt it. The Tsar himself has realized it, and is ferociously brutal in his opposition to universities, to ideas, to knowledge; he is trying to cut Russia off from Europe, and to destroy culture. He is doing his job.

Will he succeed in it?

I have already tried to answer this.

We should have no blind faith in the future; every seed has its claim to growth, but not every one actually grows up. The future of Russia does not depend on her alone, it is bound up with the future of Europe. Who can fortell the fate of the Slav world, if reaction and absolutism finally suppress the revolution in Europe?

Perhaps it will perish.

But in that case Europe too will perish.

And history will pass over to continue in America.

After writing the above I received the last two instalments of your legend. My first impulse on reading them was to throw what I had written in the fire. Your warm and generous heart has not waited for someone else to raise a voice on behalf of the wronged Russian people. You are too magnanimous to play the part you had assumed of relentless judge and avenger of the Polish people. You have been drawn into inconsistency, but it is the inconsistency of a noble mind.

I thought, however, on reading over my letter that you might find in it some new views on Russia and the Slav world, and I made up my mind to send it to you. I do hope that you will forgive the passages in which I have been carried away by my Scythian impetuosity. Alas, the blood of the barbarians flows in my veins! I so longed to change your opinion of the Russian people—it caused me such grief to find you hostile to us that I could not conceal my bitterness and let my pen run away with me. But now I see that you do not despair of us; under the coarse armyak of the Russian peasant you discern a human being. I can see this and, in my turn, confess that I fully understand the impression the very name of Russia must produce on every free man. We ourselves often curse our unhappy land. You know it—you say that everything you have written of the moral worthlessness of Russia is feeble compared with what Russians say themselves.

But the time for funeral orations on Russia is past for us too, and we say with you: "that thought conceals the spark of life." You have divined that spark by the power of your love; we see it, too. That spark will not be quenched by streams of blood, or the snows of Siberia, or the suffocating atmosphere of mines and prisons. May it go on smoulder-ing under the ashes! Or else, the cold, deadly breath which blows from Europe may extinguish it.

For us the hour of action has not come; France may still be justly proud of her foremost position. That arduous task is hers until 1852. Europe will doubtless reach the grave or the new life before us. The day of action is perhaps still far away from us; but the day of the mature consciousness of free thought and speech has already come. We have lived long enough in sleep and silence; the time is ripe for us to describe the fabric of our dreams and the conclusions we have reached.

And indeed whose fault is it that we have had to wait until 1847 for a German (Haxthausen) to *discover*, as you express it, the Russia of common people, which was as unknown before his time as America be-fore Columbus?

Of course, it is we who are to blame for it, we poor dumb creatures with our faint-heartedness, our faltering speech, our terrified imagination. Even when abroad we are afraid to confess the hatred with which we look upon our fetters. Convicts from our birth up, doomed all our lives to drag the cannon ball fastened to our shackles, we are offended when we are spoken of as though we were voluntary slaves, frozen Negroes, and yet we do not protest openly.

Ought we to submit meekly to these denunciations, or resolve to check them, raising our voice on behalf of Russian free speech? It is better for us to die suspected of human dignity than to live with the shameful brand of slavery on our brow, and hear the reproach that we are slaves by choice.

Unhappily, free speech arouses terror and amazement in Russia. I have just tried to lift a corner of the heavy curtain that hides us from Europe, I have indicated merely the theoretical tendencies, the remote hopes, the organic elements of our future development; and yet my book of which you speak in such flattering terms has made an unfavourable impression in Russia. Voices of friends whom I respect condemn it. In it they see a condemnation of Russia. A condemnation! Of what? Of our sufferings, our hardships, our desire to break away from this hateful position. . . . Poor dear friends, forgive me this crime, I am afraid, I am committing it again.

Heavy and dreadful is the yoke of years of slavery with no struggle, no hope at all! In the end it crushes even the noblest, the strongest heart. Where is the hero who is not overcome at last by weariness, who does not prefer peace in old age to the everlasting fret of vain struggle?

No, I will not be silent! My word shall avenge those unhappy lives crushed by the Russian autocracy which prostrates men morally, kills them spiritually.

We are in duty bound to speak, else no one will know how much that is fine and lofty is sealed for ever in the martyrs' breasts and perishes with them in the snows of Siberia, where their *criminal* name is not even traced upon their tombstones, but is only cherished in the hearts of friends who dare not utter it aloud.

Scarcely have we opened our mouth and murmured two or three words of our desires and hopes when they try to silence us, to stifle free speech in its cradle!

But they will not succeed. A time comes when thought reaches its maturity and can no longer be kept in fetters by the censorship or by prudence. Propaganda becomes a passion. And then can one be content with a whisper when the sleep is so deep that it can scarcely be broken by a tocsin? Since the mutiny of the Streltsi and up to the conspiracy of December 14, there was no political movement of consequence in Russia. The cause is obvious: there was no clearly defined yearning for independence in the people. In many things they were at one with the government, in many things the government was in advance of the people. The peasants alone, who had no share in the imperial benefits and were more oppressed than ever, tried to revolt. Russia, from the Urals to Penza and Kazan, was, for three months, in the power of Pugachov. The imperial army was defeated and put to flight by the rebellious Cossacks. General Bibikov, sent from Petersburg to take command of the army, wrote, if I am not mistaken, from Nizhni Novgorod: "Things are in a very bad way; what is most to be feared is not the armed hordes of the rebels, but the spirit of the peasants, which is dangerous, very dangerous." The insurrection was at last crushed with incredible difficulty. The people turned dumb, silent, submissive.

Meanwhile the nobility had developed, education had begun to enrich their minds, and like a living proof of that political maturity, of that moral development which must inevitably find expression in action, there appeared remarkable figures, those heroes, as you justly call them, who "alone in the very jaws of the dragon dared the bold stroke of December 14."

Their defeat and the terror of the present reign crushed every idea of success, every premature attempt. Other questions arose; no one cared to risk his life again in the hope of a constitution; it became too clear that a charter won in Petersburg would be cancelled by the treachery of the Tsar: the fate of the Polish Constitution served as an example.

For ten years no intellectual activity could betray itself by a single word, and the oppressive misery reached the point when men "would give their life for the happiness of being free for one moment" and giving voice to some of their thoughts.

Some, with the recklessness which is only met with in us and in the Poles, renounced their possessions and went abroad to seek distraction; others, unable to endure the stifling atmosphere of Petersburg, sought seclusion in the country. The young people went in for Pan-Slavism, or German philosophy, or history or political economy. In short, not one of those Russians whose natural vocation was intellectual activity could or would submit to the stagnation.

The case of Petrashevsky and his friends, condemned to penal servitude for life, and exiled in 1849, for forming political societies not two steps away from the Winter Palace, certainly proved, by the insane recklessness of the attempt and the obvious impossibility of success, that the time for rational reflection had passed, that feeling had overpowered good sense, and certain death seemed easier to face than dumb, agonizing submission to the Petersburg discipline.

A fairy-tale very widely known in Russia tells how a Tsar, suspecting his wife of infidelity, put her and her son in a barrel, and then had the barrel sealed up and thrown into the sea.

For many years the barrel floated on the sea.

Meanwhile, the Tsarevich grew not by days but by hours, and his feet and his head began to press against the ends of the barrel. Every day he felt more and more cramped. At last he said to his mother: "Queen Mother, let me stretch myself out and feel freedom."

"My darling Tsarevich," answered the mother, "don't do that—the barrel will burst and you will drown in the salt water."

The Tsarevich thought awhile in silence, and then said: "I will, Mother—I'd rather stretch out just once, feel freedom, and then die."

That fable, sir, tells our whole history.

Woe to Russia if bold men, risking everything to stretch out for freedom just once are no more to be found.

But there is no fear of that.

These words involuntarily bring to my mind Bakunin who has given Europe the sample of a free Russian. I was deeply touched by your fine reference to him. Unhappily, those words will not reach him.

An international crime has already been committed: Saxony has handed over the victim to Austria, Austria to Nicholas. He is in the Schlüsselburg, that fortress of evil memory where once Ivan, the grandson of the Tsar Alexei, was kept caged like a wild beast. He was finally killed by Catherine II, who, not yet stained by her husband's blood, first ordered the captive's murder, and then executed the luckless officer who carried out her command.

In that damp dungeon by the icy waters of Lake Ladoga there is no place for dreams or hopes!

May he sleep his last sleep in peace, that martyr betrayed by two governments, stained with his blood.

Glory to his name! And revenge! But where is the avenger?—We too, like him, shall perish with our work half done; then lift up your stern and majestic voice, and tell once more our children that they have a debt to pay. . . .

I will close with this memory of Bakunin, and warmly press your hand for him and for myself.

Nice, September 22, 1851

25

The Emancipation Manifesto, March 3, 1861

Russia's defeat in the Crimean War (1853–1855) at the hands of English, French, and Turkish forces and the humiliating peace terms which the victors imposed at Paris (March 1856) injured her prestige. The defeat also destroyed the myth of Russia's military might, demonstrated her backwardness, and exposed the economic, administrative, and social ineptness of her autocracy. Finally, it convinced Tsar Alexander II (1855–1881) and some of his advisers that the long-overdue reforms demanded by Radishchev, the Decembrists, and other enlight-

From *Polnoe Sobranie Zakonov Russkoi Imperii* . . . (*Complete Collection of the Laws of the Russian Empire*), 2d Series, vol. 36, no. 36,490, pp. 130–134. Translation mine. Items in brackets are mine.

ened men, could no longer be postponed, even though these reforms were opposed by the conservative elements of Russian society. The reform era, as the period after 1861 is commonly known, began with the emancipation of the serfs on March 3, 1861. Because that act shattered the entire structure of Russian society, between 1861 and 1874 the government was forced to introduce educational, legal, municipal, military, and other reforms. The emancipation thus laid a foundation for the vast transformation of Russian society which, despite obstacles and pressures, was productive and constructive.

By the Grace of God We, Alexander II, Emperor and Autocrat of All Russia, King of Poland, Grand Duke of Finland, etc., make known to all our faithful subjects:

Called by Divine Providence and by the sacred right of inheritance to the throne of Our Russian ancestors, We vowed in Our heart to respond to the mission which is entrusted to Us and to surround with Our affection and Our Imperial solicitude all Our faithful subjects of every rank and condition, from the soldier who nobly defends the country to the humble artisan who works in industry; from the career official of the state to the plowman who tills the soil.

Examining the condition of classes and professions comprising the state, We became convinced that the present state legislation favors the upper and middle classes, defines their obligations, rights, and privileges, but does not equally favor the serfs, so designated because in part from old laws and in part from custom they have been hereditarily subjected to the authority of landowners, who in turn were obligated to provide for their well being. Rights of nobles have been hitherto very broad and legally ill defined, because they stem from tradition, custom, and the good will of the noblemen. In most cases this has led to the establishment of good patriarchal relations based on the sincere, just concern and benevolence on the part of the nobles, and on affectionate submission on the part of the peasants. Because of the decline of the simplicity of morals, because of an increase in the diversity of relations, because of the weakening of the direct paternal attitude of nobles toward the peasants, and because noble rights fell sometimes into the hands of people exclusively concerned with their personal interests, good relations weakened. The way was opened for an arbitrariness burdensome for the peasants and detrimental to their welfare, causing them to be indifferent to the improvement of their own existence.

These facts had already attracted the attention of Our predecessors of glorious memory, and they had adopted measures aimed at improving the conditions of the peasants; but these measures were ineffective, partly because they depended on the free, generous action of nobles, and partly because they affected only some localities, by virtue of special circumstances or as an experiment. Thus Alexander I issued a decree on free agriculturists, and the late Emperor Nicholas, Our beloved father, promulgated one dealing with the serfs. In the Western *gubernias*, inventory regulations determine the peasant land allotments and their obligations. But decrees on free agriculturists and serfs have been carried out on a limited scale only.

We thus became convinced that the problem of improving the condition of serfs was a sacred inheritance bequeathed to Us by Our predecessors, a mission which, in the course of events, Divine Providence has called upon Us to fulfill.

We have begun this task by expressing Our confidence toward the Russian nobility, which has proven on so many occasions its devotion to the Throne, and its readiness to make sacrifices for the welfare of the country.

We have left to the nobles themselves, in accordance with their own wishes, the task of preparing proposals for the new organization of peasant life—proposals that would limit their rights over the peasants, and the realization of which would inflict on them [the nobles] some material losses. Our confidence was justified. Through members of the *gubernia* committees, who had the trust of the nobles' associations, the nobility voluntarily renounced its right to own serfs. These committees, after collecting the necessary data, have formulated proposals on a new arrangement for serfs and their relationship with the nobles.

These proposals were diverse, because of the nature of the problem. They have been compared, collated, systematized, rectified and finalized in the main committee instituted for that purpose; and these new arrangements dealing with the peasants and domestics of the nobility have been examined in the Governing Council.

Having invoked Divine assistance, We have resolved to execute this task.

On the basis of the above mentioned new arrangements, the serfs will receive in time the full rights of free rural inhabitants.

The nobles, while retaining their property rights on all the lands belonging to them, grant the peasants perpetual use of their domicile in return for a specified obligation; and, to assure their livelihood as well as to guarantee fulfillment of their obligations toward the government, [the nobles] grant them a portion of arable land fixed by the said arrangements, as well as other property.

While enjoying these land allotments, the peasants are obliged, in return, to fulfill obligations to the noblemen fixed by the same arrangements. In this state, which is temporary, the peasants are temporarily bound.

At the same time, they are granted the right to purchase their domicile, and, with the consent of the nobles, they may acquire in full ownership the arable lands and other properties which are allotted them for permanent use. Following such acquisition of full ownership of land, the peasants will be freed from their obligations to the nobles for the land thus purchased and will become free peasant landowners.

A special decree dealing with domestics will establish a temporary status for them, adapted to their occupations and their needs. At the end of two years from the day of the promulgation of this decree, they shall receive full freedom and some temporary immunities.

In accordance with the fundamental principles of these arrangements, the future organization of peasants and domestics will be determined, the order of general peasant administration will be established, and the rights given to the peasants and to the domestics will be spelled out in detail, as will the obligations imposed on them toward the government and the nobles.

Although these arrangements, general as well as local, and the special supplementary rules affecting some particular localities, estates of petty nobles, and peasants working in factories and enterprises of the nobles, have been as far as possible adapted to economic necessities and local customs; nevertheless, to preserve the existing order where it presents reciprocal advantages, we leave it to the nobles to reach a friendly understanding with the peasants and to reach agreements on the extent of the land allotment and the obligations stemming from it, observing, at the same time, the established rules to guarantee the inviolability of such agreements.

This new arrangement, because of its complexity, cannot be put into effect immediately; a time of not less than two years is necessary. During this period, to avoid all misunderstanding and to protect public and private interests, the order actually existing on the estates of nobles should be maintained until the new order shall become effective.

Towards that end, We have deemed it advisable:

1. To establish in each *gubernia* a special Office of Peasant Affairs, which will be entrusted with the affairs of the peasant communes established on the estates of the nobility.

2. To appoint in every district justices of the peace to solve all misunderstandings and disputes which may arise from the new arrangement, and to organize from these justices district assemblies.

3. To organize Peace Offices on the estates of the nobles, leaving the village communes as they are, and to open volost offices in the large villages and unite small village communes under one volost office.

4. To formulate, verify, and confirm in each village commune or

estate a charter which would enumerate, on the basis of local conditions, the amount of land alloted to the peasants for permanent use, and the scope of their obligations to the nobleman for the land as well as for other advantages which are granted.

5. To put these charters into practice as they are gradually approved on each estate, and to put them into effect everywhere within two years from the date of publication of this manifesto.

6. Until that time, peasants and domestics must be obedient towards their nobles, and scrupulously fulfill their former obligations.

7. The nobles will continue to keep order on their estates, with the right of jurisdiction and of police, until the organization of volost and of volost courts.

Aware of the unavoidable difficulties of this reform, We place Our confidence above all in the graciousness of Divine Providence, which watches over Russia.

We also rely upon the zealous devotion of Our nobility, to whom We express Our gratitude and that of the entire country as well, for the unselfish support it has given to the realization of Our designs. Russia will not forget that the nobility, motivated by its respect for the dignity of man and its Christian love of its neighbor, has voluntarily renounced serfdom, and has laid the foundation of a new economic future for the peasants. We also expect that it will continue to express further concern for the realization of the new arrangement in a spirit of peace and benevolence, and that each nobleman will realize, on his estate, the great civic act of the entire group by organizing the lives of his peasants and his domestics on mutually advantageous terms, thereby setting for the rural population a good example of a punctual and conscientious execution of state regulations.

The examples of the generous concern of the nobles for the welfare of peasants, and the gratitude of the latter for that concern, give Us the hope that a mutual understanding will solve most of the difficulties, which in some cases will be inevitable during the application of general rules to the diverse conditions on some estates, and that thereby the transition from the old order to the new will be facilitated, and that in the future mutual confidence will be strengthened, and a good understanding, and a unanimous tendency towards the general good will evolve.

To facilitate the realization of these agreements between the nobles and the peasants, by which the latter may acquire in full ownership their domicile and their land, the government will lend assistance, under special regulations, by means of loans or transfer of debts encumbering an estate.

We rely upon the common sense of Our people. When the government advanced the idea of abolishing serfdom, there developed a partial misunderstanding among the unprepared peasants. Some were concerned about freedom and disconcerned about obligations. But, generally, the common sense of the country has not wavered, because it has realized that every individual who enjoys freely the benefits of society owes it in return certain positive obligations; according to Christian law every individual is subject to higher authority (Romans, chap. xiii., 1); everyone must fulfill his obligations, and, above all, pay tribute, dues, respect, and honor (*Ibid.*, chap. xiii., 7). What legally belongs to nobles cannot be taken away from them without adequate compensation, or through their voluntary concession; it would be contrary to all justice to use the land of the nobles without assuming responsibility for it.

And now We confidently expect that the freed serfs, on the eve of a new future which is opening to them, will appreciate and recognize the considerable sacrifices which the nobility has made on their behalf.

They should understand that by acquiring property and greater freedom to dispose of their possessions, they have an obligation to society and to themselves to live up to the letter of the new law by a loyal and judicious use of the rights which are now granted to them. However beneficial a law may be, it cannot make people happy if they do not themselves organize their happiness under protection of the law. Abundance is acquired only through hard work, wise use of strength and resources, strict economy, and above all, through an honest God-fearing life.

The authorities who prepared the new way of life for the peasants and who will be responsible for its inauguration will have to see that this task is accomplished with calmness and regularity, taking the timing into account in order not to divert the attention of cultivators away from their agricultural work. Let them zealously work the soil and harvest its fruits so that they will have a full granary of seeds to return to the soil which will be theirs.

And now, Orthodox people, make the sign of the cross, and join with Us to invoke God's blessing upon your free labor, the sure pledge of your personal well being and the public prosperity.

Given at St. Petersburg, March 3, the year of Grace 1861, and the seventh of Our reign.

Alexander

26

Katkov's Views on the Polish Situation, 1863

After he ascended the throne in 1855, Alexander II
made it known that he would improve not only the
position of peasants but that of some of Russia's
minority groups as well. Most excited at this prospect were the Poles, who, since the three partitions
of Poland at the end of the eighteenth century, had
presented Russian officialdom and the educated public of Russia with the most immediately troublesome
aspect of their national problem. Polish hopes for
independence were further stimulated by sympathies
in their behalf expressed abroad in England and
France. When, by 1863, the Russians had failed to
satisfy Polish ambitions, the Poles rebelled. Russian
forces crushed the uprising and in the process committed a number of excesses. These received much
attention and additional sympathy for the Poles
abroad, but the anti-Russian sentiment, in turn,
aroused Russian nationalism. Its spokesman was
Michael N. Katkov (1818–1887). As editor of the
Russkii Vestnik (The Russian Herald), Katkov bitterly assailed foreign interference in Russo-Polish
relations and denounced those Russian revolutionaries .who sympathized with the Polish cause.
Though in his youth he subscribed to moderately
liberal views, after 1863 Katkov's name came to be
synonymous with reaction in Russian political and
literary history.

Nothing is more deceitful in the realm of politics than general rules
and abstract formulas. By their very nature they are either dead or have
a double meaning. Being abstract they may simultaneously apply to
diametrically opposed circumstances; and two hostile sides may, quite
often with equal right, place the same slogans on their banners. Because
of this it is dangerous to judge life by abstract maxims. In reality, every-

From *Russkii Vestnik*, no. I (1863). Translation mine. Items in brackets are mine.

thing forever and ever is definite and particular. Everything requires a definite viewpoint and special appraisal, and our views will be valid in such an appraisal only if we are able to approach the fact and familiarize ourselves with all of its peculiarities. Without this ability our views will be opened but we will be unable to see.

Lately in Europe one has been hearing quite frequently and loudly stated views about rights of nationalities and the principle of non-interference. Rights of nationalities and the principle of non-interference are quite good concepts deserving a prominent place in the realm of ideas. Nothing can be said against them; on the contrary, one only wishes that they could acquire an increasing force and clarity in peoples' minds. It is one thing to acknowledge the existence of a rule, and it is another thing to use it to appraise given phenomena. Understanding is one thing; judgment is another matter. We may have beautiful understanding but our judgments can be grossly invalid. To have valid judgments it is not enough to have beautiful understanding; it is essential that our beautiful views correspond to the fact. Two and two without any doubt make four; and if in this sum, which our facts give us, there should appear other numbers, no matter how much we should argue, the inescapable truth remains that two and two make four and nothing else. If there be something else we must correct the figures and those that do not belong must be discarded.

The problem of the rights of nationalities was lately awakened and defended, primarily due to the Italian situation. Who is not familiar with the circumstances in which this matter was resolved? Who is unaware of what caused its success and why it received sympathy everywhere? As a consequence of this affair, the idea of non-interference into the domestic affairs of an independent state was re-stated with added emphasis. Because in its own right this idea is quite basic, and because the popular view was everywhere sympathetic to the Italian problem, all manifestations of these principles with respect to the Italian situation were everywhere approved without reservations. Whether Emperor Napoleon III or a minister of Her Britannic Majesty referred in this matter to the principle of nationalities or to the theory of non-interference, the result was always quite satisfactory, even though frequently the same sound rule was declared by the adversaries with a diametrically opposed meaning.

The theory of non-interference did not prevent Western states from interfering quite actively in the course of the Italian problem; neither did the principle of nationality hinder France from annexing Nice; which, according to this principle, belongs really to Italy, similarly as does Venice. Right of nationalities and the principle of non-interference are now knocking in vain at the gates of Rome; French armies are not leaving the Eternal City. The theory of non-interference has not prevented England from administering Turkish affairs and from controlling the

Greek revolution; rights of nationalities have not prevented her from killing Turkish Slavs whenever they raised their heads, not only in the name of nationality, but even when they petitioned because of burdensome oppression. Montenegrins were neither subjects nor tributaries of the Sultan; yet the same British minister, who earlier had announced the principle of nationalities, treated the Montenegrins as rebels. Ships with volunteers and war supplies were dispatched from English ports to Italy when the struggle was in full progress, and no one paid any attention to this; but now heated debate goes on to discover by what right Serbia received arms with Tula markings. All this means that power centers not in general ideas but in their application. It means that power centers in the particularity of every situation, in its circumstances and in its peculiarities. The English government found it appropriate to apply the theory of non-interference and the rights of nationalities to the Italian situation, but finds it inappropriate to apply the same theory to the Turkish situation; equally as France considers it inappropriate to apply it to the problem of Rome. . . .

You should never talk to an Englishman about minority rights in India; he will consider you an insane person; a Frenchman will consider you similarly if you should talk to him about minority rights in Algeria. They will raise all sorts of objections. Neither will you gain much if you think to carry on a conversation with an Englishman about granting rights to the Celtic people in Ireland, or with a Frenchman about the possibility of an independent political existence of the same people in Britanny. In vain will you expound the theory of rights that belong to each nationality; in vain, too, will you talk about independent existence; no one will listen to you. They will tell you that you speak of utterly impossible things. They will tell you that you are applying the theory unintelligently; that the theory as such is very meritorious but that it cannot be applied to cases of your own choosing; that not every nationality is entitled to aspire to an independent political existence; and that great chaos would result if one should suddenly endorse such pretentious aspirations. They will tell you that only that nationality has that right which has proven it by its own history and which knows how to maintain and protect it. They will tell you that this right centers not in the letter, not in a word, not in a phrase, but in the reality, in existing conditions, and in given interpretations of vital forces. They will tell you that reality is the best and the only verifiable measure of real rights; and that, until such a verification, outside sympathies and verdicts decide nothing. Public opinion will side with one or the other view on the basis of various impulses or interests, which often have no bearing whatsoever on the rights of minorities. If a man whom we do not like has a heated argument with another, and we know very little about the cause of their argument, then unwittingly we will side with his adversary. As can individuals, so people and states can become an object of sympathy or antipathy; just as in the case of an argument between two individuals, public opinion is capable of siding with one or the other on the basis of its own mood, irrespctive of the nature of the arisen argument. Sometimes the cause of prejudice is the very power of the victorious people, and public opinion will sympathize with the weaker side even over an unrealizable and desperate cause. While England struggled with the bloody Sepoy rebellion in India, did not European journalists howl about the rights of nationalities and did it not express its sympathies with the victims of perfidious and mighty Albion? Was not public opinion in France ready to applaud every success of Indian mutineers, including their violent excesses? If one could imagine a serious attempt in Ireland to separate from Great Britain, would they not rejoice in France even over a slight success in such a desperate case, and would not they raise throughout the world protests of indignation over the ultimate British victory, and would not they beat on a drum all possible tunes about the rights of nationalities? But this uproar would not produce any impression in England; the affair would take its own course and not one Englishman would attach any significance to these shouts and howls, just as now no Yankee in North America is disturbed by the Englishman's opinions of the bloody discord in the secessionist states; he is not confused by the hostile criticism from abroad; he snaps at his critics, and for each cruel word he responds with ten or twelve harsher ones. Meanwhile he goes on with his business and fights to the exhaustion of his strength in order to restore the seceding parts of his country.

Everyone knows that every case can be seen from different viewpoints and that contradicting interests will view differently the same situation. The Englishman does not count on French sympathy and the Frenchman in turn does not count on English sympathy in their respective successes or failures. They both find in foreign sympathy or indifference exactly that which is alien to them; both will try to understand their respective problems with their own intellect and appraise and judge them with their own feelings; neither one nor the other will stop perplexed and listen to someone else's opinion in order to define for themselves the line of action; both will operate from the position of their own strength, interests, and incentives. Is it possible to imagine that in case of a struggle or of a crisis, both would try to assess themselves with a foreign yardstick, or, God forbid, with the yardstick of their enemies?

In this uninterrupted struggle for existence which we call life, and even call history, every cause has its defenders and its opponents. If there were no defenders then there would be no causes; and if there were no opponents then one would be unable to manifest oneself and to show ones own strength, and ones own right to existence and development. In the midst if this struggle called life and history, all truth is relative and all interest is unilateral. If there are defenders then there must be opponents; if there are opponents then there must also be defenders. And both opponents and defenders have their own more or less valid interests, their own more or less valid rights. Life and history show that whose power is mightiest his right is most righteous. But in a struggle one cannot support both sides or not support either. Whoever does not want to take a side in the struggle should leave the field, and on the battlefield each must be either a defender or an opponent of the given cause.

What causes the English or the French to seek truths in an argument between the Russians and the Poles? An outside observer will judge the affair guided not by the causes of the affair, but by his own personal sympathies or his own interests, should he ever become involved in someone else's argument. It is quite natural that neither an Englishman nor a Frenchman burns with zeal for Russian interests and would not be chagrined if a Russian cause suffered a setback somewhere. Not long ago Europe viewed with distrust and fear the Northern colossus, and not too long ago she feared its military despotism. Now these fears have abated. Russia has stopped being a bugbear. But, while no one is particularly afraid of her power, no one would grieve if an external or internal misfortune should afflict her. No foreigner has asked himself this serious question: is this power that has so dangerously and slowly emerged in the wastes of North Eastern Europe true, or is it a meteor, an apparition, that rose accidentally, and which must vanish? No one, except a Russian, is obligated, and no one can, take to his heart the Russian cause—no one can suffer for it, hope for it, and die for it. Our historical destiny, our national character, our fortunes, our sufferings and triumphs are unable to get any sympathetic consideration anywhere except here in Russia among ourselves. Every cause has two endings, every cause has both defenders and opponents and not one Russian cause can have better defenders than Russians themselves, while it can have a multitude of opponents everywhere.

This Polish problem is as much Russian as it is Polish. The Polish problem will always be a problem of Russia. Since ancient times history has placed the fatal question of life and death between these two related peoples. Both states were not simply rivals, but enemies unable to exist side by side—enemies to the very end. Between them the question was no longer that of who would take the priority or who would be more powerful: the question between them was which of them should exist. Sovereign Poland was unable to get along with an independent Russia. Agreements were impossible; either one or the other had to renounce its political independence and its pretensions to a mighty and independent state. And it was not Russia but Poland who felt the pressure of this vital question. It was Poland who started the historical struggle, and there was a time when Russia vanished, and there was another when

Poland disappeared. Will this fatal question keep its momentum forever or will the time come when alongside a powerful and strong Russia an independent Poland will be able to live and flourish? One can meditate about this question at leisure, but in time of crisis, in the midst of a struggle, it is natural for a Pole to advocate the Polish cause and for a Russian to defend the Russian cause. Poland lost its independence, but it has not reconciled itself to its fate; Polish feeling protests against this decision; feeling for his own people is still alive and vigorous in a Pole; it starts in infancy and is then jealously guarded and supported. It feeds itself and gains its strength on sufferings. The Pole did not repudiate his nationality after he lost his political independence. He is trying to free himself from his captivity and does not want to reconcile himself with any future if that future should not promise him a rebirth of a Polish nation with all of its claims. To him a simple independence is insufficient; he wants predominance. To him it is insufficient to liberate himself from alien domination; he wants the destruction of the opponent over whom he has triumphed. To him it is insufficient to be a Pole; he wants the Russian to become a Pole or else to be pushed beyond the Ural mountain range. He renounces all racial ties with us, turns us into a phantom of history, and in place of present Russia he does not want to see any one except Poles and degenerate Chuds and Tartars. What is neither Polish nor Tartar must be banished to Siberia, and in place of present powerful Russia there must arise a powerful Poland, up to Kiev, and Smolensk—Poland from the Baltic to the Black Sea. Are we to blame or condemn a Polish patriot for holding such pretensions? There is no need to blame and condemn the talk! Logical arguments will lead nowhere in such a controversy; no amount of eloquence can assist its settlement. In such an argument only events can speak, because only they possess persuasive eloquence and irresistable logic. In such controversy not words but facts decide, and facts have already decided. Be that as it may, reasonable or not, Polish pretensions are understood by and are natural with a Pole. You may condemn and dispute them, you may contest them with both word and deed, but you will agree that in its extremity, even in its own madness, Polish patriotism nevertheless is a natural phenomenon in a Pole. Events have decided, but the Pole is appealing. He has not lost his hope and is consoling himself with foreign sympathies. He does not try to discover how much sense these sympathies have, or more specifically how much sympathy there is for him and how much hostility there is for his opponent. They applaud him, they grieve for him, but in the last analysis he alone is able to feel fully the call of his nation. He has no need to subscribe to diverse theories; he doesn't need to be told about the rights of nationalities and varied truths. All he needs is to be called a Pole so that everyone can know what he wants and what he doesn't want. Common sense and experience can teach him how to understand better and clearer the interest of his nationality and how to act in its behalf with greater understanding and advantage. Be he on true or false paths, a Pole is a natural defender of his cause. Who would want to become a Pole if a Pole were not there?

Thus at least it would seem. But fate has not completely severed its ties with Poland. It struck her, but at the same time it predestined her to a rare happiness. In the midst of a battle, a Pole is finding among his adversaries his allies who are ready without any investigation to subscribe to all of his conditions. He finds on the Russian side people who, with touching generosity, are prepared to sacrifice the interests of their native land and the unity and political significance of their people. He finds people prepared to serve him honorably as obedient tools, people prepared to repeat with enthusiasm everything that is spoken against the Russian name by her enemies, everything that defames and disgraces the Russian cause, everything that extols and beautifies the enemy side, people who are prepared to be Poles more than the Poles themselves.

On February 19 [1862], the very anniversary of the ascension to the throne of the present reigning Emperor, which also coincided with the first anniversary of the emancipation of so many millions of people from serfdom, there was distributed in Moscow a new product of our underground writers. We thought that this form of amusement had tired out our progressives, but here before us is a new proclamation with the stamp of *Zemlia i Volia* [Land and Liberty]. The authors of this anonymous leaflet, speaking in behalf of the Russian people, make an appeal to our officers and soldiers in Poland, trying to convince them to abandon their own flag and to turn their arms against their own motherland. It was impossible to expect such an action even from our progressives! This is worse than fire. One would like to think that this proclamation, like many others, is the work of emissaries of the Polish revolution. It is outrageous and sickening to our national feeling that our enemies think so basely of us, and that they count on the success of such tricks. Is it really possible, indeed, that the Russian people gave any ground for such a contemptuous opinion of themselves? However that may be, the fact before our eyes seems to mean that there is something within us that justifies such tactics of our enemies, that we have amidst ourselves shameless elements on whom they can count and, who, by their very existence bring slander upon their country. Polish agitators have organized our domestic revolutionaries, and while they despise them in their souls, they know how to utilize them. These prophets and heroes of the Russian land (as Polish agitators speak of them in flattering their stupidity) are unaware of whose creatures they are. Indeed, think a little: how far would they have been able to advance in our society, what group would they have been able to join, or what position been able to hold? That we have enough stupidity is certainly true. But that one quality alone would have been insufficient to organize people, to arouse them to action, to implant in them a belief that, without rhyme or reason, they are acting in behalf of their own people and in their name, while in reality they are disgracing it and are infringing upon all the foundations of its historical existence. Why have all of these absurdities expressed themselves with such conviction and enthusiasm at a time when the Russian people have started a new life, when every Russian should stand at his post and perform honestly his duties? To do this, stupidity was not enough! It was necessary for the native stupidity to have been joined by an alien influence, and for some kind of adroit hand to hold this delusion, to give support to these absurdities and to galvanize this rot. Such a hand was found. It operated skillfully and it operates even now. But results have deceived it. Our enemies over-reached themselves. They were carried away by their own scorn for the Russian people. They operated with deception on weak minds and thus they cruelly deceived themselves. They undertook their bloody trick because they considered Russia not only a "sick colossus" but also a decomposing carcass. They imagined that because they called them their friends our soldiers would either scatter or join their banner. They relied on diverse proclamations and addresses, allegedly from the Russian army, and, hoping for quick success, they gave the signal to revolt. Who then is to blame for these sorrowful events that are now taking place in Poland?

The authors of the above-mentioned anonymous leaflet reproach the government for the blood that is now being shed there. But whoever they may be, Poles or Russians, let them know that they themselves were immediately responsible for this blood. If, to our shame, they really are Russians, then with their own scornful nihilism they have involved Polish agitators in a delusion disastrous for them concerning the true strength and feelings of the Russian people. If, however, they are Poles, then they put this nihilism on themselves and have deceived themselves by their own work.

The authors of this proclamation do not feel that Poland should remain united with Russia. What right have we, they exclaim, to be masters in Poland, when she herself does not wish it? What right! What kind of metaphysics will our patriots not adopt! They want to blame all the evil in the entire world on our people. They do not inquire why something happens elsewhere. They do not ask by what right Poles did own and now want to own regions that from time immemorial had been settled by the Russian people; they do not ask in what legal code this right is written, or which potentate granted this right to the Poles. This they do not ask. But they ask with a magnanimous indignation: Why do the Russians govern Poland?

They demand that Russia restore to Poland its independence! Return independence to Poland! But what is Poland? Where does it begin and where does it end? Do the Poles themselves know it? Have our patriots asked them about this? If these pitiful creatures would only free themselves from their own stupidity and foreign deception, they would realize that possession of the Kingdom of Poland is not completely a joy for Russia, that it was a necessary evil similar to those sacrifices which the Russian people assumed elsewhere to fulfill their historical destiny. But who said that Polish pretensions confine themselves to the present Kingdom of Poland? Any sober Polish patriot who understands the true interests of his people knows that in its present dimensions the Kingdom of Poland would fare better if it would retain its close ties with Russia, rather than to separate itself from her and form an independent state, insignificant in size, surrounded on all sides by powerful states, and devoid of any opportunity to gain European significance. For a Pole, the separation of Poland has never signified only a separation of the present Kingdom of Poland. No, the very thought of separation arouses pretensions to alter history and to put Poland in place of Russia. Here then is the source of all the present sufferings of the Polish people; here is the root of all of Poland's evils! If Poland were able to free herself from these pretensions, her fortunes would have been completely different, and Russia would not have any necessity to hold Poland with an armed hand. The trouble is that Polish patriotism does not renounce its pretensions: it considers to be Polish all ancient Russian territories where, in former times, Polish dominion and Catholic propaganda were spread with sword and fire.

If the question centered on whether to grant to Poland better institutions or fuller self-government and national administration, then the answer would be easy; then every Russian would be able to sympathize fully with the Poles without becoming a traitor to his motherland. But this is not the case. We know the longing of the best of Polish patriots. We know what demand was made in the name of Polish landowners by Count [Andrew] Zamojski. We also know what Polish nobles demanded in one of the Russian gubernias adjacent to Poland. Let foreign politicians express themselves sympathetically for the Polish cause, and let them censure Russia with reproaches. We know without them our own weaknesses and shortcomings. But we also know that with every passing year and day our position is getting brighter, and that on our horizon are unquestionable signs of a better future. No, our struggle with Poland is not a struggle over political foundations; it is a struggle of two nations, and to give in to the pretensions of Polish patriotism would mean signing a death warrant for the Russian people. Let our enemies know this: the Russian people are still alive and know how to stand for one another. If the struggle should assume the dimensions desired by Polish patriotism and our foreign critics, then not one Russian will be found who would not be ready to give his life in this struggle. Let our enemies not deceive

themselves by apparitions and let them not arouse the slu
strength of the people. This will not serve them any good. A
this struggle will be the last test of history, the last consecratic
national destiny. It is easy to understand the proper significance of all
friendly manifestations of public opinion in Europe towards us, and the
meaning of the unanimous blaming of Russia and praise of the Poles
that has been expressed in the British House of Commons. Why
shouldn't one be able to understand it? Why shouldn't England sympathize now with the Polish cause when there is hope that it may entangle
us with our difficulties and thereby place into her hands the whole Eastern question over which we both collide? As for the true aspirations of
the Polish people, we view these with greatest sincerity. From the depth
of our hearts we wish a better lot for the Poles. But to realize their
aspirations it is necessary that the Poles not only stop exciting their
pretensions but also quiet and moderate them. With the Poles lies the
choice of whether both nations will live in harmony or whether they will
carry on a merciless struggle conducted not just by a government but by
the whole great people.

27

Turgenev's "Definition" of Nihilism

The emancipation of the serfs in 1861 coincided
with the emergence in Russia of a movement known
as nihilism. Attracting young Russian radicals who
thought of themselves as socialists and democrats,
and accordingly were sworn enemies of the bourgeoisie, political liberalism, and aristocracy, the
movement was hostile to all forms of authority and
sought to destroy superstition. In their efforts to
change Russia the Nihilists renounced the Russian

From Ivan Turgenev, *Fathers and Sons*. Translated from the Russian by Bernard
Isaacs (Moscow: Foreign Languages Publishing House, n.d.), pp. 29–35.

state and its Orthodox Church. At the same time
they maintained a peculiar, almost sacred love for
Russia and its people. They idealized education in
general and the study of natural science in particular, and through such study they desired earnestly
to create a "new man." Because the older generation disapproved of the aims, attitudes, and behavior
of the materialistic young radicals, a conflict developed between "fathers and sons." Russia's great
novelist Ivan S. Turgenev (1818–1883) depicted
this conflict in his novel *Fathers and Sons*, published
in 1862. Turgenev's portrayal of the new generation
as having blind faith in science at first offended
many of them. Later, however, they accepted the
name of nihilist for themselves and hailed Bazarov,
the hero of the novel, as their ideal of the new man.

"Where's that new friend of yours?" he asked Arkady.

"He's gone out; he's usually up and about early. The main thing is
not to pay any attention to him; he doesn't like ceremony."

"Yes, that's obvious," and Pavel Petrovich began leisurely to butter
his bread. "Will he be staying here long?"

"It all depends. He's stopping over on his way to his father's."

"And where does his father live?"

"In our gubernia, about eighty *versts* from here. He has a little estate
there. He used to be an army surgeon."

"Tut, tut, tut! And I've been wondering all the time where I'd heard
that name—Bazarov! Nikolai, if I am not mistaken, there was a medical
chap in our father's division by the name of Bazarov, wasn't there?"

"I think there was."

"Why, of course. So that medical fellow is his father. Hm!" Pavel
Petrovich twitched his moustache. "Well, and what about Mr. Bazarov
himself, what is he?" he said slowly.

"What is Bazarov?" Arkady looked amused. "Shall I tell you what he
really is, Uncle?"

"Please do, nephew."

"He is a nihilist."

"A what?" Nikolai Petrovich asked, while Pavel Petrovich stopped
dead, his knife with a dab of butter on the tip arrested in mid-air.

"He is a nihilist," Arkady repeated.

"A nihilist," Nikolai Petrovich said. "That's from the Latin *nihil*—
nothing, as far as I can judge; does that mean a person who . . . who
believes in nothing?"

"Say, 'Who respects nothing,' " put in Pavel Petrovich, applying himself to the butter again.

"Who regards everything critically," Arkady observed.

"Isn't that the same thing?" asked Pavel Petrovich.

"No, it isn't. A nihilist is a person who does not look up to any authorities, who does not accept a single principle on faith, no matter how highly that principle may be esteemed."

"Well, and is that a good thing?" Pavel Petrovich broke in.

"It all depends, Uncle. It may be good for some people and very bad for others."

"I see. Well, this, I see, is not in our line. We are men of the old school—we believe that without principles," (he pronounced the word softly, in the French manner, whereas Arkady clipped the word and accentuated the first syllable) "principles taken on faith, as you put it, one cannot stir a step or draw a breath. *Vous avez changé tout cela*, God grant you good health and a generalship, but we'll be content to look on and admire, *Messieurs les* . . . what do you call them?"

"Nihilists," Arkady said distinctly.

"Yes. We used to have *Hegelists*, now we have nihilists. We shall see how you manage to live in a void, in a vacuum; and now please ring the bell, brother Nikolai Petrovich—it's time for my cocoa."

Nikolai Petrovich rang the bell and called, "Dunyasha!" But instead of Dunyasha, Fenichka herself appeared on the terrace. She was a young woman of about 23, all daintily soft and fair-skinned, with dark hair and eyes, childishly full red lips and delicate little hands. She wore a neat print dress; a new blue kerchief lay lightly upon her rounded shoulders. She carried a large cup of cocoa and having placed it before Pavel Petrovich, stood overcome with bashfulness: the hot blood spread in a deep blush under the delicate skin of her pretty face. She dropped her eyes and stood there by the table, leaning lightly on her finger-tips. She seemed to be ashamed of having come, yet looked as though she felt she was within her rights in coming.

Pavel Petrovich knit his brows sternly, while Nikolai Petrovich felt embarrassed.

"Good morning, Fenichka," he mumbled.

"Good morning, sir," she answered in a clear yet quiet voice, and with a sidelong glance at Arkady, who gave her a friendly smile, she quietly withdrew. She walked with a slightly waddling gait, but even that was becoming to her.

Silence reigned a while on the terrace. Pavel Petrovich sipped his cocoa then suddenly looked up.

"Here comes Mr. Nihilist," he murmured.

Indeed, Bazarov was striding down the garden, stepping over the flower-beds. His duck coat and trousers were muddy; a clinging marsh

weed was twined round the crown of his old round hat; in his right hand
he held a small bag with something alive squirming in it. He quickly
approached the terrace and said with a nod, "Good morning, gentlemen; sorry I'm late for tea; I'll be back in a moment; must fix up a
place for these captives."

"What have you got there, leeches?" asked Pavel Petrovich.

"No, frogs."

"Do you eat them or breed them?"

"I use them for experiments," Bazorov said indifferently and went
into the house.

"He's going to dissect them," Pavel Petrovich said. "He doesn't believe in principles, but he believes in frogs."

Arkady glanced regretfully at his uncle, and Nikolai Petrovich furtively
shrugged his shoulders. Pavel Petrovich perceived that his joke had fallen
flat, and began talking about the farm and the new steward, who had
recently come to him complaining that Foma, one of the hired labourers,
was a "rowdy customer" and had completely got out of hand. "That's
the kind of Aesop he is," he had said among other things; "he's earned
himself a disgraceful 'repitation'; he'll come to a bad end, he will, you
mark my words."

Bazarov reappeared, sat down at the table and began hurriedly drinking his tea. The two brothers regarded him in silence, while Arkady's
eyes travelled stealthily from Uncle to Father and back again.

"Did you go far?" Nikolai Petrovich presently asked Bazarov.

"You've got a little swamp here, close to the aspen wood. I flushed
five snipe; you can shoot them, Arkady."

"Don't you go in for shooting?"

"No."

"You're studying physics, I understand?" Pavel Petrovich asked in his
turn.

"Yes, physics; the natural sciences generally."

"The Deutschländer are said to have made considerable progress in
this field."

"Yes, the Germans are our teachers in that subject," Bazarov answered
casually.

Pavel Petrovich had used the word Deutschländer instead of Germans
for the sake of irony, but this had passed unnoticed.

"Do you have as high an opinion of the Germans as all that?" inquired Pavel Petrovich with studied suavity. He was beginning to feel
a secret irritation. His aristocratic nature was up in arms at Bazarov's
sheer insouciance. This son of an army sawbones, far from being dif-
fident, answered bluntly and reluctantly, and there was something rude,
almost insolent in the tone of his voice:

"Their men of science are a practical lot."

"So they are. Well, I suppose you have no such flattering opinion about Russian scientists, have you?"

"I suppose so."

"That's very praiseworthy selflessness," retorted Pavel Patrovich, drawing himself up erect and throwing his head back. "But Arkady Nikolaich has just been telling us that you recognize no authorities. Don't you believe them?"

"Why should I recognize them? And what am I to believe in? When anyone talks sense, I agree—that's all."

"Do the Germans all talk sense?" Pavel Petrovich murmured, and his face assumed an expression so impassive and detached as though his thoughts had gone woolgathering.

"Not all of them," Bazarov said stifling a yawn. He was obviously unwilling to continue the word-play.

Pavel Petrovich glanced at Arkady as much as to say: "A polite fellow, this friend of yours, I must say."

"For my part," he went on, not without some effort, "I must plead guilty to disliking the Germans. I say nothing of the Russian Germans: we know that type. But I can't even stomach the German Germans. Those of the old days, well—one could put up with in a pinch; they then had their—well, Schiller, Goethe, you know. . . . My brother, for instance, thinks a lot of them. Now they've all become chemists and materialists. . . ."

"A decent chemist is twenty times more useful than any poet," broke in Bazarov.

"Is that so?" commented Pavel Petrovich with a slight lift of his eyebrows, looking as if he were going to doze off. "You don't believe in art then, I suppose?"

"The Art of Making Money, or No More Piles!" Bazarov said with a sneer.

"So, so. You are having your joke, I see. You repudiate everything then, is that it? All right. Does that mean you believe only in science?"

"I've already told you that I believe in nothing; and what is science, science in general? There are sciences, as there are trades and callings; but science in general does not exist at all."

"Very good, sir. But what about the other conventions, those accepted in human society—do you maintain the same negative attitude here as well?"

"What's this, a cross-examination?" Bazarov said.

Pavel Petrovich paled slightly. Nikolai Petrovich deemed it necessary to intervene.

"We shall discuss this matter more fully with you some day, my dear Yevgeny Vasilich; we shall learn your views and let you know our own. For my part, I'm very glad to know you are studying natural science. I hear that Liebig has made some surprising discoveries in soil fertilization. You might help me in my agricultural pursuits; you might be able to give me some useful advice."

"I am at your service, Nikolai Petrovich; but it's a far cry to Liebig! A person has to learn his abc first before he can begin to read, whereas we haven't set eyes on our alphabet yet."

"Well, you certainly are a nihilist, I see," thought Nikolai Petrovich.

"Still, I hope you won't mind me bothering you in case of need," he added aloud. "And now, brother, I think it's time for us to be seeing the steward."

Pavel Petrovich stood up.

"Yes," he said, looking at nobody in particular. "It's a sad thing to live five years in the country as we do, enjoying no intercourse with the great minds of the age! You become a silly ass before you know it. Here you are, trying not to forget what you've been taught, when—lo and behold!—it turns out to be all tommyrot, and you're told that sensible people no longer waste time on such trifles and that you yourself are an old dunderhead, if you please. Ah, well! The young people are cleverer than us, it seems."

Pavel Patrovich turned slowly on his heel and slowly walked out; Nikolai Petrovich followed him.

"Is he always like that?" Bazarov asked coolly, as soon as the door had closed behind the two brothers.

"Look here, Yevgeny, you handled him rather roughly, you know," Arkady said. "You've insulted him."

"I'll be blowed if I'm going to humor these rustic aristocrats! It's nothing but conceitedness, swell habits, foppery! Why didn't he carry on in St. Petersburg, if that's the way he's made? Well, enough of him! I've found a water beetle, a rather rare specimen—*Dytiscus marginatus*—do you know it? I'll show it to you."

"I promised to tell you his story—" began Arkady.

"The beetle's?"

"Come, come, Yevgeny. My uncle's story. You'll see he's not at all the man you think he is. He deserves sympathy rather than sneers."

"I'm not denying it, but what makes you harp on him?"

"One must be fair, Yevgeny."

"What's the implication?"

"No, just listen. . . ."

And Arkady told him his uncle's story.

28

The Catechism
of the Revolutionary, 1868

In its prime, Russian nihilism produced a number of devoted fanatics. In dedication, however, few surpassed the enthusiasm of Michael A. Bakunin (1814–1876) and Sergei G. Nechaev (1847–1882). The prominence of these two men stems largely from their compilation, during exile in Geneva, of practical advice for conspirators entitled *Katekhizis revolutsionera* (The Catechism of the Revolutionary). In it they advocated total destruction of Russia's political, social, and economic structure in order to lay the foundation for a new and better state. To attain that aim they felt it was necessary to turn every member-conspirator into a blind instrument of the leader, and accordingly they emphasized that everything which "promotes the success of the revolution is moral and everything which hinders it is immoral."

Paragraph 1

The revolutionary is a doomed man. He has no interests, no affairs, no feelings, no habits, no property, not even a name. Everything in him is wholly absorbed by a single, exclusive interest, a single thought, a single passion—the revolution.

Paragraph 2

In the very depth of his being, not just in words but in deed, he has severed every tie with the civil order, with the educated world, and with all laws, conventions, ethics, and generally accepted rules of this world. He is an implacable enemy of this world and if he continues to inhabit it, it is only to destroy it more effectively.

From A. Shilov, " 'Katekhizis revolutsionera' [K istorii 'nechaevskogo' dela]" (The Catechism of the Revolutionary [The History of the Nechaev Affair]), *Borba Klassov* (*Class Struggle*), no. 1–2 (1924), pp. 268–272. Translation mine.

Paragraph 3

The revolutionary despises every form of doctrinarism. He has rejected peaceful science, leaving it to the next generation. He knows only one science, the science of destruction. For that reason, and that reason alone, he now studies mechanics, physics, chemistry, and even medicine. For that reason, too, day and night he studies living people, individuals, conditions, and all problems of contemporary society in every conceivable ramification. The aim is always the same: the speediest and the most thorough destruction of this ugly system.

Paragraph 4

He despises public opinion. He despises and hates the existing social customs and all of their motivations and manifestations. For him everything that promotes the revolution is moral; everything that hinders it is immoral.

Paragraph 5

The revolutionary is a doomed man. He has no pity for the state nor for the privileged and educated world in general, and expects no pity for himself. Between the two there exists, whether openly or secretly, a continuous and irreconcilable war for life and death. Every day he must be prepared for death. He must condition himself to bear tortures.

Paragraph 6

Merciless towards himself, he must be merciless towards others. A single, cold passion for the revolutionary cause must suppress within him all tender feelings for family life, friendship, love, gratitude, and even honor. For him there exists only one pleasure, one consolation, one reward, and one satisfaction—the success of the revolution. Day and night he must have one single purpose: merciless destruction. To attain this goal, tirelessly and in a cold-blooded fashion, he must always be prepared to be destroyed and to destroy with his own hands everything that hinders its attainment.

Paragraph 7

The character of a true revolutionary excludes every romanticism; every sentimentality, enthusiasm, and seduction. It excludes even personal hatred or revenge. The revolutionary passion, which becomes a daily and hourly passion, must be combined with cold calculation. He must become always and everywhere not what his personal inclinations dictate, but what the general interests of the revolution demand.

Paragraph 8

For a revolutionary, that individual is dear and friendly who truly supports the revolutionary cause as he himself does. The degree of friendship, trust, and other obligations toward such a friend is determined exclusively by its usefulness to the cause of the all-destructive practical revolution.

Paragraph 9

There is no need to talk about solidarity among revolutionaries. In it centers the entire strength of the revolutionary cause. Revolutionary comrades who equally understand the revolutionary meaning and passion, should if possible discuss all major problems jointly and resolve them unanimously. In the execution of the jointly agreed upon plan, each member should act independently. In the execution of a number of destructive actions, each member must act alone, seeking advice and comradely help only when it is essential to the total success.

Paragraph 10

Every comrade must have under his control several revolutionaries of second and third ranks, those who are not entirely dedicated. He must consider them as a portion of a general revolutionary capital entrusted to his disposal. He must dispose of his part of the capital economically, striving always to get most advantage from it. He considers himself expendable capital designated to the success of the revolutionary cause. He cannot dispose of this capital alone without first consulting all the comrades who are totally dedicated.

Paragraph 11

When a comrade runs into trouble, the question of whether to rescue him or not must be decided by the revolutionary not because of any personal feeling but on the basis of whether such rescue would benefit the revolutionary cause. Therefore, on the one hand, he must weigh the usefulness which the comrade contributes to the cause against, on the other, the losses of revolutionary forces needed for his rescue. Whichever side is weightier gets his decision.

Paragraph 12

The acceptance into the organization of a new member who declares his readiness not in words but in deeds must be resolved unanimously.

Paragraph 13

The revolutionary joins the state, society, and so-called civilized world and lives in it only for the purpose of its more total and speedier destruction. He is not a revolutionary if he feels compassion for something in this world. If he would pause before carrying out a decision affecting any individual of this world, he must always be aware of the fact that he hates everything equally. He would be in jeopardy if he should have family, friends, or love relations. He cannot be considered a revolutionary if such matters could stop his hand.

Paragraph 14

With the aim of merciless destruction, the revolutionary can, and in fact should, often live in society without revealing his true identity. Revolutionaries should infiltrate everywhere into all layers of society: higher, middle, business, church, and estate; the bureaucratic world, the military, the literary, the Third Section, and even the Winter Palace.

Paragraph 15

The whole vile society should be divided into several categories. The first category should consist of those condemned to death. A list of those condemned should be prepared by our organization on the basis of their relative harm to the success of the revolutionary cause and their numbers should come up in order of priority.

Paragraph 16

In preparing such a list as well as in establishing the above-mentioned priority of execution, one should be influenced neither by personal thievery committed by the condemned man nor even by the hatred which he arouses in our organization or among the people. This thievery and this hatred can sometimes even be useful in awakening popular uprising. One should be guided solely by the benefits which his death will bring to the revolutionary cause. Consequently, the first to be destroyed are people who are especially harmful to the revolutionary organization and those whose sudden and violent death will create the greatest fear in the government, since deprivation of its resourceful and energetic states-men will weaken its power.

Paragraph 17

The second category should consist of those people who have been granted a partial reprieve on their life so that, by their bestial actions, they will provoke people into an inescapable uprising.

Paragraph 18

The third category should include the majority of high placed beasts, individuals who are distinguished neither by their wisdom nor energy, but who possess riches, influence, connections, and power. These should be exploited in every conceivable manner and way. They should be en-tangled, confused, seized by means of blackmail, and transformed into revolutionary slaves. Their authority, influence, connections, wealth and power will thus become an inexhaustible source of and a strong support for various revolutionary undertakings.

Paragraph 19

The fourth category should consist of ambitious state bureaucrats and liberals of all shades. The revolutionary should conspire with their pro-grams and pretend that he follows them. While doing this he should gain control of them, seize all of their secrets, compromise them to such an extent that their escape is impossible, and thus with their own hands cause chaos within the state.

Paragraph 20

The fifth category should consist of doctrinaires, conspirators and revo-lutionaries of the empty-phrase and paper variety.

Paragraph 21

The sixth category, an extremely vital one, should consist of women, who should be divided into three basic groups.

The first group should be composed of dumb, stupid, and callous women who should be utilized in the same manner as the third and fourth categories of men.

The second group should consist of ardent women, dedicated and practical, but not our own, because they have failed to attain yet the real, phrase-free and factual revolutionary understanding. They should be utilized similarly as the men of the fifth category.

Finally, our own women: those who are completely dedicated and who have accepted our program. They are our comrades. We should consider them as our precious resource without whose aid we cannot succeed.

Paragraph 22

Our organization has no other aim than complete freedom and happiness of the people; that is, the toiling people. Aware that this freedom and the attainment of that happiness is possible only by means of a total popular revolution, our organization will strive with all forces and means at its disposal to publicize and single out those miseries and evils that in the end should lead the people out of sufferings and arouse them to a spontaneous uprising.

Paragraph 23

By popular revolution, our organization understands not a regulated movement in the classical Western pattern—a movement which always has been kept in check by respect for property, tradition, the social order, and the morality of the so-called civilization—a movement which hitherto has limited itself everywhere to the replacement of one political order by another in an effort to create the so-called revolutionary state. The only revolution that can save the people is that revolution which will destroy totally the entire state apparatus and will eliminate all state traditions, orders, and social classes in Russia.

Paragraph 24

Our organization, therefore, has not been destined to superimpose any system upon the people. The future order will emerge without doubt from the popular movement and from life itself. But this problem we leave to future generations. Our task is a passionate, total, universal, and merciless destruction.

Paragraph 25

To accomplish this we must draw closer to the people and above all we must ally ourselves with those elements in people's lives which, ever since the establishment of the power of the Moscovite state, have never stopped protesting, not just in words but in deeds, against everything that is either directly or indirectly associated with the state: against nobles, against officialdom, against priests, against the world of guilds, and against the kulak. We must ally ourselves with the evil world of brigands, who in Russia comprise the true and only revolutionaries.

Paragraph 26

To unite this world into a single, invincible, and omnidestructive force is the prime task of our organization, our conspiracy, and our purpose.

29

Demands of the Narodnaia Volia

Throughout the nineteenth century, the Russian revolutionary movement was stalked by the authorities and torn by the inability of its members to resolve the question of whether to use terror as a political instrument. Beginning with the Decembrists, the revolutionaries had been divided on this issue. Many of them favored the unrestrained application of terror, both as a means of self-defense and as a weapon to bring a basic transformation to Russia. The question acquired new dimensions after dismal failure of the populist movement to peacefully penetrate the Russian villages during the mid-1870's. In June 1879, such proponents of terror as Alexander Mikhailov, Michael Grachevskii, Andrei Zheliabov, and Sophia Perovskaia, founded an organization, *Narodnaia Volia* (People's Will). It advocated control of factories for Russian workers and peasant control of land; absolute freedom of thought, speech, press, and assembly; universal suffrage; and the replacement of standing armies by a popular militia. On March 13, 1881, members of the *Narodnaia Volia* assassinated Tsar Alexander II.

The regicide caused the arrest of many members

From George Kennan, *Siberia and the Exile System* (London: Century Co., 1891), vol. 2, pp. 495–503.

of the terrorist organization, and inaugurated a
period of blind and arrogant reaction. Before the
reaction set in, members of the executive committee
of the Narodnaia Volia sent a letter to the new tsar,
Alexander III (1881–1894), in which they sought
to explain candidly the causes that led to the tragedy.

Program of the Narodnaia Volia, 1879

By fundamental conviction we are socialists and democrats. We are
satisfied that only through socialistic principles can the human race
acquire liberty, equality, and fraternity; secure the full and harmonious
development of the individual as well as the material prosperity of all;
and thus make progress. We are convinced that all social forms must
rest upon the sanction of the people themselves, and that popular development is permanent only when it proceeds freely and independently,
and when every idea that is to be embodied in the people's life has first
passed through the people's consciousness and has been acted upon by
the people's will. The welfare of the people and the will of the people
are our two most sacred and most inseparable principles.

A

1. If we look at the environment in which the Russian people are
forced to live and act, we see that they are, economically and politically,
in a state of absolute slavery. As laborers they work only to feed and
support the parasitic classes; and as citizens they are deprived of all
rights. Not only does the actual state of things fail to answer to their
will, but they dare not even express and formulate their will; they cannot even think what is good and what is bad for them; the very thought
that they can have a will is regarded as a crime against the State. Enmeshed on all sides, they are being reduced to a state of physical degeneration, intellectual stolidity, and general inferiority.

2. Around the enchained people we see a class of exploiters whom the
state creates and protects. The state itself is the greatest capitalistic
power in the land; it constitutes the sole political oppressor of the
people, and only through its aid and support can the lesser robbers
exist. This bourgeois excrescence in the form of a government sustains
itself by mere brute force—by means of its military, police, and bureaucratic organization—in precisely the same way that the Mongols of
Genghis Khan sustained themselves in Russia. It is not sanctioned by the
people; it rules by arbitrary violence, and it adopts and enforces governmental and economic forms and principles that have nothing whatever
in common with the people's wishes and ideals.

3. In the nation we can see, crushed but still living, its old traditional principles, such as the right of the people to the land, communal and local self-government, freedom of speech and of conscience, and the rudiments of federal organization. These principles would develop broadly, and would give an entirely different and a more popular direction to our whole history, if the nation could live and organize itself in accordance with its own wishes and its own tendencies.

B

1. We are of opinion, therefore, that it is our first duty, as socialists and democrats, to free the people from the oppression of the present government, and bring about a political revolution, in order to transfer the supreme power to the nation. By means of this revolution we shall afford the people an opportunity to develop, henceforth, independently, and shall cause to be recognized and supported, in Russian life, many purely socialistic principles that are common to us and to the Russian people.

2. We think that the will of the people would be sufficiently well expressed and executed by a national Organizing Assembly, elected freely by a general vote, and acting under the instructions of the voters. This, of course, would fall far short of an ideal manifestation of the people's will; but it is the only one that is practicable at present, and we therefore think best to adopt it. Our plan is to take away the power from the existing Government, and give it to an Organizing Assembly, elected in the manner above described, whose duty it will be to make an examination of all our social and governmental institutions, and remodel them in accordance with instructions from the electors.

C

Although we are ready to submit wholly to the popular will, we regard it as none the less our duty, as a party, to appear before the people with our program. This program we shall use as a means of propaganda until the revolution comes, we shall advocate it during the election campaign, and we shall support it before the Organizing Assembly. It is as follows:

1. Perpetual popular representation, constituted as above described and having full power to act in all national questions.

2. General local self-government, secured by the election of all officers, and the economic independence of the people.

3. The self-controlled village commune as the economic and administrative unit.

4. Ownership of the land by the people.

5. A system of measures having for their object the turning over to the laborers of all mining works and factories.

6. Complete freedom of conscience, speech, association, public meeting, and electioneering activity.

7. Universal right of franchise, without any class or property limitation.

8. The substitution of a territorial militia for the army.

We shall follow this program, and we believe that all of its parts are so interdependent as to be impracticable one without the other, and that only as a whole will the program insure political and economic freedom and the harmonious development of the people.

D

In view of the stated aim of the party its operations may be classified as follows:

1. *Propaganda and agitation*. Our propaganda has for its object the popularization, in all social classes, of the idea of a political and democratic revolution as a means of social reform, as well as popularization of the party's own program. Its essential features are criticism of the existing order of things, and a statement and explanation of revolutionary methods. The aim of agitation should be to incite the people to protest, as generally as possible, against the present state of affairs; to demand such reforms as are in harmony with the party's purposes; and, especially, to demand the summoning of an Organizing Assembly. The popular protest may take the form of meetings, demonstrations, petitions, leading addresses, refusals to pay taxes, etc.

2. *Destructive and terroristic activity*. Terroristic activity consists in the destruction of the most harmful persons in the Government, the protection of the party from spies, and the punishment of official lawlessness and violence in all the more prominent and important cases in which such lawlessness and violence are manifested. The aim of such activity is to break down the prestige of Governmental power, to furnish continuous proof of the possibility of carrying on a contest with the Government, to raise in that way the revolutionary spirit of the people and inspire belief in the practicability of revolution, and, finally, to form a body suited and accustomed to warfare.

3. *The organization of secret societies and the arrangement of them in connected groups around a single center*. The organization of small secret societies with all sorts of revolutionary aims is indispensable, both as a means of executing the numerous functions of the party and of finishing the political training of its members. In order, however, that the work may be carried on harmoniously, it is necessary that these small bodies should

be grouped about one common center, upon the principle either of complete identification or of federal union.

4. *The acquirement of ties, and an influential position in the administration, in the army, in society, and among the people.* The administration and the army are particularly important in connection with a revolution, and serious attention should also be devoted to the people. The principal object of the party, so far as the people are concerned, is to prepare them to cooperate with the revolution, and to carry on a successful electioneering contest after the revolution—a contest that shall have for its object the election of purely democratic delegates to the Organizing Assembly. The party should enlist acknowledged partizans among the more prominent classes of the peasantry, and should prearrange for the active cooperation of the masses at the more important points and among the more sympathetic portions of the population. In view of this, every member of the party who is in contact with the people must strive to take a position that will enable him to defend the interests of the peasants, give them aid when they need it, and acquire celebrity among them as an honest man and a man who wishes them well. In this way he must keep up the reputation of the party and support its ideas and aims.

5. *The organization and consummation of the revolution.* In view of the oppressed and cowed condition of the people, and of the fact that the Government, by means of partial concessions and pacifications, may retard for a long time a general revolutionary movement, the party should take the initiative, and not wait until the people are able to do the work without its aid.

6. *The electioneering canvass before the summoning of the Organizing Assembly.* However the revolution may be brought about—as the result of an open revolution, or with the aid of a conspiracy—the duty of the party will be to aid in the immediate summoning of an Organizing Assembly, to which shall be transferred the powers of the Provisional Government created by the revolution or the conspiracy. During the election canvass the party should oppose, in every way, the candidacy of kuláks of all sorts, and strive to promote the candidacy of purely communal people.

A Letter from The Revolutionary Executive Committee of the Narodnaia Volia to Alexander III, March 22, 1881

Your Majesty:

Although the Executive Committee understands fully the grievous oppression that you must experience at this moment, it believes that it has no right to yield to the feeling of natural delicacy which would perhaps dictate the postponement of the following explanation to another time. There is something higher than the most legitimate human feeling, and that is duty to one's country—the duty for which a citizen must sacrifice himself and his own feelings, and even the feelings of others. In obedience to this all-powerful duty we have decided to address you at once, waiting for nothing, as will wait for nothing the historical process that threatens us with rivers of blood and the most terrible convulsions.

The tragedy enacted on the Ekaterínski canal was not a mere casualty, nor was it unexpected. After all that had happened in the course of the previous decade it was absolutely inevitable; and in that fact consists its deep significance for a man who has been placed by fate at the head of governmental authority. Such occurrences can be explained as the results of individual malignity, or even of the evil disposition of "gangs," only by one who is wholly incapable of analyzing the life of a nation. For ten whole years—notwithstanding the strictest prosecution; notwithstanding the sacrifice by the late Emperor's Government of liberty, the interests of all classes, the interests of industry and commerce, and even its own dignity; notwithstanding the absolute sacrifice of everything in the attempt to suppress the revolutionary movement—that movement has obstinately extended, attracting to itself the best elements of the country —the most energetic and self-sacrificing people of Russia—and the revolutionists have carried on, for three years, a desperate partizan warfare with the administration.

You are aware, your Majesty, that the Government of the late Emperor could not be accused of a lack of energy. It hanged the innocent and the guilty, and filled prisons and remote provinces with exiles. Tens of so-called "leaders" were captured and hanged, and died with the courage and tranquillity of martyrs; but the movement did not cease—on the contrary it grew and strengthened. The revolutionary movement, your Majesty, is not dependent upon any particular individuals; it is a process of the social organism; and the scaffolds raised for its more energetic exponents are as powerless to save the out-grown order of things as the cross that was erected for the Redeemer was powerless to save the ancient world from the triumph of Christianity. The Government, of course, may yet capture and hang an immense number of separate individuals, it may break up a great number of separate revolutionary groups, it may even destroy the most important of existing revolutionary organizations; but all this will not change, in the slightest degree, the condition of affairs. Revolutionists are the creation of circumstances; of the general discontent of the people; of the striving of Russia after a new social framework. It is impossible to exterminate the whole people; it is impossible, by means of repression, to stifle its discontent. Discontent only grows the more when it is repressed. For these reasons the places of slain revolutionists are constantly taken by new individuals, who come forth from among the people in ever-increasing numbers, and who are still more embittered, still more energetic. These persons, in order to carry on the conflict, form an association in the light of the experience of their predecessors, and the revolutionary organization thus grows stronger, numerically and in quality, with the lapse of time. This we actually see from the history of the last ten years. Of what use was it to destroy the Dolgúshintsi, the Chaikóftsi, and the workers of 1874? Their places were taken by much more resolute democrats. Then the awful repressive measures of the Government called upon the stage the terrorists of 1878–1879. In vain the Government put to death the Koválskis, the Dubróvins, the Ossínskis, and the Lisogúbs. In vain it destroyed tens of revolutionary circles. From among those incomplete organizations, by virtue of natural selection, arose only stronger forms, until, at last, there has appeared an Executive Committee with which the Government has not yet been able successfully to deal.

A dispassionate glance at the grievous decade through which we have just passed will enable us to forecast accurately the future progress of the revolutionary movement, provided the policy of the Government does not change. The movement will continue to grow and extend; deeds of a terroristic nature will increase in frequency and intensity, and the revolutionary organization will constantly set forth, in the places of destroyed groups, stronger and more perfect forms. Meanwhile the number of the discontented in the country will grow larger and larger; confidence in the Government, on the part of the people, will decline; and the idea of revolution—of its possibility and inevitability—will establish itself in Russia more and more firmly. A terrible explosion, a bloody hurly-burly, a revolutionary earthquake throughout Russia, will complete the destruction of the old order of things. Upon what depends this terrible prospect? Yes, your Majesty, "terrible" and lamentable! Do not take this for a mere phrase. We understand, better than any one else can, how lamentable is the waste of so much talent and energy, the loss, in bloody skirmishes and in the work of destruction, of so much strength that, under other conditions, might have been expended in creative labor and in the development of the intelligence, the welfare, and the civil life of the Russian people. Whence proceeds this lamentable necessity for bloody conflict? It arises, your Majesty, from the lack in Russia of a real government in the true sense of that word. A government, in the very nature of things, should only give outward form to the aspirations of the people and effect to the people's will. But with us—excuse the expression—the Government has degenerated into a mere camarilla, and deserves the name of a usurping "gang" much more than does the Executive Committee.

Whatever may be the *intentions* of the Tsar, the *actions* of the Government have nothing in common with the popular welfare, or popular aspirations. The Imperial Government subjected the people to serfdom, put the masses into the power of the nobility, and is now openly creating the most injurious class of speculators and jobbers. All of its reforms result merely in a more perfect enslavement and a more complete exploitation of the people. It has brought Russia to such a pass that, at the present time, the masses of the people are in a state of pauperism and ruin; are subjected to the most humiliating surveillance, even at their own domestic hearths; and are powerless even to regulate their own communal and social affairs. The protection of the law and of the Government is enjoyed only by the extortionist and the exploiter, and the most exasperating robbery goes unpunished. But, on the other hand, what a terrible fate awaits the man who sincerely considers the general good! You know very well, your Majesty, that it is not only socialists who are exiled and prosecuted. Can it be possible that the Government is the guardian of such "order"? Is it not rather probable that this is the work of a "gang" —the evidence of a complete usurpation?

These are the reasons why the Russian Government exerts no moral influence, and has no support among the people. These are the reasons why Russia brings forth so many revolutionists. These are the reasons why even such a deed as Tsaricide excites in the minds of a majority of the people only gladness and sympathy. Yes, your Majesty! Do not be deceived by the reports of flatterers and sycophants—Tsaricide, in Russia, is popular.

From such a state of affairs there can be only two exits: either a revolution, absolutely inevitable and not to be averted by any punishments, or a voluntary turning of the Supreme Power to the people. In the interest of our native land, in the hope of preventing the useless waste of energy, in the hope of averting the terrible miseries that always accompany revolution, the Executive Committee approaches your Majesty with the advice to take the second course. Be assured, so soon as the Supreme Power ceases to rule arbitrarily, so soon as it firmly resolves to accede to the demands of the people's conscience and consciousness, you may, without fear, discharge the spies that disgrace the administration, send your guards back to their barracks, and burn the scaffolds that are demoralizing the people. The Executive Committee will voluntarily terminate its own existence, and the organizations formed about it will disperse, in order that their members may devote themselves to the work of culture among the people of their native land.

We address your Majesty as those who have discarded all prejudices, and who have suppressed the distrust created by the actions of the Government throughout a century. We forget that you are the representative of the authority that has so often deceived and that has so injured the people. We address you as a citizen and as an honest man. We hope that the feeling of personal exasperation will not extinguish in your mind your consciousness of your duties and your desire to know the truth. We also might feel exasperation. You have lost your father. We have lost not only our fathers, but our brothers, our wives, our children and our dearest friends. But we are ready to suppress personal feeling if it be demanded by the welfare of Russia. We expect the same from you.

We set no conditions for you—do not let our proposition irritate you. The conditions that are prerequisite to a change from revolutionary activity to peaceful labor are created, not by us, but by history. These conditions, in our opinion, are two.

1. A general amnesty to cover all past political crimes; for the reason that they were not crimes but fulfillments of civil duty.

2. The summoning of representatives of the whole Russian people to examine the existing framework of social and governmental life, and to remodel it in accordance with the people's wishes.

We regard it as necessary, however, to remind you that the legalization of the Supreme Power, by the representatives of the people, can be valid only in case the elections are perfectly free. For this reason such elections must be held under the following conditions.

1. Delegates are to be sent from all classes, without distinction, and in number are to be proportionate to the number of inhabitants.

2. There shall be no limitations, either for voters or delegates.

3. The canvass and the elections shall be absolutely unrestricted, and therefore the Government, pending the organization of the National Assembly, shall authorize, in the form of temporary measures; (a) Complete freedom of the press; (b) Complete freedom of speech; (c) Complete freedom of public meeting; (d) Complete freedom of election program. This is the only way in which Russia can return to the path of normal and peaceful development.

We declare solemnly, before the people of our native land and before the whole world, that our party will submit unconditionally to the decisions of a National Assembly elected in the manner above indicated, and that we will not allow ourselves, in future, to offer violent resistance to any Government that the National Assembly may sanction.

And now, your Majesty, decide! Before you are two courses, and you are to make your choice between them. We can only trust that your intelligence and conscience may suggest to you the only decision that is compatible with the welfare of Russia, with your own dignity, and with your duty to your native land.

The Executive Committee

30

Russian Pan-Slavism: Danilevskii's Views

There were many Russian intellectuals in the nineteenth century who applauded the achievements of
Western Europe, believed in scientific progress, favored the constitutional form of government, and
advocated freedom of thought and of the press.
There were also those who were highly critical of
"the decadent West" and extolled the virtues of the
Slavic and above all of the Russian character. While
each of these two positions had numerous spokesmen, few matched Nikolai Ia. Danilevskii (1822–
1885) in color and bluntness. A philosopher of Slavophilism and a recognized spokesman of Pan-Slavism,
Danilevskii is remembered most for his work *Rossiia
i Evropa* (Russia and Europe), originally published
in 1871. Because the history of Russia was unlike
the history of the Latin and Germanic peoples,
Danilevskii argued, Russia should remain indifferent
to the West and should unite with all Slavs as the
first step toward an inevitable confrontation between
Europe and the Slavic world. The Slavic union he
envisaged was to be under Russian leadership and
was to stretch from Stettin in the Baltic to Trieste
in the Adriatic, antedating by many years the concept expressed in Winston Churchill's famed Iron
Curtain speech of 1946.

[Constantinople has been] the aim of the aspirations of the Russian
people from the dawn of our statehood, the ideal of our enlightenment;
the glory, splendor and greatness of our ancestors, the center of Orthodoxy, and the bone of contention between Europe and ourselves. What

From Nikolai Ia. Danilevskii, *Rossiia i Evropa. Vzgliad na kulturnyia i politi-
cheskiia otnosheniia Slavianskogo mira k Germansko-Romanskomu* (*Russia and
Europe. A View on Cultural and Political Relations Between the Slavic and
German-Roman Worlds*) (St. Petersburg: 1871), pp. 407–408, 413–414, 421,
426–434, and 436–438. Translation mine. Items in brackets are mine.

historical significance Constantinople would have for us if we could wrest her away from the Turks regardless of Europe! What delight would our hearts feel from the radiance of the cross that we would raise atop the dome of St. Sophia! Add to this all the other advantages of Constantinople . . . , her world significance, her commercial significance, her exquisite location, and all the charms of the south. One should be cautious, however, that Constantinople, if she should become Russia's capital, should not unduly attract to herself the moral, intellectual and material forces of Russia, and thereby disrupt her vital balance.

But Constantinople should not become Russia's capital, she should not concentrate [on herself] her national and state life, and consequently she should not become an inseparable part of the Russian state. In order to provide Russia with the above enumerated advantages, without imposing obvious dangers upon her, Constantinople, once freed and transformed into the real Tsargrad, must *ipso facto* be more than just a capital of the Russian state. She cannot have close ties and be a mother image for Russia. Moscow alone has the exclusive prerogative on that. Tsargrad, in a word, should not be the capital of Russia, but the capital of a Pan-Slav Union. . . .

[This] Pan-Slav Union should consist of the following states:

The Russian Empire, to which should be added all of Galicia and Hungarian Rus [present-day Carpatho-Ukraine];

The Bohemian-Moravian-Slovak Kingdom, consisting, in addition to Bohemia proper, of that part of Moravia and Northwest Hungary inhabited exclusively or predominantly by Slovaks, with approximately 9,000,-000 inhabitants and 1800 square miles;

The Serbo-Croatian-Slovene Kingdom, consisting of the Principality of Serbia, Montenegro, Bosnia, Herzegovina, Old Serbia, Northern Albania, Serbian Voivodina and Banat, Croatia, Slovenia, Dalmatia, the Military Frontiers, the duchy of Krajna, Hertz, Gradishche, Istria, the Trieste District, two-thirds of Corinthia, and one-fifth of Styria up to the Drava River, with a combined population of about 8,000,000, and a territory of about 4500 square miles.

The Bulgarian Kingdom, with Bulgaria and a large part of Rumelia and Macedonia, with 6,000,000 to 7,000,000 inhabitants, and about 3000 square miles.

The Rumanian Kingdom with Wallachia, Moldavia, a portion of Bukovina, half of Transylvania approximately to the Maros River, and that part of Western Bessarabia inhabited predominantly by the Moldavians. In return for this exchange, Russia should receive the severed part of southern Bessarabia, including the Danube Delta and the Dobrudgea Peninsula. This [Rumanian Kingdom] would comprise about 7,000,000 inhabitants, and more than 3000 square miles.

The Greek Kingdom with the addition to its present territory of Thessaly, Epirus, southwestern parts of Macedonia, all of the islands of the Aegean Archipelago, Rhodes, Crete, Cyprus, and the coasts of Asia Minor and of the Aegean Sea, with approximately 2,800 or 3,000 square miles, and a population of about 4,000,000.

The *Magyar Kingdom*, with Hungary and Transylvania, excluding those parts which are inhabited by non-Magyar peoples and which should be added to Russia, Bohemia, Serbia, and Rumania, respectively, with a population of about 7,000,000, and 3000 square miles.

The *Tsargrad* [Constantinople] *District*, with the adjacent portions of Rumelia and Asia Minor which surround the Bosphorus, the Sea of Marmora, and the Dardanelles with the Gallipoli Peninsula, and Tenedos Island, with approximately 2,000,000 inhabitants.

Such a union, about 125,000,000 strong, consisting largely of peoples homogeneous in spirit and blood who would find in Tsargrad a natural center of their moral and material unity, would provide complete, wise, and therefore the only possible solution of the Eastern problem. Controlling only that which legally belongs to it, not endangering anyone, and not being afraid of any threats, such a union could withstand all storms and adversities and march peacefully along the road of independent development. . . .

The Pan-Slav Union is the only firm ground on which a distinctive Slavic culture can rise—it is the condition *sine qua non* of its development. Such is the general purport, the main conclusion of our entire investigation. Therefore we shall not stop now to cite evidence of the significance, value, and necessity of such an arrangement of the Slavic world from a cultural-historical viewpoint. In this chapter I intend to develop, from a more specialized political viewpoint, the importance, value, and need for unity of the Slavic family in a unified federal system.

We have seen above that from a general cultural-historical viewpoint Russia cannot, either by origin or adoption, be considered an integral part of Europe; that only two possibilities are available to her: either to form a distinct, independent cultural unity with other Slavs, or be devoid of any cultural-historical significance—to be nothing. . . .

Her internal structure being alien to the European world, and in addition being strong and powerful enough to occupy a role as one of the members of the European family and as one of the great European powers, Russia can acquire a distinguished place in history for herself and for Slavdom in no other way than as the leader of a unique, independent political system of states; she would serve as a counterweight to Europe in her totality and unity. These are the advantages, the benefits, and the essence of the Pan-Slav Union for Russia.

The significance of the Union is even more important for Western Slavdom. A Russia which has not become the representative of the Slavic world will inevitably be deprived thereby of the historic goal of her existence. She will present to the world in vast dimensions a pitiful model of the historical ignoramus. Viewed, however, from a more immediate perspective, she still can for a long time—for years and centuries—not only preserve her external independence, but even be a great political force, however devoid she is of internal meaning and content. For the other Slavic nations the question is put more bluntly. Here the concern is not with the historical essence of their life, nor with their great historical role, but simply with existence—the daily bread of their national life, so to speak. The question of *to be or not to be* presents itself in the most prosaic and therefore in the most fearful and tragic form. We examined this question in sufficient depth in the thirteenth chapter, and there is no need to repeat it here. Here I consider it necessary to advance only those particular, special advantages which must accrue from the Pan-Slav Union for each of the units that should become members.

Let us begin with Greece. . . . Let us look at the existing real advantages which will result from her entrance into the Union. Neither topography nor the soil of Greece will permit her to become an agricultural or an industrial state. Trade must serve as the prime basis of wealth and prosperity for the Hellenic peoples. This stems from the natural inclinations of the Greeks, from their long standing habit, and from local conditions of the continental part of Greece, the islands of the Aegean Archipelago, and the Western Coast of Asia Minor. Not only geographic and ethnographic conditions, but historical experience itself, point to this. The prosperity of Greece in glorious times was based on trade. Trade was also the basic preoccupation of the Greeks during the time of their decline and enslavement. Following the restoration of the political independence to a portion of Greece, the Greek people again turned their main activity to that direction.

Trade in the Eastern Mediterranean, in the archipelago and in the Black Sea, is to a large degree in Greek hands and is carried aboard Greek ships. This fact has aroused the envy of England, as evidenced in the Pacifico Affair [in 1850]. The opening of the Suez Canal should immeasurably broaden the trading area of Greece, transforming its significance from local to world-wide. In addition to the Eastern Mediterranean with all of its gulfs and branches, the Red Sea, the Indian Ocean, and the Bay of Bengal will become domestic seas for the Greek merchant fleet. They will be, so to speak, under Greek influence; and no one's trade routes will be shortened to the same degree as the Greeks'. But a voluminous trade (especially in distant seas) can be carried on successfully only if it is supported by a strong navy capable of protecting the merchant flag at all points of the globe. Without it there cannot be necessary confidence and necessary support for trading enterprises. . . . The Pacifico Affair points out quite clearly how vulnerable a country is in its maritime trade if it is not supported by an ample military power. But where is Greece, who has all the prerequisites to become a world-wide maritime nation, to obtain a sufficiently powerful fleet to support her maritime trade? No one can provide her this naval might except a powerful Slavic-Greek Union—the only form under which the Eastern Roman Empire can be resurrected.

A general union of Slavs, headed by Russia, has a particularly real importance for *Bulgaria*. Of all the Slavic nations she is under the most severe oppression because she lives close to her oppressors. Moreover, she least remembers the tradition of statehood and of independent political existence. She feels, however, her oppression, and feels her own uniqueness from her oppressors; therefore she cannot merge with them, she cannot betray her cultural foundations and consequently she aspires for freedom. But how to utilize this freedom, how to make the transition from national to political existence, and to an independent statehood? We have seen similar examples in Greece, Serbia and Rumania. The Bulgar example therefore is not unique. It is simply a rock that must be avoided in order not to encounter a disaster. The examples of Greece and Serbia differ in many ways from that which is in prospect for Bulgaria. They achieved their independence as a result of prolonged struggles, in the course of which there emerged from the people progressive representatives who lived a national life and who understood the spirit and needs of the people. The people accepted them, and thus the people themselves created essential institutions of public administration. In Serbia even the memory of national representation was preserved—the *skupshchina*. There is nothing of this in Bulgaria. . . .

In order to prevent Bulgaria from falling under an alien influence, she must organize herself under the protective wing of Russia and under the influence of other states of the Slavic Union that are politically more developed. She must develop close relations with them, first as a distinct administrative region and subsequently as a distinct political entity. Such protection and such guardianship of an impartial Russia for all Slavic peoples is especially necessary for Bulgaria for yet another reason; namely, that this country which is inhabited by an independent Slavic people should preserve its independence and not become a victim of the ambitions of neighboring Serbia.

A close connection between Russia and all Slavdom is not less useful for *Serbia* as well, in order to suppress incorrect ambitious instincts within her and to guide these in the proper direction, not toward Bulgaria, but toward the lands under the control of Austria, lands populated by Serbs and the related Croat and Slovene peoples. The vigorous and strong Serbian people must guard against the Polish tradition of eagerness to appropriate what belongs to others while relinquishing their own. The Serbian people can find the necessary strength and hope for success in their struggle against Italianization, Magyarizition, and Germanization of their land only in a political union with all the Slavs under the leadership of Russia.

This truism applies to an even greater degree to the *Czech* nation, whose territory juts out into German land like a bastion, inside of which German settlement has achieved great success. Neither the internal struggle with the Germans nor external attacks, which this bone of contention between Slavdom and Germandom cannot escape, can be successfully carried out without a close unity with all Slavdom.

The *Rumanians* can count on the annexation of half of Transylvania, Bukovina, and part of Bessarabia only with the agreement and cooperation of Russia; only under her impartial and peaceful influence is opposition to the usurpation of Magyarism possible. Only by relying on Slavdom, incomparably more kindred to them, can the Rumanians struggle with the corroding Gallomania and the imitativeness of their pitiful intelligentsia.

In the preceding chapter we saw that even *Poland* can find a satisfactory solution to her long torment exclusively in the womb of the Pan-Slav Union, in close unity and friendship with Russia.

For *Hungary* alone, the perspective of such a union that would place a limit on all her ambitions and lofty plans cannot present itself in an optimistic light. But even she can rely on the satisfaction of all of her legal aspirations. She would have to abandon only her illicit love of power.

Such are the advantages for each of the peoples who could and should form independent states in the great Pan-Slav Federation, a union that would unite them. If one should add to all this the brilliant, majestic, universal historical role which such a union promises to all Slavdom, it would seem that such a union must be, if not a spontaneous goal of the ambitions of all Slavs conscious of their Slavic identity, at least an object of their desires—their political ideal. And we actually cannot recall one famous Slavic name for whom the thought of Slavic unity in one form or another did not represent such an ideal. We will name several who expressed it more or less, as for example Khomiakov, Pogodin, Hanka, Kollár and Štur.* It is sad that many of the non-Europe oriented Slavs do not regard the political unity of their nations under Russia's leadership with the sympathy that one could and should expect.

The slanders by the Poles and by Europe, with little, and one can even say with absolutely no knowledge of Russia, with no acquaintance with our affairs, are presented in a totally false light, yet have penetrated so deeply that even many of the leading Slavic thinkers, who are fully de-

---

* Alexander S. Khomiakov (1804–1860), a Russian Slavophile writer; Michael P. Pogodin (1799–1875), a Russian Slavophile historian; Václav Hanka (1791–1861), a Czech nationalist; Jan Kollár (1793–1852), a Czech poet; and Ludevit Štur (1815–1856), a Slovak poet. All were outspoken proponents of the Panslav idea.—Ed.

voted to the Slavic cause, are frightened by some kind of ghosts. On the one hand they are frightened by the ghost of power-loving Russia, which supposedly desires to destroy the distinctiveness of the Slavic nationalities, to devour them like she devoured Poland; on the other hand, viewing the fate of mankind and civilization in general, they are frightened by the ghost of universal sovereignty, which appears as something terrible for the Slavic heart, saturated with humanism, even if this sovereignty belongs to no one else but the very poor, downtrodden Slavs—whose own oppression horrifies no one and of whom no one says it is incompatible with true humanity. That Slavic independence and the development of Slavic power are not appreciated in Europe is obvious. It would be fruitless and silly on our part or on anyone else's part to try to reassure Europeans of this. But it is sad that Slavs, even the Russians themselves, are able to argue in such a way. As far as possible we will try to dissipate here this unnatural fog, beginning with Russia's love of power.

The facts themselves will serve as an answer and refutation. Nothing will be elaborated here. We will only point to the well known examples of Russia's dealings with regions annexed to her territory. Finland, which had been won from Sweden, was given full autonomy and independence: a separate military force, which has not gone outside the limits of Finland; a separate monetary, trade, and financial system, even a constitution and a parliament; a territorial region which had belonged to Russia for over one hundred years was given to Finland; the Russian language was not introduced in Finnish schools; Orthodoxy did not become the dominant religion; she was not turned into a market for our manufactures; not one copeck of Finnish revenues went to Russia. In a word, Russia not only did not exploit Finland morally or materially, but to the contrary, she has always extended her a helping hand. The Baltic territory was not only not Russified but, on the contrary, the most powerful agent of Germanization—the Dorpat-German University—was founded and has been maintained by the Russian government. Not only did the Russian government not assist in the Russification of the territory, it placed barriers in opposition to it, even when it was called forth by the natural course of events. All this was done to eliminate the fear of being branded an oppressor of the nationalities who were politically united with Russia. The Polish example itself, so often advanced against Russia, is in essence a good proof of that. Following her unity with Russia, Poland enjoyed statelike independence and a constitutional life; under Russian control Polish influence in Western Russia was extended by means of Vilna University, through a whole system of public education, and much else. Only the obvious, crude attempts of Poles to add West Russia to Poland by force opened our eyes—and that, it seems, only for a time. Although, of course, I do not at all say this in praise of Russia, her government, and her public opinion, these events nonetheless clearly show that no associate

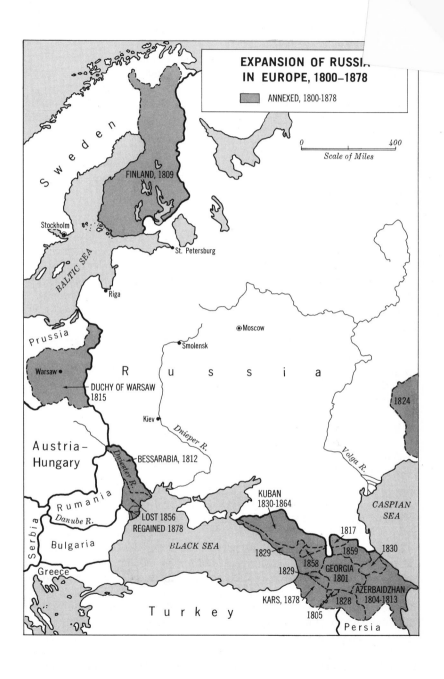

EXPANSION OF RUSSIA IN EUROPE, 1800–1878

ANNEXED, 1800–1878

0 — 400
Scale of Miles

Sweden

FINLAND, 1809

Stockholm

St. Petersburg

BALTIC SEA

Riga

Prussia

Moscow

Smolensk

R   u   s   s   i   a

Warsaw

DUCHY OF WARSAW
1815

Kiev

Dnieper R.

1824

Volga R.

Austria–
Hungary

BESSARABIA, 1812

Dniester R.

Rumania

Danube R.

CASPIAN
SEA

KUBAN
1830–1864

Serbia

LOST 1856
REGAINED 1878

1817

Bulgaria

BLACK SEA

1829

1859

1830

Greece

1829

1858

GEORGIA
1801

AZERBAIDZHAN
1804–1813

KARS, 1878

1828

T   u   r   k   e   y

1805

Persia

of a state that has dealt with the integral parts of its territory in such a manner has anything to fear about its independence, both political and national, or has anything to fear about the violation of the bounds of clearly external-political unified hegemony. Any closer alliance would certainly only allow for that kindred, national sympathy which could not help but draw the members of the Slavic family to one another after the external barriers dividing them were broken and they had undertaken the general historical task.

But this is not enough. If Russia would often act to her own detriment in that way, would she act otherwise when the most obvious, simplest calculation would prompt her to refrain from any interference in the internal affairs of her allies, to touch neither their political nor national independence? . . .

What would Russia achieve if she were to try to destroy the internal independence of Slavic and other powers allied with her by trying to include them in her own state system—even if such a desire proved to be successful? Instead of 40,000,000 loyal, amicably disposed allies she would acquire 40,000,000 discontented subjects: how much such a situation increases the strength of a state can be seen from abundant examples in the relations of Poland to Russia, Ireland to England, and, above all, Hungary and Venice to Austria. . . .

Thus, the freedom of the Slavs and the other peoples in the union, amongst themselves and with Russia, would be assured, on the one hand by simple, healthy, political common sense, and by Russia's instinct of self-preservation; on the other hand, the entire past of Russia, the very flaws of Russian and Slavic virtue in general, would serve as a guarantee of the just, inoffensive character of those mutual relations which would develop between the head of the union and its members. He who gave the most can expect the least: he who gave national and even political freedom to the parts comprising a state, as for instance to Finland and even to hostile Poland—having taken it away only after the most sense-less, doublecrossing abuse by them and in view of the preservation and securing of the freedom of a part of the Russian people whom the Poles schemed against—will not encroach on the independence of his own allies.

Another scarecrow frightening people away from Pan-Slavism is the fear of a world-wide monarchy, the fear of world sovereignty. It is clear from the above explanation that if such a world sovereignty was the natural, necessary consequence of the Panslav Union, then in any case it would not be especially Russian, but Panslav; and there would be nothing for the Slavs to fear. The thought of world sovereignty did not frighten the ancient Romans; England does not fear the idea of world-wide sovereignty on the seas; the extension of her control, spanning the seas and oceans with a chain of large and small British colonies; the thought of limitless sovereignty from Greenland to the Tierra del Fuego does not frighten America either. What strange modesty—to recoil before a great future, to shun it because of a dread of being too powerful and strong, and even parodying the thought of Voltaire about God (that if He did not exist it would be necessary to invent Him), to apply it to Austria in the view of the prevention of such a misfortune?

But this is not the question. The fright itself does not have any basis. The Pan-Slav Union, having assured the freedom of the Slavs and their fruitful interaction on one another, would not be able to threaten the independence of anyone, nor of anyone's legal rights. Again the most simple statistical calculation convinces one of this. The population of only that part of Europe which currently plays an active political role, that is, Germany (with the exclusion of the entire non-German portion of Austria), France, and England, with the addition of only Belgium and Holland (who are surrounded by them, and who must voluntarily or involuntarily follow them), would equal the population of the entire Slavic Union. With the addition of Italy, Spain, Portugal, and the Scandinavian states, there would be at least an excess of fifty million souls on the side of Europe. Consequently, the Slavic system of states would still be significantly weaker than Europe by the amount of its population, and could consider itself invincible only in the defense and protection of Slavic independence and originality. The strength would be only slightly equalized by the previously discussed strategic location of Constantinople and the Czech bastion.

31

Pobedonostsev's Criticism of Modern Society

The emancipation of the serfs in 1861 profoundly affected all aspects of Russian life. It contributed to the decline of the power of the nobility, discontent

From K. P. Pobyedonostseff, *Reflections of a Russian Statesman*. Translated from the Russian by Robert Crozier Long (London: Grant Richard, 1898), pp. 23–30, 32–46, 52–54, 62–74.

among the peasantry, restlessness among the workers, dissatisfaction among the intelligentsia, and
increasing reaction among the advocates of autocracy.
The principal spokesman of the latter from 1880 to
1905 was Constantine P. Pobedonostsev (1827–
1907). A constitutional lawyer by training, Pobedonostsev taught civil law at Moscow University from
1860 to 1865. He left teaching to become first a
member of the Senate (Russia's Supreme Court),
then a member of the Council of State (a consulta-
tive body that advised the tsar in legislative matters),
and from 1880 to 1905 he acted as Procurator of the
Holy Synod (lay administrator of the Orthodox
Church). Since Pobedonostsev was also a tutor in law
of Alexander III and Nicholas II, he was, between
1881 and 1905, the most influential member of the
government and the prime inspirer of its reactionary
policies.

The New Democracy

What is this freedom by which so many minds are agitated, which
inspires so many insensate actions, so many wild speeches, which leads
the people so often to misfortune? In the democratic sense of the word,
freedom is the right of political power, or, to express it otherwise, the
right to participate in the government of the State. This universal aspiration for a share in government has no constant limitations, and seeks no
definite issue, but incessantly extends, so that we might apply to it the
words of the ancient poet about dropsy: *crescit indulgens sibi.** Forever
extending its base, the new Democracy now aspires to universal suffrage—
a fatal error, and one of the most remarkable in the history of mankind.
By this means, the political power so passionately demanded by Democracy would be shattered into a number of infinitesimal bits, of which each
citizen acquires a single one. What will he do with it, then? How will he
employ it? In the result it has undoubtedly been shown that in the attainment of this aim Democracy violates its sacred formula of "Freedom indissolubly joined with Equality." It is shown that this apparently equal
distribution of "freedom" among all involves the total destruction of
equality. Each vote, representing an inconsiderable fragment of power, by
itself signifies nothing; an aggregation of votes alone has a relative value.
The result may be likened to the general meetings of shareholders in
public companies. By themselves individuals are ineffective, but he who
controls a number of these fragmentary forces is master of all power, and

---

* "It grows as it indulges itself."—Ed.

directs all decisions and dispositions. We may well ask in what consists the superiority of Democracy. Everywhere the strongest man becomes master of the State; sometimes a fortunate and resolute general, sometimes a monarch or administrator with knowledge, dexterity, a clear plan of action, and a determined will. In a Democracy, the real rulers are the dexterous manipulators of votes, with their place-men, the mechanics who so skillfully operate the hidden springs which move the puppets in the arena of democratic elections. Men of this kind are ever ready with loud speeches lauding equality; in reality, they rule the people as any despot or military dictator might rule it. The extension of the right to participate in elections is regarded as progress and as the conquest of freedom by democratic theorists, who hold that the more numerous the participants in political rights, the greater is the probability that all will employ this right in the interests of the public welfare, and for the increase of the freedom of the people. Experience proves a very different thing. The history of mankind bears witness that the most necessary and fruitful reforms —the most durable measures—emanated from the supreme will of statesmen, or from a minority enlightened by lofty ideas and deep knowledge, and that, on the contrary, the extension of the representative principle is accompanied by an abasement of political ideas and the vulgarisation of opinions in the mass of the electors. It shows also that this extension—in great States—was inspired by secret aims to the centralisation of power, or led directly to dictatorship. In France, universal suffrage was suppressed with the end of the Terror, and was re-established twice merely to affirm the autocracy of the two Napoleons. In Germany, the establishment of universal suffrage served merely to strengthen the high authority of a famous statesman who had acquired popularity by the success of his policy. What its ultimate consequences will be, Heaven only knows!

The manipulation of votes in the game of Democracy is of the commonest occurrence in most European states, and its falsehood, it would seem, has been exposed to all; yet few dare openly to rebel against it. The unhappy people must bear the burden, while the Press, herald of a supposititious public opinion, stifles the cry of the people with its shibboleth, "Great is Diana of the Ephesians." But to an impartial mind, all this is nothing better than a struggle of parties, and a shuffling with numbers and names. The voters, by themselves inconsiderable unities, acquire a value in the hands of dexterous agents. This value is realised by many means—mainly, by bribery in innumerable forms, from gifts of money and trifling articles, to the distribution of places in the services, the financial departments, and the administration. Little by little a class of electors has been formed which lives by the sale of votes to one or another of the political organisations. So far has this gone in France, for instance, that serious, intelligent, and industrious citizens in immense numbers abstain from voting, through the difficulty of contending with the cliques of political agents. With bribery go violence and threats, and reigns of terror are organised at elections by the help of which the respective cliques advance their candidates; hence the stormy scenes at electoral demonstrations, in which arms have been used, and the field of battle strewn with the bodies of the killed and wounded.

Organisation and bribery—these are the two mighty instruments which are employed with such success for the manipulation of the mass of electors. Such methods are in no way new. Thucydides depicts in vivid colours their employment in the ancient republics of Greece. The history of the Roman Republic presents monstrous examples of corruption as the chief instrument of factions at elections. But in our times a new means has been found of working the masses for political aims, and joining them in adventitious alliances by provoking a fictitious community of views. This is the art of rapid and dexterous generalisation of ideas, the composition of phrase and formulas, disseminated with the confidence of burning conviction as the last word of science, as dogmas of politicology, as infallible appreciations of events, of men, and of institutions. At one time it was believed that the faculty of analysing facts, and deducing general principles, was the privilege of a few enlightened minds and deep thinkers; now it is considered an universal attainment, and, under the name of convictions, the generalities of political science have become a sort of current money, coined by newspapers and rhetoricians. . . .

The Greatest Falsehood of Our Time

That which is founded on falsehood cannot be right. Institutions founded on false principles cannot be other than false themselves. This truth has been demonstrated by the bitter experience of ages and generations.

Among the falsest of political principles is the principle of the sovereignty of the people, the principle that all power issues from the people, and is based upon the national will—a principle which has unhappily become more firmly established since the time of the French Revolution. Thence proceeds the theory of Parliamentarism, which, up to the present day, has deluded much of the so-called "intelligence," and unhappily infatuated certain foolish Russians. It continues to maintain its hold on many minds with the obstinacy of a narrow fanaticism, although every day its falsehood is exposed more clearly to the world.

In what does the theory of Parliamentarism consist? It is supposed that the people in its assemblies makes its own laws, and elects responsible officers to execute its will. Such is the ideal conception. Its immediate realisation is impossible. The historical development of society necessitates that local communities increase in numbers and complexity; that separate races be assimilated, or, retaining their polities and languages, unite under a single flag, that territory extend indefinitely: under such conditions direct government by the people is impracticable. The people must, therefore, delegate its right of power to its representatives, and invest them with administrative autonomy. These representatives in turn cannot govern immediately, but are compelled to elect a still smaller number of trustworthy persons—ministers—to whom they entrust the preparation and execution of the laws, the apportionment and collection of taxes, the appointment of subordinate officials, and the disposition of the militant forces.

In the abstract this mechanism is quite symmetrical: for its proper operation many conditions are essential. The working of the political machine is based on impersonal forces constantly acting and completely balanced. It may act successfully only when the delegates of the people abdicate their personalities; when on the benches of Parliament sit mechanical fulfillers of the people's behests; when the ministers of State remain impersonal, absolute executors of the will of the majority; when the elected representatives of the people are capable of understanding precisely, and executing conscientiously the programme of activity, mathematically expressed, which has been delivered to them. Given such conditions the machine would work exactly, and would accomplish its purpose. The law would actually embody the will of the people; administrative measures would actually emanate from Parliament; the pillars of the State would rest actually on the elective assemblies, and each citizen would directly and consciously participate in the management of public affairs.

Such is the theory. Let us look at the practice. Even in the classic countries of Parliamentarism it would satisfy not one of the conditions enumerated. The elections in no way express the will of the electors. The popular representatives are in no way restricted by the opinions of their constituents, but are guided by their own views and considerations, modified by the tactics of their opponents. In reality, ministers are autocratic, and they rule, rather than are ruled by, Parliament. They attain power, and lose power, not by virtue of the will of the people, but through immense personal influence, or the influence of a strong party which places them in power, or drives them from it. They dispose of the force and resources of the nation at will, they grant immunities and favours, they maintain a multitude of idlers at the expense of the people, and they fear no censure while they enjoy the support in Parliament of a majority which they maintain by the distribution of bounties from the rich tables which the State has put at their disposal. In reality, the ministers are as irresponsible as the representatives of the people. Mistakes, abuse of power, and arbitrary acts, are of daily occurrence, yet how often do we hear of the grave responsibility of a minister? It may be once in fifty years a minister is tried for his crimes, with a result contemptible when compared with the celebrity gained by the solemn procedure.

Were we to attempt a true definition of Parliament, we should say that Parliament is an institution serving for the satisfaction of the personal ambition, vanity, and self-interest of its members. The institution of Parliament is indeed one of the greatest illustrations of human delusion. Enduring in the course of centuries the tyranny of autocratic and oligarchical governments, and ignoring that the evils of autocracy are the evils of society itself, men of intellect and knowledge have laid the responsibility for their misfortunes on their rulers and on their systems of government, and imagined that by substituting for these systems government by the will of the people, or representative government, society would be delivered from all the evils and violence which it endured. What is the result? The result is that, *mutato nomine*, all has remained essentially as before, and men, retaining the weaknesses and failings of their nature, have transfused in the new institutions their former impulses and tendencies. As before, they are ruled by personal will, and in the interests of privileged persons, but this personal will is no longer embodied in the person of the sovereign, but in the person of the leader of a party; and privilege no longer belongs to an aristocracy of birth, but to a majority ruling in Parliament and controlling the State.

On the pediment of this edifice is inscribed: "All for the Public Good." This is no more than a lying formula: Parliamentarism is the triumph of egoism—its highest expression. All here is calculated to the service of the ego. In the Parliamentary fiction, the representative, as such, surrenders his personality, and serves as the embodiment of the will and opinions of his constituents; in reality, the constituents in the very act of election surrender all their rights in favour of their representatives. In his addresses and speeches the candidate for election lays constant emphasis upon this fiction; he reiterates his phrases about the public welfare; he is nothing but a servant of the people; he will forget himself and his interests for its sake. But these are words, words, words alone—temporary steps of the staircase by which he climbs to the height he aspires to, and which he casts away when he needs them no longer. Then, so far from beginning to work for society, society becomes the instrument of his aims. To him his constituents are a herd, an aggregation of votes, and he, as their possessor, resembles those rich nomads whose flocks constitute their whole capital—the foundation of their power and eminence in society. Thus is developed to perfection the art of playing on the instincts and passions of the mass, in order to attain the personal ends of ambition and power. The people loses all importance for its representative, until the time arrives when it is to be played upon again; then false and flattering and lying phrases are lavished as before; some are suborned by bribery, others terrified by threats—the long chain of manoeuvres spun which forms an invariable factor of Parliamentarism. Yet this electoral farce continues to deceive humanity, and to be regarded as an institution which crowns the edifice of State. Poor humanity! In truth may it be said, *mundus vult decipi, decipiatur.**

Thus the representative principle works in practice. The ambitious man comes before his fellow-citizens, and strives by every means to convince them that he more than any other is worthy of their confidence. What motives impel him to this quest? It is hard to believe that he is impelled by disinterested zeal for the public good.

In our time, nothing is so rare as men imbued with a feeling of solidarity with the people, ready for labour and self-sacrifice for the public good; this is the ideal nature, but such natures are little inclined to come into contact with the baseness of the world. He who, in the consciousness of duty, is capable of disinterested service of the community does not descend to the soliciting of votes, or the crying of his own praise at election meetings in loud and vulgar phrases. Such men manifest their strength in their own work, in a small circle of congenial friends, and scorn to seek popularity in the noisy market-place. If they approach the crowd, it is not to flatter it, or to pander to its basest instincts and tendencies, but to condemn its follies and expose its depravity. To men of duty and honour the procedure of elections is repellent; the only men who regard it without abhorrence are selfish, egoistic natures, which wish thereby to attain their personal ends. To acquire popularity such men have little scruple in assuming the mask of ardour for the public good. They cannot and must not be modest, for with modesty they would not be noticed or spoken of. By their positions, and by the parts which they have chosen, they are forced to be hypocrites and liars; they must cultivate, fraternise with, and be amiable to their opponents to gain their suffrages; they must lavish promises, knowing that they cannot fulfil them; and they must pander to the basest tendencies and prejudices of the masses to acquire majorities for themselves. What honourable nature would accept such a role? Describe it in a novel, the reader would be repelled, but in elections the same reader gives his vote to the living *artiste* in the same role.

Parliamentary elections are a matter of art, having, as the military art, their strategy and tactics. The candidate is not brought into direct relations with his constituents. As intermediary stands the committee, a self-constituted institution, the chief weapon of which is impudence. The candidate, if he is unknown, begins by assembling a number of friends and patrons. Then all together organise a hunt among the rich and weak-minded aristocrats of the neighbourhood, whom they convince that it is their duty, their prerogative, and their privilege to stand at the head as

---

* "The world wishes to be deceived, let it be deceived."—Ed.

leaders of public opinion. There is little difficulty in finding stupid or idle people who are taken in by this trickery; and then, above their signatures, appear manifestos in the newspapers and on the walls and pillars, which seduce the mass, eager always in the pursuit of names, titles, and wealth. Thus are formed the committees which direct and control the elections. They resemble in much public companies. The composition of the committee is carefully elaborated: it contains some effective forces—energetic men who pursue at all costs material ends; while simple and frivolous idlers constitute the ballast. The committees organise meetings, where speeches are delivered, where he who possesses a powerful voice, and can quickly and skillfully string phrases together, produces always an impression on the mass, and acquires notoriety—thus comes out the candidate for future election, who, with favouring conditions, may even supersede him whom he came to help. Phrases, and nothing but phrases, dominate these meetings. The crowd hears only him who cries the loudest, and who with impudence and with flattery conforms most artfully to the impulses and tendencies of the mob.

On the day of polling few give their votes intelligently: these are the individual, influential electors whom it has been worthwhile to convince in private. The mass of the electors, after the practice of the herd, votes for one of the candidates nominated by the committees. Not one exactly knows the man, or considers his character, his capacity, his convictions; all vote merely because they have heard his name so often. It would be vain to struggle against this herd. If a levelheaded elector wished to act intelligently in such a grave affair, and not to give way to the violence of the committee, he would have to abstain altogether, or to give his vote for his candidate according to his conviction. However he might act, he could not prevent the election of the candidate favoured by the mass of frivolous, indifferent, and prejudiced electors.

In theory, the elected candidate must be the favourite of the majority; in fact, he is the favourite of a minority, sometimes very small, but representing an organised force, while the majority, like sand, has no coherence, and is therefore incapable of resisting the clique and the faction. In theory, the election favours the intelligent and capable; in reality, it favours the pushing and impudent. It might be thought that education, experience, conscientiousness in work, and wisdom in affairs, would be essential requirements in the candidate; in reality, whether these qualities exist or not, they are in no way needed in the struggle of the election, where the essential qualities are audacity, a combination of impudence and oratory, and even some vulgarity, which invariably acts on the masses; modesty, in union with delicacy of feeling and thought, is worth nothing.

Thus comes forth the representative of the people, thus he acquires his power. How does he employ it, how will he turn it to advantage? If energetic by nature he will attempt to form a party; if he is of an ordinary nature, then he joins himself to one party or another. The leader of a party above all things requires a resolute will. This is an organic quality, like physical strength, and does not by any means inevitably accompany moral excellence. With limited intellect, with infinite egoism, and even wickedness, with base and dishonest tendencies, a man with a strong will may become a leader in Parliament, and may control the decisions of a party which contains men far surpassing him in moral and intellectual worth. Such may be the character of a ruling force in Parliament. To this should be joined another decisive force—eloquence. This also is a natural faculty, involving neither moral character, nor high intellectual culture. A man may be a deep thinker, a poet, a skilful general, a subtle jurist, an experienced legislator, and at the same time may not enjoy the gift of fluent speech, while, on the contrary, one with ordinary intellectual capacity and knowledge may possess a special gift of eloquence. The union of this gift with a plentitude of intellectual power is a rare and exceptional phenomenon in Parliamentary life. The most brilliant improvisations, which have given glory to orators, and determined grave decisions, when read are as colourless and contemptible as descriptions of scenes enacted in former times by celebrated actors and singers. Experience shows that in great assemblies the decision does not belong to reason, but to daring and brilliancy; that the arguments most effective on the mass are not the most symmetrical—the most truly taken from the nature of things, but those expressed in sounding words and phrases, artfully selected, constantly reiterated, and calculated on the instinct of baseness always dominant in the people. The masses are easily drawn by outbursts of empty declamation, and under such influences often form sudden decisions, which they regret on cold-blooded consideration of the affair.

Therefore, when the leader of a party combines with a strong will the gift of eloquence, he assumes his first role on an open stage before the whole world. If he does not possess this gift he stands like a stage manager behind the scenes and directs thence all the movements of the Parliamentary spectacle, allotting the parts to others, appointing orators to speak for him, employing in his work all the rich but irresolute intellects of his party to do his thinking for him.

What is a Parliamentary party? In theory, it is an alliance of men with common convictions, joining forces for the realisation of their views in legislation and administration. But this description applies only to small parties; the large party, which alone is an effective force in Parliament, is formed under the influence only of personal ambition, and centres itself around one commanding personality. By nature, men are divided into two classes—those who tolerate no power above them, and therefore of necessity strive to rule others; and those who by their nature dread the responsibility inseparable from independent action, and who shrink from any resolute exercise of will. These were born for submission, and together constitute a herd, which follows the men of will and resolution, who form the minority. Thus the most talented persons submit willingly, and gladly entrust to stronger hands the control of affairs and the moral responsibility for their direction. Instinctively they seek a leader, and become his obedient instruments, inspired by the conviction that he will lead them to victory—and, often, to spoil. Thus all the important actions of Parliament are controlled by the leaders of the party, who inspire all decisions, who lead in combat, and profit by victory. The public sessions are no more than a spectacle for the mass. Speeches are delivered to sustain the fiction of Parliamentarism, but seldom a speech by itself affects the decision of Parliament in a grave affair. Speech-making serves for the glory of orators, for the increase of their popularity, and the making of their careers; only on rare occasions does it affect the distribution of votes. Majorities and minorities are usually decided before the session begins.

Such is the complicated mechanism of the Parliamentary farce; such is the great political lie which dominates our age. By the theory of Parliamentarism, the rational majority must rule; in practice, the party is ruled by five or six of its leaders who exercise all power. In theory, decisions are controlled by clear arguments in the course of Parliamentary debates; in practice, they in no wise depend from debates, but are determined by the wills of the leaders and the promptings of personal interest. In theory, the representatives of the people consider only the public welfare; in practice, their first consideration is their own advancement, and the interests of their friends. In theory, they must be the best citizens; in practice, they are the most ambitious and impudent. In theory, the elector gives his vote for his candidate because he knows him and trusts him; in practice the elector gives his vote for a man whom he seldom knows, but who has been forced on him by the speeches of an interested party. In theory, Parliamentary business is directed by experience, good sense, and unselfishness; in practice, the chief motive powers are a firm will, egoism, and eloquence.

Such is the Parliamentary institution, exalted as the summit and crown of the edifice of State. It is sad to think that even in Russia there are men who aspire to the establishment of this falsehood among us; that our professors glorify to their young pupils representative government as the ideal of political science; that our newspapers pursue it in their articles and feuilletons, under the name of justice and order, without troubling to examine without prejudice the working of the parliamentary machine. Yet even where centuries have sanctified its existence, faith already decays; the Liberal intelligence exalts it, but the people groans under its despotism, and recognises its falsehood. We may not see, but our children and grandchildren assuredly will see, the overthrow of this idol, which contemporary thought in its vanity continues still to worship. . . .

The prevalent doctrine of the perfection of Democracy and of democratic government stands on the same delusive foundation. This doctrine presupposes the capacity of the people to understand subtleties of political science which have a clear and substantial existence in the minds of its apostles only. Precision of knowledge is attainable only by the few minds which constitute the aristocracy of intellect; the mass, always and everywhere, is *vulgus*, and its conceptions of necessity are vulgar.

Democracy is the most complicated and the most burdensome system of government recorded in the history of humanity. For this reason it has never appeared save as a transitory manifestation, with few exceptions giving place before long to other systems. It is in no way surprising. The duty of the State is to act and to ordain: its dispositions are manifestations of a single will; without this government is inconceivable. But how can a multitude of men, or a popular assembly act with a single will? The upholder of Democracy takes little trouble over the decision of this question, but evades it by means of those favourite phrases and formulas: "The will of the people," "public opinion," "the supreme decision of the nation," "the voice of the people is the voice of God," and others of a like nature. All these phrases signify that a multitude of men on a multitude of questions may form a common conclusion, and, conformably with their conclusion, arrive at a common decision. This may be possible sometimes, but only on the simplest questions. Where questions present the slightest complexity their decision by a numerous assembly is possible only through the medium of men capable of judging them in all their details, and of persuading the people to accept their judgment. In the number of complex questions may be counted all political questions requiring great concentration of the intellectual forces of the most capable and experienced statesmen; on such questions it would be absurd to rely upon unanimity of thought and will in a numerous assembly; the decision of the people could only be ruinous to the State. The enthusiasts of Democracy contend that the people may manifest its will in affairs of State: this is a shallow theory. In reality, we find that popular assemblies are capable only of accepting—through enthusiasm—the opinion expressed by individuals or by a small minority—the opinion, for instance, of the recognised leader of their party, of some local worker of repute, of some organised association, or the impersonal opinion of an influential journal. Thus the discussions which precede decision become an absurd comedy played on a vast stage by a multitude of hands and voices, the greater the multitude the more unintelligible is the comedy, and the more the *dénouement* depends upon fortuitous and disorderly impulses. . . .

The greatest evil of constitutional government lies in the formation of ministries on parliamentary or party principles. Each political party aspires to seize the reins of government at any cost. The chief of the State must submit to the party which commands a majority in Parliament; a ministry is formed from the members of this party, and to maintain itself in power, enters upon a contest with the Opposition, which, in its turn, puts forth its whole strength to overthrow its rivals and take their places. If the chief of the State were to favour the minority and nominate his own ministry from its ranks, the new ministry would dissolve Parliament, and direct all its strength towards gaining a majority at the general election—with the support of this majority being enabled to withstand the Opposition. The placemen of the ministerial party vote always for the Government, not for the sake of upholding authority, not from intimate community of opinions, but because this Government in its turn supports the members of its party in power, and in its concomitant privileges, advantages, and emoluments. The natural instinct of all parties is to support their own in all circumstances, either on account of common interests, or simply by virtue of that gregarious instinct which impels mankind to unite in societies and to march into battle side by side.

It is evident, then, that unanimity of opinion has little influence, and that the pretended solicitude for the public welfare serves as the concealment of motives and instincts in no way related to it. This is the ideal of parliamentary government! It is a gross delusion to regard it as a guarantee of freedom. The absolute power of the sovereign is replaced by the absolute power of Parliament, with this difference only, that the person of the sovereign may embody a rational will, while in Parliament all depends upon accident, as the decisions of Parliament are brought about by the majority. But as, by the side of the majority constituted under the influence of party gambling, a powerful minority exists, the will of the majority is in no way the will of Parliament. Still less can it be regarded as the will of the people, the healthy mass of which abstains from participation in the comedy of parties, and turns away from it with abhorrence. On the other hand, the corrupt part of the population mingles willingly in politics, and thereby is driven to a worse corruption, for the chief motive of this comedy is appetite for power and plunder. Political freedom becomes a fiction maintained on paper by the paragraphs and phrases of the constitution; the principles of monarchical power disappear; the Liberal Democracy triumphs, bringing into society disorder and violence with the principles of infidelity and materialism, and proclaiming Liberty, Equality and Fraternity—where there is place neither for Liberty nor for Equality. Such conditions inevitably lead to anarchy, from which society can be saved alone by dictatorship—that is, by the rehabilitation of autocracy in the government of the world. . . .

The Press

From the day that man first fell falsehood has ruled the world—ruled it in human speech, in the practical business of life, in all its relations and institutions. But never did the Father of Lies spin such webs of falsehood of every kind as in this restless age when we hear so many falsehoods uttered everywhere on Truth. With the growing complexity of social problems increases the number of relations and institutions pervaded with falsehood through and through. At every step appears some splendid edifice bearing the legend, "Here is Truth." Do you enter—you tread on falsehoods at every step. Would you expose the falsehoods which have angered you, the world will turn on you with anger greater still, and bid you trust and preach that this is truth, and truth unassailable.

Thus we are bidden to believe that the judgments of newspapers and periodicals, the judgments of the so-called Press, are the expression of public opinion. This, too, is a falsehood. The Press is one of the falsest institutions of our time.

But who will dare to stand against the forces of *opinion*—the opinion of the world on men and institutions? Such is the nature of man that each one of us, whatever his words or actions may be, takes care that he shall conform with the opinions of the people. The man is yet unborn who can truly boast himself free from this servility.

In our age the judgment of others has assumed an organised form, and calls itself Public Opinion. Its organ and representative is the Press. In truth, the importance of the Press is immense, and may be regarded as the most characteristic fact of our time—more characteristic than our remarkable discoveries and inventions in the realm of technical science. No government, no law, no custom can withstand its destructive activity when, from day to day, through the course of years, the Press repeats and disseminates among the people its condemnations of institutions or of men.

What is the secret of this strength? Certainly not the novelties and sensations with which the newspaper is filled, but its declared policy— the political and philosophical ideas propagated in its articles, the selection and classification of its news and rumours, and the peculiar illumination which it casts upon them. The newspaper has usurped the position of judicial observer of the events of the day; it judges not only the actions and words of men, but affects a knowledge of their unexpressed opinions, their intentions, and their enterprises; it praises and condemns at discretion; it incites some, threatens others; drags to the pillory one, and others exalts as idols to be adored and examples worthy of the emulation of all. In the name of Public Opinion it bestows rewards on some, and punishes others with the severity of excommunication. The question naturally occurs: Who are these representatives of this terrible power, Public Opinion? Whence is derived their right and authority to rule in the name of the community, to demolish existing institutions, and to proclaim new ideals of ethics and legislation?

But no one attempts to answer this question; all talk loudly of the liberty of the Press as the first and essential element of social well-being. Even in Russia, so libelled by the lying Press of Europe, such words are heard. Our so-called Slavophiles, with amazing inconsistency, share the same delusion, although their avowed object is to reform and renovate the institutions of their country upon a historic basis. Having joined the chorus of Liberals, in alliance with the propagandists of revolution, they proclaim exactly in the manner of the West: "Public Opinion—that is, the collective thought, guided by the natural love of right in all—is the final judge in all matters of public interest; therefore no restriction upon freedom of speech can be allowed, for such restriction can only express the tyranny of the minority over the will of the mass."

Such is the current proposition of the newest Liberalism. It is accepted by many in good faith, and there are few who, having troubled to analyse it have discerned how it is based upon falsehood and self-deception.

It conflicts with the first principles of logic, for it is based on the fallacious premiss that the opinions of the public and of the Press are identical.

To test the validity of this claim it is only needful to consider the origin of newspapers, and the characters of their makers.

Any vagabond babbler or unacknowledged genius, any enterprising tradesman, with his own money or with the money of others, may found a newspaper, even a great newspaper. He may attract a host of writers and feuilletonists, ready to deliver judgment on any subject at a moment's notice; he may hire illiterate reporters to keep him supplied with rumors and scandals. His staff is then complete. From that day he sits in judgment on all the world, on ministers and administrators, on literature and art, on finance and industry. It is true that the new journal becomes a power only when it is sold in the market—that is, when it circulates among the public. For this talent is needed and the matter published must be attractive and congenial for the readers. Here, we might think, was some guarantee of the moral value of the undertaking—men of talent will not serve a feeble or contemptible editor or publisher; the public will not support a newspaper which is not a faithful echo of public opinion. This guarantee is fictitious. Experience proves that money will attract talent under any conditions, and that talent is ready to write as its paymaster requires. Experience proves that the most contemptible persons—retired money lenders, Jewish factors, newsvendors, and bankrupt gamblers—may found newspapers, secure the services of talented writers, and place their editions on the market as organs of public opinion.

The healthy taste of the public is not to be relied upon. The great mass of readers, idlers for the most part, is ruled less by a few healthy instincts than by a base and despicable hankering for idle amusement; and the support of the people may be secured by any editor who provides for the satisfaction of these hankerings, for the love of scandal, and for intellectual pruriency of the basest kind. Of this we meet with evidence daily: even in our own capital no search is necessary to find it; it is enough to note the supply and demand at the newsvendors' shops, and at the railway stations. All of us have observed the triviality of conversation in society; in provincial towns, in the government capitals, the recreations of the people are well known—gambling, scandal, and anecdotes are the chief. Even conversation on the so-called social and political questions takes in a great measure the form of censure and aphorisms, plentifully supplemented with scandal and anecdote. This is a rich and fruitful soil for the tradesmen of literature, and there, as poisonous fungi, spring up organs of calumny, ephemeral and permanent, impudently extolling themselves as organs of public opinion. The great part which in the idle life of government towns is played by anonymous letters and lampoons, which unhappily, are so common among us, is played in the newspaper by "correspondence," sent from various quarters or composed in the editorial offices, by the reports and rumors invented by ignorant reporters, and by the atrocious practice of blackmailing, often the strongest weapon of the newspaper press. Such a paper may flourish, attain consideration as an organ of public opinion, and be immensely remunerative to its owners, while no paper conducted upon firm moral principles, or founded to meet the healthier instincts of the people, could compete with it for a moment.

This phenomenon is worthy of close inspection, for we find in it the most incongruous product of modern culture, the more incongruous where the principles of the new Liberalism have taken root, where the sanction of election, the authority of the popular will, is needed for every institution, where the ruling power is vested in the hands of individuals and derived from the suffrages of the majority in the representative assemblies. For the journalist with a power comprehending all things, requires no sanction; he derives his authority from no election, he receives support from no one. His newspaper becomes an authority in the State, and for this authority no endorsement is required. The man in the street may establish such an organ, and exercise the concomitant authority with an irresponsibility enjoyed by no other power in the world. That this is in no way exaggeration there are innumerable proofs. How often have superficial and unscrupulous journalists paved the way for revolution, fomented irritation into enmity, and brought about desolating wars! For conduct such as this a monarch would lose his throne, a minister would be disgraced, impeached, and punished; but the journalist stands dry above the waters he has disturbed, from the ruin he has caused he rises triumphant, and briskly continues his destructive work.

This is by no means the worst. When a judge has power to dishonour us, to deprive us of our property and of our freedom, he receives his power from the hands of the State only after such prolonged labour and experience as qualify him for his calling. His power is restricted by rigorous laws, his judgments are subject to revision by higher powers, and his sentence may be altered or commuted. The journalist has the fullest power to defame and dishonour me, to injure my material interests, even to restrict my liberty by attacks which force me to leave my place of abode. These judicial powers he has usurped; no higher authority has conferred them upon him; he has never proven by examination his fitness to exercise them; he has in no way shown his trustworthiness or his impartiality; his court is ruled by no formal procedure; and from his judgment there lies no appeal. Its defenders assure us that the Press itself heals the wounds it has inflicted; but any thinking mind can see that these are mere idle words. The attacks of the Press on individuals may cause irreparable injury. Retractions and explanations can in no way give them full satisfaction. Not half of those who read the denunciatory article will read the apology or the explanation, and in the minds of the mass of frivolous readers insulting or calumnious suggestions leave behind an ineffaceable stain. Criminal prosecution for defamation is but the feeblest defence, and civil action seldom succeeds in exposing the offender, while it subjects the offended to fresh attack. The journalist, moreover, has a thousand means of wounding and terrifying individuals without furnishing them with sufficient grounds for legal prosecution.

It is hard to imagine a despotism more irresponsible and violent than the despotism of printed words. Is it not strange and irrational, then, that those who struggle most for the preservation of this despotism are the impassioned champions of freedom, the ferocious enemies of legal restrictions and of all interference by the established authority. We cannot help remembering those wise men who went mad because they knew of their wisdom. . . .

There is nothing more remarkable in this century of advancement than the development of journalism to its present state as a terribly active social force. The importance of the Press first began to increase after the Revolution of July 1830, it doubled its influence after the Revolution of 1848; since then it has grown in power not only year by year but day by day. Already Governments have begun to measure their strength against this new force, and it has become impossible to imagine not only public but even individual life without the newspaper; so that the suppression of newspapers, if it were possible, would mean as much to daily life as the cessation of railway communications. Without doubt, the newspaper serves the world as a powerful instrument of culture. But while we acknowledge the convenience and profit derived from the dissemination of knowledge among the people, and from the interchange of thought and opinion, we cannot ignore the dangers imminent from the unbounded growth of the Press; we cannot refuse to recognise with a feeling of terror, the fatal, mysterious, and disintegrating force which threatens the future of humanity.

Every day the newspaper brings us a mass of varied news. How much of this is of real use to our lives, and to our educational development? How much is it fit to feed in our souls the sacred flame of aspiration unto good? How much is there not to flatter our baser instincts and impulses? We are told that the newspaper gives what the taste of readers demands, that its level reaches the level of the reader's taste. But to this we may reply that the demand would not be so great were the supply less energetically pushed.

If news alone were published the case would be different; but no, it is offered in a special form, embellished with personal opinions, and accompanied by anonymous but very decided commentaries. Papers controlled by serious persons of course exist, but such are few, while to the making of newspapers there is no end; and no morning passes without some writer, unknown to me, whom, perhaps, I should not care to know, obtruding upon me his views, expressed with all the authority of public opinion. What is graver still, however, is that this newspaper addresses not only a single class, but all men, some of whom can barely spell out a page of print, and offers to each a ready-made judgment upon everything, in such a seductive form that, little by little, by force of habit, the reader loses all wish for, and feels absolved from the duty of, forming his own opinions. Some have no ability for forming opinions, and accept mechanically the opinions of their newspapers; while others, born with a capacity for original thought in the trials and anxieties of daily life have not the time to think, and welcome the newspaper which does their thinking for them. The harm that results from this is too visible, especially in our time when powerful currents of thought are everywhere in action, wearing down the corners and distinctions of individual thought, reducing to uniformity the so-called public opinion, and weakening all independent development of thought, of will, and of character. Moreover, for many of the people the newspaper is the only source of education—a contemptible, pretended education—the varied mass of news and information found in the newspaper being taken by its readers as real knowledge, with which he proceeds to arm himself complacently. This we may take as one of the reasons why our age brings forth so few *complete* individuals, so few men of character. The modern Press is like the fabled hero who, having inscribed upon his visor some mysterious characters, the symbols of divine truth, struck all his enemies with terror, till one intrepid warrior rubbed from his helm the mysterious letters. On the visor of our Press today is written the legend "Public Opinion," and its influence is irresistible.

In the present constitution of society the Press has become an *institution* which cannot be ignored, but which must be considered side by side with the existing institutions which constitute the State and are subject to control and responsibility, for there is no institution which may be accounted uncontrolled and irresponsible. The greater the growth of the Press, the more clearly appear, side by side with the apparent advantages of rational and conscientious publicity, those social dangers which it creates. One of these dangers is the production and multiplication of a class of journalists, adventurers, and writers, who feed and grow fat upon the pen. The more serious workers on the serious Press never cease to complain bitterly of the multiplication of these fellows, with whom they are ashamed to be associated, even in name. In all the great States, in all the great markets, out of this rabble of scribbling brethren springs a class of men whom it is no exaggeration to describe as parasites on society.

In fact, these men stand on a special footing in relation to the general welfare, which should unite and inspire all institutions. They are in no way directly interested in the preservation of social order, in the reconciliation of opposing minds and contending parties. This is in the nature of things. The newspaper lives and is nourished by daily events and news. In troubled times its circulation increases; then its energies are expended in the dissemination of rumours and sensations which alarm and irritate the minds of the people; while on the other hand in times of quietude its circulation is sensibly diminished. Hardly has trouble begun when the streets are flooded with new publications which discord nourishes till peace returns, when they vanish as quickly as they appeared. But even in quiet times some must live, and for that end, new agitations are fomented, new interests developed, and sensations invented or exaggerated.

Those journals which pretend to seriousness find matter in the consideration of political questions and in the frothy polemics which daily appear. The journalist is ready at a moment's notice to decide any imaginable political question; and by his position he is bound to consider and decide it immediately, for he is a servant not of thought, or of reason, but a servant of the actual day. No sooner does the thought occur than it flies to paper, thence to the printing press; there must be no delay, no time is allowed for the ripening of his thought. You ask these men are they ashamed. Not at all. They would laugh in your face at such a question; they are persuaded that they render great services to society. They resemble in this the ancient augurs who made merry both over themselves and over their dupes.

If the journalist is to attract attention, he must raise his voice to a scream. This his trade requires, and exaggeration capable of passing into pathos becomes for him his second nature. When he enters upon a controversy he is ready to denounce his adversary as a fool, a rascal, or a dunce, to heap upon him unimaginable insults—this costs his conscience nothing; it is required by journalistic etiquette. His cries resemble the protestations of a trader in the market-place when he cheats his customers.

These are the practices and qualities which unhappily flourish in the Press and among its workers. It would be very laughable were it not so harmful. It is harmful because the Press now occupies an arena in which are discussed and decided the gravest questions of internal and external policy—questions of economy and administration indissolubly bound with the vital interests of peoples. For all this passion is but a weak equipment; sage reasoning and maturity and sanity of thought are also needed; needed, too, is knowledge of the history of peoples, and of practical life. Yet in Europe things have gone so far that from the ranks of journalism rise orators and statesmen who, together with the advocates with whom they share the capacity for abusive language, constitute in Parliament an overwhelming force. In the French Chamber there are but twenty-two representatives of large and fifty of small property, while all the talking strength belongs to journalists, of whom there are fifty-nine, and to advocates, of whom there are a hundred and seven.

And these are the representatives of their country, and the judges of the lives and requirements of the people! The people groan at this confusion of legislators. But it cannot deliver itself. . . .

32

Program of Plekhanov's
Group for the Emancipation of Labor,
1884

Until the early 1880s the Russian revolutionary
movement was predominantly oriented toward the
peasant and his commune. This was natural, as
Russia's economy was agricultural, her society rural,
and the bulk of her population peasant of one kind
or another. The emancipation in 1861, mainly because of its resulting inequities and inadequacies, intensified this orientation, with the result that two
vocal and active revolutionary groups emerged:
Zemlia i Volia (Land and Liberty) and V *Narod*
(To the People). The aim of the groups was simple:
to educate Russian peasants as the first step toward
instilling in them self-confidence while at the same
time acquainting them with the revolutionary message. This goal, however, was frustrated by the alert-
ness of the police and by the peasants' suspicion and
misunderstanding of the motives of the young revolutionaries. While painful, the failure was not catas-
trophic for, following their disappointment with the
peasants, some of the Russian revolutionaries turned
their attention to the rapidly emerging Russian industrial proletariat and to Marxism. The man most
responsible for the shift was George V. Plekhanov
(1856–1918), who is known as "the father of Russian Marxism." A prolific writer and an original
thinker, Plekhanov embraced Marxism shortly after
he fled from Russia to Geneva, where in 1884 he
prepared the first program of the Group for the
Emancipation of Labor. From this group evolved the
future Russian Social Democratic Workers' party
(the present Communist party of the Soviet Union).

From G. V. Plekhanov, *Selected Philosophical Works* (Moscow: Foreign Languages Publishing House, 1959), vol. 1, pp. 400–405.

> While Plekhanov was primarily a Marxist, his program nevertheless advocated a separate path of development for Russia.

The *Emancipation of Labour* group sets itself the aim of spreading socialist ideas in Russia and working out the elements for organizing a Russian workers' *socialist party*.

The essence of its outlook can be expressed in the following few propositions:*

1. The economic emancipation of the working class will be achieved only by the transfer to collective ownership by the working people of the means and products of production and the organization of all the functions of social and economic life in accordance with the requirements of society.

2. The modern development of technology in civilized societies not only provides the *material possibility* for such an organization but makes it *necessary and inevitable* for solving the contradictions which hinder the quiet and all-round development of those societies.

3. This radical economic revolution will entail most fundamental changes in the entire constitution of social and international relationships.

Abolishing the class struggle by destroying the classes themselves; making the economic struggle of individuals impossible and unnecessary by abolishing commodity production and the competition resulting from it; briefly, putting an end to the struggle for existence between individuals, classes and whole societies, it renders unnecessary all those social organs which have developed as the weapons of that struggle during the many centuries it has been proceeding.

Without falling into utopian fantasies about the social and international organization of the future, we can already now foretell the abolition of the most important of the organs of chronic struggle inside society, namely, *the state as a political organization opposed to society* and safeguarding mainly the interests of the ruling section. In exactly the same way we can already now foresee the international character of the impending economic revolution. The contemporary development of international exchange of products necessitates the participation of all civilized societies in this revolution.

That is why the socialist parties in all countries acknowledge the

---

* We by no means regard the programme which we submit to the judgment of the comrades as something finished and complete, not subject to partial changes or additions. On the contrary, we are ready to introduce into it any kind of corrections, provided they do not contradict the basic concepts of scientific socialism and that they correspond to the practical conclusions following from these concepts concerning the work of the socialists in Russia.

international character of the present-day workingclass movement and proclaim the principle of international solidarity of producers.

The *Emancipation of Labour* group also acknowledges the great principles of the former *International Working Men's Association* and the identity of interests among the working people of the whole civilized world.

4. Introducing *consciousness* where *blind economic necessity* now dominates, replacing the modern mastery of the *product* over the *producer* by that of the *producer* over the *product*, the socialist revolution simplifies all social relationships and gives them a purpose, at the same time providing each citizen with the real possibility of participating directly in the discussion and decision of all social matters.

This direct participation of citizens in the management of all social matters presupposes the abolition of the modern system of political representation and its replacement by *direct popular legislation*.

In their present-day struggle, the socialists must bear in mind this necessary political reform and aim at its realization by all means in their power.

This is all the more necessary as the political self-education and the rule of the working class are a necessary preliminary condition of its economic emancipation. Only a completely *democratic* state can carry out the economic revolution which conforms to the interests of the producers and demands their intelligent participation in the organization and regulation of production.

At present the working class in the advanced countries is becoming increasingly clear on the necessity of the social and political revolution referred to and is organizing into a special labour party which is hostile to parties of exploiters.

Being accomplished according to the principles of the *International Working Men's Association*, this organization, however, has mainly in view the achievement by the workers of political domination within each of the respective states. "The proletariat of each country must, of course, first of all settle matters with its own bourgeoisie."

This introduces an element of variety into the programmes of the socialist parties in the different states, compelling each of them to conform to the social conditions in its country.

It goes without saying that the practical tasks, and consequently the programmes of the socialists, are bound to be more original and complicated in countries where capitalist production has not yet become dominant and where the working masses are oppressed under a double yoke—that of rising capitalism and that of obsolescent patriarchal economy.

In those countries, the socialists must at the same time organize the workers for the struggle against the bourgeoisie and wage war against the survivals of old-pre-bourgeois social relationships, which are harmful both to the development of the working class and to the welfare of the whole people.

That is precisely the position of the Russian socialists. The working population of Russia is oppressed directly by the whole burden of the enormous police-despotic state and at the same time suffers all the miseries inherent in the epoch of capitalist *accumulation;* and in places—in our industrial centres—it suffers from the oppression of capitalist *production* which is not as yet limited by any decisive intervention of the state or by the organized resistance of the workers themselves. Present-day Russia is suffering—as Marx once said of the West European continent—not only from the development of capitalist production, but also from insufficiency of that development.

One of the most harmful consequences of this backward state of production was and still is the underdevelopment of the middle class, which, in our country, is incapable of taking the *initiative* in the struggle against absolutism.

That is why our socialist intelligentsia has been obliged to head the present-day emancipation movement, whose direct task must be to set up free political institutions in our country, the socialists on their side being under the obligation to provide the working class with the possibility to take an active and fruitful part in the future political life of Russia.

The first means to achieve this aim must be agitation for a democratic constitution guaranteeing:

(a) The right to vote and to be elected to the Legislative Assembly as well as to the provincial and village self-government bodies for every citizen who has not been sentenced by court to deprivation of political rights* for certain *shameful* activities strictly specified by law.

(b) A money payment fixed by law for the representatives of the people, which will allow them to be elected from the poorest classes of the population.

(c) Inviolability of the person and home of citizens.

(d) Unlimited freedom of conscience, speech, the press, assembly and association.

(e) Freedom of movement and of employment.

(f) Complete equality of all citizens irrespective of religion and racial origin.†

---

* Such actions may include, for example, *bribing at elections*, outrageous repression of workers by employers, etc.

† This point is logically included in item 4, which requires, among other things, complete freedom of conscience; but we consider it necessary to set it in relief in view of the fact that there are in our country whole sections of the population, for instance the *Jews*, who do not even enjoy the wretched "rights" made available to other "residents."

(g) The replacement of the standing army by general arming of the people.

(h) A revision of all our civil and criminal legislation, the abolition of division according to estates and of punishments incompatible with human dignity.

But this aim will not be achieved, the political initiative of the workers will be unthinkable, if the fall of absolutism finds them completely unprepared and unorganized.

That is why the socialist intelligentsia has the obligation to organize the workers and prepare them as far as possible for the struggle against the present-day system of government as well as against the future bourgeois parties.

The intelligentsia must *immediately set to work to organize* the workers in our industrial centers, as the formost representatives of the whole working population of Russia, in secret groups with links between them and a definite social and political programme corresponding to the present-day needs of the entire class of producers in Russia and the basic task of socialism.

Understanding that the details of such a programme can be worked out only in the future and by the working class itself when it is called on to participate in the political life of the country and is united in its own party, the *Emancipation of Labour* group presumes that the main points of the *economic section* of the workers' programme must be the *demands:*

(a) Of a radical revision of our agrarian relations, i.e., the conditions for the redemption of the land and its distribution to peasant communities. Of the right to renounce allotments and leave the community for those peasants who find this convenient for themselves, etc.

(b) Of the abolition of the present system of dues and the institution of a progressive taxation system.

(c) Of the legislative regulation of relations between workers (in town and country) and employers, and the organization of the appropriate *inspection with representation of the workers.*

(d) Of state assistance for production *associations* organized in all possible branches of agriculture, the mining and manufacturing industries (by peasants, miners, factory and plant workers, craftsmen, etc.).

The *Emancipation of Labour* group is convinced that not only the success but even the mere possibility of such a purposeful movement of the Russian working class depends in a large degree upon the work referred to above being done by the intelligentsia among the working class.

But the group assumes that the intelligentsia themselves must as a preliminary step adopt the standpoint of modern scientific socialism, adhering to the Narodnaya Volya [Peoples' Will] traditions only inasmuch as they are not opposed to its principles.

In view of this, the Emancipation of Labour group sets itself the aim of spreading modern socialism in Russia and preparing the working class for a conscious social and political movement; to this aim it devotes all its energies, calling upon our revolutionary youth for help and collaboration.

Pursuing this aim by all means in its power, the Emancipation of Labour group at the same time recognizes the necessity for terrorist struggle against the absolute government and differs from the Narodnaya Volya party only on the question of the so-called seizure of power by the revolutionary party and of the *tasks of the immediate activity of the socialists among the working class.*

The Emancipation of Labour group *does not in the least ignore the peasantry, which constitutes an enormous portion of Russia's working population.* But it assumes that the work of the intelligentsia, especially under present-day conditions of the social and political struggle, must be aimed first of all at the most developed part of this population, which consists of the industrial workers. Having secured the powerful support of this section, the socialist intelligentsia will have far greater hope of success in extending their activity to the peasantry as well, especially if they have by that time won freedom of agitation and propaganda. Incidentally, it goes without saying that the distribution of the forces of our socialists *will have to be changed if an independent revolutionary movement becomes manifest among the peasantry,* and that even at present people who are in direct touch with the peasantry could, by their work among them, render an important service to the socialist movement in Russia. The Emancipation of Labour group, far from rejecting such people, will exert all its efforts to agree with them on the basic propositions of the programme.

33

Lenin's Concept
of the Revolutionary Party

Until 1900 the Russian revolutionary movement had
many prominent spokesmen, such as Pestel, Herzen,
Bakunin, and Nechaev, to name only a few. After
1900 the dominant figure was Nikolai Lenin (1870–
1924). Born Vladimir Illich Ulianov, Lenin became
a Russian revolutionary agitator, organizer, and a convinced Marxist in his student days, first at the University of Kazan and later at St. Petersburg. Late in
1895 he was arrested, imprisoned, and then released,
only to be banished in 1897 to Siberia for three
years. On his release in 1900 Lenin emigrated to
Geneva where he joined Plekhanov and other Russian Social Democrats in publishing a newspaper,
Iskra [The Spark]. Directing his attention to the
organizational aspects of the Russian Social Democratic movement, he conceived what in retrospect has
been an important contribution to twentieth-century
politics: the concept of a tightly organized and
disciplined party of professional revolutionaries as a
creative history-making force and also as the general
staff of the world revolution. Lenin developed this
idea in a pamphlet entitled *What Is to Be Done?*,
a lengthy polemic against those Marxist revolutionaries in Russia known as "economists" who preferred
to emphasize the economic struggle of the workers
rather than a separate revolutionary movement.
When he published his pamphlet in 1902, Lenin
not only launched Leninism but also pioneered the
totalitarian age, for the movement he led inspired
other totalitarian parties.

From V. I. Lenin, *Collected Works*. 4th Edition. 2d Impression (Moscow:
Progress Publishers, 1964), vol. 5, pp. 17–24, 352–355, 369–370, 373–376,
382–385, 399–401, 413–414, 422, 424–427, 431–432, 452–453, 459–460, 464–
467.

In recent years the question of "what is to be done" has confronted Russian Social-Democrats with particular insistence. It is not a question of what path we must choose (as was the case in the late eighties and early nineties), but of what practical steps we must take upon the known path and how they shall be taken. It is a question of a system and plan of practical work. And it must be admitted that we have not yet solved this question of the character and the methods of struggle, fundamental for a party of practical activity, that it still gives rise to serious differences of opinion which reveal a deplorable ideological instability and vacillation. On the one hand, the "Economist" trend, far from being dead, is endeavoring to clip and narrow the work of political organisation and agitation. On the other, unprincipled eclecticism is again rearing its head, aping every new "trend," and is incapable of distinguishing immediate demands from the main tasks and permanent needs of the movement as a whole. This trend, as we know, has ensconced itself in *Rabocheye Dyelo*. This journal's latest statement of "programme," a bombastic article under the bombastic title "A Historic Turn" (*"Listok" Rabochevo Dyela*, No. 6), bears out with special emphasis the characterisation we have given. Only yesterday there was a flirtation with "Economism," a fury over the resolute condemnation of *Rabochaya Mysl*, and Plekhanov's presentation of the question of the struggle against autocracy was being toned down. But today Liebknecht's words are being quoted: "If the circumstances change within twenty-four hours, then tactics must be changed within twenty-four hours." There is talk of a "strong fighting organisation" for direct attack, for storming the autocracy; of "broad revolutionary political agitation among the masses" (how energetic we are now—both revolutionary and political!); of "ceaseless calls for street protests"; of "street demonstrations of a pronounced [sic] political character"; and so on, and so forth.

We might perhaps declare ourselves happy at *Rabocheye Dyelo's* quick grasp of the programme we put forward in the first issue of *Iskra*, calling for the formation of a strong well-organised party, whose aim is not only to win isolated concessions but to storm the fortress of the autocracy itself; but the lack of any set point of view in these individuals can only dampen our happiness.

Rabocheye Dyelo, of course, mentions Liebknecht's name in vain. The tactics of agitation in relation to some special question, or the tactics with regard to some detail of party organisation may be changed in twenty-four hours; but only people devoid of all principle are capable of changing, in twenty-four hours, or, for that matter, in twenty-four months, their view on the necessity—in general, constantly, and absolutely—of an organisation of struggle and of political agitation among the masses. It is ridiculous to plead different circumstances and a change of periods: the building of a fighting organisation and the conduct of political agitation are essential under any "drab, peaceful" circumstances, in any period, no matter how marked by a "declining revolutionary spirit"; moreover, it is precisely in such periods and under such circumstances that work of this kind is particularly necessary, since it is too late to form the organisation in times of explosion and outbursts; the party must be in a state of readiness to launch activity at a moment's notice. "Change the tactics within twenty-four hours"! But in order to change tactics it is first necessary to have tactics; without a strong organisation skilled in waging political struggle under all circumstances and at all times, there can be no question of that systematic plan of action, illumined by firm principles and steadfastly carried out, which alone is worthy of the name of tactics. Let us, indeed, consider the matter; we are now being told that the "historic moment" has presented our Party with a "completely new" question— the question of terror. Yesterday the "completely new" question was political organisation and agitation; today it is terror. Is it not strange to hear people who have so grossly forgotten their principles holding forth on a radical change in tactics?

Fortunately, *Rabocheye Dyelo* is in error. The question of terror is not a new question at all; it will suffice to recall briefly the established views of Russian Social-Democracy on the subject.

In principle we have never rejected, and cannot reject, terror. Terror is one of the forms of military action that may be perfectly suitable and even essential at a definite juncture in the battle, given a definite state of the troops and the existence of definite conditions. But the important point is that terror, at the present time, is by no means suggested as an operation for the army in the field, an operation closely connected with and integrated into the entire system of struggle, but as an independent form of occasional attack unrelated to any army. Without a central body and with the weakness of local revolutionary organisations, this, in fact, is all that terror can be. We, therefore, declare emphatically that under the present conditions such a means of struggle is inopportune and unsuitable; that it diverts the most active fighters from their real task, the task which is most important from the standpoint of the interests of the movement as a whole; and that it disorganises the forces, not of the government, but of the revolution. We need but recall the recent events. With our own eyes we saw that the mass of workers and "common people" of the towns pressed forward in struggle, while the revolutionaries lacked a staff of leaders and organisers. Under such conditions, is there not the danger that, as the most energetic revolutionaries go over to terror, the fighting contingents, in whom alone it is possible to place serious reliance, will be weakened? Is there not the danger of rupturing the contact between the revolutionary organisations and the disunited masses of the discontented, the protesting, and the disposed to struggle, who are weak precisely because they are disunited? Yet it is this contact that is the sole guarantee of our success. Far be it from us to deny the significance of heroic individual blows, but it is our duty to sound a vigorous warning against becoming infatuated with terror, against taking it to be the chief and basic means of struggle, as so many people strongly incline to do at present. Terror can never be a regular military operation; at best it can only serve as one of the methods employed in a decisive assault. But can we *issue the call* for such a decisive assault at the present moment? *Rabocheye Dyelo* apparently thinks we can. At any rate, it exclaims: "Form assault columns!" But this, again, is more zeal than reason. The main body of our military forces consists of volunteers and insurgents. We possess only a few small units of regular troops, and these are not even mobilised; they are not connected with one another, nor have they been trained to form columns of any sort, let alone assault columns. In view of all this, it must be clear to anyone who is capable of appreciating the general conditions of our struggle and who is mindful of them at every "turn" in the historical course of events that at the present moment our slogan cannot be "To the assault," but has to be, "Lay siege to the enemy fortress." In other words, the immediate task of our Party is not to summon all available forces for the attack right now, but to call for the formation of a revolutionary organisation capable of uniting all forces and guiding the movement in actual practice and not in name alone, that is, an organisation ready at any time to support every protest and every outbreak and use it to build up and consolidate the fighting forces suitable for the decisive struggle.

The lesson of the February and March events has been so impressive that no disagreement in principle with this conclusion is now likely to be encountered. What we need at the present moment, however, is not a solution of the problem in principle but a practical solution. We should not only be clear on the nature of the organisation that is needed and its precise purpose, but we must elaborate a definite *plan* for an organisation, so that its formation may be undertaken from all aspects. In view of the pressing importance of the question, we, on our part, take the liberty of submitting to the comrades a skeleton plan to be developed in greater detail in a pamphlet now in preparation for print.

In our opinion, the starting-point of our activities, the first step towards creating the desired organisation, or, let us say, the main thread which, if followed, would enable us steadily to develop, deepen, and extend that organisation, should be the founding of an All-Russian political newspaper. A newspaper is what we most of all need; without it we cannot conduct that systematic, all-round propaganda and agitation, consistent in principle, which is the chief and permanent task of Social-Democracy in general and, in particular, the pressing task of the moment, when interest in politics and in questions of socialism has been aroused among the broadest strata of the population. Never has the need been felt so acutely as today for reinforcing dispersed agitation in the form of individual action, local leaflets, pamphlets, etc., by means of generalised and systematic agitation that can only be conducted with the aid of the periodical press. It may be said without exaggeration that the frequency and regularity with which a newspaper is printed (and distributed) can serve as a precise criterion of how well this cardinal and most essential sector of our militant activities is built up. Furthermore, our newspaper must be All-Russian. If we fail, and as long as we fail, to combine our efforts to influence the people and the government by means of the printed word, it will be utopian to think of combining other means, more complex, more difficult, but also more decisive, for exerting influence. Our movement suffers in the first place, ideologically, as well as in practical and organisational respects, from its state of fragmentation, from the almost complete immersion of the overwhelming majority of Social-Democrats in local work, which narrows their outlook, the scope of their activities, and their skill in the maintenance of secrecy and their preparedness. It is precisely in this state of fragmentation that one must look for the deepest roots of the instability and the waverings noted above. The first step towards eliminating this shortcoming, towards transforming divers local movements into a single, All-Russian movement, must be the founding of an All-Russian newspaper. Lastly, what we need is definitely a *political* newspaper. Without a political organ, a political movement deserving that name is inconceivable in the Europe of today. Without such a newspaper we cannot possibly fulfil our task—that of concentrating all the elements of political discontent and protest, of vitalising thereby the revolutionary movement of the proletariat. We have taken the first step, we have aroused in the working class a passion for "economic," factory exposures; we must now take the next step, that of arousing in every section of the population that is at all politically conscious a passion for *political* exposure. We must not be discouraged by the fact that the voice of political exposure is today so feeble, timid, and infrequent. This is not because of a wholesale submission to police despotism, but because those who are able and ready to make exposures have no tribune from which to speak, no eager and encouraging audience, they do not see anywhere among the people that force to which it would be worth while directing their complaint against the "omnipotent" Russian Government. But today all this is rapidly changing. There is such a force—it is the revolutionary proletariat, which has demonstrated its readiness, not only to listen to and support the summons to political struggle, but boldly to engage in battle. We are now in a position to provide a tribune for the nation-wide exposure of the tsarist government, and it is our duty to do this. That tribune must be a Social-Democratic newspaper. The Russian working class, as distinct from the other classes and strata of Russian society, displays a constant interest in political knowledge and manifests a constant and extensive demand (not only in periods of intensive unrest) for illegal literature. When such a mass demand is evident, when the training of experienced revolutionary leaders has already begun, and when the concentration of the working class makes it virtual master in the working-class districts of the big cities and in the factory settlements and communities, it is quite feasible for the proletariat to found a political newspaper. Through the proletariat the newspaper will reach the urban petty bourgeoisie, the rural handicraftsmen, and the peasants, thereby becoming a real people's political newspaper.

The role of a newspaper, however, is not limited solely to the dissemination of ideas, to political education, and to the enlistment of political allies. A newspaper is not only a collective propagandist and a collective agitator, it is also a collective organiser. In this last respect it may be likened to the scaffolding round a building under construction, which marks the contours of the structure and facilitates communication between the builders, enabling them to distribute the work and to view the common results achieved by their organised labour. With the aid of the newspaper, and through it, a permanent organisation will naturally take shape that will engage, not only in local activities, but in regular general work, and will train its members to follow political events carefully, appraise their significance and their effect on the various strata of the population, and develop effective means for the revolutionary party to influence those events. The mere technical task of regularly supplying the newspaper with copy and of promoting regular distribution will necessitate a network of local agents of the united party, who will maintain constant contact with one another, know the general state of affairs, get accustomed to performing regularly their detailed functions in the All-Russian work, and test their strength in the organisation of various revolutionary actions. This network of agents will form the skeleton of precisely the kind of organisation we need—one that is sufficiently large to embrace the whole country; sufficiently broad and many-sided to effect a strict and detailed division of labour; sufficiently well tempered to be able to conduct steadily *its own* work under any circumstances, at all "sudden turns," and in face of all contingencies; sufficiently flexible to be able, on the one hand, to avoid an open battle against an overwhelming enemy, when the enemy has concentrated all his forces at one spot, and yet, on the other, to take advantage of his unwieldiness and to attack him when and where he least expects it. Today we are faced with the relatively easy task of supporting student demonstrations in the streets of big cities; tomorrow we may, perhaps, have the more difficult task of supporting, for example, the unemployed movement in some particular area, and the day after to be at our posts in order to play a revolutionary part in a peasant uprising. Today we must take advantage of the tense political situation arising out of the government's campaign against the Zemstvo;

tomorrow we may have to support popular indignation against some tsarist bashi-bazouk on the rampage and help, by means of boycott, indictment demonstrations, etc., to make things so hot for him as to force him into open retreat. Such a degree of combat readiness can be developed only through the constant activity of regular troops. If we join forces to produce a common newspaper, this work will train and bring into the foreground, not only the most skilful propagandists, but the most capable organisers, the most talented political party leaders capable, at the right moment, of releasing the slogan for the decisive struggle and of taking the lead in that struggle.

In conclusion, a few words to avoid possible misunderstanding. We have spoken continuously of systematic, planned preparation, yet it is by no means our intention to imply that the autocracy can be overthrown only by a regular siege or by an organised assault. Such a view would be absurd and doctrinaire. On the contrary, it is quite possible, and historically much more probable, that the autocracy will collapse under the impact of one of the spontaneous outbursts or unforeseen political complications which constantly threaten it from all sides. But no political party that wishes to avoid adventurous gambles can base its activities on the anticipation of such outbursts and complications. We must go our own way, and we must steadfastly carry on our regular work, and the less our reliance on the unexpected, the less the chance of our being caught unawares by any "historic turns". . . .

It is no secret for anyone that two trends have taken form in present-day international Social-Democracy. The conflict between these trends now flares up in a bright flame and now dies down and smoulders under the ashes of imposing "truce resolutions." The essence of the "new" trend, which adopts a "critical" attitude towards "obsolete dogmatic" Marxism, has been clearly enough *presented* by Bernstein and *demonstrated* by Millerand.

Social-Democracy must change from a party of social revolution into a democratic party of social reforms. Bernstein has surrounded this political demand with a whole battery of well-attuned "new" arguments and reasonings. Denied was the possibility of putting socialism on a scientific basis and of demonstrating its necessity and inevitability from the point of view of the materialistic conception of history. Denied was the fact of growing impoverishment, the process of proletarisation, and the intensification of capitalistic contradictions; the very concept, "*ultimate aim*," was declared to be unsound, and the idea of the dictatorship of the proletariat was completely rejected. Denied was the antithesis in principle between liberalism and socialism. Denied was *the theory of the class struggle*, on the alleged grounds that it could not be applied to a strictly democratic society governed according to the will of the majority, etc. . . .

He who does not deliberately close his eyes cannot fail to see that the new "critical" trend in socialism is nothing more nor less than a new variety of opportunism. And if we judge people, not by the glittering uniforms they don or by the high-sounding appellations they give themselves, but by their actions and what they actually advocate, it will be clear that "freedom of criticism" means freedom for an opportunist trend in Social-Democracy, freedom to convert Social-Democracy into a democratic party of reform, freedom to introduce bourgeois ideas and bourgeois elements into socialism.

"Freedom" is a grand word, but under the banner of freedom for industry the most predatory wars were waged, under the banner of freedom of labour, the working people were robbed. The modern use of the term "freedom of criticism" contains the same inherent falsehood. Those who are really convinced that they have made progress in science would not demand freedom for the new views to continue side by side with the old, but the substitution of the new views for the old. The cry heard today, "Long live freedom of criticism," is too strongly reminiscent of the fable of the empty barrel. . . .

Without revolutionary theory there can be no revolutionary movement. This idea cannot be insisted upon too strongly at a time when the fashionable preaching of opportunism goes hand in hand with an infatuation for the narrowest forms of practical activity. Yet, for Russian Social-Democrats the importance of theory is enhanced by three other circumstances, which are often forgotten: first, by the fact that our Party is only in process of formation, its features are only just becoming defined, and it has as yet far from settled accounts with the other trends of revolutionary thought that threaten to divert the movement from the correct path. On the contrary, precisely the very recent past was marked by a revival of non-Social-Democratic revolutionary trends (an eventuation regarding which Axelrod long ago warned the Economists). Under these circumstances, what at first sight appeared to be an "unimportant" error may lead to most deplorable consequences, and only short-sighted people can consider factional disputes and a strict differentiation between shades of opinion inopportune or superfluous. The fate of Russian Social-Democracy for very many years to come may depend on the strengthening of one or the other "shade."

Secondly, the Social-Democratic movement is in its very essence an international movement. This means, not only that we must combat national chauvinism, but that an incipient movement in a young country can be successful only if it makes use of the experiences of other countries. In order to make use of these experiences it is not enough merely to be acquainted with them, or simply to copy out the latest resolutions. What is required is the ability to treat these experiences critically and to test them independently. He who realises how enormously the modern working-class movement has grown and branched out will understand what a reserve of theoretical forces and political (as well as revolutionary) experience is required to carry out this task.

Thirdly, the national tasks of Russian Social-Democracy are such as have never confronted any other socialist party in the world. We shall have occasion further on to deal with the political and organisational duties which the task of emancipating the whole people from the yoke of autocracy imposes upon us. At this point, we wish to state only that the *role of vanguard fighter can be fulfilled only by a party that is guided by the most advanced theory.* To have a concrete understanding of what this means, let the reader recall such predecessors of Russian Social-Democracy as Herzen, Belinsky, Chernyshevsky, and the brilliant galaxy of revolutionaries of the seventies; let him ponder over the world significance which Russian literature is now acquiring; let him . . . but be that enough! . . . .

The Russian proletariat will have to undergo trials immeasurably graver; it will have to fight a monster compared with which an anti-socialist law in a constitutional country seems but a dwarf. History has now confronted us with an immediate task which is the *most revolutionary* of all the *immediate* tasks confronting the proletariat of any country. The fulfillment of this task, the destruction of the most powerful bulwark, not only of European, but (it may now be said) of Asiatic reaction, would make the Russian proletariat the vanguard of the international revolutionary proletariat. And we have the right to count upon acquiring this honourable title, already earned by our predecessors, the revolutionaries of the seventies, if we succeed in inspiring our movement, which is a thousand times broader and deeper, with the same devoted determination and vigour. . . .

Strikes occurred in Russia in the seventies and sixties (and even in the first half of the nineteenth century), and they were accompanied by the "spontaneous" destruction of machinery, etc. Compared with these "revolts," the strikes of the nineties might even be described as "conscious," to such an extent do they mark the progress which the working class movement made in that period. This shows that the "spontaneous element," in essence, represents nothing more nor less than consciousness in an *embryonic form.* Even the primitive revolts expressed the awakening of consciousness to a certain extent. . . . The strikes of the nineties revealed far greater flashes of consciousness; definite demands were advanced, the strike was carefully timed, known cases and instances in other places were discussed, etc. The revolts were simply the resistance of the oppressed, whereas the systematic strikes represented the class struggle in embryo, but only in embryo. Taken by themselves, these strikes were simply trade union struggles, not yet Social-Democratic struggles. They marked the awakening antagonisms between workers and employers; but the workers were not, and could not be, conscious of the irreconcilable antagonism of their interests to the whole of the modern political and social system, i.e., theirs was not yet Social-Democratic consciousness. In this sense, the strikes of the nineties, despite the enormous progress they represented as compared with the "revolts," remained a purely spontaneous movement.

We have said that there could not have been Social-Democratic consciousness among the workers. It would have to be brought to them from without. The history of all countries shows that the working class, exclusively by its own effort, is able to develop only trade-union consciousness, i.e., the conviction that it is necessary to combine in unions, fight the employers, and strive to compel the government to pass necessary labour legislation, etc. The theory of socialism, however, grew out of the philosophic, historical, and economic theories elaborated by educated representatives of the propertied classes, by intellectuals. By their social status, the founders of modern scientific socialism, Marx and Engels, themselves belonged to the bourgeois intelligentsia. In the very same way, in Russia, the theoretical doctrine of Social-Democracy arose altogether independently of the spontaneous growth of the working-class movement; it arose as a natural and inevitable outcome of the development of thought among the revolutionary socialist intelligentsia. In the period under discussion, the middle nineties, this doctrine not only represented the completely formulated programme of the Emancipation of the Labour group, but had already won over to its side the majority of the revolutionary youth in Russia.

Hence, we had both the spontaneous awakening of the working masses, their awakening to conscious life and conscious struggle, and a revolutionary youth, armed with Social-Democratic theory and straining towards the workers. In this connection it is particularly important to state the oft-forgotten (and comparatively little-known) fact that, although the early Social-Democrats of that period zealously carried on economic agitation (being guided in this activity by the truly useful indications contained in the pamphlet On Agitation, then still in manuscript), they did not regard this as their sole task. On the contrary, from the very beginning they set for Russian Social-Democracy the most far-reaching historical tasks, in general, and the task of overthrowing the autocracy, in particular. . . .

All worship of the spontaneity of the working-class movement, all belittling of the role of "the conscious element" of the role of Social-Democracy, means, quite independently of whether he who belittles that role desires it or not, a strengthening of the influence of bourgeois ideology upon the workers. All those who talk about "overrating the importance of ideology," about exaggerating the role of the conscious element, etc., imagine that the labour movement pure and simple can elaborate, and will elaborate, an independent ideology for itself, if only the workers "wrest their fate from the hands of the leaders." But this is a profound mistake. . . .

Since there can be no talk of an independent ideology formulated by the working masses themselves in the process of their movement, the only choice is—either bourgeois or socialist ideology. There is no middle course (for mankind has not created a "third" ideology, and, moreover, in a society torn by class antagonisms there can never be a non-class or an above-class ideology). Hence, to belittle the socialist ideology *in any way, to turn aside from it in the slightest degree means to strengthen bourgeois ideology.* There is much talk of spontaneity. But the *spontaneous* development of the working-class movement leads to its subordination to bourgeois ideology, *to its development along the lines of the Credo programme;* for the spontaneous working-class movement is tradeunionism, is *Nur-Gewerkschaftlerei,* and trade-unionism means the ideological enslavement of the workers by the bourgeoisie. Hence, our task, the task of Social-Democracy, is *to combat spontaneity,* to divert the working-class movement from this spontaneous, trade-unionist striving to come under the wing of the bourgeoisie, and to bring it under the wing of revolutionary Social-Democracy. The sentence employed by the authors of the "Economist" letter published in *Iskra,* No. 12, that the efforts of the most inspired ideologists fail to divert the working-class movement from the path that is determined by the interaction of the material elements and the material environment *is therefore tantamount to renouncing socialism.* . . .

The overwhelming majority of Russian Social-Democrats have of late been almost entirely absorbed by this work of organising the exposure of factory conditions. Suffice it to recall *Rabochaya Mysl* to see the extent to which they have been absorbed by it—so much so, indeed, that they have lost sight of the fact that this, *taken by itself,* is in essence still not Social-Democratic work, but merely trade-union work. As a matter of fact, the exposures merely dealt with the relations between the workers *in a given trade* and their employers, and all they achieved was that the sellers of labour-power learned to sell their "commodity" on better terms and to fight the purchasers over a purely commercial deal. These exposures could have served (if properly utilised by an organisation of revolutionaries) as a beginning and a component part of Social-Democratic activity; but they could also have led (and, given a worshipful attitude towards spontaneity, were bound to lead) to a "purely trade-union" struggle and to a non-Social-Democratic working-class movement. Social-Democracy leads the struggle of the working class, not only for better terms for the sale of labour-power, but for the abolition of the social system that compels the propertyless to sell themselves to the rich. Social-Democracy represents the working class, not in its relation to a given group of employers alone, but in its relation to all classes of modern society and to the state as an organised political force. Hence, it follows that not only must Social-Democrats not confine themselves exclusively to the economic struggle, but that they must not allow the organisation of economic exposures to become the predominant part of their activities. We must take up actively the political education of the working class and the development of its political consciousness. Now that *Zarya* and *Iskra* have made the first attack upon Economism, "all are agreed" on this (although some agree only in words, as we shall soon see).

The question arises: what should political education consist in? Can it be confined to the propaganda of working-class hostility to the autocracy? Of course not. It is not enough *to explain* to the workers that they are politically oppressed (any more than it is *to explain* to them that their interests are antagonistic to the interests of the employers). Agitation must be conducted with regard to every concrete example of this oppression (as we have begun to carry on agitation round concrete examples of economic oppression). Inasmuch as *this* oppression affects the most diverse classes of society, inasmuch as it manifests itself in the most varied spheres of life and activity—vocational, civic, personal, family, religious, scientific, etc., etc.—is it not evident that *we shall not be fulfilling our task* of developing the political consciousness of the workers if we do not *undertake* the organisation of the *political exposure* of the autocracy *in all its aspects?* In order to carry on agitation round concrete instances of oppression, these instances must be exposed (as it is necessary to expose factory abuses in order to carry on economic agitation). . . . .

Why do the Russian workers still manifest little revolutionary activity in response to the brutal treatment of the people by the police, the persecution of religious sects, the flogging of peasants, the outrageous censorship, the torture of soldiers, the persecution of the most innocent cultural undertakings, etc.? Is it because the "economic struggle" does not "stimulate" them to this, because such activity does not "promise palpable results," because it produces little that is "positive"? To adopt such an opinion, we repeat, is merely to direct the charge where it does not belong, to blame the working masses for one's own philistinism (or Bernsteinism). We must blame ourselves, our lagging behind the mass movement, for still being unable to organise sufficiently wide, striking, and rapid exposures of all the shameful outrages. When we do that (and we must and can do it), the most backward worker will understand, or *will feel*, that the students and religious sects, the peasants and the authors, are being abused and outraged by those same dark forces that are oppressing and crushing him at every step of his life. Feeling that, he himself will be filled with an irresistible desire to react, and he will know how to hoot the censors one day, on another day to demonstrate outside the house of a governor who has brutally suppressed a peasant uprising, on still another day to teach a lesson to the gendarmes in surplices who are doing the work of the Holy Inquisition, etc. As yet we have done very little, almost nothing, to *bring* before the working masses prompt exposures on all possible issues. Many of us as yet do not recognise this as our *bounden duty* but trail spontaneously in the wake of the "drab everyday struggle," in the narrow confines of factory life. Under such circumstances to say that "*Iskra* displays a tendency to minimise the significance of the forward march of the drab everyday struggle in comparison with the propaganda of brilliant and complete ideas" means to drag the Party back, to defend and glorify our unpreparedness and backwardness.

As for calling the masses to action, that will come of itself as soon as energetic political agitation, live and striking exposures come into play. To catch some criminal red-handed and immediately to brand him publicly in all places is of itself far more effective than any number of "calls"; the effect very often is such as will make it impossible to tell exactly who it was that "called" upon the masses and who suggested this or that plan of demonstration, etc. Calls for action, not in the general but in the concrete sense of the term, can be made only at the place of action; only those who themselves go into action, and do so immediately, can sound such calls. Our business as Social-Democratic publicists is to deepen, expand, and intensify political exposures and political agitation. . . .

Class political consciousness can be brought to the workers *only from without*, that is, only from outside the economic struggle, from outside the sphere of relations between workers and employers. The sphere from which alone it is possible to obtain this knowledge is the sphere of relationships of *all* classes and strata to the state and the government, the sphere of the interrelations between *all* classes. For that reason, the reply to the question as to what must be done to bring political knowledge to the workers cannot be merely the answer with which, in the majority of cases, the practical workers, especially those inclined towards Economism, mostly content themselves, namely: "To go among the workers." To bring political knowledge to the *workers* the Social-Democrats must *go among all classes of the population;* they must dispatch units of their army *in all directions.* . . .

Let us return, however, to our thesis. We said that a Social-Democrat, if he really believes it necessary to develop comprehensively the political consciousness of the proletariat, must "go among all classes of the population." This gives rise to the questions: how is this to be done? have we enough forces to do this? is there a basis for such work among all the other classes? will this not mean a retreat, or lead to a retreat, from the class point of view? Let us deal with these questions.

We must "go among all classes of the population" as theoreticians, as propagandists, as agitators, and as organisers. No one doubts that the theoretical work of Social-Democrats should aim at studying all the specific features of the social and political condition of the various classes. But extremely little is done in this direction, as compared with the work that is done in studying the specific features of factory life. In the committees and study circles, one can meet people who are immersed in the study even of some special branch of the metal industry; but one can hardly ever find members of organisations (obliged, as often happens, for some reason or other to give up practical work) who are especially engaged in gathering material on some pressing question of social and political life in our country which could serve as a means for conducting Social-Democratic work among other strata of the population. In dwelling upon the fact that the majority of the present-day leaders of the working-class movement lack training, we cannot refrain from mentioning training in this respect also, for it too is bound up with the "Economist" conception of "close organic connection with the proletarian struggle." The principal thing, of course, is *propaganda* and *agitation* among all strata of the people. The work of the West-European Social-Democrat is in this respect facilitated by the public meetings and rallies which all are free to attend, and by the fact that in parliament he addresses the representatives of all classes. We have neither a parliament nor freedom of assembly; nevertheless, we are able to arrange meetings of workers who desire to listen to a Social-Democrat. We must also find ways and means of calling meetings of representatives of all social classes that desire to listen to a *democrat*; for he is no Social-Democrat who forgets in practice that "the Communists support every revolutionary movement," that we are obliged for that reason to expound and emphasise *general democratic tasks before the whole people*, without for a moment concealing our socialist convictions. He is no Social-Democrat who forgets in practice his obligation to be *ahead of all* in raising, accentuating, and solving *every* general democratic question. . . .

For it is not enough to call ourselves the "vanguard," the advanced contingent; we must act in such a way that all the other contingents recognise and are obliged to admit that we are marching in the vanguard. And we ask the reader: Are the representatives of the other "contingents" such fools as to take our word for it when we say that we are the "vanguard"? Just picture to yourselves the following: a Social-Democrat comes to the "contingent" of Russian educated radicals, or liberal constitutionalists, and says, We are the vanguard; "the task confronting us now is, as far as possible, to lend the economic struggle itself a political character." The radical, or constitutionalist, if he is at all intelligent (and there are many intelligent men among Russian radicals and constitutionalists), would only smile at such a speech and would say (to himself, of course, for in the majority of cases he is an experienced diplomat): "Your 'vanguard' must be made up of simpletons. They do not even understand that it is our task, the task of the progressive representatives of bourgeois

democracy to lend the workers' economic struggle *itself* a political character. Why, we too, like the West-European bourgeois, want to draw the
workers into politics, *but only into trade-unionist, not into Social-Democratic politics*. Trade-unionist politics of the working class is precisely
bourgeois politics of the working class, and this 'vanguard's' formulation
of its task is the formulation of trade-unionist politics! Let them call
themselves Social-Democrats to their heart's content, I am not a child
to get excited over a label. But they must not fall under the influence of
those pernicious orthodox doctrinaires, let them allow 'freedom of criticism' to those who unconsciously are driving Social-Democracy into trade-
unionist channels."

And the faint smile of our constitutionalist will turn into Homeric
laughter when he learns that the Social-Democrats who talk of Social-
Democracy as the vanguard, today, when spontaneity almost completely
dominates our movement, fear nothing so much as "belittling the spontaneous element," as "underestimating the significance of the forward
movement of the drab everyday struggle, as compared with the propaganda of brilliant and completed ideas," etc., etc.! A "vanguard" which
fears that consciousness will outstrip spontaneity, which fears to put
forward a bold "plan" that would compel general recognition even among
those who differ with us. Are they not confusing "vanguard" with "rearguard"? . . .

In our time only a party that will *organise* really *nation-wide* exposures
can become the vanguard of the revolutionary forces. The word "nation-
wide" has a very profound meaning. The overwhelming majority of the
non-working-class exposers (be it remembered that in order to become
the vanguard, we must attract other classes) are sober politicians and
level-headed men of affairs. They know perfectly well how dangerous it
is to "complain" even against a minor official, let alone against the
"omnipotent" Russian Government. And they will come *to us* with their
complaints only when they see that these complaints can really have
effect, and that we represent a *political force*. In order to become such a
force in the eyes of outsiders, much persistent and stubborn work is required *to raise* our own consciousness, initiative, and energy. To accomplish this it is not enough to attach a "vanguard" label to rearguard
theory and practice.

But if we have to undertake the organisation of a really nation-wide
exposure of the government, in what way will then the class character of
our movement be expressed?—the overzealous advocate of "close organic
contact with the proletarian struggle" will ask us, as indeed he does. The
reply is manifold: we Social-Democrats will organise these nation-wide
exposures; all questions raised by the agitation will be explained in a consistently Social-Democratic spirit, without any concessions to deliberate or
undeliberate distortions of Marxism; the all-round political agitation will

be conducted by a party which unites into one inseparable whole the assault on the government in the name of the entire people, the revolutionary training of the proletariat, and the safeguarding of its political independence, the guidance of the economic struggle of the working class, and the utilisation of all its spontaneous conflicts with its exploiters which rouse and bring into our camp increasing numbers of the proletariat. . . .

The political struggle of Social-Democracy is far more extensive and complex than the economic struggle of the workers against the employers and the government. Similarly (indeed for that reason), the organisation of the revolutionary Social-Democratic Party must inevitably be of a kind different from the organisation of the workers designed for this struggle. The workers' organisation must in the first place be a trade-union organisation; secondly, it must be as broad as possible; and thirdly, it must be as public as conditions will allow (here, and further on, of course, I refer only to absolutist Russia). On the other hand, the organisation of the revolutionaries must consist first and foremost of people who make revolutionary activity their profession (for which reason I speak of the organisation of *revolutionaries*, meaning revolutionary Social-Democrats). In view of this common characteristic of the members of such an organisation, all distinctions as between workers and intellectuals, not to speak of distinctions of trade and profession, in both categories, must be effaced. Such an organisation must perforce not be very extensive and must be as secret as possible. . . .

A small, compact core of the most reliable, experienced, and hardened workers, with responsible representatives in the principal districts and connected by all the rules of strict secrecy with the organisation of revolutionaries, can, with the widest support of the masses and without any formal organisation, perform all the functions of a trade-union organisation, in a manner, moreover, desirable to Social-Democracy. Only in this way can we secure the *consolidation* and development of a *Social-Democratic* Trade-union movement, despite all the gendarmes.

It may be objected that an organisation which is so loose that it is not even definitely formed, and which has not even an enrolled and registered membership, cannot be called an organisation at all. Perhaps so. Not the name is important. What is important is that this "organisation without members" shall do everything that is required, and from the very outset ensure a solid connection between our future trade unions and socialism. Only an incorrigible utopian would have a broad organisation of workers, with elections, reports, universal suffrage, etc., under the autocracy.

The moral to be drawn from this is simple. If we begin with the solid foundation of a strong organisation of revolutionaries, we can ensure the stability of the movement as a whole and carry out the aims both of Social-Democracy and of trade unions proper. If, however, we begin with a broad workers' organisation, which is supposedly most "accessible" to the masses (but which is actually most accessible to the gendarmes and makes revolutionaries most accessible to the police), we shall achieve neither the one aim nor the other; we shall not eliminate our rule-of-thumb methods, and, because we remain scattered and our forces are constantly broken up by the police, we shall only make trade unions of the Zubatov and Ozerov type the more accessible to the masses. . . .

As I have stated repeatedly, by "wise men," in connection with organisation, I mean *professional revolutionaries*, irrespective of whether they have developed from among students or working men. I assert: (1) that no revolutionary movement can endure without a stable organisation of leaders maintaining continuity; (2) that the broader of the popular mass drawn spontaneously into the struggle, which forms the basis of the movement and participates in it, the more urgent the need for such an organisation, and the more solid this organisation must be (for it is much easier for all sorts of demagogues to side-track the more backward sections of the masses); (3) that such an organisation must consist chiefly of people professionally engaged in revolutionary activity; (4) that in an autocratic state, the more we confine the membership of such an organisation to people who are professionally engaged in revolutionary activity and who have been professionally trained in the art of combating the political police, the more difficult will it be to unearth the organisation; and (5) the *greater* will be the number of people from the working class and from the other social classes who will be able to join the movement and perform active work in it.

I invite our Economists, terrorists, and "Economist-terrorists" to confute these propositions. At the moment, I shall deal only with the last two points. The question as to whether it is easier to wipe out "a dozen wise men" or "a hundred fools" reduces itself to the question, above considered, whether it is possible to have a mass *organisation* when the maintenance of strict secrecy is essential. We can never give a mass organisation that degree of secrecy without which there can be no question of persistent and continuous struggle against the government. To concentrate all secret functions in the hands of as small a number of professional revolutionaries as possible does not mean that the latter will "do the thinking for all" and that the rank and file will not take an active part in the *movement*. On the contrary, the membership will promote increasing numbers of the professional revolutionaries from its ranks; for it will know that it is not enough for a few students and for a few working men waging the economic struggle to gather in order to form a "committee," but that it takes years to train oneself to be a professional revolutionary; and the rank and file will "think," not only of amateurish methods, but of such training. Centralisation of the secret functions of the *organisation* by no means implies centralisation of all the functions of the movement. Active participation of the widest masses in the illegal press will not diminish because a "dozen" professional revolutionaries centralise the secret functions connected with this work; on the contrary, it will increase tenfold. In this way, and in this way alone, shall we ensure that reading the illegal press, writing for it, and to some extent even distributing it, will almost cease to be secret work, for the police will soon come to realise the folly and impossibility of judicial and administrative red-tape procedure over every copy of a publication that is being distributed in the thousands. This holds not only for the press, but for every function of the movement, even for demonstrations. The active and widespread participation of the masses will not suffer; on the contrary, it will benefit by the fact that a "dozen" experienced revolutionaries, trained professionally no less than the police, will centralise all the secret aspects of the work—the drawing up of leaflets, the working out of approximate plans; and the appointing of bodies of leaders for each urban district, for each factory district, and for each educational institution, etc. (I know that exception will be taken to my "undemocratic" views, but I shall reply below fully to this anything but intelligent objection.) Centralisation of the most secret functions in an organisation of revolutionaries will not diminish, but rather increase the extent and enhance the quality of the activity of a large number of other organisations that are intended for a broad public and are therefore as loose and as non-secret as possible, such as workers' trade unions; workers' self-education circles and circles for reading illegal literature; and socialist, as well as democratic, circles among all other sections of the population; etc., etc. We must have such circles, trade unions, and organisations everywhere in as large a number as possible and with the widest variety of functions; but it would be absurd and harmful to confound them with the organisation of revolutionaries, to efface the border-line between them, to make still more hazy the all too faint recognition of the fact that in order to "serve" the mass movement we must have people who will devote themselves exclusively to Social-Democratic activities, and that such people must train themselves patiently and steadfastly to be professional revolutionaries.

Yes, this recognition is incredibly dim. Our worst sin with regard to organisation consists in the fact that by our primitiveness we have lowered the prestige of revolutionaries in Russia. A person who is flabby and shaky on questions of theory, who has a narrow outlook, who pleads the spontaneity of the masses as an excuse for his own sluggishness, who resembles a trade-union secretary more than a spokes-man of the people, who is unable to conceive of a broad and bold plan that would command the respect even of opponents, and who is inexperienced and clumsy in his own professional art—the art of combating the political police—such a man is not a revolutionary, but a wretched amateur!

Let no active worker take offence at these frank remarks, for as far as insufficient training is concerned, I apply them first and foremost to myself. I used to work in a study circle that set itself very broad, all-embracing tasks; and all of us, members of that circle, suffered painfully and acutely from the realisation that we were acting as amateurs at a moment in history when we might have been able to say, varying a well-known statement: "Give us an organisation of revolutionaries, and we will overturn Russia!" The more I recall the burning sense of shame I then experienced, the bitterer become my feelings towards those pseudo-Social-Democrats whose preachings "bring disgrace on the calling of a revolutionary," who fail to understand that our task is not to champion the degrading of the revolutionary to the level of an amateur, but *to raise* the amateurs to the level of revolutionaries.

34

Father Gapon's Petition to Nicholas II, January 22, 1905

The Pobedonostsev-directed reaction and persecution, designed to maintain autocracy intact, succeeded in driving the revolutionaries underground, where they became more active, and in increasing popular discontent. This discontent increased sharply following Russia's involvement with Japan in a war which the people neither supported nor understood and which inflicted several military and naval disasters (Port Arthur, Tsushima, Mukden) on Russian forces. In the midst of these reverses, zemstvo representatives (representatives of local self-governing districts which had emerged in 1864) unanimously

From N. S. Trusova, A. A. Novoselskii and L. N. Pushkarev, eds., *Nachalo pervoi Russkoi revolutsii, ianuar-mart, 1905 goda* (*The Beginning of the First Russian Revolution, January–March, 1905*), (Moscow: Akademiia Nauk, 1955), pp. 28–31. Translation mine. Items in brackets are mine.

called for a reform of Russian political life. They demanded what other revolutionaries had insisted on: civil rights; freedom of speech, assembly, press, thought, and conscience; equality before the law; and a parliamentary system of government. Official rejection of these modest proposals widened the existing gulf between government bureaucracy and the people, and on January 22, 1905, the tension exploded in a crisis known as "Bloody Sunday." A priest, George A. Gapon (1870–1906), led a peaceful procession of striking workers of St. Petersburg toward the Winter Palace, bearing a petition to Nicholas II listing their grievances and wishes. Instead of the expected audience with the tsar, the petitioners met with police bullets that killed scores and wounded hundreds. The incident caused a great public indignation, intensified the existing radicalism, led to nationwide antigovernment strikes and demonstrations, and triggered the 1905 Revolution.

Sovereign!

We, the workers and the inhabitants of various social strata of the city of St. Petersburg, our wives, children, and helpless old parents, have come to you, Sovereign, to seek justice and protection. We are impoverished; our employers oppress us, overburden us with work, insult us, consider us inhuman, and treat us as slaves who must suffer a bitter fate in silence. Though we have suffered, they push us deeper and deeper into a gulf of misery, disfranchisement, and ignorance. Despotism and arbitrariness strangle us and we are gasping for breath. Sovereign, we have no strength left. We have reached the limit of endurance. We have reached that terrible moment when death is preferable to the continuance of unbearable sufferings.

And so we left our work and informed our employers that we shall not resume work until they meet our demands. We do not demand much; we only want what is indispensable to life and without which life is nothing but hard labor and eternal suffering. Our first request was that our employers discuss our needs jointly with us. But they refused to do this; they even denied us the right to speak about our needs, saying that the law does not give us such a right. Also unlawful were our requests to reduce the working day to eight hours, to set wages jointly with us; to examine our disputes with lower echelons of factory administration; to increase the wages of unskilled workers and women to one ruble per day; to abolish overtime work; to provide medical care without insult; to build shops in such a way that one could work there and not die because of awful drafts, rains, and snow.

Our employers and factory administrators considered all this to be unlawful; they regarded every one of our requests as a crime and inter- preted our desire to improve our condition as audacity.

Sovereign, there are thousands of us here; outwardly we resemble human beings, but in reality neither we nor the Russian people as a whole enjoy any human right, have any right to speak, to think, to assemble, to discuss our needs, or to take measures to improve our conditions. They have enslaved us and they did it under the protection of your officials, with their aid and with their cooperation. They imprison and [even] send into exile any one of us who has the courage to speak on behalf of the interests of the working class and of the people. They punish us for our good heartedness and sympathy as if for a crime. To pity a down- trodden, disfranchised, and oppressed man is to commit a major crime. All the workers and the peasants are at the mercy of bureaucratic ad- ministrators consisting of embezzlers of public funds and thieves who not only disregard the interests of the people but also scorn these in- terests. The bureaucratic administration has brought the country to com- plete ruin, has brought upon it a disgraceful war, and continues to lead it further and further into destruction. We, the workers and the people, have absolutely nothing to say in the matter of expenditure of huge taxes that are collected from us. In fact, we do not know where or for what the money collected from the impoverished people goes. The people are deprived of the opportunity to express their wishes and their demands and to participate in determining taxes and expenditures. The workers are deprived of the opportunity to organize themselves in unions to pro- tect their interests.

Sovereign! Is all this compatible with God's laws, by the grace of which you reign? And is it possible to live under such laws? Wouldn't it be better for all of us if we, the toiling people of all Russia, died? Let the capitalist-exploiters of the working class, the bureaucratic embezzlers of public funds, and the pillagers of the Russian people live and enjoy them- selves. Sovereign, these are the problems that we face and these are the reasons that we have gathered before the walls of your palace. Here we seek our last salvation. Do not refuse to come to the aid of your people; lead them out of the grave of disfranchisement, poverty, and ignorance; grant them an opportunity to determine their own destiny, and remove from them the unbearable yoke of bureaucrats. Tear down the wall that separates you from your people and let them rule the country with you. You have been placed [on the throne of Russia] for the happiness of the people; the bureaucrats, however, pull this happiness out of our hands and hence it never reaches us; we receive only grief and humiliation. Sovereign, examine our requests attentively and without any anger; they

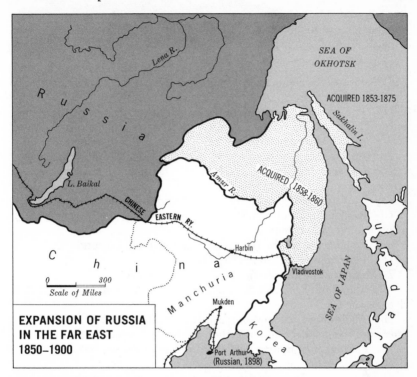

EXPANSION OF RUSSIA
IN THE FAR EAST
1850–1900

are intended not for any evil but for a good [cause] for both of us. It is not arrogance that forces us to speak but the realization of the need to escape from a situation unbearable for all of us. Russia is too great, her needs too diverse and numerous to be administered by bureaucrats only. It is essential to have a popular representation; it is essential that the people help themselves and that they govern themselves. Only they know their real needs. Do not spurn their help; accept it; decree immediately to summon at once representatives of the Russian land from all classes, from all strata, including workers' representatives. Let there be present a capitalist, a worker, a bureaucrat, a priest, a doctor, and a teacher—let everyone regardless of who they are elect their own representatives. Let everyone be equal and free to elect or be elected, and toward that end decree that the elections to the Constituent Assembly be carried out on the basis of universal, secret, and equal suffrage.

This is our chief request because everything is based within it and upon it; this is the main and the only bandage for our painful wounds; without it they will bleed severely and will soon cause our death.

One measure, however, cannot heal all of our wounds. Other [measures] are indispensable and, Sovereign, we speak about them to you directly and openly, as to our father, in behalf of the entire toiling class of Russia.

[The following measures] are indispensable:

1. Measures to eliminate the ignorance and disfranchisement of the Russian people.

(a) The immediate release and return [from exile] of all those who have suffered because of their political or religious beliefs, or because of strikes or peasant disturbances.

(b) An immediate declaration of freedom and inviolability of person, freedom of speech and press, freedom of assembly, and freedom of conscience.

(c) Universal and compulsory public education, financed by the state.

(d) Responsibility of Ministers before the people and a guarantee of a law abiding administration.

(e) Equality before the law for everyone, without exception.

(f) Separation of the church from the state.

2. Measures to eliminate the poverty of the people.

(a) Abolition of indirect taxes and the substitution of a direct progressive income tax.

(b) Abolition of redemption payments, [introduction of] low interest rates, and the gradual transfer of the land to the people.

(c) Placement of military and naval orders in Russia, not abroad.

(d) Termination of the war by the will of the people.

3. Measures to eliminate the oppression of labor by capital:

(a) Abolition of the institution of factory inspectors.

(b) Establishment at the factories and mills of permanent committees elected by the workers which, jointly with the management, would consider complaints of individual workers. The dismissal of a worker would not take place other than by the decision of this committee.

(c) Immediate freedom for consumer and trade unions.

(d) An eight-hour working day and standardization of overtime work.

(e) Immediate freedom for the struggle between labor and capital.

(f) Immediate standardization of a minimum wage.

(g) Immediate and continued participation of representatives of the working classes in the preparation of legislation for a state insurance for workers.

Here, Sovereign, are our principal needs with which we came to you. Only if and when they are fulfilled will it be possible to free our country from Slavery and poverty; will it be possible for it to flourish; will it be possible for the workers to organize themselves to protect their interests against the insolent exploitation of the capitalists and the thievish government of bureaucrats who strangle the people. Decree and swear that you will realize these [requests] and you will make Russia happy, famous and will imprint forever your name in our hearts and in the hearts of our descendants. And if you will not decree it, if you will not respond to our plea, we shall die here, in this square, before your palace. We have nowhere else to go and it is useless to go. We have only two roads open to us: one leading to freedom and happiness, the other to the grave. Let our life be a sacrifice for suffering Russia. We do not regret this sacrifice. We offer it willingly.

George Gapon, Priest
Ivan Vasimov, Worker

35

Concessions of Nicholas II in the Revolution of 1905

The "Bloody Sunday" massacre had an electrifying effect on all segments of Russian society. It intensified radicalism, increased agitation, and brought on clashes with authorities; it precipitated strikes and demands for a constitutional government, equal rights, and autonomy for minorities; and even led to mutiny. Under the mounting nationwide radicalism, which was accompanied by critical military reverses in the war with Japan, Nicholas II was forced to yield. On October 30, 1905, he issued a manifesto (drafted by Sergei J. Witte) which granted the people of the Empire "personal inviolability, freedom of conscience, speech, assembly and association," and promised to allow the disfranchised elements of society to participate in the election to the Duma. Finally, it established as an "unbreakable rule" that

The following two items are from *Polnoe Sobranie Zakonov Russkoi Imperii* . . . (*Complete Collection of the Laws of the Russian Empire*), 3d Series, vol. 25. "The October Manifesto" from no. 26, 803, pp. 754–755. "The Cancellation of Redemption Payments" from no. 26,871, p. 790. Translation mine. Items in brackets mine.

no law should be promulgated without the sanction of the Parliament. The October Manifesto marked the end of absolute monarchy in Russia.

Then on November 16, 1905, the tsar canceled peasant redemption payments, which since the emancipation in 1861 had been one of the main deterrents to progress in the Russian villages. The cancellation paved the way to the agrarian reform commonly known as the Stolypin Land Reforms (1906–1911). These concessions, while failing to satisfy the extreme radicals, pacified the liberals and the majority of the people, thus enabling the authorities to restore order and direct Russia to a period of "constitutional experiment."

The October Manifesto, October 30, 1905

By the grace of God, We Nicholas II, Emperor and Autocrat of all Russia, Tsar of Poland, Grand Duke of Finland, etc.

Make known to all Our loyal subjects: Rioting and disturbances in the capitals and in many localities of Our Empire fill Our heart with great and heavy grief. The well-being of the Russian Sovereign is inseparable from the national well-being; and the national sorrow is His sorrow. The disturbances which have appeared may cause a grave national tension that may endanger the integrity and unity of Our State.

By the great vow of Tsarist service We are obligated to use every resource of wisdom and Our authority to bring a speedy end to an unrest dangerous to Our State. We have [already] ordered the responsible authorities to take measures to terminate direct manifestations of disorder, lawlessness, and violence, and to protect peaceful people who quietly seek to fulfill the duties incumbent upon them. To successfully fulfill general measures which We have designed for the pacification of State life, We feel it is essential to coordinate the activity of the higher government.

We impose upon the government the duty to execute Our inflexible will:

1. To grant the population the inviolable foundations of civic freedom based on the principles of genuine personal inviolability, freedom of conscience, speech, assemblies and associations.

2. Without postponing the scheduled elections to the State Duma, to admit in the participation of the Duma insofar as possible in the short time that remains before its scheduled meeting all those classes of the population which presently are completely deprived of voting rights, and

to leave further development of general elective law to the future legislative order;

3. To establish as an unbreakable rule that no law shall become effective without the confirmation by the State Duma, and that the elected representatives of the people shall be guaranteed an opportunity of real participation in the supervision of the legality of the acts by authorities whom We shall appoint.

We summon all loyal sons of Russia to remember their duties towards their country, to assist in terminating this unprecedented unrest, and together with Us to make every effort to restore peace and tranquility in Our native land.

Given in Peterhof, October 30, the year of Our Lord 1905, and eleventh of Our reign.

Nicholas

The Cancellation of Redemption Payments, November 16, 1905

By the Grace of God, We, Nicholas II, Emperor and Autocrat of All-Russia, Tsar of Poland, Grand Duke of Finland, etc.

Make known to all Our loyal subjects: Our heart is filled with deep sorrow over disturbances that have developed in villages of certain districts where the peasants have resorted to violence. We can tolerate neither violation of the law nor high-handed actions, and have instructed Our military and civil authorities to use every means to prevent and terminate the disorder and to punish the guilty.

We have the needs of the peasants close to Our heart and do not ignore them. Violence and crime do not, however, aid the peasant; [on the contrary] they may bring much sorrow and misery to the country. The only way to permanently improve the well-being of the peasant is through peaceful and legal means; to improve his condition has always been one of Our first concerns. We have lately issued orders to gather and submit to Us information concerning the measures that might be adopted immediately to benefit the peasants. After consideration, We have decided:

1. To reduce by half, from January 1, 1906, and to terminate completely after January 1, 1907, [redemption] payments from peasants for land which prior to the Emancipation belonged to nobles, state, and Crown.

2. To increase the resources of the Peasant Land Bank, in order to enable it to offer better terms for loans to petty peasants to buy additional land.

We have issued special instructions to realize these measures. We are convinced that if We unite Our efforts with those of the best men to be elected in Russia by Our loyal subjects, including peasants, We shall succeed in satisfying the other peasant needs without harming the interests of nobles.

We hope that the peasant population, which is so dear to Our heart, will follow Christian teachings of love and good and will listen to Our Tsarist call to maintain peace and order and to not violate the laws and rights of others.

Given at Tsarskoe Selo, November 16, the year of Our Lord, 1905, and the twelfth of Our reign.

Nicholas

36

The Constitution of Imperial Russia, April 23, 1906

Until the Revolution of 1905, imperial Russia's autocratic tsars embodied the executive, the legislative, and the judicial branches of the government. Moreover, since each tsar was also nominal head of the Russian Orthodox Church, his power was not only absolute but divine as well. The tsars jealously guarded their prerogatives and rebuffed all suggestions—even the most moderate ones—to alter this arrangement.

The Revolution of 1905 changed the situation. In his October Manifesto Nicholas II granted Russia a parliament, and by April 1906, when the country received its first constitution, imperial Russia had begun its slow development from an autocratic to a constitutional regime. It was an erratic process be-

From *Polnoe Sobranie Zakonov Russkoi Imperii* . . . (*Complete Collection of the Laws of the Russian Empire*), 3d Series, vol. 26, no. 27,805, pp. 456–461. Translation mine. Items in brackets are mine.

cause the country lacked many necessary prerequisites for a constitutional system: established political parties, a literate population, the experience of self-government, and an atmosphere of mutual trust between the elected legislators and government bureaucrats. The transition was painful also because the tsar, as the following articles indicate, still retained power over matters which in parliamentary countries belonged within the competence of the legislative branch of government. He retained, for instance, his historic title of Autocrat (Article 4), and under Article 45 he had the right to issue imperial decrees in emergencies between sessions of the parliament, which later, however, were to be submitted for approval by the legislature. No longer was he an absolute monarch.

The Fundamental Laws

1. The Russian state is unified and indivisible.

2. The Grand Duchy of Finland, while comprising an inseparable part of the Russian state, is governed in its internal affairs by special decrees based on special legislation.

3. The Russian language is the official state language and its use is obligatory in the Army, the Fleet, and in all state and public institutions. The use of local languages and dialects in state and public institutions is determined by special laws.

Chapter I. The Essence of the Supreme Autocratic Power

4. The All-Russian Emperor possesses the supreme autocratic power. Not only fear and conscience, but God himself, commands obedience to his authority.

5. The person of the Sovereign Emperor is sacred and inviolable.

6. The same supreme autocratic power belongs to the Sovereign Empress, should the order of succession to the throne pass to a female line; her husband, however, is not considered a sovereign; except for the title, he enjoys the same honors and privileges reserved for the spouses of all other sovereigns.

7. The Sovereign Emperor exercises the legislative authority jointly with the State Council and the State Duma.

8. The Sovereign Emperor enjoys the legislative initiative in all legislative matters. The State Council and the State Duma may examine the Fundamental State Laws only on his initiative.

9. The Sovereign Emperor approves laws; and without his approval no legislative measure can become law.

10. The Sovereign Emperor possesses the administrative power in its totality throughout the entire Russian state. On the highest level of administration his authority is direct; on subordinate levels of administration, in conformity with the law, he determines the degree of authority of subordinate branches and officials who act in his name and in accordance with his orders.

11. As supreme administrator, the Sovereign Emperor, in conformity with the existing laws, issues decrees for the organization and functioning of diverse branches of state administration as well as directives essential for the execution of the laws.

12. The Sovereign Emperor alone is the supreme leader of all foreign relations of the Russian state with foreign countries. He also determines the direction of foreign policy of the Russian state.

13. The Sovereign Emperor alone declares war, concludes peace, and negotiates treaties with foreign states.

14. The Sovereign Emperor is the Commander-in-Chief of the Russian Army and of the Fleet. He possesses supreme command over all the land and sea forces of the Russian state. He determines the organization of the Army and of the Fleet, and issues decrees and directives dealing with: the distribution of the armed forces, their transfer to a war footing, their training, the duration of service by various ranks of the Army and of the Fleet, and all other matters related to the organization of the armed forces and the defense of the Russian state. As supreme administrator, the Sovereign Emperor determines limitation on the rights of residence and the acquisition of immovable property in localities that have fortifications and defensive positions for the Army and the Fleet.

15. The Sovereign Emperor has the power to declare martial law or a state of emergency in localities.

16. The Sovereign Emperor has the right to coin money and to determine its physical appearance.

17. The Sovereign Emperor appoints and dismisses the Chairman of the Council of Ministers, Ministers, and Chief administrators of various departments, as well as other officials whose appointment or dismissal has not been determined by law.

18. As supreme administrator the Sovereign Emperor determines the scope of activity of all state officials in accordance with the needs of the state.

19. The Sovereign Emperor grants titles, medals and other state distinctions as well as property rights. He also determines conditions and procedure for gaining titles, medals, and distinctions.

20. The Sovereign Emperor directly issues decrees and instructions on matters of property that belongs to him as well as on those properties that bear his name and which have traditionally belonged to the ruling Em-

peror. The latter cannot be bequeathed or divided and are subject to a different form of alienation. These as well as other properties are not subject to levy or collection of taxes.

21. As head of the Imperial Household, the Sovereign Emperor, in accordance with Regulations on the Imperial Family, has the right to issue regulations affecting princely properties. He also determines the composition of the personnel of the Ministry of the Imperial Household, its organization and regulation, as well as the procedure of its administration.

22. Justice is administered in the name of the Sovereign Emperor in courts legally constituted, and its execution is also carried out in the name of His Imperial Majesty.

23. The Sovereign Emperor has the right to pardon the accused, to mitigate the sentence, and even to completely forgive transgressions; including the right to terminate court actions against the guilty and to free them from trial and punishment. Stemming from royal mercy, he also has the right to commute the official penalty and to generally pardon all exceptional cases that are not subject to general laws, provided such actions do not infringe upon civil rights or the legally protected interests of others.

24. Statutes of the *Svod Zakonov* (Vol. I, part 1, 1892 edition) on the order of succession to the throne (Articles 3–17), on the coming of age of the Sovereign Emperor, on government and guardianship (Articles 18–30), on the ascension to the throne and on the oath of allegiance (Articles 31–34 and Appendix V), on the sacred crowning and anointing (Articles 35 and 36), and on the title of His Imperial Majesty and on the State Emblem (Articles 37–39 and Appendix I), and on the faith (Articles 40–46), retain the force of the Fundamental Laws.

25. The Regulation on the Imperial Family (*Svod Zakonov*, Vol. I, part 1, 1892 edition, Articles 82–179 and Appendices II–IV and VI), while retaining the force of the Fundamental Laws, can be changed or amended only by the Sovereign Emperor personally in accordance with the procedure established by him, provided these changes or amendments of these regulations do not infringe upon general laws or provided they do not call for new expenditures from the treasury.

26. Decrees and commands that are issued directly or indirectly by the Sovereign Emperor as supreme administrator are implemented either by the Chairman of the Council of Ministers, or a subordinate minister, or a department head, and are published by the Governing Senate.

Chapter II. Rights and Obligations of Russian Subjects

27. Conditions for acquiring rights of Russian citizenship, as well as its loss, are determined by law.

28. The defense of the Throne and of the Fatherland is a sacred

obligation of every Russian subject. The male population, irrespective of social status, is subject to military service determined by law.

29. Russian subjects are obliged to pay legally instituted taxes and dues and also to perform other obligations determined by law.

30. No one shall be subjected to persecution for a violation of the law except as prescribed by the law.

31. No one can be detained for investigation otherwise than prescribed by law.

32. No one can be tried and punished other than for criminal acts considered under the existing criminal laws, in force during the perpetration of these acts, provided newly enacted laws do not exclude the perpetrated criminal acts from the list of crimes.

33. The dwelling of every individual is inviolable. Breaking into a dwelling without the consent of the owner and search and seizure are allowed only in accordance with the legally instituted procedures.

34. Every Russian subject has the right to freely select his place of dwelling and profession, to accumulate and dispose of property, and to travel abroad without any hindrance. Limits on these rights are determined by special laws.

35. Private property is inviolable. Forcible seizure of immovable property, should state or public need demand such action, is permissible only upon just and decent compensation.

36. Russian subjects have the right to organize meetings that are peaceful, unarmed, and not contrary to the law. The law determines the conditions of meetings, rules governing their termination, as well as limitations on places of meetings.

37. Within the limits determined by law everyone can express his thoughts orally or in writing, as well as distribute these thoughts through publication or other means.

38. Russian subjects have the right to organize societies and unions for purposes not contrary to the law. Conditions for organization of societies and unions, their activity, terms and rules for acquiring legal rights as well as closing of societies and unions, is determined by law.

39. Russian subjects enjoy freedom of religion. Terms to enjoy this freedom are determined by law.

40. Foreigners living in Russia enjoy the rights of Russian subjects, with limitations established by law.

41. Exceptions to the rules outlined in this chapter include localities where martial law is declared or where there exist exceptional conditions that are determined by special laws.

Chapter III. Laws

42. The Russian Empire is governed by firmly established laws that have been properly enacted.

43. Laws are obligatory, without exception, for all Russian subjects and foreigners living within the Russian state.

44. No new law can be enacted without the approval of the State Council and the State Duma, and it shall not be legally binding without the approval of the Sovereign Emperor.

45. Should extraordinary circumstances demand, when the State Duma is not in session, and the introduction of a measure requires a properly constituted legal procedure, the Council of Ministers will submit such a measure directly to the Sovereign Emperor. Such a measure cannot, however, introduce any changes into the Fundamental Laws, or to the organization of the State Council or the State Duma, or to the rules governing elections to the Council or to the Duma. The validity of such a measure is terminated if the responsible minister or the head of a special department fails to introduce appropriate legislation in the State Duma during the first two months of its session upon reconvening, or if the State Duma or the State Council should refuse to enact it into law.

46. Laws issued especially for certain localities or segments of the population are not made void by a new law unless such a voiding is specifically intended.

47. Every law is valid for the future, except in those cases where the law itself stiuplates that its force is retroactive or where it states that its intent is to reaffirm or explain the meaning of a previous law.

48. The Governing Senate is the general depository of laws. Consequently, all laws should be deposited in the Governing Senate in the original or in duly authorized lists.

49. Laws are published for general knowledge by the Governing Senate according to established rules and are not legally binding before their publication.

50. Legal decrees are not subject to publication if they were issued in accordance with the rules of the Fundamental Laws.

51. Upon publication, the law is legally binding from the time stipulated by the law itself, or, in the case that such a time is omitted, from the day on which the Senate edition containing the published law is received locally. The law itself may stipulate that telegraph or other media of communication be used to transmit it for execution before its publication.

52. The law cannot be repealed otherwise than by another law. Consequently, until a new law repeals the existing law, the old law retains fully its force.

53. No one can be excused for ignorance of the law once it is duly published.

54. Regulations governing combat, technical, and supply branches of the Armed Forces, as well as rules and orders to institutions and authorized personnel of the military and naval establishments are, as a rule, submitted directly to the Sovereign Emperor upon review by the Military

and Admiralty Councils, provided that these regulations, rules, and orders affect primarily the above mentioned establishments, do not touch on matters of general laws, and do not call for new expenditures from the treasury; or, if they call for new expenditure, are covered by expected savings by the Military or Naval Ministries. In cases where the expected saving is insufficient to cover the projected expenditure, submission of such regulations, rules, and orders for the Emperor's approval is permitted only upon first requesting, in a prescribed manner, the necessary appropriation.

55. Regulations governing military and naval courts are issued in accordance with Regulations on Military and Naval Codes.

Chapter IV. The State Council, State Duma, and the Scope of Their Activity

56. The Sovereign Emperor, by a decree, annually convenes the session of the State Council and of the State Duma.

57. The Sovereign Emperor determines by a decree the length of the annual session of the State Council and of the State Duma, as well as the interval between the sessions.

58. The State Council is composed of members appointed by His Majesty and of elected members. The total number of appointed members of the Council called by the Emperor to deliberate in the Council's proceedings cannot exceed the total number of the elected members of the Council.

59. The State Duma consists of members elected by the population of the Russian Empire for a period of five years, on the basis of rules governing elections to the Duma.

60. The State Council examines the credentials of its members. Equally, the State Duma examines the credentials of its members.

61. The same person cannot serve simultaneously as a member of the State Council and as a member of the State Duma.

62. The Sovereign Emperor, by a decree, can replace the elected membership of the State Council with new members before its tenure expires. The same decree sets new elections of members of the State Council.

63. The Sovereign Emperor, by a decree, can dissolve the State Duma and release its members from their five-year tenure. The same decree must designate new elections to the State Duma and the time of its first session.

64. The State Council and the State Duma have equal rights in legislative matters.

65. The State Council and the State Duma enjoy the constitutional right to submit proposals to repeal or to amend the existing laws as well

as to issue new laws, except the Fundamental Law whose review belongs exclusively to the Sovereign Emperor.

66. The State Council and the State Duma have a constitutional right to address questions to Ministers and heads of various departments, who legally are under the jurisdiction of the Governing Senate, on matters that stem from violations of laws by them or by their subordinates.

67. The jurisdiction of the State Council and of the State Duma includes those matters that are listed in the Rules of the Council and of the Duma.

68. Those legislative measures that are considered and approved by the State Duma are then submitted to the State Council for its approval. Those legislative measures that have been initiated by the State Council are reviewed by the Council and, upon approval, are submitted to the Duma.

69. Legislative measures that have been rejected either by the State Council or by the State Duma are considered defeated.

70. Those legislative measures that have been initiated either by the State Council or by the State Duma [and approved by both], but which have failed to gain Imperial approval, cannot be re-submitted for legislative consideration during the same session. Those legislative measures that have been initiated by either the State Council or by the State Duma and are rejected by either one of the Chambers, can be resubmitted for legislative consideration during the same session, provided the Emperor agrees to it.

71. Legislative measures that have been initiated in and approved by the State Duma and then by the State Council, equally as the legislative measures initiated and approved by the State Council and then by the State Duma, are submitted by the Chairman of the State Council to the Sovereign Emperor.

72. Deliberations on the state budget [by the State Council and/or by the State Duma] cannot exclude or reduce the set sums for the payment of state debts or other obligations assumed by the Russian state.

73. Revenues for the maintenance of the Ministry of the Imperial Household, including institutions under its jurisdiction that do not exceed the allocated sum of the state budget for 1906, are not subject to review by either the State Council or the State Duma. Equally not subject to review are such changes in specific revenues as stem from decisions based on Regulations of the Imperial Family that have resulted from internal reorganizations.

74. If the state budget is not appropriated before the appropriation deadline, the budget that had been duly approved in the preceding year will remain in force with only such changes as have resulted from those legislative measures that became laws after the budget was approved. Prior to publication of the new budget, on the decision of the Council

of Ministers and rulings of Ministries and Special Departments, necessary funds will be gradually released. These funds will not exceed in their totality during any month, however, one-twelfth of the entire budgetary expenditures.

75. Extraordinary budgetary expenditures for war-time needs and for special preparations preceding a war are unveiled in all departments in accordance with existing law on the decision of highest administration.

76. State loans to cover both the estimated and non-estimated expenditures are contracted according to the system established to determine state budgetary revenues and expenditures. State loans to cover expenditures in cases foreseen in Article 74, as well as loans to cover expenditures stipulated in Article 75, are determined by the Sovereign Emperor as supreme administrator. Time and conditions to contract state loans are determined on the highest level of government.

77. If the State Duma fails to act on a proposal submitted to it reasonably in advance on the number of men needed for the Army and the Fleet, and a law on this matter is not ready by May 1, the Sovereign Emperor has the right to issue a decree calling to military service the necessary number of men, but not more than the number called the preceding year.

Chapter V. Council of Ministers, Ministers, and Heads of Various Departments

78. By law, the Council of Ministers is responsible for the direction and coordination of activities of Ministers and Heads of various departments on matters affecting legislation as well as the highest state administration.

79. Ministers and Heads of various departments have the right to vote in the State Council and in the State Duma only if they are members of these institutions.

80. Binding resolutions, instructions, and decisions issued by the Council of Ministers, and Ministers and Heads of various departments, as well as by other responsible individuals entitled by law, should not be contrary to existing laws.

81. The Chairman of the Council of Ministers, Ministers, and Heads of various departments, are responsible to the Sovereign Emperor for state administration. Each individual member is responsible for his actions and decisions.

82. For official misconducts in office, the Chairman of the Council of Ministers, Ministers and Heads of various departments are subject to civil and criminal punishment established by law.

37

Programs of Russian Political Parties

The Russian revolutionaries relied on careful political planning methods as well as terror and agitation to attain their objectives. This planning led sometimes to brief appeals to the people, sometimes to elaborate programs for social, economic, and political reforms. In either case the aim was to capture the imagination of the Russian populace. Because open discussion of political issues was not possible before 1905, many of the revolutionary leaders lived, dreamed, and conspired abroad. The Revolution of 1905 changed the situation. When, in the October Manifesto, Tsar Nicholas II promised a constitutional form of government he unintentionally triggered a political ferment and several new political parties appeared. Some of these subscribed to the ideas of the extreme Left (Bolsheviks, Socialist Revolutionaries, Mensheviks); others advocated a moderate program (Cadets, Octobrists); still others supported tsarism (Monarchists, Union of the Russian People); and some favored an autonomous national existence (various Polish, Finnish, and Ukrainian parties, and the Jewish Bund). Regardless of their aims, the rise of political parties in Russia at the beginning of the twentieth century—each operating openly and each trying to attract followers by its appeals—was a new phenomenon. It was not only a sign of mounting dissatisfaction with autocracy, but a manifestation of the developing political restlessness.

Program of the Russian Social Democratic Workers' Party (Bolshevik), August, 1903

The development of exchange has created such close ties among all the peoples of the civilized world that the great proletarian movement toward

The following four items are from V. Ivanovich, ed. *Rossiiskiia partii, soiuzy i ligi* (*Russian Parties, Unions, and Leagues*) (St. Petersburg: 1906), pp. 3–7, 8–13, 14–18, 117–122. Translation mine. Items in brackets are mine.

emancipation was bound to become—and has long since become—international.

Considering itself one of the detachments of the universal army of the proletariat, Russian social democracy is pursuing the same ultimate goal as that for which the social democrats in other countries are striving. This ultimate goal is determined by the nature of contemporary bourgeois society and by the course of its development. The main characteristic of such a society is production for the market on the basis of capitalist production relations, whereby the largest and most important part of the means of production and exchange of commodities belongs to a numerically small class of people, while the overwhelming majority of the population consists of proletarians and semi-proletarians who, by their economic conditions, are forced either continuously or periodically to sell their labor power; that is, to hire themselves out to the capitalists, and by their toil to create the incomes of the upper classes of society.

The expansion of the capitalist system of production runs parallel to technical progress, which, by increasing the economic importance of large enterprises, tends to eliminate the small independent producers, to convert some of them into proletarians, to reduce the socio-economic role of others and, in some localities, to place them in more or less complete, more or less open, more or less onerous dependence on capital.

Moreover, the same technical progress enables the entrepreneurs to utilize to an ever greater extent woman and child labor in the process of production and exchange of commodities. And since, on the other hand, technical improvements lead to a decrease in the entrepreneur's demand for human labor power, the demand for labor power necessarily lags behind the supply, and there is in consequence greater dependence of hired labor upon capital, and increased exploitation of the former by the latter.

Such a state of affairs in the bourgeois countries, as well as the ever growing competition among those countries on the world market, render the sale of goods which are produced in greater and greater quantities ever more difficult. Overproduction, which manifests itself in more or less acute industrial crises—which in turn are followed by more or less protracted periods of industrial stagnation—is the inevitable consequence of the development of the productive forces in bourgeois society. Crises and periods of industrial stagnation, in their turn, tend to impoverish still further the small producers, to increase still further the dependence of hired labor upon capital and to accelerate still further the relative, and sometimes the absolute, deterioration of the condition of the working class.

Thus, technical progress, signifying increased productivity of labor and the growth of social wealth, becomes in bourgeois society the cause of increased social inequalities, of wider gulfs between the wealthy and the poor, of greater insecurity of existence, of unemployment, and of numerous privations for ever larger and larger masses of toilers.

But together with the growth and development of all these contradictions inherent in bourgeois society, there grows simultaneously dissatisfaction with the present order among the toiling and exploited masses; the number and solidarity of the proletarians increases, and their struggle against the exploiters sharpens. At the same time, technical progress, by concentrating the means of production and exchange, by socializing the process of labor in capitalist enterprises, creates more and more rapidly the material possibility for replacing capitalist production relations by socialist ones; that is, the possibility for social revolution, which is the ultimate aim of all the activities of international social democracy as the class-conscious expression of the proletarian movement.

By replacing private with public ownership of the means of production and exchange, by introducing planned organization in the public process of production so that the well being and the many sided development of all members of society may be insured, the social revolution of the proletariat will abolish the division of society into classes and thus emancipate all oppressed humanity, and will terminate all forms of exploitation of one part of society by another.

A necessary condition for this social revolution is the dictatorship of the proletariat; that is, the conquering by the proletariat of such political power as would enable it to crush any resistance offered by the exploiters. In its effort to make the proletariat capable of fulfilling its great historical mission, international social democracy organizes it into an independent political party in opposition to all bourgeois parties, directs all the manifestations of its class struggle, discloses before it the irreconcilable conflict between the interests of the exploiters and those of the exploited, and clarifies for it the historical significance of the imminent social revolution and the conditions necessary for its coming. At the same time, it reveals to the other sections of the toiling and exploited masses the hopelessness of their condition in capitalist society and the need of a social revolution if they wish to be free of the capitalist yoke. The party of the working class, the social democracy, calls upon all strata of the toiling and exploited population to join its ranks insofar as they accept the point of view of the proletariat.

On the road toward their common final goal, which is determined by the prevalence of the capitalist system of production throughout the civilized world, the social democrats of different countries must devote themselves to different immediate tasks—first, because that system is not everywhere developed to the same degree; and second, because in different countries its development takes place in a different socio-political setting.

In Russia, where capitalism has already become the dominant mode of production, there are still preserved numerous vestiges of the old pre-capitalist order, when the toiling masses were serfs of the landowners, the state, or the sovereign. Greatly hampering economic progress, these vestiges interfere with the many-sided development of the class struggle of the proletariat, help to preserve and strengthen the most barbarous forms of exploitation by the state and the propertied classes of the millions of peasants, and thus keep the whole people in darkness and subjection.

The most outstanding among these relics of the past, the mightiest bulwark of all this barbarism, is the tsarist autocracy. By its very nature it is bound to be hostile to any social movement, and cannot but be bitterly opposed to all the aspirations of the proletariat toward freedom.

By reason of the above, the first and immediate task put before itself by the Russian Social Democratic Workers' Party is to overthrow the tsarist autocracy and to replace it with a democratic republic whose *constitution* would guarantee the following:

1. The sovereignty of the people; that is, the concentration of all supreme state power in the hands of a legislative assembly, consisting of people's representatives, and forming one chamber.

2. Universal, equal, and direct suffrage for all male and female citizens, twenty years old or over, at all elections to the legislative assembly and to the various local organs of self-government; the secret ballot at elections; the right of every voter to be elected to any representative institution; biennial parliaments; salaries to be paid to the people's representatives.

3. Broad local self-government; home rule for all localities where the population is of a special composition and characterized by special conditions of life.

4. Inviolability of person and dwelling.

5. Unlimited freedom of religion, speech, press, assembly, strikes, and unions.

6. Freedom of movement and occupation.

7. Abolition of classes; equal rights for all citizens, irrespective of sex, religion, race, or nationality.

8. The right of any people to receive instruction in its own language, to be secured by creating schools at the expense of the state and the local organs of self-government; the right of every citizen to use his native language at meetings; the introduction of the use of the native language on a par with the state language in all local, public, and state institutions.

9. The right of self-determination for all nations included in the composition of the state.

10. The right of any person to sue any official before a jury in the regular way.

11. Election of judges by the people.

12. Replacement of the standing army by a general armament of the people.

13. Separation of church and state, and of school and church.

14. Free and compulsory general and professional education for all children of both sexes up to the age of sixteen; provision by the state of food, clothing, and school supplies for poor children.

As a basic condition for the democratization of our state economy, the Russian Social Democratic Workers' Party demands the abolition of all indirect taxes and the establishment of a progressive tax on income and inheritances.

In order to safeguard the working class against physical and moral degeneration, as well as to insure the development of its power to carry on the struggle for freedom, the party demands the following:

1. Eight-hour working day for all hired labor.

2. A law providing a weekly uninterrupted forty-two-hour respite for all hired labor, of both sexes, in all branches of the national economy.

3. Complete prohibition of overtime work.

4. Prohibition of night work (from 9 p.m. to 6 a.m.) in all branches of the national economy, with the exception of those in which this is absolutely necessary because of technical considerations approved by labor organizations.

5. Prohibition of the employment of children of school age (up to sixteen) and restriction of the working day of minors (from sixteen to eighteen) to six hours.

6. Prohibition of female labor in those branches of industry which are injurious to women's health; relief from work four weeks before and six weeks after childbirth, with regular wages paid during all this period.

7. Establishment of nurseries for infants and children in all shops, factories, and other enterprises that employ women; permission for freedom of at least a half-hour's duration to be granted at three-hour intervals to all nursing mothers.

8. Old-age state insurance, and insurance against total or partial disability; such insurance to be based on a special fund formed from a tax levied on the capitalists.

9. Prohibition of payment of wages in kind; establishment of regular weekly pay days when all wages shall be paid in money in absolute conformity with all the agreements relating to the hire of workers; wages to be paid during working hours.

10. Prohibition of deductions by employers from workers' wages, on any ground or for any purpose (fines, spoilage, and so forth).

11. Appointment of an adequate number of factory inspectors in all branches of the national economy and extension of their supervision to all enterprises employing hired labor, including government enterprises (domestic service also to be within the sphere of their supervision); ap-

pointment of special women inspectors in those industries where female labor is employed; participation of representatives, elected by the workers and paid by the state, in supervising the enforcement of the factory laws, the fixing of wage scales, and in accepting or rejecting the finished products and other results of labor.

12. Control by organs of local self-government, together with representatives elected by the workers, over sanitation in the dwellings assigned to the workers by the employers, as well as over internal arrangements in those dwellings and the renting conditions—in order to protect the workers against the employers' interference with their life and activity as private citizens.

13. Establishment of properly organized sanitary control over all establishments employing hired labor, the medico-sanitary organization to be entirely independent of the employers; in time of illness, free medical aid to be rendered to the workers at the expense of the employers, with the workers retaining their wages.

14. Establishment of criminal responsibility in the case of employers' infringement upon the laws intended to protect the workers.

15. Establishment in all branches of the national economy of industrial courts to be composed of representatives of workers and employers in equal numbers.

16. Imposition upon the organs of local self-government of the duty of establishing employment agencies (labor exchanges) to deal with the hiring of local and out-of-town labor in all branches of industry, and participation of workers' and employers' representatives in their administration.

In order to *remove the vestiges of serfdom* that fall directly and heavily upon the peasants, and to encourage the free development of the class struggle in the *village*, the party demands above all:

1. Abolition of redemption payments and quit rents as well as all obligations which presently fall on the peasantry, the tax-paying class.

2. Repeal of all laws which restrict the peasant in disposing of his land.

3. Return to peasants of money collected from them in the form of redemption payments and quit rents; confiscation of monastery and church properties as well as property belonging to princes, government agencies, and members of the royal family; imposition of a special tax on lands of nobles who have sold it on loan terms; transfer of the money thus procured into a special reserve fund to meet cultural and charitable needs of villages.

4. Organization of peasant committees: (a) to return to villages (by means of expropriation . . .) those lands which were taken away from the peasants at the emancipation, and which are held by the nobles as a means of enserfment of peasants; (b) to transfer to peasant ownership

those lands in the Caucasus which they use now on a temporary basis; (c) to eliminate the remnants of serfdom still in effect in the Urals, the Altai, the Western Provinces, and other parts of the country.

5. Grant to the courts the right to lower unusually high rents and to annul those contracts which contain slave characteristics.

To attain its immediate goals, the Russian Social Democratic Workers' Party will support every opposition and revolutionary movement directed against the existing social and political system in Russia. At the same time it rejects all reformist projects whose aim is to extend or to consolidate bureaucratic-police protection over the toiling classes.

On its own part, the Russian Social Democratic Workers' Party is firmly convinced that a full, consistent, and thorough realization of the indicated political and social changes can only be attained by the overthrow of autocracy and by the convocation of a Constituent Assembly freely elected by the entire people.

Program of the Socialist Revolutionary Party, 1905

In its cultural and social relations, contemporary Russia increasingly enters into closer and closer ties with the advanced countries of the civilized world, while at the same time it preserves a number of peculiarities that have been formulated by the course of its past history, its local conditions, and its international situation.

All the advanced countries of the civilized world, parallel to the growth of the population and its basic needs, experience the growth of man's power over nature, the improved means of utilizing its natural forces, and the increase of creative power of human work in all the spheres of activity. This growth is an indispensable condition for social progress and for the struggle toward a balanced and harmonious development of human individuality.

But this growth of human control over nature takes place in contemporary society under a condition of bourgeois competition of uncoordinated economic units, of private control of the means of production, of transformation of the latter into capital, and of advance exploitation of the direct producers or their indirect subordination to capital. Parallel to the development of the foundations of contemporary society, society itself increasingly transforms itself into two classes: a class of exploited toilers who receive increasingly lower rewards for the wealth their work creates, and a class of exploiters who have a monopoly on the control of natural forces and the social means of production.

As long as in those narrow frames of bourgeois capitalist relations there develop—albeit one sided and incomplete—forms of collective labor and mass production, so long will the contemporary economic development reveal positive, creative aspects, because it prepares certain material elements for a higher socialist system of life and unites in a compact social force the industrial armies of hired workers.

However, since bourgeois capitalist forms tend to narrow, limit, and impede the development of collective forms of labor and socially productive forces, the contemporary economic development strengthens its negative, destructive aspects: the anarchy of commodity production and competition; sterile waste of its economic forces; crises which shatter the national economy to its foundation; the growth of exploitation; dependence and insecurity of the toiling masses; the corrupting power of money on all moral standards; the selfish struggle of all against all for existence and privileged position.

Mutual relations between the positive and negative aspects of contemporary economic development vary from one branch of industry to another and from one country to another. They are relatively good in more advanced branches of industry and in countries of classical capitalism; they become less and less good in other branches of industry, especially in agriculture, and in countries situated less advantageously in the international economic struggle.

But, regardless of those distinctions, the incompatibility and contradiction between the positive and the negative aspects of contemporary economic development represents a general and growing fact fraught with serious historical consequences.

With the growth of social division between the exploiters and the exploited, with the growth of contradictions between the productivity of labor and the inconsequential reward of workers for their products, and with the increase of the norms of their exploitation, there also grows dissatisfaction among the exploited with their conditions in contemporary society.

Because of the spontaneous process of intensifying class relations there is developing, with systematic tactics, a conscious and planned interference into attempts at organizing collective forces in the name of one or another social ideal or the ultimate goal. This expediently directed struggle encompasses simultaneously all aspects of life—economic, political, and spiritual.

The exploiting classes are trying to perpetuate the basis of their existence—exploitation through rent, profit on capital in all of its forms, and increased taxes of the toiling masses. By means of syndicates, cartels, and trusts they are trying to control, for their egoistic gains, the means of production as well as consumption. They are trying to appropriate for their class interest all the institutions of the contemporary state and to transform it completely into a weapon of their rule and impoverishment of the exploited. Finally, they are striving to subjugate spiritual and material literature, art, science, and public opinion in order to keep the toiling masses not only in economic but in intellectual dependence as well.

Not possessing any other resources, or having lost them already in the struggle, they are joining hands with the reactionary forces of the dead past, are resurrecting racial and religious animosity, are poisoning national consciousness with chauvinism or nationalism, and are entering into alliances with the remnants of monarchial and Church-clerical institutions.

The bourgeois system has gradually abandoned its former progressive content, has brought intellectual sterility to its ruling classes, has caused the alienation of the intellectual and moral flower of the nation, and has left it to suffer in the hostile camp of the oppressed and the exploited.

The exploited classes naturally are trying to protect themselves from the pressing burden, and in proportion to the growth of their consciousness they are uniting themselves in this struggle and are directing it against the very foundations of bourgeois exploitation. International by its nature, this movement is becoming increasingly a movement of the great majority in the interest of the great majority, a factor that represents the key to its victory.

International revolutionary socialism represents a conscious expression, scientific illumination, and formulation of this movement. Its aim is intellectual, political, and economic emancipation of the working class. It advances above all as an initiating revolutionary minority, as the fighting vanguard of the toiling masses, trying constantly at the same time to merge with the masses and incorporate them into its ranks. Its basic practical aim is to make all layers of the toiling and exploited people aware that they are one working class, that that class is the only hope of their freedom by means of a planned, organized struggle to create a socio-revolutionary uheaval that consists of:

1. Freeing of all public institutions from control of the exploiting classes.

2. Eliminating, alongside private property in natural forces and in public means of production, the very division of the society into classes.

3. Eliminating the contemporary, stratified, compulsory, repressive nature of public institutions while at the same time preserving and developing their normal cultural functions; that is, planned organization of public work for public good.

The realization of this program will make possible an uninterrupted, free, and unhampered development of all spiritual and material forces of mankind. It will also turn the growth of public wealth from a source of dependence and oppression of the working class into a source of prosperity and balanced harmonious development of human dignity. It will also halt the degeneration of mankind from uselessness and superfluity on the one hand, and, on the other, the presence of excessive work and semi-starvation. Finally, only through the introduction of a free socialist society will mankind be able to develop fully its physical, mental, and moral capabilities and introduce realism, truth, and solidarity ever fully into the social life. Consequently, the essence of contemporary socialism is the freeing of all mankind. It seeks elimination of all forms of civil strife among peoples, of all forms of violence and exploitation of man by man; instead, it seeks to introduce freedom, equality and brotherhood of all regardless of sex, race, religion or nationality.

The Socialist Revolutionary Party of Russia views its task as an organic, component part of a universal struggle of labor against the exploitation of human dignity, against all barriers that prevent its development into social forms, and conducts it in the spirit of general interests of that struggle in ways that are determined by concrete conditions of Russian reality.

The mutual cooperation between the patriarchal nobility-bureaucratic autocracy and new bourgeois exploitation intensifies the social problem in Russia. The development of capitalism reveals here, more than anywhere else, its dark aspects and, less than anywhere else, it balances the organized creative influence of the growth of public productive forces. The abnormally growing bureaucratic apparatus of the state, as a result of the emancipation of serfs and the development of the kulak system in all of its aspects and forms, increasingly paralyzes the productive forces of the village. The toiling peasantry is forced to a large degree to seek help either in subsidiary enterprises or hired labor, and receives from all of its labor an earning that corresponds to the lowest wage earning of an industrial worker. This factor also limits and undermines the domestic market of industry, which in addition suffers from shortages of foreign markets. Surplus population and the capitalist surplus labor force progressively increase, which, because of the competition, lowers the living standards of the city proletariat. The labor movement is forced to develop in conditions of an autocratic regime based on the all-embracing police protection and suppression of individual and public initiative. The class of great industrialists and merchants, more reactionary than everywhere else, depends increasingly on the support of autocracy against the proletariat, and against the toiling masses of the village. In the interest of self preservation the autocracy has intensified the oppression of the subjugated nationalities of Imperial Russia, has paralyzed their spiritual renaissance, has imposed national, racial, and religious antagonism in order to becloud the understanding of socio-political interests of the toiling masses. The existence of autocracy represents an irreconcilable and progressively intensifying contradiction with all of the economic, socio-political and cultural growth of the country. As a reliable ally and pillar of the most exploiting and parasitical classes in Russia, beyond its frontiers Russian autocracy is also one of the main bulwarks of reaction and a great danger to the cause of the freedom struggle of the working parties of other countries. Its overthrow should be the immediate and undelayed objective of the Socialist Revolutionary Party, not only as the first indispensable condition for the solution of the social problem in Russia, but also as a major factor of international progress.

The burden of the struggle with autocracy, irrespective of the liberal-democratic opposition, which primarily includes middle class elements of the "educated society," falls on the proletariat, the toiling peasantry, and the revolutionary-socialist intelligentsia. The immediate task of the Socialist Revolutionary Party, which assumes the leading role in this struggle, is to broaden and deepen the social and property changes to pave the way thereby for the overthrow of autocracy.

To realize fully its program, namely the expropriation of capitalist property and the reorganization of production and of the entire social system on socialist foundations, it is essential that there be a complete victory of the working class, organized by the Socialist Revolutionary Party, and, in case of need, that there be established a temporary revolutionary dictatorship.

So long as the organized working class, as the revolutionary minority, can exert only partial influence on the change of the social system and legislation, the Socialist Revolutionary Party must see to it that the working class is not blinded by its partial gains and does not lose sight of its ultimate goal; that by its revolutionary struggle the proletariat would seek in this period such changes that would develop and strengthen its solidarity and ability to fight for freedom, would help to elevate its intellectual and cultural needs, and would strengthen its fighting position and eliminate barriers that hinder its organization.

Since the process of the transformation of Russia is led by nonsocialist forces, the Socialist Revolutionary Party, on the basis of the above principles, will advocate, defend, and seek by its revolutionary struggle the following reforms:

In the Realm of Politics and Legislation

The establishment of a democratic republic with broad autonomy for *oblasts* and communes, both urban and rural; increased acceptance of federal principles in relations between various nationalities; granting them unconditional right to self-determination; direct, secret, equal, and universal right to vote for every citizen above twenty years of age regardless of sex, religion, or national origin; proportional representation; direct popular legislation (referenda and initiatives); election, removability at all times, and accountability of all officials; complete freedom of conscience, speech, press, meetings, strikes, and unions; complete and general civil equality; inviolability of the individual and home; complete separation of the church from the state and declaration that religion is a private affair for every individual; introduction of a compulsory, equal-for-all general public education at government expense; equality of languages; free justice; abolishment of permanent armies and their replacement by a people's militia.

In the Realm of National Economy

1. In the matter of labor legislation the Socialist Revolutionary Party sets as its aim the safeguarding of spiritual and material forces of the working class and increasing its capability of further struggle to whose goals should be subordinated all expedient, direct, local, and professional interests of the diverse working strata. In this sphere the Party will advocate: a reduction of the working time in order to relieve surplus labor; establishment of a legal maximum of working time based on norms determined by health conditions (an eight-hour working norm for most branches of industry as soon as possible, and lower norms in dangerous or harmful-to-health work); establishment of a minimum wage in agreement between administration and labor unions; complete government insurance (for accident, unemployment, sickness, old age, and so on), administered by the insured at the expense of the state and employers; legislative protection of labor in all branches of industry and trade, in accordance with the health conditions supervised by factory inspection commissions elected by workers (normal working conditions, hygienic conditions of buildings; prohibition of work for youngsters below sixteen years of age, limitation of work for youngsters, prohibition of woman and child labor in some branches of industry and during specified periods, adequate and uninterrupted Sunday rest, and so forth); professional organization of workers and their increased participation in determining internal rules in industrial enterprises.

2. In matters of agricultural policy and land relations, the Socialist Revolutionary Party sets its task to be, in the interests of socialism and the struggle against the bourgeois property system, the utilization of the communal as well as the labor views, the traditions and forms of life of Russian peasantry, and especially their views on land as the public property of all the toilers. Consequently the Party will support socialization of all privately owned lands; that is, their transfer from private property of individual owners to public domain and administration by democratically organized communes and territorial associations of communes on the basis of equalized utilization. Should this basic demand of the agrarian minimum program not be realized at once as a revolutionary measure, the Socialist Revolutionary Party in its future agrarian policy will be guided by consideration of a possible realization of this demand in its entirety, advocating such related measures as: broadening of the rights of com-

munes and their territorial associations in expropriating privately owned lands; confiscation of lands belonging to monasteries, princes, ministers, and so forth, and their transfer, together with state properties, to communes, in order that they would have an adequate amount, and also for the needs of resettlement and redistribution; limiting of payments for the use of land to the amount of clear profit from the farm (less gross revenue of the cost of production and normal remuneration for labor); reimbursement for improvements on land when it is transferred from one user to another; conversion of rent through a special tax into a source of revenue for the communes and self-governing institutions.

3. In matters of financial policy the Party will agitate for the introduction of a progressive tax on income and inheritance, and for complete freedom from taxation of small incomes below an established norm; it will agitate for the elimination of indirect taxes (except luxury taxes), protective duties, and all other taxes that burden labor.

4. In matters of municipal and land economy, the Party will support the development of all kinds of public services, land agronomy organizations, communalization of water supply, education, ways and means of communication, and so forth; will support the granting of broad powers to urban and rural communes to tax immovable property as well as the right to confiscate it if this be necessary to improve the living standards of the toiling population; will support communal and zemstvo as well as governmental policy aimed at helping the development of cooperatives on solid democratic foundations.

5. With respect to various measures aimed at nationalization of one or another sectors of the national economy within the framework of a bourgeois state, the Socialist Revolutionary Party will support these measures, provided they are accompanied by a democratization of the political system, by a change in social forces, and that the very nature of these measures themselves would provide sufficient guarantee against the increase of dependence of the working class on ruling bureaucracy. In general the Socialist Revolutionary Party warns the working class against "state socialism," which is partly a system of half measures for the strengthening of the working class and partly a peculiar type of state capitalism that concentrates various branches of production and trade in the hands of the ruling bureaucracy for their financial and political aims.

The Socialist Revolutionary Party, in commencing its direct revolutionary struggle with autocracy, agitates for the calling of the *Zemskii Sobor* [Constituent Assembly] freely elected by the people regardless of sex, social status, nationality, or religion, to liquidate the autocratic regime and to reform all present systems. The Party will support its program of reform in the Constituent Assembly and it will also try to realize it directly during the revolutionary period.

Program of the Russian Constitutional Democratic Party (Cadet), 1905

I. Basic Rights of Citizens

1. All Russian citizens, irrespective of sex, religion, or nationality, are equal before the law. All class distinctions and all limitations of personal and property rights of Poles, Jews, and all other groups of the population, should be repealed.

2. Every citizen is guaranteed freedom of conscience and religion. No persecution for religious beliefs or convictions, or for change or refusal to accept religious indoctrination, can be allowed. The celebration of religious and church ceremonies and the spread of beliefs is free, provided these activities do not include any general transgressions contrary to the criminal code of law. The Orthodox Church and other religions should be freed from state protection.

3. Anyone who wishes to express his thoughts orally or in writing has the right to publish and spread them through printing or any other media. Censorship, both general and special, regardless of its name, must be abolished and cannot be reinstituted. For their oral or written transgressions the guilty ones will answer before the court.

4. All Russian citizens have the right to organize public or private meetings, in dwellings as well as in the open air, to examine any problem they wish.

5. All Russian citizens have the right to organize unions or societies without needing permission for it.

6. The right to petition is granted to every citizen as well as to all groups, unions, gatherings, and so forth.

7. The person and home of every individual should be inviolable. Entering of a private dwelling, search, seizure, and opening of private correspondence, are allowed only in cases permitted by law or on order of the court. Any individual detained in cities or places where courts are located should be freed within twenty-four hours; in other localities of the Empire not later than three days, or be brought before the court. Any detention undertaken illegally, or without proper grounds, gives a detained person the right to be compensated by the state for losses suffered.

8. No one can be subjected to persecution or punishment except on the basis of law by court authorities in a legally constituted court. No extraordinary courts are allowed.

9. Every citizen has freedom of movement and travel abroad. The passport system is abolished.

10. All the above mentioned rights of citizens must be incorporated into the Constitution of the Russian Empire and be guaranteed by courts.

11. The Constitution of the Russian Empire should guarantee all the minorities inhabiting the Empire, in addition to full civil and political equality enjoyed by all citizens, the right of cultural self-determination, namely: full freedom of usage of various languages and dialects in public, the freedom to found and maintain educational institutions and meetings of all sorts having as their aim the preservation and development of language, literature and culture of every nationality.

12. Russian language should be the official language of central administration, army, and fleet. The use of local languages alongside the official language in state and public institutions and educational establishments supported by the state or organs of local self-government is determined by general and local laws, and within their competence by the institutions concerned. The population of each locality should be guaranteed education in the native language in elementary schools, and possibly in subsequent education.

II. Government Apparatus

13. The constitutional system of the Russian state will be determined by the constitution.

14. People's representatives are elected by a general, equal, direct and secret ballot, irrespective of their religion, nationality or sex.

The party allows within its midst a difference of opinion on the question of national representation, consisting of one or two chambers in which case the second chamber should consist of representatives of the local organs of self-government, organized on the basis of a general vote and spread throughout all of Russia.

15. National representation participates in the realization of legislative power, in the determination of government revenues and expenditures, and in control of the legality and expedience of actions of higher and lower organs of administration.

16. No decision, decree, ukaz, order, or a similar act not based on the legislative measure of national representation, regardless of its name or place of origin, can have the force of law.

17. A government inventory, which should include all revenues and expenditures of the state, should be established by law, every year. No taxes, dues, and collections for the state, as well as state loans, can be established other than by legislation.

18. Members of national representative assemblies should have the right of legislative initiative.

19. Ministers are responsible to the representatives of the national assembly, and the latter have the right of questioning and interpellation.

III. Local Self-Government and Autonomy

20. Local self-government should be extended throughout the entire Russian state.

21. Representatives in the organs of local self-government, being close to the population by virtue of the organization of small self-governing units, should be elected on the basis of universal, equal, direct, and secret ballot, regardless of sex, religion, and nationality, while the assemblies of higher self-governing units can be selected by lower assemblies. Gubernia zemstvos should have the right to enter into temporary or permanent unions among themselves.

22. The competence of the organs of local self-government should include the entire field of local administration, including police, but excluding only those branches of administration which, under the condition of present state life, must be located in the hands of the central government. Organs of the local self-government should receive partial support from sources which now go to the budget of the central government.

23. The activity of representatives of the central government should be limited to supervision of the legality of acts of the organs of local self government; the final decision on any disputes or doubts is reserved for the courts.

24. Following the establishment of rights of civil freedom and proper representation with constitutional rights for the entire Russian state, there should be opened a legal way within the framework of state legislation for the establishment of local autonomy and *oblast* representative assemblies, with the right to participate in the realization of legislative authority on familiar matters in accordance with the needs of the population.

25. Immediately following the introduction of the imperial democratic government with constitutional rights, there should be established in the Polish kingdom an autonomous administration with a *sejm* [Parliament] elected on the same basis as the state parliament of Russia, preserving its state unity and participation in the central parliament on an equal footing with other parts of the Empire. Frontiers between the Polish kingdom and neighboring *gubernias* shall be established in accordance with the native population and desires of the local population. In the Polish kingdom there should be instituted national guarantees of civil freedom and rights of nationalities on cultural self-determination as well as protection of the rights of minorities.

26. *Finland*. The Finnish Constitution, which safeguards its special

state status, should be fully reinstated. All future measures common to the Empire and the grand duchy of Finland should be solved by an agreement between legislative branches of the Empire and the grand duchy.

IV. Courts

27. All departures from the bases of the Judicial Statute of November 20, 1864, which separated judicial from administrative power (irremovability of judges, independence of courts, and equality of all citizens before the court) as well as the introduction of subsequent novelties are to be abolished . . . Courts with class representatives are abolished. Matters of volost justice are subject to the competence of an elected justice of the peace. The volost court and the institution of *zemskii nachalniks* [land administrators] are abolished. The demand for property qualifications to perform the functions of a justice of the peace as well as that of a sworn deputy is abolished. The principle of the unity of appelate court is reestablished. Advocacy is organized on the foundation of true self-administration.

28. In addition to this, the aim of penal policy should consist of: (a) unconditional abolishment forever of the death penalty; (b) introduction of conditional conviction; (c) establishment of protection during preliminary investigation; and (d) introduction into court proceedings of controvertible rule.

29. The immediate task centers in the full examination of the criminal code, the annulment of decrees which are contrary to the foundations of political freedom, and the reworking of the project of the civil code.

V. Financial and Economic Policy

30. There should be re-examination of government expenditure in order to eliminate unproductive expenses, and to bring about an appreciable increase of state resources for the real needs of the people.

31. The redemption payments should be repealed.

32. There should be replacement of indirect by direct taxes, general lowering of indirect taxes, and gradual repeal of indirect taxes on items of general consumption.

33. There should be a reform of direct taxes on the basis of progressive income, a reform of property taxation, and a progressive tax on inheritance.

34. In conformity with the condition of individual industries there should be a lowering of custom duties in order to cut down the cost of products of general consumption and to improve the technical level of industry and agriculture.

35. Saving banks should be used for the development of small loans.

VI. Agrarian Legislation

36. There should be an increase of arable land for that part of the population which works the land with its own labor, namely landless and petty peasants—as well as other peasants—by state, princely, cabinet, monastery, and private estates at the state's expense, with private owners being compensated at a fair (not market) price for their land.

37. Expropriated land should be transfered to a state and land reserve. Rules by which the land from this reserve should be given to a needy population (ownership, or personal or communal use, and so forth) should be determined in accordance with peculiarities of land ownership and land usage in different parts of Russia.

38. There should be broad organization of government aid to migration, resettlement, and arrangement of the economic life of peasants. There should be reorganization of the Boundary Office, termination of surveying and introduction of other measures for bringing prosperity to the rural population and improving the rural economy.

39. Legislation dealing with the lease relationship should be promulgated in order to protect the right of tenants and the right to re-lease . . .

40. The existing rules on hiring of agricultural workers should be repealed and labor legislation should be extended to agricultural workers. . . .

VII. Labor Legislation

41. There should be freedom of labor unions and assemblies.

42. The right to strike should be granted. Punishment for violations of law which occur during or as a result of strikes should be determined in general terms and under no circumstances should be extreme.

43. Labor legislation and independent inspection of labor should be extended to all forms of hired labor; there should be participation of workers' elected representatives in inspections aimed at safeguarding the interests of workers.

44. Legislation should introduce the eight-hour working day. Where possible, this norm should be immediately realized everywhere, and systematically introduced in other industries. Night work and overtime work should be prohibited except where technically and socially indispensable.

45. Protection of female and child labor and the establishment of special measures to protect male labor should be developed in dangerous enterprises.

46. Arbitration offices consisting of an equal number of representatives of labor and capital to regulate all kinds of hiring which are not

regulated by labor legislation, and solving of disputes which may arise between workers and employers, should be established.

47. Obligatory state medical care (for a definite period), accident and work-connected illness compensations, which are to be contributed to by the employers, should be established.

48. State old age security and disability allowances for all individuals who make a living by their own work should be introduced.

49. Criminal responsibility for violation of laws dealing with the protection of labor should be established.

VIII. Problems of Education

Public education should be founded on freedom, democracy, and decentralization in order to realize the following goals:

50. The elimination of all restrictions on school admissions based on sex, origin or religion.

51. Freedom of private and public initiative to found and organize all sorts of educational institutions, including education outside the school; freedom of instruction.

52. Better liaison should be organized between various school classes in order to make easier a transfer from one school to another.

53. There should be full autonomy and freedom of instruction in universities and other institutions of higher learning. Their numbers should increase. The fee for attending lectures should be lowered. Institutions of higher learning should organize education to meet the needs of broad layers of society. Students should have freedom to organize themselves.

54. The number of institutions of secondary learning should increase in accordance with public needs; the fee for these should be reduced. Local public institutions should have the right to participate in the formulation of the education curriculum.

55. A universal, free, and obligatory system of education should be introduced in elementary schools. Local self-government should extend material aid to those who need it.

56. Local self-government should organize institutions for the education of the adult population—elementary schools for the adult, as well as public libraries and public universities.

57. Professional education should be developed.

Program of the Union of the Russian People, 1905

Russian People!

The great manifesto of October 30 granted us civil freedom on the basis of inviolability of person, freedom of expression, conscience, meetings and unions. In spite of this Tsarist grace, under the cover of promised freedom, many of us in fact have joined the darkest slavery of a mysterious, unknown, coarse, and all-destructive force which arbitrarily determines our fate without any legal authority, issues its own "manifestoes" and openly advocates a whole series of impractical demands, such as complete destruction of the Russian army and its replacement by militia subordinate to city administration, organization of a social democratic republic, and so forth. The enemies of the Tsar and of the country, by means of deception, threats, and violence, cause strikes in factories and mills, stop trains, disrupt trade, inflict tremendous loss to the entire state, and deprive hundreds of thousands of poor people of work in order to force them into violence through hunger. Our children are deprived of the possibility of education, the sick are dying, not being able to obtain medicine . . . The trouble has not stopped in spite of the fact that we have received freedom, the same "freedom" which everyone has demanded so ardently. God only knows how far this anarchy will lead. One thing, however, is certain: we are proceeding directly to the downfall and destruction of the Russian state. This is why we call upon all those honest Russian people, irrespective of their profession or status, who are loyal to the Tsar, the country, and traditional Russian principles, to unite in order to conduct an active struggle by every legal means against arbitrariness, violence, and other repulsive manifestations of the recently granted freedom.

The ultimate aim which this Union of the Russian People must seek is the introduction of a firm, durable, legal order, on the basis of the following foundations:

1. Unity and indivisibility of the Russian Empire and stability of the basic foundations of Russian statehood, because only firm Tsarist authority, based on a direct union between the Tsar and the people, or their elected representatives, can provide unconditional guarantees for a durable legal order in such a multi-national state as Russia.

2. Establishment of a State Duma with the right to report directly to the Sovereign, the right to address an inquiry to the ministers, the right to control the activity of the ministers, and the right to petition the Emperor that the former be dismissed and tried in the courts.

3. Coordination of the activity of ministers and establishment of their firm, actual responsibility, similar to the responsibility of all other officials, for every irregularity connected with their service and for damages suffered by private individuals, including bringing them to the attention of the Procurator.

4. Allowing the election of Jews to the State Duma, not more than three persons, elected by the entire Jewish population of the Russian Empire to present in the Duma the special needs of the Jewish population. Such limitation is necessary because of the disruptive, anti-state

activity of the united Jewish masses, their unceasing hatred of everything Russian, and the unscrupulousness which they so openly demonstrated during the recent revolutionary movement.

5. The realization of freedom and inviolability granted by the Manifesto of October 30; that is, protection of individuals from the arbitrariness and violence of officials, of private individuals as well as of all sorts of societies, unions, and committees, both open and secret.

6. Establishment of a firm criminal responsibility of the press to protect the basic foundation of the state system, based on special legislation similar to that which exists in the countries of Western Europe.

7. Firm, severe, and actual protection of property rights of private individuals, of societies, and of the state.

The basis of our Union is brotherly love towards neighbors, and we therefore do not allow any of the arbitrariness, force, falsehoods, rumors, distortions, secret or similar means of struggle used by our enemies, by the Tsar's enemies, or by enemies of the country.

The Statute of the Union of the Russian People

I. *The Aim of the Union* 1. The Union of the Russian People sets as its undeviating goal a durable unity of the Russian people of all classes and professions to work for the general good of our fatherland—a Russia united and indivisible.

II. *Program* 2. The well being of the country should consist of a firm preservation of Russian autocracy, orthodoxy, and nationality, and of the establishment of a State Duma, order, and legality.

3. Russian autocracy was created by national wisdom, sanctified by the Church, and justified by history. Our autocracy consists of unity between the Tsar and the people.

Note: Convinced that national well being consists of the unity between the Russian Tsar and the people, the Union acknowledges that the present ministerial bureaucratic system, which separates the pure soul of the Russian Tsar from the people, and which has appropriated a number of rights that truly belong to the Russian autocratic power, has brought our country to grave troubles and should therefore be changed fundamentally. At the same time the Union firmly believes that a change of the existing order should be accomplished not through the introduction of certain restrictive institutions such as constitutional or constituent assemblies, but rather through convocation of a State Duma as an institution which would represent a direct tie between the autocratic will of the Tsar and the right of the people.

4. The Russian people are Orthodox people and therefore the Orthodox faith remains steadfastly the official religion of the Russian Empire.

All subjects of the Empire, however, have the freedom of religious worship.

5. The Russian nation, as the gatherer of Russian lands and the creator of the great might of the state, enjoys a preferential position in national life and in national administration.

Note: All institutions of the Russian state should be united and should constantly strive to maintain the greatness of Russia and the preferential rights of the Russian nation that legally belong to them, so that the numerous minorities that inhabit our country would consider it their privilege to be a part of the Russian Empire and would not consider themselves oppressed.

Note: The Russian language is and should be the official language of the Russian Empire for all of its people.

6. The State Duma, the bulwark of autocracy, should not demand any limitations on the supreme authority of the Tsar. It should only inform him of the real needs of the people and of the state and help the Lawgiver to realize the necessary reforms.

7. The immediate activity of authorities should be directed toward the introduction of a firm order and legality guaranteeing freedom of speech, press, assembly, and unions, and the inviolability of the individual. There should be established a rule that would determine the limits of these freedoms in order to prevent the violation of the established system, the endangering of the rights of other individuals, and thus to protect freedom itself.

III. *The Activity of the Union* 8. The Union sets as its continuous aim active participation in elections, from among its midst, of members to the State Duma to realize the aims to which the Union subscribes.

Note: Problems which the Union believes should be dealt with as soon as possible by the State Duma have been listed in Appendix 1 of the present statute.

9. The Union intends to assume the responsibility of providing people with sound education, of developing among the people consciousness in the spirit of autocracy, and of spreading among them Christian foundations, thereby strengthening their patriotism and feelings of debt to the nation, society, and family.

Note: The proposed educational activity of the Union will be accomplished through the opening of a greater number of schools, through the preparation of readings, meetings, talks, distribution of appropriate books and pamphlets, and through the publication of newspapers and journals. The foundation of educational activity of Union schools are included in Appendix 2 of the present charter.

10. Within the limits of its possibilities, the Union intends to build churches and to open hospitals, shelters, industries, and similar useful

buildings, and to aid in the founding of mutual banks and other industrial-protective unions.

11. The Union considers as its immutable obligation the extension, within its capabilities, of brotherly help to all of its members; that is, material and moral support.

12. The Union has the right to enter into relations with governmental and public institutions on matters that relate to the aims of the Union.

13. The Union has the right to appropriate in its own name, using legal means, immovable property and operate these as legally its own.

IV. *The Organization of the Union* 14. Members of the Union can be only native Russians of both sexes, of all classes and professions, who are dedicated to the aims of the Union, who show an indication that they are firmly acquainted with the aims of the Union and who, when they join the Union, will promise not to enter into any association with a secret organization or an organization that pursues aims that are contrary to those of the Union.

15. All other persons can be accepted as members of the Union only by the decision of the General Meeting of the members of the Union.

Note: Jews cannot become members of the Union.

16. Members of the Union pay membership dues of fifty copecks annually, and any payment above the indicated sum is considered a gift; the name of a person making such a gift will be listed on a special list to be published twice a year indicating the amount given.

Note: Persons who cannot afford membership dues are freed from the payment.

17. Members of the Union who distinguish themselves by their useful work, either for the well-being of the nation or in executing the goals of the Union, as well as those who contribute appreciable gifts, will receive the title of Distinguished Members of the Union to be designated by the General Meeting of the members of the Union.

18. The Union is governed by a Council consisting of twelve members of the Union elected by a general meeting which also elects three candidate members of the Council. Candidates in turn replace absent members of the Council. Members of the Council elect from their members a Chairman of the Council of the Union and two Associate Chairmen. The Chairman is obligated to execute the decision of the Council and of the General Meeting.

19. The first membership of the Council of the Union is to be elected by the founding members from among their midst for a period of three years. Subsequently at the expiration of three years three members of the Council will be replaced annually by new members of the Council elected by the General Meeting. Retired members of the Council may be re-elected at the next General Meeting.

20. The Council of the Union is responsible for the organization of

provincial branches of the Union in *gubernias, oblasts,* cities, settlements, villages, and hamlets. Members of the Council of the Union may delegate this activity to individual members of the Union.

Note: Members of the Union pledge not to assume any organizational activity without the decision of the Council of the Union, and have no right to act without such a decision in behalf of the Union.

21. Members of the Council elect from their midst a Secretary of the Council.

22. All matters in the Council of the Union are decided by a simple majority of votes. The Chairman of the Council, in case of a tie vote, casts the deciding vote.

23. Members of the Council elect from their membership a clerk of the Council of the Union and a Treasurer of the Union.

24. The Council of the Union has its own press, and the Chairman of the Council of the Union is responsible for it.

25. Upon joining the Union every member receives the insignia of the Union, which is uniform throughout the Russian Empire.

26. Members of the Union form a General Meeting which can be called by the Council twice a year or more if necessary. The General Meeting can also be called on demand of the members themselves if the number of those desiring a General Meeting is more than fifty members.

27. The Union may enter into relations with other Unions or societies if the latter's aim does not contradict the aims and activities of the Union of the Russian People.

V. *Resources of the Union* 28. Resources of the Union Consist of membership dues and other offerings.

29. Monetary funds of the Union, upon the decision of the Council, are deposited in either government or private banks.

30. Monetary funds of the Union are safe deposited to draw interest, but they can be converted into securities, guaranteed by the government, if the Council deems it more useful.

31. Monetary funds of the Union are disposed of by the decision of the Council; their withdrawal from the bank must be done only by a check bearing three signatures, including that of the Chairman or his assistant.

32. The decisions of the Council of the Union are considered binding if the meeting of the Council is attended by not fewer than seven members.

VI. *The Accountability of the Union* 33. The Council will present before every General Meeting an account of its revenues and expenditures, the finances of the Union, and will account for the activity of the Union and of individual members.

34. The General Meeting has the right to audit finances of the Union.

To do so it selects an Auditing Commission consisting of three members of the Union for every individual audit.

Appendix 1 (to Article 8 of the Statute) Of the problems that the State Duma should first consider, the Union lists among others: the peasant problem; the improvement of living conditions of all the toiling classes, irrespective of their profession; the responsibility of all officials for illegal acts in the performance of their duties.

1. The Union believes that one of the most important national problems is to resolve whether the village commune among the peasants should be retained or abolished. The Union, believing that the peasants themselves without any outside compulsion express themselves on this issue, publicly states that it will not assume any initiative in resolving this problem; until the peasants themselves resolve this problem, the Union considers its obligation to be to provide the peasants a peaceful atmosphere for an absolutely free solution of the communal organization without any outside interference, whether by institutions or individuals.

While limiting its support to advocating free expression by the peasants on the commune problem until its solution by the peasants themselves, the Union, to improve peasant conditions, considers that its immediate task is to advocate that poor peasants be given more land, or that such peasants be either resettled or permitted to transfer their land to other peasants by a freely reached bargain.

The Union also takes note of the extreme unproductivity of Russian agriculture and suggests that a broad program of education be instituted to acquaint the Russian agricultural population with a more rational form of farming and to provide them with every needed assistance for a more rational increase of the productivity of land.

2. The Union considers that its special obligation is to do everything possible to improve the condition of all the toiling classes regardless of their occupation; toward the workers the Union considers that its particular obligation is to declare that their difficult situation in many enterprises demands that relations between the workers and employers be regulated without delay by means of legislation, taking into account the location and the nature of the enterprise.

3. The Union believes that the existing system of accountability for responsible officials is one of the causes of the current difficult situation in Russia. Presently, all those who have suffered from abuses and illegal acts by responsible officials have no recourse against them in the courts to seek legal compensations for their losses from the guilty ones, and can only complain to administrators who, by virtue of the powers vested in them by the law, take note only of those cases which have endangered the interests of the treasury. The impunity of present officials has given rise to an infinite abuse which can easily be stopped by repealing the appropriate articles of the law and by allowing every individual who has

suffered the right to turn freely and directly to the Procurator's Office and/or to the Court with his complaint against illegal acts of officials, and to demand compensation for the losses suffered as a result of official negligence. To prevent abuses of this system the law should severely punish those who accuse unjustly or report falsely.

Appendix 2 (to Article 9 of the Statute) The elementary school does not at all correspond either to the spirit or the needs of the Russian people.

The Union sets as one of its main objectives the education of peasant, city, and working population on firm foundations and the development in them of political consciousness and principles of Christianity. Village schools should equip the peasant for the necessities of rural life, agriculture, crafts, and domestic industry.

38

Witte's Account of His Premiership

One of the most forceful statesmen during the closing years of imperial Russia was Count Sergei J. Witte (1849–1915). A nobleman by birth and a financier by profession, Witte was Minister of Finance from 1892 to 1903. In that capacity he secured large foreign loans (mainly from France), encouraged extensive railroad construction, placed Russia on the gold standard, supported protectionist tariffs, and in every possible way fostered industrial development. He vigorously opposed Russia's adventurist policy in the Far East, which had led to war with Japan (1904–1905) and following Russia's defeat, he headed the Russian delegation to the

Reprinted with permission of Avrahm Yarmolinsky from *The Memoirs of Count Witte.* Translated from the original Russian manuscript and edited by Abraham Yarmolinsky. (Garden City, N.Y.: Doubleday, Page & Company, 1921), pp. 285–298, 307–309.

peace conference at Portsmouth, New Hampshire. There he not only gained advantageous terms for Russia but universal respect as a statesman. Upon his triumphant return, Witte was selected by Nicholas II to be Russia's first premier, and guide the revolution-agitated country back to normalcy. As Premier, Witte drafted the October Manifesto, restored order throughout the country, put the final touches on the Fundamental Laws, and secured for Russia what was at the time the largest foreign loan ever made. While he was respected abroad, Witte was never really popular at home. In court circles he was accused of republicanism; the nobles thought he sought to ruin them for the benefit of the peasants; and revolutionaries saw him as a monarchist who tried to deceive the peasants for the benefit of the nobles. In April 1906, after he had secured the enormous foreign loan that started Russia on the way to economic stability, Nicholas II, as a first major reaction step, summarily dismissed Witte.

Shortly after my arrival from my peace mission in the United States, I had a heart-to-heart talk with Count Dimitry Solski, President of the Imperial Council, about Russian home affairs. "Count," he repeated, "you alone can save the situation." When I declared that it was my intention to keep aloof by all means, and to go abroad for a few months' rest, he burst into tears and reproached me for my egoism and lack of patriotism. "Go abroad!" he exclaimed. "In the meantime we shall all perish here!"

Unwilling to shirk the duty I owed to my Monarch and country, I did not go abroad. Although I had no illusions about the difficulty and thanklessness of the task, I assumed the burden of power and bore it for six months. My appointment as President took place immediately upon the publication of the historical manifesto of October 17th, which granted the Russian people civic liberties and a parliamentary regime.

In October, 1905, the Government had neither troops nor funds with which to fight the revolution. I soon perceived that only two things could save the dynasty and enable Russia to weather the revolutionary storm, namely, a large foreign loan and the return of the army from Transbaikalia and Manchuria to the European part of the country. These two measures, coupled with a determination on the part of the Government to carry out in good faith the promises of the constitutional manifesto, I was certain, would pacify the country.

At the time when I assumed the task of ruling the country, the bulk of the army, about a million men, was in far Manchuria. Those units which remained in Russia were largely depleted, both in their personnel and military equipment. As a matter of fact, the whole vast body of the Russian army was in a state of complete physical and moral prostration. Owing its existence, as it did, to universal military conscription, the army could not help being affected by the spirit of general discontent which prevailed in the country. Indeed, the most extreme subversive ideas found a fertile soil among the military, who felt more keenly than the civilian population the pain and disgrace of the disastrous war into which the country had been dragged by its irresponsible rulers. It should be noted that actual cases of mutinies in the army were rather infrequent, this being perhaps due to the energy Grand Duke Nikolai Nikolaievich displayed in dealing with the outbreaks.

Several days before my appointment I conferred with the Minister of War and General Trepov, then commander of the St. Petersburg garrison, for the purpose of ascertaining to what extent we could depend on the troops in case it should be decided to crush the revolution by armed force. The impression I gained from that conference was that the army was unreliable for two reasons, namely, because of its numerical weakness and its dangerous state of mind. This circumstance perhaps accounts for His Majesty's decision in preferring the road of reforms to the unstinted application of sheer force. I cannot explain His Majesty's choice otherwise, for like all weak people he believes most in physical force.

After the ratification of the Portsmouth treaty, in accordance with the letter of the law, it was necessary to discharge the reservists who had been called to the colours for the duration of the war. Since these soldiers were the most troublesome element of the army and had infected with revolutionary ideas both the Transbaikalian troops and the units stationed in European Russia, I had them demobilized immediately. As a result, the army at my disposal diminished in numbers, but it was purged of the troublesome element, which was at any moment liable to break out in uncontrollable mutinies. Thus, European Russia was practically denuded of troops. A sufficient number of them was available only in the St. Petersburg, Warsaw and Caucasian military districts, but as the situation in those regions was threatening the commanders there were extremely reluctant to part with their units for the benefit of other regions. Central Russia was almost completely deprived of troops. The disorganization was so great that the military authorities themselves did not know how many men were available and where they were stationed. Most of the units in the rear were far below their normal strength, but the military authorities were in many cases ignorant of the extent to which the units had been depleted. At the request of the local administration, a battalion would be dispatched, after long delay, to quell a peasant riot. We would next hear that, instead of a battalion no more than, say, a dozen men had arrived. We would then turn to the army authorities and learn that most of the personnel of the battalion in question was at the front. Such cases, I remember, were by no means exceptional. This chaotic condition, I later found out, was the result of General Kuropatkin's activity as Minister of War.

As we had at our disposal neither troops nor rural police, it was impossible to combat the agrarian disorders with any degree of efficiency. In the course of my premiership I succeeded in increasing and improving the police force, both municipal and rural. But at the height of the disturbances in some places there was no police at all, and even in Moscow the force was poorly armed. The policemen often reported for duty with empty revolver cases for all arms.

Since the local administration was in many places demoralized, I conceived the plan of sending His Majesty's Adjutant Generals to those districts where the situation was most alarming. Thus, Adjutant General Sakharov was sent to the government of Saratov, Adjutant General Strukov to the governments of Tambov and Voronezh, and Adjutant General Dubasov to the governments of Chernigov and Kursk. General Dubasov acted very energetically, but in such a way as not to arouse anyone's animosity. He was profoundly impressed by the extent and importance of the agrarian disturbances. He urged me, I recall, without waiting for the opening of the Duma to enact a law whereby the land forcefully seized by the peasants would be made their legitimate property. This, he argued, would pacify the peasants. As for the land-owners, he said, it would be best for them, too, for otherwise the peasants would seize all the private estates and leave nothing to their owners.

The peasant riots were caused by Russian conditions and also, to a certain extent, by the propaganda of the socialists.

In shaping the course of the revolution an exceedingly important role was played by the whole gamut of socialistic doctrines, from Tolstoy's Christian communism to "anarchistic socialism," which served as a disguise for plain robbery—all these teachings having in common a denial of property rights as defined in Roman law. During the last fifty years the ideas of socialism have advanced with vigorous strides throughout the whole of Europe. They found a fertile soil in Russia, owing to the constant violation of every right, especially of property rights, on the part of the authorities, and also because of the lack of culture among the population. The revolutionists promised the factories to the workmen and the land of *pomieshchiki* (landowners) to the peasants, declaring that these commodities belong to the people by right, and had been unjustly taken away from them. The workers naturally responded with strikes, while the peasants began to practise what, in imitation of an orator of the French Revolution, Deputy Herzenstein in the First Duma called "the illumination" of the landowners' estates, i.e., they began to burn and loot the property of the landed gentry.

The Manchurian armies were naturally anxious to get home. Owing to the railroad strikes in European Russia and in Siberia, the Far East was oftentimes cut off from the rest of Russia for weeks together. As a result the most fantastic rumours spread among the troops like wildfire. Making his way home through Siberia, after the conclusion of the Portsmouth treaty, Prince Vasilchikov did not know, until he reached Cheliabinsk, whether the Emperor was still in Russia, for he had heard rumours to the effect that the Imperial family had escaped abroad and that my colleagues and myself had been strung up on lamp-posts on the Champ de Mars in St. Petersburg. This story I have from His Majesty himself.

I am under the impression that toward the end of 1905 the army at the front was thoroughly demoralized and revolutionary. If this was not a matter of common knowledge, it is because it was the policy of the military authorities to hide the plagues which were corroding the very heart of the army.

The first revolutionary wave, originating in the West, moved eastward and infected the Transbaikalian army. A movement in the opposite direction began toward the end of 1905, some of the discharged soldiers from the front bringing the revolutionary germ into the interior of the country. Alarming news of the state of mind of the Manchurian army had reached St. Petersburg in previous months. Under the influence of this news, the Minister of Agriculture, Schwanebach, laid before the Committee of Ministers a plan for allotting the crown lands in Siberia to the soldiers in active service who would consent to settle there. After a short discussion of this singular scheme, the committee declined to consider it further, and the whole matter came to nothing.

The strike on the Great Siberian Railroad, coupled with the eagerness of the troops to return home, completely disorganized the Eastern Chinese Railway, which circumstance added to the dissatisfaction of the army. The railroad strikes were responsible for the delay in assembling recruits and in transporting the Manchurian armies home. At one time the Siberian railroads were in the hands of self-constituted bands and organizations which refused to obey the governmental authorities. The revolutionists perceived that no sooner did the troops reach their homes than they lost all their revolutionary ardour and turned into a bulwark of law and order. For that reason they made every effort to keep up the railroad strikes in Siberia.

Traffic on the Siberian and Eastern Chinese Railways oftentimes ceased completely, and the troops indulged in rioting as they made their way westward. Then the strike of the telegraph operators came to increase the confusion. Day after day passed and the armies were still far away from Central Russia, their absence complicating both the internal and the international position of the country. I repeatedly pointed out the seriousness of the situation to Grand Duke Nikolai Nikolaievich, to the Minister of War, and to the Chief of the General Staff, General Palitzyn. They replied quite correctly that the matter was within the province of General Linevich, Commander-in-Chief of the armies in active service. The only official communication I received from the Commander-in-chief throughout the six months of my premiership was a dispatch informing me that fourteen (I remember that number very distinctly) anarchist-revolutionists had arrived at the front to stir up trouble in the army. I showed this telegram to His Majesty and he returned it to me with the following words written on the margin: "I hope they will be hanged."

At this juncture, I hit upon the idea of dispatching two military trains, one from Kharbin westward, the other from European Russia eastward, under the command of two firm and resolute generals, instructed to open up normal traffic on the Siberian roads and remove the causes which hindered the regular functioning of the roads. His Majesty was pleased by this idea and adopted my plan. General Meller-Zakomelski was placed at the head of the expedition which had Moscow as its starting-point, while the train dispatched from Kharbin was put under the command of General Rennenkampf. The two generals were ordered to reopen normal traffic and restore order along the Siberian railways *at any price.* They acquitted themselves of their task with eminent success, and the two trains effected a junction near Chita. Naturally enough, this extraordinary measure could not be carried into effect without severe repressions. On reaching Chita, which was entirely in the hands of revolutionists, General Rennenkampf proceeded to execute a number of people. While he was restoring order at Chita, my wife once came to me in alarm and showed me a telegram sent to her from Brussels, in the name of the Russian revolutionary group of that city. It read as follows: "If your husband does not immediately cancel Rennenkampf's death sentences, he and the following men (names follow) will be executed, your daughter and grandson will be killed on the same day." As a matter of fact, my daughter lived in Brussels with her husband, K. V. Naryshkin, who served at our Embassy, and they had a one-year old boy for whom both my wife and myself had an affection almost morbid in its intensity. Of course, I paid no heed to this threat, which, by the way, the revolutionists failed to carry out. This incident illustrates the perfection to which the revolutionists carried their system of underground communication, and also the difficult position in which we were in those days.

Simultaneously Commander-in-Chief Linevich was dismissed and General Grodekov appointed in his stead, at my recommendation. He succeeded in restoring order in the army and transporting the Manchurian armies into the interior of the country. At my suggestion, the location of the troops was altered, with a view to the most effective suppression of local insurrections and riots. My principle was to oppose force to force and to take the most drastic measures against an open uprising, but at the same time I was against the practice of mass executions months and years after order had been restored.

My next great task was to secure a foreign loan. As early as 1904 the need for a foreign loan became apparent. At that time our financial system was already giving way under the pressure of the war expenditures. In concluding our second commercial treaty with Germany in 1904, I succeeded in securing Germany's permission to float our loan in that country. The next year I made an effort to prepare the ground for the loan in France and in the United States, where I went on the Portsmouth peace mission. My intention was to conclude the loan before the opening of the Imperial Duma. As I felt sure that the first Duma would be unbalanced and to a certain extent revengeful, I was afraid that its interference might thwart the loan negotiations and render the bankers less tractable. As a result, the Government, without funds, would lose the freedom of action which is so essential during a period of upheaval.

I had a keen personal interest in the loan. It must be borne in mind that I was responsible for the adoption by Russia (in 1896) of the gold standard of currency, and it was doubly painful for me to see this standard seriously threatened by the financial crisis brought about by the war, on the one hand, and by the nearsighted policy of the Minister of Finances, on the other. He waited for the end of the war to conclude a large loan, but he failed to foresee the outbreak of the revolution, with its disastrous effect on our credit.

France was willing to open its money market to us, but as a preliminary condition the French Government demanded the conclusion of peace with Japan. When the Portsmouth treaty was concluded, new obstacles presented themselves, notably the Franco-German conflict over Morocco, and the Paris Government made the conclusion of the loan contingent upon the peaceable settlement of that conflict. Elsewhere, in my remarks on the Kaiser, I tell the story of how I succeeded in having the clash arbitrated by an international conference at Algeciras. The conference lasted till the end of March, 1906, and until its termination the conclusion of the loan was out of the question.

The loan was to be an international one, but in view of its large amount the French group of bankers was to play the leading part. In 1905 I opened preliminary negotiations with Neutzlin, the head of the Banque de Paris et des Pays Bas. After the death of Germain, of the Crédit Lyonnais, the Banque de Paris et des Pays Bas became the chief banking institution in the so-called Christian group of bankers' syndicates. The other group of banks, known as the Jewish group, was headed by the Rothschild firm. Old Baron Alphonse Rothschild, with whom I had been on very friendly terms, was already dead, and Lord Rothschild of London was now the head of the family. Consequently, I instructed Rafalovich, our financial agent in Paris, to go to London and find out what was the attitude of the Rothschilds toward our loan. Rafalovich's reply was to the effect that out of respect for Count Witte as a statesman they would willingly render full assistance to the loan, but that they would not be in a position to do so until the Russian Government had enacted legal measures tending to improve the conditions of the Jews in Russia. As I deemed it beneath our dignity to connect the solution of our Jewish question with the loan, I decided to give up my intention of securing the participation of the Rothschilds.

The Constitutional Democrats ("Cadets") were fully aware of the stabilizing effect the loan would have upon the Government. Consequently, they sought to defeat my efforts to conclude the loan before the opening of the Duma. Their representatives, chiefly Prince Dolgoruki and Maklakov, acted in Paris, trying to persuade the French Government that it was illegal for the Imperial Government to conclude the loan without the sanction of the Duma. It is not without shame, I am sure, that these public leaders, who were very decent men for all that, recall this activity of theirs, which could hardly be termed patriotic. Their only excuse lies in the fact that in those days the greater part of thinking Russia was in a state of intoxication. People were actually drunk with the old wine of freedom, which had been brewing for many generations.

As for our press, it did nothing to inspire the foreign investor with confidence. For instance, nearly all the papers printed the appeal of the revolutionists to the population enjoining it to withdraw their deposits from the banks and local treasuries, so as to force the Government to cease the exchange of credit bills and reduce the Treasury to a state of insolvency. On the other hand, the foreign press displayed a great deal of hostility toward us. . . .

Already in November, 1905, our money circulation was in a very critical state and I found it necessary to keep the financial committee informed about the situation. With my approval, the committee appointed two of its members, V. N. Kokovtzev and Schwanebach, Minister of Agriculture, together with the Minister of Finances, I. P. Shipov, to watch the transactions of the Imperial Bank, but, of course, they were unable to suggest anything to improve matters. As the situation was rapidly growing worse and as some of the members of the financial committee thought it was possible to conclude a foreign loan immediately, I proposed to Kokovtzev that he go abroad with full powers to contract a loan. I knew very well that before the settlement of the Morocco conflict, this was out of the question, but I did not judge it possible to take the financial committee into my confidence with regard to the political aspect of the situation.

Kokovtzev went to Paris late in December, 1905, and was told, of course, by Rouvier that we could not conclude the loan before the peaceable termination of the Morocco affair. He also had an interview with President Loubet. Kokovtzev succeeded in getting an advance of 100 million rubles on account of the future loan. This sum was but a drop in the bucket, for the short-term bonds issued by Kokovtzev in Berlin were soon to fall due. Accordingly I asked Kokovtzev to stop in Berlin on his way back and try to obtain an extension of time for these bonds. This extension he secured, for the reason that the German Government was still undecided as to what course I would follow in matters pertaining to Russia's external policy. For, though I was instrumental in annulling the monstrous Björke agreement, I nevertheless made it clear that I was in favour of a coalition between Russia, Germany, and France, which would dominate the whole of Europe, if not the world. If this plan, which was my chief political idea, was not realized, it was because of insufficient political farsightedness on our part and also on the part of Emperor William of Germany. . . .

In January, 1906, I decided to push further the negotiations for the loan, which I had initiated in Paris on my way back from the United States. As I could not go abroad and as there was no one who could be entrusted with the task of conducting the negotiations, I asked Neutzlin to come to Russia. It was a matter of extreme importance that his visit should be a secret to the public, for otherwise it would have had an undesirable effect upon the course of the Algeciras Conference and upon the Russian Stock Exchange. I may mention in passing that since I had left the post of Minister of Finances, in 1903, the Russian securities had fallen twenty per cent. Accordingly, Neutzlin came to Russia incognito and put up at the palace of Grand Duke Vladimir Alexandrovich, at Tsarskoye Selo. He arrived on February 2nd, and his visit lasted five days. In the course of that period I had several conferences with Neutzlin, and in the presence of the Minister of Finance, Shipov, we agreed upon the terms of the loan. At first, Neutzlin insisted that the loan should not be realized before the opening of the Duma, but I succeeded in convincing him of the undesirability of such an arrangement, and it was then agreed that the loan should be effected immediately upon the termination of the Algeciras Conference. It was also agreed that the amount of the loan should be made as large as possible, so as to enable us to get along for a considerable period of time without new loans and also in order to cancel the temporary loans contracted by Kokovtzev in France and in Germany. I insisted on 2,750,000,000 francs—as the nominal amount of the loan. Anticipating upon the course of events, I may say that, owing to the treachery of Germany and of the American syndicate of bankers headed by Morgan, we had to reduce the amount to 2,250,-000,000 francs—843,750,000 rubles. Neutzlin insisted on six and a quarter per cent, but I could not agree to that rate of interest, and it was fixed at six per cent, the loan certificates becoming convertible after ten years. The syndicate which was to handle the loan was to be made up, we agreed, of French, Dutch, English, German, American, and Russian banking firms. Austrian banks were also permitted to participate in the loan. The sums realized were to be left in the hands of the syndicate at one and a quarter per cent and then transferred to the Russian Government in definite instalments in the course of one year. Not less than half of the amount of the loan the syndicate was to take upon itself. We also agreed upon the secondary details. Neutzlin returned home, conferred with the other members of the syndicate and they all indorsed the main terms of the agreement which was formulated at Tsarskoye Selo. I continued to advise him all the while, and until the very conclusion of the loan he turned to me personally for instructions. . . .

The loan was indeed an achievement of the highest importance. It was the largest foreign loan in the history of the modern nations. After the Franco-Prussian War, Thiers succeeded in securing a somewhat greater loan, but it was largely an internal loan, while this one was almost exclusively subscribed abroad. By means of it Russia maintained intact its gold standard of currency, which I introduced in 1896. This, in its turn, served to sustain all the basic principles of our financial system, which were mostly inaugurated by myself, and which Kokovtzev preserved with laudable firmness. It was these principles that enabled Russia to recover after that ill-starred war and the subsequent senseless turmoil, known as the Russian revolution. This loan enabled the Imperial Government to weather all the vicissitudes of the period extending from 1906 to 1910 by providing it with funds, which together with the troops recalled from Transbaikalia restored consistency and assurance to the acts of the Government.

In view of all this, what was the Emperor's attitude toward the loan? His Majesty fully appreciated how important it was to conclude the loan and what a disaster failure to secure it would mean. In all financial matters throughout the time when I held the office of Minister of Finances he had full confidence in me and did not in the least thwart my activity. In this case, too, as on previous occasions, he granted me full liberty of action, as far as this financial operation depended upon political action. He stood there like a spectator, as it were, watching a great politico-financial game of chess, but a spectator fully cognizant of the momentous importance of the game's outcome for Russia and deeply engrossed in its course.

In the months of February and March I had already begun to lose patience with the reactionary attacks directed against the reform of October 17th. In certain circles people began to brand me as a traitor. At the same time, Durnovo, the Temporary Governors-General and others carried out many measures without my knowledge, although the responsibility for those measures fell upon me as the head of the Government. As a result I began to intimate that I had no objection to surrendering my post to a man enjoying more confidence. The invariable reply was to the effect that this was impossible before the conclusion of the loan. The Emperor was fully aware of the fact that I alone could negotiate it: first, because of my prestige in financial circles abroad; second, because of my vast experience in financial affairs. The following is from a letter written to me by His Majesty in his own hand and dated April 15th:

> The successful conclusion of the loan forms the best page in the history of your ministerial activity. It is for the Government a great moral triumph and a pledge of Russia's undisturbed and peaceful development in the future.

39

Rasputin: The Holy Devil

The last years of imperial Russian history are closely linked with the name of Gregory Efimovich Rasputin (1872–1916). To his admirers Rasputin was a "holy man" whose mission was to save the Romanov dynasty. To his opponents he was a pernicious pervert whose activity accelerated the downfall of imperial Russia. A Siberian peasant by birth, Rasputin was a half-literate, unordained religious teacher who wandered through rural Russia and lived on donations from simple-minded believers. The essence of his preaching seems to have been a belief that "sexual indulgence is the true path to humility and, through humility, to eternal salvation." In 1905, through the efforts of a group of ladies of St. Petersburg society, he was introduced to the imperial family. His ap-

Reprinted with permission of the publisher from M. V. Rodzianko, *The Reign of Rasputin: An Empire's Collapse*. Translated by Catherine Zvegintzoff. Introduction by Sir Bernard Pares (London: Philpot, 1927), pp. 41–47, 49–59, 61–62.

parent hypnotic and clairvoyant powers and his seeming ability to control the bleeding of the hemo-philic heir to the Russian throne immediately captured the imagination of Empress Alexandra, who felt him to be an instrument of Providence sent to save Russia and the Romanov dynasty. She sought his advice on all matters, family as well as state, and denounced criticism of his loose morals and crude manners as slanderous. Because he wielded such powerful influence, Rasputin attracted as followers all kinds of adventurers and their activities soon became a national scandal. In 1911 and 1912 he was severely criticized by the leaders of the Duma and bitterly indicted by M. V. Rodzianko (1859–1924), the President of the Duma, whose charges against Ras-putin are presented below.

"Your Majesty, my report to-day [February 26, 1912, O. S.]* extends to matters far beyond its usual scope. Granted the gracious permission of your Majesty, I intend to lay before you the detailed and documentary evidence concerning a process of destruction which has begun, pregnant with the most disastrous consequences to all concerned. . . ."

The Tsar glanced at me in some astonishment.

I continued:

"I refer to the *starets* Rasputin and to the inadmissible fact of his presence at your Majesty's Court. I beseech you, Sire, as your Majesty's most loyal subject—will it be your pleasure to hear me to the end? If not, say but one word, and I will remain silent."

With bowed head and averted gaze the Tsar murmured in a low voice:

"Speak."

"Your Majesty, the presence of this man of more than tarnished reputation in the most intimate Court circles is an event unparalleled in the history of the Russian Monarchy. The entire nation, all circles of the community, view with profound apprehension the influence this man exercises on the affairs of Church and State. The whole machinery of government, from Ministers to the inferior ranks of the secret police, is mobilized for the purpose of shielding this adventurer. Rasputin is a tool in the hands of Russia's enemies; he is their instrument for under-mining the Church and the Monarchy itself. No revolutionary propa-ganda could achieve as much as Rasputin's mere presence at Court. Everyone fears his intimacy with the Imperial Family. Public feeling is running very high."

---

* All dates given here are according to the Julian Calendar.—Ed.

"But why such attacks on Rasputin?" interrupted the Tsar; "why is he considered so harmful?"

"Your Majesty, the fact that Rasputin has created a split in the Synod has become common knowledge, both by hearsay and through the Press. Everyone knows that bishops are being transferred from their posts owing to his intrigues."

"Which bishops?" asked the Tsar.

"The case of Mgr. Hermogen aroused universal indignation, as being an undeserved insult to a prelate. Mgr. Hermogen has many supporters. I have received a petition signed by ten thousand people, begging me to intercede on his behalf before your Majesty."

"I think Mgr. Hermogen is a good man," said the Tsar; "he will soon be permitted to return. Still, I could not allow him to remain unpunished for his flagrant disobedience to my Imperial order."

"Your Majesty, according to the canons of the Church, an episcopal court can alone sit in judgment on a bishop. Mgr. Hermogen was sentenced to banishment on the sole charge of the High Procurator and on the strength of his personal report. It was an infringement of the canons of the Church."

The Tsar listened in silence.

"The case of Iliodor, too, has made a most painful impression on the people. After the inquiry held by order of your Majesty, his trial was cancelled a year ago. Now, without trial, he is confined in the Floristchevo hermitage —and this was done after he had dared to speak openly against Rasputin. These two were not the only ones to suffer. Bishop Feofan was deprived of his office of the Empress's confessor and removed to Simferopol. Bishop Anthony of Tobolsk, who was the first to inform the Synod of Rasputin's adherence to the *khlysty* sect and to demand his trial, was transferred to Tver. Anyone who dares utter a word against Rasputin is persecuted by the Synod. Such a state of affairs cannot be tolerated, your Majesty. How can Orthodox Christians stand by in silence, when Orthodoxy is being defiled and destroyed by the pernicious activities of this rogue? One may well understand the general outburst of indignation which followed the disclosure that Rasputin was a *khlyst*."

"What proofs have you?"

"The police discovered that he went to the baths with women. That is one of the peculiarities of their religious practices."

"What of that? It is merely a custom among common people."

"No, your Majesty, there is no such custom. Perhaps husbands and wives go together, but what we have here is sheer debauchery. Permit me, in the first place, to read you letters from those of his victims who fell into the trap and repented afterwards. Here is a letter from a priest in Siberia, addressed to several members of the Duma [I did not like to mention Gutchkoff by name], and imploring them to inform the authorities of Rasputin's exploits, his immoral conduct and the rumours he circulated concerning his position and influence at the Imperial Court." (This letter I read out from end to end.)

"Here is another letter written by a lady confessing having been seduced and morally corrupted by Rasputin. She afterwards recoiled from him and repented of her fall . . . and met him one evening coming out of the baths in the company of her two daughters. . . . The wife of an engineer, Mme. L., also fell a victim to Rasputin's teachings. She became insane and is now in a lunatic asylum. Will your Majesty order this evidence to be verified?"

"I believe you," said the Tsar.

I read him other letters and extracts from Novoseloff's pamphlet; I laid stress on the painful impression which the prohibition of any publication in the Press concerning Rasputin had made on the public mind. He did not belong to the category of persons of whom it was forbidden to write. He occupied no exalted position, neither was he a member of the Imperial Family. Ministers of the Crown, the presidents of the Imperial Duma or of the Council of the Empire were freely criticized in the Press. Why, then, this enforced silence concerning Rasputin? Such a policy naturally led the public to suppose him to be intimately connected with the Imperial Family.

"But why do you assume him to be a *khlyst?*"

"Your Majesty should read Novoseloff's pamphlet. He made a special investigation of the case. He states that Rasputin was prosecuted on the charge of belonging to that sect, but that for some reason or other the prosecution was stopped. Moreover, as has been ascertained, meetings of Rasputin's followers were held at Sazonoff's flat, where Rasputin himself was staying at the time. Permit me to show you a foreign newspaper cutting, in which it is said that at the Masonic Congress in Brussels Rasputin was mentioned as being a useful instrument for carrying out the freemason's policy in Russia. The whole intrigue, with all its subsequent developments, is as clear as daylight. It is not the fate of the dynasty and the prestige of the Imperial Family alone which are involved."

"How?" inquired the Tsar, greatly agitated.

"Your Majesty, there is no serious or responsible person in charge of the Tsarevitch; he is entrusted to the care of a country yokel, Derevenko, who may be a very good man, but is a simple peasant. Ignorant folk are naturally inclined towards mysticism. What if anything were to happen to the Heir Apparent? This is a subject of profound anxiety to all. . . . Such a charming child, so universally beloved."

The Tsar was evidently struggling to overcome his emotion. He nervously lit one cigarette after another, then threw them down again.

I here decided to approach the subject from another side and to persuade the Emperor that Rasputin was a sycophant. I produced a photograph of the *starets* wearing a pectoral cross.

"Your Majesty knows Rasputin is not in holy orders; yet here he is depicted as a priest."

The Tsar replied:

"Yes, this is really going too far. He has no right to wear a pectoral cross."

"It is blasphemy, your Majesty. He is an illiterate peasant and not entitled to wear a cowl, which appertains to the priesthood. Here is another photograph. It is a '*khlysty* ship.' This was reproduced in the *Ogonek** and circulated throughout the country. Here is Rasputin surrounded by young girls; there are also boys with him in their midst. Here he is with two young men. They are carrying a placard inscribed with *khlysty* texts, and he is holding a *khlysy* ikon of Our Lady in his hands. It is a 'ship' bearing its inmates towards fornication."

"What is that?" asked the Tsar.

"Read Novoseloff's pamphlet, which I will submit to you. Here is another photograph of Rasputin with two women, and inscribed: 'The Way to Salvation.' . . ."

"The suppression of any mention of Rasputin in the Press encourages the idea that the *khlysty* enjoy the patronage of the Tsar. What if a war broke out? Where is the prestige of the Tsar's name and authority? A number of persons closely connected with the Court are openly designated as Rasputin's followers. Rumours are current that the highest society is contaminated with his sectarian teachings. Thus a slur is cast on society and on the Court. In defiance of the censorship all the rumours and stories about Rasputin are being feverishly seized upon and reproduced by the provincial Press."

"Have you read Stolypin's report?" asked the Emperor.

"No, I have heard it spoken of, but never read it."

"I rejected it," said the Tsar.

"It is a pity," I replied, "for all this would not have happened. Your Majesty, you witness my profound emotion. It pains me exceedingly to be obliged to speak the cruel truth. But I dared not keep silent, I had no right to conceal from my Sovereign the menacing state of affairs with their possible terrible consequences. I believe that God has placed me as a mediator between the Tsar and the representatives of the people summoned together by his august command. It is my duty, Sire, as a Russian and as your Majesty's loyal subject to warn you that our enemies are striving to undermine the Throne and the Church and to cast a shadow on the beloved name of the Tsar. I always bear in mind the text of the oath of allegiance. In the name of all you hold sacred, in the name

---

* An illustrated weekly.—Ed.

of Russia, and for the sake of the welfare and happiness of your successors—I implore you to banish this villainous rogue, and so dispel the
fears which assail those who are loyal to the Throne."

"He is not here now," replied the Tsar in a low voice.

"Will you authorize me to tell everyone that he will not return?"

The Tsar remained silent for a while, then said:

"No, I cannot promise you that. Nevertheless, I fully believe all you
have told me."

"Do you believe, Sire, in the absolute loyalty and trustworthiness of all
those who raised the question in the Duma? Will you believe that they were
inspired by the same motives which prompted my coming to lay the
whole case before you?"

"I feel the sincerity of your report, and I trust the Duma because I
trust you."

I was anxious to learn whether the Emperor was pleased with my report.
I continued:

"Your Majesty, I came here fully prepared to pay the penalty if I had
the misfortune to incur your Majesty's displeasure. If I have overstepped
my rights, you have but to say a word, and I will resign my office of President of the Imperial Duma. I sought but to do my duty in laying the whole
matter before you. In view of the excitement raised by this affair in the
Duma, I did not think it right to conceal it from my Sovereign."

"I thank you. You acted as an honourable man and a loyal subject." . . .

That same evening I drove to the Duma, where I was immediately
surrounded by groups of deputies. I gave them a brief account of the interview and of the gracious reception accorded me by the Emperor. My
narrative produced a most excellent impression on all. I gave a *verbatim*
account of the whole interview to my most intimate associates.

On the morning of February 28, General V. N. Dediulin, Commandant
of the Imperial Palace and A.D.C. to the Emperor, telephoned to me
from Tsarskoe Selo, asking me to call on him at his flat in town. General Dediulin was an old schoolfellow of mine and a personal friend;
hence the conversation which ensued was of an intimate nature. Dediulin
imparted to me the following news.

"After your visit to Tsarskoe Selo," he said to me, "it became known
that the Tsar had scarcely touched his dinner and remained all the time
extremely taciturn and thoughtful. When I reported to him next morning
I took the liberty of saying to him: 'Your Majesty, you have received
Rodzianko. It appears he has fatigued you very much.'"

The Tsar replied: "No, I am not in the least tired. I see that
Rodzianko is a loyal subject who is not afraid of speaking the truth. He
told me much that I knew nothing about. You are an old schoolfellow
of his. Tell him, from me, to investigate Rasputin's case. Let him take

from the Synod all the secret documents concerning Rasputin, thoroughly examine them and report the results to me. But tell him to keep the whole affair secret for the time being."

I was astounded by the news. That same evening I invited V. I. Karpoff, a member of the Council of the Empire, and the members of the Duma Kamensky, Shubinsky and Gutchkoff, to come to see me. We discussed far into the night the best means for proceeding with the mission entrusted to me by the Tsar. Next day I asked M. Damansky, Assistant High Procurator of the Synod, to come to the Duma and bring me the secret *dossier* on Rasputin's case. Damansky arrived. In order the better to draw him out, I decided to feign complete ignorance. This manoeuvre met with complete success. My informant divulged all I wished to know. In his endeavours to persuade me of Gregory's holiness and purity, he declared that the *starets* was honoured and respected by many highly placed persons, who enjoyed and found edification in his conversations. Damansky revealed many names and confirmed much evidence already familiar to me through other channels. He said that Resputin lodged with the Sazonoffs, a very respectable family with whom he, Damansky, was on intimate terms; that the house was visited by M. Taneieff, Gentleman Usher to the Emperor, by the wife of General Orloff, Countess Witte,* "such a universally respected man" as Bishop Barnabas, and many others. I expressed my astonishment at all this, and nodded in assent.

All this time Damansky kept a firm hold on the file of documents in his hands, and kept repeatedly assuring me that the case was in itself too trivial to be worth looking into. While dwelling on the virtues of the *starets*, Damansky professed profound indignation at the gossip and calumny of which he was the subject. "He is accused of being a *khlyst* and a libertine. Some people go so far as to allege an intimacy between him and the Empress Alexandra Feodorovna. . . ."

Here I dropped the mask, struck the table with my fist, drew myself up to my full height,† and looking as ferocious as I could, shouted at the top of my voice so as to be heard in the adjoining room:

"Are you mad, sir? How dare you utter such abominations in my presence? You forget of whom and to whom you are speaking! I refuse to listen to you any further."

My outburst was so unexpected that he turned pale, cowered and hastened to excuse himself. The object of his mean behaviour was obvious. He imagined me to be his dupe, and hoped to lead me on to talk scandal with the intention of reporting it in certain quarters afterwards. He expected to convince me by his explanations, and prevent my claiming the documents. He was, therefore, completely taken aback when I

---

* Wife of the ex-Prime Minister.—Ed.
† M. Rodzianko was an exceptionally tall and powerful man.—Ed.

wrenched the file from his grasp, locked it up in my desk and, placing the key in my pocket, declared: "By order of his Majesty the Emperor, I shall examine these documents, and inform you later of the results."

Having obtained possession of these important documents, I at once ordered the clerical staff of the Duma and the sworn-in lady typists to make complete copies of them. With the aid of J. V. Glinka, the head of the Duma clerks' office, I myself proceeded to draft a plan of procedure for the task in hand—a task demanding great circumspection in view of the extremely delicate nature of the case.

The very next day Damansky telephoned asking for a private interview at my flat. Suspecting a trap, I replied that I did not give private interviews on matters of State; I therefore requested his presence in my room at the Duma at three o'clock that afternoon, and to avoid any further explanations I immediately hung up the receiver.

On my arrival at the Duma I found Damansky waiting for me. To my astonishment he was accompanied by the Archpriest Alexander Vasilieff, the religious teacher of the Imperial children. The reverend father's presence at the Duma was rather surprising. I at once realized that some plan for putting pressure on me was afoot, and decided to separate them. They were, therefore, shown into different rooms.

First I tackled Damansky. He explained that he was entrusted with a mission to reclaim from me the file containing the documents on Rasputin. I expressed surprise at this request, and replied that the documents had been placed in my keeping by the Emperor's orders, and that their surrender could only be claimed by a similar act, i.e., by an Imperial order transmitted either verbally through an adjutant-general or a Secretary of State, or by written decree. At this juncture, looking somewhat perturbed and agitated, and lowering his voice, Damansky explained that though he did not bear an order from the Emperor, the demand came from a very exalted person.

"Who was it?" I asked. "Sabler?"

Damansky made a deprecating gesture.

"No, someone much more highly placed," he replied.

"Who was it, then?" I repeated, putting on an expression of astonishment.

"The Empress Alexandra Feodorovna."

"If that is the case, will you kindly inform her Majesty that she is as much a subject of her August Consort as myself, and that it is the duty of us both to obey his commands. I am, therefore, not in a position to comply with her wishes."

"What!" exclaimed Damansky, "must I really tell her that? But it is her desire."

"I am very sorry," I replied, "but nevertheless I am unable to accede to it." And to prevent further insistence on Damansky's part, I ended the interview.

I then passed on to Father Vasilieff. He was instructed by the Empress Alexandra Feodorovna, he said, to communicate to me his opinion on the *starets*.

"He really is a God-fearing and pious man, absolutely harmless and even rather useful to the Imperial Family," said Father Vasilieff.

"What part does he play in the intimate life of the Imperial Family, particularly in relation to the children?"

"He has talks with them about God and about religion. . . ."

At these words I flew into a passion.

"You dare tell me that! You, an orthodox priest and the religious teacher of the Tsar's children! You tolerate that a stupid, ignorant *mouzhik* should speak to them on matters of faith; you tolerate his pernicious hypnotic influence on their pure childish souls? You are a witness to the part played by this sectarian *khlyst* in the family life of the Tsar, and yet you keep silent. By countenancing this man's criminal activities you betray your holy office and your oath of allegiance. You know everything that is going on, and yet out of cowardice and servility you prefer to hold your tongue when, as a servant of the Church of God, your duty bids you raise your voice in defence of our faith. By your criminal connivance you, too, become a sectarian and a participator in the devilish conspiracy engineered by the enemies of Russia and of the Tsar, who aim at defiling the Throne and the Orthodox Church."

The unfortunate priest, completely taken aback by my vehemence, grew pale and murmured tremulously:

"No one has ever spoken to me like this before. You have opened my eyes. Tell me what I am to do."

"Go and tell the Empress from me, that if she does not want to see the ruin of her husband and son and the collapse of the Throne, she must dismiss this obscene *khlyst* from her presence for ever. The position is serious. No revolutionary propaganda could inflict greater injury on the Monarchy nor degrade the prestige of the Imperial House as does Rasputin's presence at the Palace. If you continue to be silent and fail to disclose the truth—then the cross you wear upon your breast will brand your very heart and soul."

He told Prince Volkonsky afterwards: "When I left the President I was trembling all over, and fully realized the force and truth of his arguments."

Father Vasilieff, however, as I was subsequently informed, gave a completely distorted account of our interview to the Empress, thereby merely strengthening the disfavour in which she already held me. He continued to encourage her infatuation for Rasputin, and persevered in his ambiguous behaviour.

From Gutchkoff I learnt that my prolonged interview with the Tsar had seriously agitated all Rasputin's followers, and that they had decided to recall him to St. Petersburg.

Princess Z. N. Yusupoff informed us by telephone that the Empress was so distressed by Rasputin's dismissal that she took to her bed. It is interesting to recall that after the questions on Rasputin in the Duma, the Empress wrote a despairing letter of eight pages to Princess Yusupoff complaining of the unjust attacks and calumnies of which they were the object. "No one loves us," wrote the Empress; "everyone is trying to do us harm. This interpellation was a revolutionary act."

The Empress's complaints of their tragic position were so bitter that Princess Yusupoff felt sorry for her and sent a telephone message that she would come to see her next day. Owing, however, in all probability to some intrigue on the part of Mme. Vyrubova, Princess Yusupoff was informed that the Empress was indisposed and unable to receive her.

It was not till March 9, 1912, that Princess Yusupoff was admitted to see the Empress. Her visit took place after Gutchkoff's speech in the Duma on the Synod estimates, in which he made a further allusion to Rasputin. Princess Yusupoff spoke very gravely on the subject and tried to impress the Empress with the same arguments I had submitted to the Tsar, but in vain. The Empress remained obdurate, working herself into a state of great indignation and excitement. She expressed her displeasure at the tenor of my report to the Tsar, and was particularly angry at my refusal to return the Rasputin documents.

"What right had he to keep them and refuse their surrender?" the Empress repeated.

Princess Yusupoff tried to persuade her to believe the word of the President of the Duma.

"He is an honest and truthful man," she said.

"No, no! You don't know what he told Father Vasilieff! Hanging is too good for men like Rodzianko and Gutchkoff!"

"How can you say such things?" the Princess exclaimed indignantly. "You ought to thank God for sending you honest men who speak the truth to the Tsar. Rasputin must be turned out. He is a *khlyst* who abuses your confidence."

"No, no, that is a calumny. He is a holy man."

A thorough examination of the documents produced by Damansky revealed the history of Rasputin in all its sordid reality.

The first time that Rasputin was arraigned as a *khlyst* was as far back as 1902, when, on the strength of an official intimation from the parish priest of Pokrovskoe, the head of the district police denounced him to the Governor of Tobolsk. The Governor handed over the case to the local bishop, Mgr. Anthony, who ordered one of the diocesan missionaries to carry out a detailed investigation. The latter, being an energetic man, made a domiciliary search in Rasputin's house, carried off various material proofs, and brought to light numerous obscure facts all tending to prove irrefutably Rasputin's adherence to the *khlysty* sect. A detailed report on the case, supported by important circumstantial evidence, was presented to the bishop. Some of the details mentioned in the report were of so obscene and revolting a nature, that it was impossible to read them without a feeling of repulsion.

On receiving the report Mgr. Anthony handed it over for study to an expert on sectarianism, a M. Berezkin, inspector of the Theological Seminary at Tobolsk. The affair dragged on indefinitely. Rasputin, meanwhile, had made his way to St. Petersburg, where, as I have previously described, he gradually wormed himself into the confidence of highly placed persons and was introduced at the Palace.

A survey of the very thorough and conscientious investigation carried out by Berezkin, confirmed, moreover, by the evidence of numerous witnesses, letters and references to the teachings of the *khlysty*, revealed beyond the shadow of a doubt Rasputin's adherence to that disgusting sect. He was, moreover, a *khlyst* of a superior order, a clever propagandist and a pernicious corrupter of souls of simple-minded Orthodox folk. The evidence in hand established beyond doubt his connection with many of the *khlysty* "prophets," among whom he occupied a more or less important position.

In his report to the Bishop of Tobolsk, M. Berezkin declared that he had no doubt whatever that Rasputin belonged to the *khlysty*, and recommended that the whole case should be referred to the civil authorities in order that Rasputin might be prosecuted. Before doing so, however, M. Berezkin advised the Bishop to collect certain additional evidence on the case. Acting on the strength of this report Bishop Anthony ordered the consistory of Tobolsk to carry out M. Berezkin's injunctions and hand over the case of Gregory Efimoff Rasputin to the judicial authorities.

While this inter-departmental procedure was going on, Rasputin returned from St. Petersburg to his native village. He brought with him considerable sums of money and proceeded to build himself a large, well-furnished house. He openly boasted of favours received from members of the Imperial Family, and exhibited to everyone the presents they had given him—for instance, a richly ornamented gold cross on a golden chain, a medallion containing a portrait of the Empress Alexandra Feodorovna, and photographs of exalted personages with appropriate inscriptions. He flaunted about in expensive sable-lined coats. In a word, the prosecuted sectarian was transformed into an influential personage, whose patronage was already beginning to be sought by many.

After Bishop Anthony's resolution recommending Rasputin's prosecution, the affair was brought to an end by an ukase of the Holy Synod appointing, by Imperial warrant, Bishop Anthony of Tobolsk to the archbishopric of Tver and Kashin, i.e., the removal of Mgr. Anthony from his former diocese. As I learnt afterwards from competent sources, to avoid a public scandal over the Rasputin case, Bishop Anthony was given the choice of two alternatives: either to withdraw his charge against Rasputin and receive promotion to the see of Tver, or to retire to a monastery. He chose the former, and Rasputin's prosecution was suppressed.

Having completed a thorough and all-round examination of the documents submitted to my investigation, I drew up a comprehensive and concise summary of the case, and on March 8, 1912, presented a request for an audience with the Emperor for the purpose of reporting on the result of the mission entrusted to me by his Majesty.

For a long time my petition remained unanswered. The Empress Alexandra Feodorovna, I learnt, was absolutely opposed to my having a second interview with the Emperor, particularly as I should confront him armed with official and incriminating evidence against Rasputin. . . .

In the meantime Rasputin again made his appearance at St. Petersburg and, according to the papers, received a great welcome from his admirers assembled at the flat of Mme. Golovina. This time he was closely tracked both by the police and by pressmen. Rasputin was brought by his friends to Tsarskoe Selo, but their attempts to gain him admittance to the Empress suffered a defeat.

In the sixth week of Lent the Imperial Family left for the Crimea. Mme. Vyrubova succeeded in smuggling Rasputin on to the suite's train, where he was concealed in Prince Tumanoff's compartment. Someone informed the Emperor, who was exceedingly angry at such flagrant disobedience to his command and ordered the train to be stopped at Tosno. Rasputin was removed from the train and, under surveillance of a secret service official, conveyed to the province of Tobolsk.

My words had struck home. After that Rasputin ceased for some time to appear at Court. Now and again he returned to St. Petersburg, never daring to remain for more than two or three days. The chief of the police department used to complain to me: "I am utterly sick of him. He has to be watched. Directly he arrives, off he goes, straight from the station to the baths, with two ladies."

The Empress, I feel sure, never forgave me for my interference. No news reached me concerning the fate of my report; I received neither reply nor reproof. Had the Tsar read it? I did not know. A rumour was current that he read it in the Crimea with his brother-in-law, the Duke of Hesse.

40

Durnovo's Memorandum, February 1914

In historical literature Peter N. Durnovo (1844–1915) is cursorily dismissed as either "an experienced policeman" or "a vicious reactionary." Durnovo acquired his reputation through his unswerving insistence on maintaining the *status quo*, first as an official of the Ministry of Justice (1872–1883), then as head of the Police Department of the Ministry of Interior (1884–1893), later as Deputy Minister of Interior (1900–1905), subsequently as Minister of Interior (1905–1907), and finally as a prominent member of the State Council, Russia's upper legislative chamber.

But while he was a reactionary—a fact that made him unpopular with liberals as well as revolutionaries—Durnovo was at the same time one of the most astute observers of Russia's domestic ills and her international position on the eve of World War I. This is clearly evident from the February 1914 memorandum he submitted to Nicholas II. In it, he pleaded for a thorough reappraisal of the goals of Russia's foreign policy, for abandonment of her association with France and England (which he called "an artificial combination") and, above all, that she stay out of any European war, not only because she was inadequately prepared but primarily because she would have to carry the main burden of fighting. Russia's probable defeat, Durnovo argued, would result in "hopeless anarchy, the issue of which cannot be foreseen." Because his analysis turned out to be remarkably correct it is reproduced here in its entirety.

From Frank Alfred Golder, ed. Documents of Russian History, 1914–1917. Translated by Emanuel Aronsberg (New York: The Century Co., 1927), pp. 3–23.

A Future Anglo-German War Will Become an Armed Conflict between Two Groups of Powers

The central factor of the period of world history through which we are now passing is the rivalry between England and Germany. This rivalry must inevitably lead to an armed struggle between them, the issue of which will, in all probability, prove fatal to the vanquished side. The interests of these two powers are far too incompatible, and their simultaneous existence as world powers will sooner or later prove impossible. On the one hand, there is an insular State, whose world importance rests upon its domination of the sea, its world trade, and its innumerable colonies. On the other, there is a powerful continental empire, whose limited territory is insufficient for an increased population. It has therefore openly and candidly declared that its future is on the seas. It has, with fabulous speed, developed an enormous world commerce, built for its protection a formidable navy, and, with its famous trademark, "Made in Germany," created a mortal danger to the industrial and economic prosperity of its rival. Naturally, England cannot yield without a fight, and between her and Germany a struggle for life or death is inevitable.

The armed conflict impending as a result of this rivalry cannot be confined to a duel between England and Germany alone. Their resources are far too unequal, and, at the same time, they are not sufficiently vulnerable to each other. Germany could provoke rebellion in India, in South Africa, and, especially, a dangerous rebellion in Ireland, and paralyze English sea trade by means of privateering and, perhaps, submarine warfare, thereby creating for Great Britain difficulties in her food supply; but, in spite of all the daring of the German military leaders, they would scarcely risk landing in England, unless a fortunate accident helped them to destroy or appreciably to weaken the English navy. As for England, she will find Germany absolutely invulnerable. All that she may achieve is to seize the German colonies, stop German sea trade, and, in the most favorable event, annihilate the German navy, but nothing more. This, however, would not force the enemy to sue for peace. There is no doubt, therefore, that England will attempt the means she has more than once used with success, and will risk armed action only after securing participation in the war, on her own side, of powers stronger in a strategical sense. But since Germany, for her own part, will not be found isolated, the future Anglo-German war will undoubtedly be transformed into an armed conflict between two groups of powers, one with a German, the other with an English orientation.

It Is Hard to Discover Any Real Advantages to Russia
in Rapprochement with England

Until the Russo-Japanese War, Russian policy had neither orientation. From the time of the reign of Emperor Alexander III, Russia had a defensive alliance with France, so firm as to assure common action by both powers in the event of attack upon either, but, at the same time, not so close as to obligate either to support unfailingly, with armed force, all political actions and claims of the ally. At the same time, the Russian Court maintained the traditional friendly relations, based upon ties of blood, with the Court of Berlin. Owing precisely to this conjuncture, peace among the great powers was not disturbed in the course of a great many years, in spite of the presence of abundant combustible material in Europe. France, by her alliance with Russia, was guaranteed against attack by Germany; the latter was safe, thanks to the tried pacifism and friendship of Russia, from *revanche* ambitions on the part of France; and Russia was secured, thanks to Germany's need of maintaining amicable relations with her, against excessive intrigues by Austria-Hungary in the Balkan peninsula. Lastly, England, isolated and held in check by her rivalry with Russia in Persia, by her diplomats' traditional fear of our advance on India, and by strained relations with France, especially notable at the time of the well-known Fashoda incident, viewed with alarm the increase of Germany's naval power, without, however, risking an active step.

The Russo-Japanese War radically changed the relations among the great powers and brought England out of her isolation. As we know, all through the Russo-Japanese War, England and America observed benevolent neutrality toward Japan, while we enjoyed a similar benevolent neutrality from France and Germany. Here, it would seem, should have been the inception of the most natural political combination for us. But after the war, our diplomacy faced abruptly about and definitely entered upon the road toward rapprochement with England. France was drawn into the orbit of British policy; there was formed a group of powers of the Triple Entente, with England playing the dominant part; and a clash, sooner or later, with the powers grouping themselves around Germany became inevitable.

Now, what advantages did the renunciation of our traditional policy of distrust of England and the rupture of neighborly, if not friendly, relations with Germany promise us then and at present?

Considering with any degree of care the events which have taken place since the Treaty of Portsmouth, we find it difficult to perceive any practical advantages gained by us in rapprochement with England. The only benefit—improved relations with Japan—is scarcely a result of the Russo-

English rapprochement. There is no reason why Russia and Japan should not live in peace; there seems to be nothing over which they need quarrel. All Russia's objectives in the Far East, if correctly understood, are entirely compatible with Japan's interests. These objectives, in their essentials, are very modest. The too broad sweep of the imagination of overzealous executive officials, without basis in genuine national interests, on the one hand, and the excessive nervousness and impressionability of Japan, on the other, which erroneously regarded these dreams as a consistently executed policy—these were the things that provoked a clash which a more capable diplomacy would have managed to avoid.

Russia needs neither Korea nor even Port Arthur. An outlet to the open sea is undoubtedly useful, but the sea in itself is, after all, not a market, but merely a road to a more advantageous delivery of goods at the consuming markets. As a matter of fact, we do not possess, and shall not for a long time possess any goods in the Far East that promise any considerable profits in exportation abroad. Nor are there any markets for the export of our products. We cannot expect a great supply of our export commodities to go to industrially and agriculturally developed America, to poor, but likewise industrial, Japan, or even to the maritime sections of China and remoter markets, where our exports would inevitably meet the competition of goods from the industrially stronger rival powers. There remains the interior of China, with which our trade is carried on, chiefly overland. Consequently, an open port would aid the import of foreign merchandise more than the export of our own products.

Japan, on her part, no matter what is said, has no desire for our Far Eastern possessions. The Japanese are by nature a southern people, and the harsh environment of our Far Eastern borderland cannot attract them. We know that even within Japan itself northern Yezo is sparsely populated, while apparently Japanese colonization is making little headway even in the southern part of Sakhalin Island, ceded to Japan under the Treaty of Portsmouth. After taking possession of Korea and Formosa, Japan will hardly go farther north, and her ambitions, it may be assumed, will turn rather in the direction of the Philippine Islands, Indo-China, Java, Sumatra, and Borneo. The most she might desire would be the acquisition, for purely commercial reasons, of a few more sections of the Manchurian railway.

In a word, peaceable coexistence, nay, more, a close rapprochement, between Russia and Japan in the Far East is perfectly natural, regardless of any mediation by England. The grounds for agreement are self-evident. Japan is not a rich country, and the simultaneous upkeep of a strong army and a powerful navy is hard for her. Her insular situation drives her to strengthen her naval power, and alliance with Russia would allow her to devote all her attention to her navy, especially vital in view of her imminent rivalry with America, leaving the protection of her interests on the continent to Russia. On our part, we, having the Japanese navy to protect our Pacific coast, could give up once for all the dream, impossible to us, of creating a navy in the Far East.

Thus, so far as our relations with Japan are concerned, the rapprochement with England has yielded us no real advantage. And it has gained us nothing in the sense of strengthening our position in Manchuria, Mongolia, or even the Ulianghai territory, where the uncertainty of our position bears witness that the agreement with England has certainly not freed the hands of our diplomats. On the contrary, our attempt to establish relations with Tibet met with sharp opposition from England.

In Persia, also, our position has been no better since the conclusion of this agreement. Every one recalls our predominant influence in that country under the Shah Nasr-Eddin, that is, exactly at a time when our relations with England were most strained. From the moment of our accord with the latter, we have found ourselves drawn into a number of strange attempts to impose upon the Persian people an entirely needless constitution, with the result that we ourselves contributed to the overthrow, for the benefit of our inveterate enemies, of a monarch who was devoted to Russia. That is, not only have we gained nothing, but we have suffered a loss all along the line, ruining our prestige and wasting many millions of rubles, even the precious blood of Russian soldiers, who were treacherously slain and, to please England, not even avenged.

The worst results, however, of the accord with England—and of the consequent discord with Germany—have been felt in the Near East. As we know, it was Bismarck who coined that winged phrase about the Balkan problem not being worth to Germany the bones of a single Pomeranian grenadier. Later the Balkan complications began to attract much more attention from German diplomacy, which had taken the "Sick Man" under its protection, but even then Germany, for a long time, failed to show any inclination to endanger relations with Russia in the interests of Balkan affairs. The proofs are patent. During the period of the Russo-Japanese War and the ensuing turmoil in our country, it would have been very easy for Austria to realize her cherished ambitions in the Balkan peninsula. But at that time Russia had not yet linked her destinies with England, and Austria-Hungary was forced to lose an opportunity most auspicious for her purposes.

No sooner had we taken the road to closer accord with England, however, than there immediately followed the annexation of Bosnia and Herzegovina, a step which might have been taken so easily and painlessly in 1905 or 1906. Next came the Albanian question and the combination with the Prince of Wied. Russian diplomacy attempted to answer Austrian intrigue by forming a Balkan league, but this combination, as might have been expected, proved to be quite unworkable. Intended to be directed against Austria, it immediately turned on Turkey and fell apart in the process of dividing the spoils taken from the latter. The final result was merely the definite attachment of Turkey to Germany, in whom, not without good reason, she sees her sole protector. In short, the Russo-British rapprochement evidently seems to Turkey as tantamount to England's renouncing her traditional policy of closing the Dardanelles to us, while the creation of the Balkan league, under the auspices of Russia, appeared as a direct threat to the continued existence of Turkey as a European power.

To sum up, the Anglo-Russian accord has brought us nothing of practical value up to this time, while for the future, it threatens us with an inevitable armed clash with Germany.

Fundamental Alignments in the Coming War

Under what conditions will this clash occur and what will be its probable consequences? The fundamental groupings in a future war are self-evident: Russia, France, and England, on the one side, with Germany, Austria, and Turkey, on the other. It is more than likely that other powers, too, will participate in that war, depending upon circumstances as they may exist at the war's outbreak. But, whether the immediate cause for the war is furnished by another clash of conflicting interests in the Balkans, or by a colonial incident, such as that of Algeciras, the fundamental alignment will remain unchanged.

Italy, if she has any conception of her real interests, will not join the German side. For political as well as economic reasons, she undoubtedly hopes to expand her present territory. Such an expansion may be achieved only at the expense of Austria, on one hand, and Turkey, on the other. It is, therefore, natural for Italy not to join that party which would safeguard the territorial integrity of the countries at whose expense she hopes to realize her aspirations. Furthermore, it is not out of the question that Italy would join the anti-German coalition, if the scales of war should incline in its favor, in order to secure for herself the most favorable conditions in sharing the subsequent division of spoils.

In this respect, the position of Italy is similar to the probable position of Rumania, which, it may be assumed, will remain neutral until the scales of fortune favor one or another side. Then, animated by normal political self-interest, she will attach herself to the victors, to be rewarded at the expense of either Russia or Austria. Of the other Balkan States, Serbia and Montenegro will unquestionably join the side opposing Austria, while Bulgaria and Albania (if by that time they have not yet formed at least the embryo of a State) will take their stand against the Serbian side. Greece will in all probability remain neutral or make common cause with the side opposing Turkey, but that only after the issue has been more or less determined. The participation of other powers will be incidental, and Sweden ought to be feared, of course, in the ranks of our foes.

Under such circumstances, a struggle with Germany presents to us enormous difficulties, and will require countless sacrifices. War will not find the enemy unprepared, and the degree of his preparedness will probably exceed our most exaggerated calculations. It should not be thought that this readiness is due to Germany's own desire for war. She needs no war, so long as she can attain her object—the end of exclusive domination of the seas. But, once this vital object is opposed by the coalition, Germany will not shrink from war, and, of course, will even try to provoke it, choosing the most auspicious moment.

The Main Burden of the War Will Fall on Russia

The main burden of the war will undoubtedly fall on us, since England is hardly capable of taking a considerable part in a continental war, while France, poor in man power, will probably adhere to strictly defensive tactics, in view of the enormous losses by which war will be attended under present conditions of military technique. The part of a battering-ram, making a breach in the very thick of the German defense, will be ours, with many factors against us to which we shall have to devote great effort and attention.

From the sum of these unfavorable factors we should deduct the Far East. Both America and Japan—the former fundamentally, and the latter by virtue of her present political orientation—are hostile to Germany, and there is no reason to expect them to act on the German side. Furthermore, the war, regardless of its issue, will weaken Russia and divert her attention to the West, a fact which, of course, serves both Japanese and American interests. Thus, our rear will be sufficiently secure in the Far East, and the most that can happen there will be the extortion from us of some concessions of an economic nature in return for benevolent neutrality. Indeed, it is possible that America or Japan may join the anti-German side, but, of course, merely as usurpers of one or the other of the unprotected German colonies.

There can be no doubt, however, as to an outburst of hatred for us in Persia, and a probable unrest among the Moslems of the Caucasus and Turkestan; it is possible that Afghanistan, as a result of that unrest, may act against us; and, finally, we must foresee very unpleasant complications in Poland and Finland. In the latter, a rebellion will undoubtedly break out if Sweden is found in the ranks of our enemies. As for Poland, it is not to be expected that we can hold her against our enemy during the war. And after she is in his power, he will undoubtedly endeavor to provoke an insurrection which, while not in reality very dangerous, must be considered, nevertheless, as one of the factors unfavorable to us, especially since the influence of our allies may induce us to take such measures in our relations with Poland as will prove more dangerous to us than any open revolt.

Are we prepared for so stubborn a war as the future war of the European nations will undoubtedly become? This question we must answer, without evasion, in the negative. That much has been done for our defense since the Japanese war, I am the last person to deny, but even so, it is quite inadequate considering the unprecedented scale on which a future war will inevitably be fought. The fault lies, in a considerable measure, in our young legislative institutions, which have taken a dilettante interest in our defenses, but are far from grasping the seriousness of the political situation arising from the new orientation which, with the sympathy of the public, has been followed in recent years by our Ministry of Foreign Affairs.

The enormous number of still unconsidered legislative bills of the war and navy departments may serve as proof of this: for example, the plan of the organization of our national defense proposed to the Duma as early as the days of Secretary of State Stolypin. It cannot be denied that, in the matter of military instruction, according to the reports of specialists, we have achieved substantial improvements, as compared with the time before the Japanese War. According to the same specialists, our field artillery leaves nothing to be desired; the gun is entirely satisfactory, and the equipment convenient and practical. Yet, it must be admitted that there are substantial shortcomings in the organization of our defenses.

In this regard we must note, first of all, the insufficiency of our war supplies, which, certainly, cannot be blamed upon the war department, since the supply schedules are still far from being executed, owing to the low productivity of our factories. This insufficiency of munitions is the more significant since, in the embryonic condition of our industries, we shall, during the war, have no opportunity to make up the revealed shortage by our own efforts, and the closing of the Baltic as well as the Black Sea will prevent the importation from abroad of the defense materials which we lack.

Another circumstance unfavorable to our defense is its far too great dependence, generally speaking, upon foreign industry, a fact which, in connection with the above noted interruption of more or less convenient communications with abroad, will create a series of obstacles difficult to overcome. The quantity of our heavy artillery, the importance of which was demonstrated in the Japanese War, is far too inadequate, and there are few machine guns. The organization of our fortress defenses has scarcely been started, and even the fortress of Reval, which is to defend the road to the capital, is not yet finished.

The network of strategic railways is inadequate. The railways possess a rolling stock sufficient, perhaps, for normal traffic, but not commensurate with the colossal demands which will be made upon them in the event of a European war. Lastly, it should not be forgotten that the impending war will be fought among the most civilized and technically most advanced nations. Every previous war has invariably been followed by something new in the realm of military technique, but the technical backwardness of our industries does not create favorable conditions for our adoption of the new inventions.

The Vital Interests of Germany and Russia Do Not Conflict

All these factors are hardly given proper thought by our diplomats, whose behavior toward Germany is, in some respects, even aggressive, and may unduly hasten the moment of armed conflict, a moment which, of course, is really inevitable in view of our British orientation.

The question is whether this orientation is correct, and whether even a favorable issue of the war promises us such advantages as would compensate us for all the hardships and sacrifices which must attend a war unparalleled in its probable strain.

The vital interests of Russia and Germany do not conflict. There are fundamental grounds for a peaceable existence of these two States. Germany's future lies on the sea, that is, in a realm where Russia, essentially the most continental of the great powers, has no interests whatever. We have no overseas colonies, and shall probably never have them, and communication between the various parts of our empire is easier overland than by water. No surplus population demanding territorial expansion is visible, but, even from the viewpoint of new conquests, what can we gain from a victory over Germany? Posen, or East Prussia? But why do we need these regions, densely populated as they are by Poles, when we find it difficult enough to manage our own Russian Poles? Why encourage centripetal tendencies, that have not ceased even to this day in the Vistula territory, by incorporating in the Russian State the restless Posnanian and East Prussian Poles, whose national demands even the German Government, which is more firm than the Russian, cannot stifle?

Exactly the same thing applies to Galicia. It is obviously disadvantageous to us to annex, in the interests of national sentimentalism, a territory that has lost every vital connection with our fatherland. For, together with a negligible handful of Galicians, Russian in spirit, how many Poles, Jews, and Ukrainian Uniates we would receive! The so-called Ukrainian, or Mazeppist, movement is not a menace to us at present, but we should not enable it to expand by increasing the number of turbulent Ukrainian elements, for in this movement there undoubtedly lies the seed of an extremely dangerous Little Russian separatism which, under favorable conditions, may assume quite unexpected proportions.

The obvious aim of our diplomacy in the rapprochement with England has been to open the Straits. But a war with Germany seems hardly necessary for the attainment of this object, for it was England, and not Germany at all, that closed our outlet from the Black Sea. Was it not because we made sure of the cooperation of the latter power, that we freed ourselves in 1871 from the humiliating restrictions imposed upon us by England under the Treaty of Paris?

Also, there is reason to believe that the Germans would agree sooner than the English to let us have the Straits, in which they have only a slight interest, and at the price of which they would gladly purchase our alliance.

Moreover, we should not cherish any exaggerated hopes from our occupation of the Straits. Their acquisition would be advantageous to us only as they served to close the Black Sea to others, making it an inland sea for us, safe from enemy attack.

The Straits would not give us an outlet to the open sea, however, since on the other side of them there lies a sea consisting almost wholly of territorial waters, a sea dotted with numerous islands where the British navy, for instance, would have no trouble whatever in closing to us every inlet and outlet, irrespective of the Straits. Therefore, Russia might safely welcome an arrangement which, while not turning the Straits over to our direct control, would safeguard us against a penetration of the Black Sea by an enemy fleet. Such an arrangement, attainable under favorable circumstances without any war, has the additional advantage that it would not violate the interests of the Balkan States, which would not regard our seizure of the Straits without alarm and quite natural jealousy.

In Trans-Caucasia we could, as a result of war, expand territorially only at the expense of regions inhabited by Armenians, a move which is hardly desirable in view of the revolutionary character of present Armenian sentiment, and of its dream of a greater Armenia; and in this region, Germany, were we allied to her, would certainly place even fewer obstacles in our way than England. Those territorial and economic acquisitions which might really prove useful to us are available only in places where our ambitions may meet opposition from England, but by no means from Germany. Persia, the Pamir, Kuldja, Kashgar, Dzungaria, Mongolia, the Ulianghai territory—all these are regions where the interests of Russia and Germany do not conflict, whereas the interests of Russia and England have clashed there repeatedly.

And Germany is in exactly the same situation with respect to Russia. She could seize from us, in case of a successful war, only such territories as would be of slight value to her, and because of their population, would prove of little use for colonization; the Vistula territory, with a Polish-Lithuanian population, and the Baltic provinces, with a Lettish-Estonian population, are all equally turbulent and anti-German.

Russia's Economic Advantages and Needs
Do Not Conflict with Germany's

It may be argued, however, that, under modern conditions in the various nations, territorial acquisitions are of secondary importance, while economic interests take first rank. But in this field, again, Russia's advantages and needs do not conflict with Germany's as much as is believed. It is, of course, undeniable that the existing Russo-German trade agreements are disadvantageous to our agriculture and advantageous to Germany's, but it would be hardly fair to ascribe this circumstance to the treachery and unfriendliness of Germany.

It should not be forgotten that these agreements are in many of their sections advantageous to us. The Russian delegates who concluded these agreements were confirmed protagonists of a development of Russian industry at any cost, and they undoubtedly made a deliberate sacrifice, at least to some extent, of the interests of Russian agriculture to the interests of Russian industry. Furthermore, we ought not to forget that Germany is far from being the direct consumer of the greater share of our agricultural exports abroad. For the greater share of our agricultural produce, Germany acts merely as middleman, and so it is for us and the consuming markets to establish direct relations and thus avoid the expensive German mediation. Lastly, we should keep in mind that the commercial relations of States depend on their political understandings, for no country finds advantage in the economic weakening of an ally but, conversely, profits by the ruin of a political foe. In short, even though it be obvious that the existing Russo-German commercial treaties are not to our advantage, and that Germany, in concluding them, availed herself of a situation that happened to be in her favor—in other words, forced us to the wall—this action should have been expected from Germany and thought of. It should not, however, be looked upon as a mark of hostility toward us, but rather as an expression of healthy national self-interest, worthy of our emulation. Aside from that, we observe, in the case of Austria-Hungary, an agricultural country that is in a far greater economic dependence upon Germany than ours, but nevertheless, is not prevented from attaining an agricultural development such as we may only dream of.

In view of what has been said, it would seem that the conclusion of a commercial treaty with Germany, entirely acceptable to Russia, by no means requires that Germany first be crushed. It will be quite sufficient to maintain neighborly relations with her, to make a careful estimate of our real interests in the various branches of national economy, and to engage in long, insistent bargaining with German delegates, who may be expected to protect the interests of their own fatherland and not ours.

But I would go still further and say that the ruin of Germany, from the viewpoint of our trade with her, would be disadvantageous to us. Her defeat would unquestionably end in a peace dictated from the viewpoint of England's economic interests. The latter will exploit to the farthest limit any success that falls to her lot, and we will only lose, in a ruined Germany without sea routes, a market which, after all, is valuable to us for our otherwise unmarketable products.

In respect to Germany's economic future, the interests of Russia and England are diametrically opposed. For England, it is profitable to kill Germany's maritime trade and industry, turning her into a poor and, if possible, agricultural country. For us, it is of advantage for Germany to develop her sea-going commerce and the industry which serves it, so as to supply the remotest world markets, and at the same time open her domestic market to our agricultural products, to supply her large working population.

But, aside from the commercial treaties, it has been customary to point out the oppressive character of German domination in Russian economic life, and the systematic penetration of German colonization into our country, as representing a manifest peril to the Russian State. We believe, however, that fears on these grounds are considerably exaggerated. The famous "Drang nach Osten" was in its own time natural and understandable, since Germany's land could not accommodate her increased population, and the surplus was driven in the direction of the least resistance, i.e., into a less densely populated neighboring country. The German Government was compelled to recognize the inevitability of this movement, but could hardly look upon it as to its own interests. For, after all, it was Germans who were being lost to the influence of the German State, thus reducing the man power of their own country. Indeed, the German Government made such strenuous efforts to preserve the connection between its emigrants and their old fatherland that it adopted even the unusual method of tolerating dual citizenship. It is certain, however, that a considerable proportion of German emigrants definitely and irrevocably settled in their new homes, and slowly broke their ties with the old country. This fact, obviously incompatible with Germany's State interests, seems to have been one of the incentives which started her upon a colonial policy and maritime commerce, previously so alien to her. And at present, as the German colonies increase and there is an attendant growth of German industry and naval commerce, the German colonization movement decreases, in a measure, and the day is not remote when the "Drang nach Osten" will become nothing more than a subject for history.

In any case, the German colonization, which undoubtedly conflicts with our State interests, must be stopped, and here, again, friendly relations with Germany cannot harm us. To express a preference for a German orientation does not imply the advocacy of Russian vassalage to Germany, and, while maintaining friendly and neighborly intercourse with her, we must not sacrifice our State interests to this object. But Germany herself will not object to measures against the continued flow of German colonists into Russia. To her, it is of greater benefit to turn the wave of emigration toward her own colonies. Moreover, even before Germany had colonies, when her industry was not yet sufficiently developed to employ the entire population, the German Government did not feel justified in protesting against the restrictive measures that were adopted against foreign colonization during the reign of Alexander III.

As regards the German domination in the field of our economic life, this phenomenon hardly justifies the complaints usually voiced against it. Russia is far too poor, both in capital and in industrial enterprise, to get along without a large import of foreign capital. A certain amount of dependence upon some kind of foreign capital is, therefore, unavoidable, until such time as the industrial enterprise and material resources of our population develop to a point where we may entirely forego the services of foreign investors and their money. But as long as we do require them, German capital is more advantageous to us than any other.

First and foremost, this capital is cheaper than any other, being satisfied with the lowest margin of profit. This, to a large extent, explains the relative cheapness of German products, and their gradual displacement of British products in the markets of the world. The lower demands of German capital, as regards returns, have for their consequence Germany's readiness to invest in enterprises which, because of their relatively small returns, are shunned by other foreign investors. Also, as a result of that relative cheapness of German capital, its influx into Russia is attended by a smaller outflow of investors' profits from Russia, as compared with French and English investments, and so a larger amount of rubles remain in Russia. Moreover, a considerable proportion of the profits made on German investments in Russian industry do not leave our country at all, but are spent in Russia.

Unlike the English or French, the German capitalists, in most cases, come to stay in Russia, themselves, with their money. It is this very German characteristic which explains in a considerable degree the amazing number of German industrialists, manufacturers, and mill owners in our midst, as compared with the British and French.

The latter live in their own countries, removing from Russia the profits produced by their enterprises, down to the last kopek. The German investors, on the contrary, live in Russia for long periods, and not infrequently settle down permanently. Whatever may be said to the contrary, the fact is that the Germans, unlike other foreigners, soon feel at home in Russia and rapidly become Russianized. Who has not seen Frenchmen and Englishmen, for example, who have spent almost their whole lives in Russia and yet do not speak a word of Russian? On the other hand, are there many Germans here who cannot make themselves understood in Russian, even though it be with a strong accent and in broken speech? Nay, more—who has not seen genuine Russians, orthodox, loyal with all their hearts dedicated to the principles of the Russian State, and yet only one or two generations removed from their German emigrant ancestry? Lastly, we must not forget that Germany herself is, to a certain extent, interested in our economic well-being. In this regard, Germany differs, to our advantage, from other countries, which are interested exclusively in obtaining the largest possible returns from capital invested in Russia, even at the cost of the economic ruin of this country. Germany, however, in her capacity of permanent—although, of course, not unselfish—middleman for our foreign trade, has an interest in preserving the productive resources of our country, as a source of profitable intermediary operations for her.

Even a Victory over Germany Promises Russia an Exceedingly Unfavorable Prospect

In any case, even if we were to admit the necessity for eradicating German domination in the field of our economic life, even at the price of a total banishment of German capital from Russian industry, appropriate measures could be taken, it would seem, without war against Germany. Such a war will demand such enormous expenditures that they will many times exceed the more than doubtful advantages to us in the abolition of the German [economic] domination. More than that, the result of such a war will be an economic situation compared with which the yoke of German capital will seem easy.

For there can be no doubt that the war will necessitate expenditures which are beyond Russia's limited financial means. We shall have to obtain credit from allied and neutral countries, but this will not be granted gratuitously. As to what will happen if the war should end disastrously for us, I do not wish to discuss now. The financial and economic consequences of defeat can be neither calculated nor foreseen, and will undoubtedly spell the total ruin of our entire national economy.

But even victory promises us extremely unfavorable financial prospects; a totally ruined Germany will not be in a position to compensate us for the cost involved. Dictated in the interest of England, the peace treaty will not afford Germany opportunity for sufficient economic recuperation to cover our war expenditures, even at a distant time. The little which we may perhaps succeed in extorting from her will have to be shared with our allies, and to our share there will fall but negligible crumbs, compared with the war cost. Meantime, we shall have to pay our war loans, not without pressure by the allies. For, after the destruction of German power, we shall no longer be necessary to them. Nay, more, our political might, enhanced by our victory, will induce them to weaken us, at least economically. And so it is inevitable that, even after a victorious conclusion of the war, we shall fall into the same sort of financial and economic dependence upon our creditors, compared with which our present dependence upon German capital will seem ideal.

However, no matter how sad may be the economic prospects which face us as a result of union with England, and, by that token, of war with Germany, they are still of secondary importance when we think of the political consequences of this fundamentally unnatural alliance.

A Struggle Between Russia and Germany Is Profoundly Undesirable to Both Sides, as It Amounts to a Weakening of the Monarchist Principle

It should not be forgotten that Russia and Germany are the representatives of the conservative principle in the civilized world, as opposed to the democratic principle, incarnated in England and, to an infinitely lesser degree, in France. Strange as it may seem, England, monarchistic and conservative to the marrow at home, has in her foreign relations always acted as the protector of the most demagogical tendencies, invariably encouraging all popular movements aiming at the weakening of the monarchical principle.

From this point of view, a struggle between Germany and Russia, regardless of its issue, is profoundly undesirable to both sides, as undoubtedly involving the weakening of the conservative principle in the world of which the above-named two great powers are the only reliable bulwarks. More than that, one must realize that under the exceptional conditions which exist, a general European war is mortally dangerous both for Russia and Germany, no matter who wins. It is our firm conviction, based upon a long and careful study of all contemporary subversive tendencies, that there must inevitably break out in the defeated country a social revolution which, by the very nature of things, will spread to the country of the victor.

During the many years of peaceable neighborly existence, the two countries have become united by many ties, and a social upheaval in one is bound to affect the other. That these troubles will be of a social, and not a political, nature cannot be doubted, and this will hold true, not only as regards Russia, but for Germany as well. An especially favorable soil for social upheavals is found in Russia, where the masses undoubtedly profess, unconsciously, the principles of Socialism. In spite of the spirit of antagonism to the Government in Russian society, as unconscious as the Socialism of the broad masses of the people, a political revolution is not possible in Russia, and any revolutionary movement inevitably must degenerate into a Socialist movement. The opponents of the Government have no popular support. The people see no difference between a government official and an intellectual. The Russian masses, whether workmen or peasants, are not looking for political rights, which they neither want nor comprehend.

The peasant dreams of obtaining a gratuitous share of somebody else's land; the workman, of getting hold of the entire capital and profits of the manufacturer. Beyond this, they have no aspirations. If these slogans are scattered far and wide among the populace, and the Government permits agitation along these lines, Russia will be flung into anarchy, such as she suffered in the ever-memorable period of troubles in 1905–1906. War with Germany would create exceptionally favorable conditions for such agitation. As already stated, this war is pregnant with enormous difficulties for us, and cannot turn out to be a mere triumphal march to Berlin. Both military disasters—partial ones, let us hope—and all kinds of shortcomings in our supply are inevitable. In the excessive nervousness and spirit of opposition of our society, these events will be given an exaggerated importance, and all the blame will be laid on the Government.

It will be well if the Government does not yield, but declares directly that in time of war no criticism of the governmental authority is to be tolerated, and resolutely suppresses all opposition. In the absence of any really strong hold on the people by the opposition, this would settle the affair. The people did not heed the writers of the Wiborg Manifesto, in its time, and they will not follow them now.

But a worse thing may happen: the government authority may make concessions, may try to come to an agreement with the opposition, and thereby weaken itself just when the Socialist elements are ready for action. Even though it may sound like a paradox, the fact is that agreement with the opposition in Russia positively weakens the Government. The trouble is that our opposition refuses to reckon with the fact that it represents no real force. The Russian opposition is intellectual throughout, and this is its weakness, because between the intelligentsia and the people there is a profound gulf of mutual misunderstanding and distrust. We need an artificial election law, indeed, we require the direct influence of the governmental authority, to assure the election to the State Duma of even the most zealous champions of popular rights. Let the Government refuse to support the elections, leaving them to their natural course, and the legislative institutions would not see within their walls a single intellectual, outside of a few demagogic agitators. However insistent the members of our legislative institutions may be that the people confide in them, the peasant would rather believe the landless government official than the Octobrist landlord in the Duma, while the workingman treats the wage-earning factory inspector with more confidence than the legislating manufacturer, even though the latter professes every principle of the Cadet party.

It is more than strange, under these circumstances, that the governmental authority should be asked to reckon seriously with the opposition, that it should for this purpose renounce the role of impartial regulator of social relationships, and come out before the broad masses of the people as the obedient organ of the class aspirations of the intellectual and propertied minority of the population. The opposition demands that the Government should be responsible to it, representative of a class, and should obey the parliament which it artificially created. (Let us recall that famous expression of V. Nabokov: "Let the executive power submit to the legislative power!") In other words, the opposition demands that the Government should adopt the psychology of a savage, and worship the idol which he himself made.

Russia Will be Flung into Hopeless Anarchy, the Issue of Which Will be Hard to Foresee

If the war ends in victory, the putting down of the Socialist movement will not offer any insurmountable obstacles. There will be agrarian troubles, as a result of agitation for compensating the soldiers with additional land allotments; there will be labor troubles during the transition from the probably increased wages of war time to normal schedules; and this, it is to be hoped, will be all, so long as the wave of the German social revolution has not reached us. But in the event of defeat, the possibility of which in a struggle with a foe like Germany cannot be overlooked, social revolution in its most extreme form is inevitable.

As has already been said, the trouble will start with the blaming of the Government for all disasters. In the legislative institutions a bitter campaign against the Government will begin, followed by revolutionary agitations throughout the country, with Socialist slogans, capable of arousing and rallying the masses, beginning with the division of the land and succeeded by a division of all valuables and property. The defeated army, having lost its most dependable men, and carried away by the tide of primitive peasant desire for land, will find itself too demoralized to serve as a bulwark of law and order. The legislative institutions and the intellectual opposition parties, lacking real authority in the eyes of the people, will be powerless to stem the popular tide, aroused by themselves, and Russia will be flung into hopeless anarchy, the issue of which cannot be foreseen.

Germany, in Case of Defeat, is Destined to Suffer Social Upheavals No Less than those of Russia

No matter how strange it may appear at first sight, considering the extraordinary poise of the German character, Germany, likewise, is destined to suffer, in case of defeat, no lesser social upheavals. The effect of a disastrous war upon the population will be too severe not to bring to the surface destructive tendencies, now deeply hidden. The peculiar social order of modern Germany rests upon the actually predominant influence of the agrarians, Prussian Junkerdom and propertied peasants.

These elements are the bulwark of the profoundly conservative German regime, headed by Prussia. The vital interests of these classes demand a protective economic policy towards agriculture, import duties on grain, and consequently, high prices for all farm products. But Germany, with her limited territory and increasing population, has long ago turned from an agricultural into an industrial State, so that protection of agriculture is, in effect, a matter of taxing the larger part of the population for the benefit of the smaller. To this majority, there is a compensation in the extensive development of the export of German industrial products to the most distant markets, so that the advantages derived thereby enable the industrialists and working people to pay the higher prices for the farm products consumed at home.

Defeated, Germany will lose her world markets and maritime commerce, for the aim of the war—on the part of its real instigator, England —will be the destruction of German competition. After this has been achieved, the laboring masses, deprived not only of higher but of any and all wages, having suffered greatly during the war, and being, naturally, embittered, will offer fertile soil for anti-agrarian and later anti-social propaganda by the Socialist parties.

These parties, in turn, making use of the outraged patriotic sentiment among the people, owing to the loss of the war, their exasperation at the militarists and the feudal burgher regime that betrayed them, will abandon the road of peaceable evolution which they have thus far been following so steadily, and take a purely revolutionary path. Some part will also be played, especially in the event of agrarian troubles in neighboring Russia, by the class of landless farmhands, which is quite numerous in Germany. Apart from this, there will be a revival of the hitherto concealed separatist tendencies in southern Germany, and the hidden antagonism of Bavaria to domination by Prussia will emerge in all its intensity. In short, a situation will be created which (in gravity) will be little better than that in Russia.

Peace Among the Civilized Nations is Imperiled Chiefly by the Desire of England to Retain Her Vanishing Domination of the Seas

A summary of all that has been stated above must lead to the conclusion that a rapprochement with England does not promise us any benefits, and that the English orientation of our diplomacy is essentially wrong.

We do not travel the same road as England; she should be left to go her own way, and we must not quarrel on her account with Germany.

The Triple Entente is an artificial combination, without a basis of real interest. It has nothing to look forward to. The future belongs to a close and incomparably more vital rapprochement of Russia, Germany, France (reconciled with Germany), and Japan (allied to Russia by a strictly defensive union). A political combination like this, lacking all aggressiveness toward other States, would safeguard for many years the peace of the civilized nations, threatened, not by the militant intentions of Germany, as English diplomacy is trying to show, but solely by the perfectly natural striving of England to retain at all costs her vanishing domination of the seas. In this direction, and not in the fruitless search of a basis for an accord with England, which is in its very nature contrary to our national plans and aims, should all the efforts of our diplomacy be concentrated.

It goes without saying that Germany, on her part, must meet our desire to restore our well-tested relations and friendly alliance with her, and to elaborate, in closest agreement with us, such terms of our neighborly existence as to afford no basis for anti-German agitation on the part of our constitutional-liberal parties, which, by their very nature, are forced to adhere, not to a Conservative German, but to a liberal English orientation.

February, 1914   P. N. Durnovo

41

Russia's Entry into World War I: Sazonov's Account

On June 28, 1914, the heir-presumptive to the Austro-Hungarian throne Archduke Francis Ferdinand, and his wife were assassinated in Sarajevo, the capital of Bosnia, by a fanatically patriotic Bosnian youth. While the Serbian government was in

Reprinted with permission of the publisher from Serge Sazonov, *Fateful Years,* *1909–1916* (London: Jonathan Cape, 1928), pp. 196–205.

no way responsible for the crime (though some of
its lesser officials probably had some knowledge of
a plot but took no steps to prevent its execution),
Austria-Hungary seized the opportunity created by
the assassination to settle accounts with its small
but turbulent southern neighbor. On July 23, the
Austro-Hungarian Foreign Minister Count von
Berchtold sent a forty-eight hour, ten-point ultimatum to Serbia demanding the immediate suppression of all forms of anti-Austrian propaganda and
permission for Austro-Hungarian officials to assist in
the suppression of the subversive movement directed
against the Dual Monarchy. Both the content and
the tenor of Berchtold's ultimatum shocked many
statesmen. Sir Edward Grey, British Secretary of
State for Foreign Affairs, called it "the most formidable document he had ever seen addressed by one
state to another, that is independent," while Russia's
Foreign Minister Sergei Sazonov (1861–1927), on
learning of the ultimatum's content, exclaimed:
"C'est la guerre européene."

Officially, the Russian government advised its
Serbian ally to exercise "extreme moderation." This
the Serbs did in their reply of July 25, wherein, while
refusing to allow Austrian officials on Serbian soil,
they expressed a desire to submit the entire matter
to the Permanent Court of Arbitration at The Hague.
The Austrians found Serbia's evasive response un-
acceptable, severed diplomatic ties with Belgrade on
July 25, ordered partial mobilization, and on July 28
declared war on Serbia. These actions prompted the
Russian government to put its armed forces on alert.
In an attempt to pose a serious warning to Austria-
Hungary without at the same time offending Germany, an ally of the Dual Monarchy, Russia ordered
partial mobilization on July 29. When this action
failed to produce the desired results, Sazonov and
the military men prevailed on Nicholas II to issue
a general mobilization order on July 30. This
prompted Austria's general mobilization on July 31,
which was followed by that of France and Germany
on August 1. World War I thus became a reality.

My object is to give a brief account of events in which I took a personal
part and thus enable my readers to form a correct view of the policy
followed by the Russian Government during those tragic days; hence it
is my rule to mention but cursorily the facts I learned from extraneous

sources, even though they confirmed and justified the Russian diplomacy. I will, therefore, content myself with saying that by July 30 our conviction of a European war being inevitable, because of the attitude of the Central Powers, was shared not only in Paris and in London but also in Rome. In spite of every one being peaceably disposed, all the Governments realized the necessity for preparing in one way or another for the gathering storm. At the same time both we and our friends were determined to continue diplomatic negotiations so long as it was at all possible, since breaking them off meant war.

In spite of the extremely difficult position in which the obduracy of the Austrian Cabinet placed us, refusing, as they did, every one of my suggestions for a peaceable settlement, I nevertheless continued, with the entire approval of the Tsar, to try and come to an understanding with the Central Powers. I informed of this the French and the English Ambassadors, with whom I worked together in friendly confidence, since we were equally concerned to preserve peace. I told them that I would continue negotiations up to the last moment.

On July 30 I had another interview with the German Ambassador, in the course of which he asked me whether we would be content with Austria's promise to leave Serbian territory intact, and begged me to state on what conditions we should be ready to stop our preparations for war. I immediately wrote down on a piece of paper and handed him the following statement: "If, admitting that the Austro-Serbian conflict has become a European question, Austria is ready to withdraw from her ultimatum the clauses which infringe upon the sovereign rights of Serbia, Russia will undertake to stop her preparations for war."

It would be hardly possible for a Great Power to give a stronger proof of its desire for peace than that contained in the formula I submitted to Count Pourtalès. Russia consented to stop her preparations for war if Austria merely renounced her attack upon Serbia's sovereign rights; she did not require that Austria should immediately stop her military operations against Serbia or demobilize on the Russian frontier. In making this offer I was really exceeding my powers, for I had no sanction for going so far in my negotiations with Germany and Austria, and I could only take upon myself the responsibility for it because I knew that in the eyes of the Tsar the sole limit to concessions for the sake of securing peace were the honour and the vital interests of Russia, and that the Russian Cabinet was no less peaceably disposed than the Emperor Nicholas II.

A few hours after I had made this statement to the German Ambassador I received a telegram from M. Sverbeyev, our Ambassador in Berlin, telling me that he had transmitted my offer to the Foreign Secretary at the same time as Count Pourtalès had done and that Herr von Jagow declared our offer to be impossible of acceptance for Austria. Evidently the unanimity between the German and the Austrian Governments was so complete that one could speak for the other. Every hour that passed robbed us of our last hopes of preserving peace and the necessity for taking measures of self-defence grew more and more urgent.

On that same day I received another message from Berlin. Sverbeyev telegraphed to me that the decree for the mobilization of the German Army had been signed. Without losing a moment, I passed this news to the Minister of War and to the Chief of the General Staff. I must confess that after my conversations with the German Ambassador I did not feel surprised. At midday on July 30 a special edition of the German official paper, the *Lokal Anzeiger*, was published, announcing the mobilization of the German Armies and Fleet. Sverbeyev's telegram, with the news, was dispatched to St. Petersburg a few minutes after the special edition appeared, and reached me some two hours later. Soon after sending the telegram Sverbeyev was called to the telephone and heard from von Jagow that the news about the German mobilization was not true. He again telegraphed to me at once, but this time his telegram was considerably delayed on the way. It is not clear to this day what exactly had happened about the German mobilization. One thing is certain—that the order appeared the day after the meeting of the Crown Council at Potsdam and was evidently connected with it. No one, of course, will be surprised to hear that in Russia the news was taken very seriously and that people believed in the mobilization decree being issued more readily than they did in its being rescinded. The German press is not unanimous on the subject. Official organs, or those supporting the Government, attach no importance to the mobilization decree, while the Opposition papers regard it as genuine. In any case, the German Government itself admits that the decree had had some influence upon Russia's decision to mobilize on July 31. Thus Bethmann-Hollweg wrote to Prince Lichnowsky that in his opinion the Russian mobilization might be explained by the false rumours of the German mobilization which spread in Berlin on July 30 and which, though they were immediately contradicted, might have been transmitted to St. Petersburg.

It was not, however, a case of rumours but of an official communication in a Government newspaper.

There is another aspect of this affair which has never been cleared up. The reason for the delay of Sverbeyev's second telegram by which, on von Jagow's authority, he contradicted his first, has never been ascertained. The explanation that naturally occurs to one is that the telegram was delayed on purpose. It cannot, of course, be proved, but many persons who commented on this circumstance in the press are agreed that the delay in the Russian Ambassador's telegram was not accidental, but was the work of the German Government which had intended thereby to cause the Russians to hasten with their mobilization under the influence of the first news in the *Lokal Anzeiger*, subsequently contradicted, and thus to make the Russian Government responsible for the war in the eyes of Europe and especially of the German public. I have no incontrovertible proofs of this, but the above interpretation deserves attention because, as had already been said, Germany was anxious for domestic reasons to put the blame for the European conflagration upon Russia.

But whether the *Lokal Anzeiger* communication was a manoeuvre of the German Government or an indiscretion on the part of some one who had heard of the mobilization being contemplated, or, perhaps already begun, it was interpreted in St. Petersburg, in connection with the news coming from the frontier, to mean exactly what the German Chancellor had said in his telegram to the German Ambassador in London.

About two o'clock on July 30 the Chief of the General Staff, General Yanushkevich, telephoned to say that he had to speak to me concerning the latest news received at his Headquarters. He said that the Minister of War was with him and that they both asked me to look in. On my way to the Staff Headquarters, which is five minutes' walk from the Ministry of Foreign Affairs, I fully guessed what I should have to hear. I found both Generals in a state of grave anxiety. From their very first words I realized that in their opinion peace could not be preserved any longer and the only safety lay in mobilizing the Army and the Fleet without delay. They hardly mentioned Austria, since she had no further surprises in store for us, her intentions about Serbia being perfectly clear, and also because the menace from Germany made the Austrian danger seem comparatively unimportant. General Yanushkevich said that the special information collected by the General Staff made him feel perfectly certain that the German mobilization had advanced much further than was generally supposed, and that, considering the quickness with which it could be carried out, Russia might find herself in an extremely dangerous situation if she mobilized partially and not as a whole. The General added that the war had become inevitable and that we were in danger of losing it before we had had time to unsheath our sword. I was too well acquainted with the German preparedness for war and with the defects of our military organization to doubt the justice of Yanushkevich's words. I merely asked him whether he had told all this to the Tsar. The Generals answered that the Tsar knew exactly how matters stood, but that they had not so far succeeded in obtaining his consent for a general mobilization decree and that it was with the utmost difficulty they had wrung from him the permission to mobilize the four Southern Districts against Austria after it had declared war on Serbia and bombarded Belgrade—and this in spite of the Tsar having told the Kaiser that our mobilization did not necessarily mean war. The difference between mobilization and war was clearly recognized at every stage of our military administration, and all foreign military attachés in St. Petersburg knew this perfectly well. During this memorable conversation General Yanushkevich told me that our mobilization might be put off for another twenty-four hours at the utmost, but after that it would be useless, for it could not be carried out properly; in that case he could not hold himself responsible for the consequences.

The moment was so critical that the Chief of the General Staff and the Minister of War begged me to telephone to the Tsar, who was in Peterhof, and try to induce him to give his consent to general mobilization.

I need not say with what feelings I regarded this request, repellent to my whole nature and way of thinking, and concerned with matters that were utterly foreign to me. Nevertheless, I consented to do what was asked of me, feeling that it was a painful duty which I had no right to shirk at a moment so full of terrible responsibility. I must make at this point a personal remark. I was by no means a friend either of General Sukhomlinov or of General Yanushkevich, and, at ordinary times, their opinion would not have been sufficient to make me change my judgment on a subject to which I attached serious importance. But now the case was different. In the first place, I had been quite prepared for what they told me, for the information which I had received, though less exact from the point of view of technical detail but obtained for the most part at first hand, confirmed my belief that the Generals were right in thinking that the war was inevitable and that it might break out suddenly at any moment. Secondly, I knew very well that neither General Yanushkevich nor General Sukhomlinov was eager for war or had any hatred for the Germans, which was sometimes found among our young officers, though less frequently at that time than immediately after the Berlin Congress at which the interests of Russia were betrayed by Bismarck to our perpetual enemy, Austria, and our enemy of the moment, England. A whole generation had grown up since then and our wound had healed. Extraordinary happenings were needed to make it open once more, and the events which were approaching with the rapidity of a thunder-storm had not yet penetrated into the minds of our Army. Besides, Russian haters of Germany were found only among the so-called political Generals—a type which had become almost extinct with the death of Skobelev and remained only as a harmless and insignificant survival. Apart from all these considerations, the tone of profound sincerity in which Yanushkevich and Sukhomlinov spoke and their deep anxiety for the national safety made me feel that I could not refuse their request, painful as it was to me to comply with it.

I telephoned to the Peterhof Palace. After several minutes of agonizing expectation I heard a voice which I did not recognize at once—the voice of a man obviously not used to speaking on the telephone—asking me who was speaking. I told the Tsar that I was speaking to him from the

office of the Chief of the General Staff. "What is it you wish?" asked the
Tsar. I answered that I begged him earnestly to see me in the afternoon
on urgent business. This time I had to wait still longer for a reply. At
last the voice was heard again and said: "I will receive you at three
o'clock." The Generals heaved a sigh of relief and I hurried home to
change and left for Peterhof before half-past two, arriving there at the
time appointed.

The Tsar was alone, and I was at once admitted to his study. I noticed at the first glance that he was tired and anxious. After greeting me
he asked whether I had anything against General Tatishtchev being present at our interview. Tatishtchev was going that very evening or the
following morning to Berlin, where he had for years occupied a post of
a General in the suite of the Emperor Wilhelm. I answered that I should
be very pleased, for I had known the General for many years and was
on friendly terms with him, but at the same time expressed a doubt as
to whether Tatishtchev would be able to return to Berlin.

"You think it is too late?" asked the Tsar.

I had to say that I did.

The Tsar rang the bell and a minute later General Tatishtchev came
in. He was one of the noblest and most devoted servants of the martyred
Tsar, and his memory is revered both by his friends and by all who know
the tragic story of his heroic death in Ekaterinburg together with the
Imperial family.

I began my report at ten minutes past three and finished at four. I
told the Tsar in detail my conversation with the Minister of War and
the Chief of the General Staff, omitting nothing of what I had heard
from them and mentioning the last news that had been received at the
Ministry of Foreign Affairs from Austria and Germany and were still unknown to His Majesty. This news left no doubt whatever that during
the two days I had not seen the Emperor the position had changed so
much for the worse that there was no more hope of preserving peace.
All our conciliatory offers, which went far beyond anything that a Great
Power, whose resources were still untouched, could be expected to con-
cede, had been rejected. The same thing happened about the offers made,
with our consent, by Sir Edward Grey, which proved that the British
Government was no less peaceably disposed than ourselves. I told the
Tsar that I fully agreed with Yanushkevich and Sukhomlinov that it was
dangerous to delay the general mobilization any longer, since, according
to the information they possessed, the German mobilization, though not
as yet proclaimed officially, was fairly advanced. The perfection of the
German military organization made it possible by means of personal
notices to the reservists to accomplish a great part of the work quietly
and then, after the formal orders have been issued, to complete the
mobilization in a very short time. This circumstance gave a tremendous

advantage to Germany, but we could counteract it to a certain extent by taking measures for our own mobilization in good time. The Tsar knew all this very well and he signified it by inclining his head without speaking. On the morning of July 30 he had received a telegram from the Emperor Wilhelm saying that if Russia continued to mobilize against Austria the Kaiser would be unable to intercede, as the Tsar had asked him. The decision rested, therefore, with the Tsar, who had alone to bear the responsibility for war or for peace. I had not yet seen that telegram and read it only in the Tsar's study. I could see from his expression how wounded he was by its tone and content. It contained nothing but threats, and there was not a single word about submitting the Austro-Serbian conflict to the decision of the Hague tribunal. If it had not been for the lucky chance to which I have referred already, no one would have known to this day that the Tsar had made that excellent suggestion.

After giving me time to read the unfortunate telegram carefully, the Tsar said in an agitated voice: "He is asking the impossible. He has forgotten, or does not wish to remember, that the Austrian mobilization had begun sooner than the Russian, and now asks us to stop ours without saying a word about the Austrian. You know I have already suppressed one mobilization decree and then consented only to a partial one. If I agreed to Germany's demands now, we should find ourselves unarmed against the Austrian Army which is mobilized already. It would be madness."

The Tsar's words expressed exactly what I had thought and felt the day before, after the visit of the German Ambassador. I said so, adding that both Wilhelm II's telegram to His Majesty and Count Pourtalès's verbal communication pointed to one conclusion only—that war was unavoidable. It had been settled long ago in Vienna, and the German Government, which might have been expected to bring the Austrians to reason, had no wish to do so, demanding that we should capitulate before the Central Powers—a thing that Russia would never forgive to the Tsar, for it would cover with shame the good name of the Russian people. In the circumstances there was nothing left for the Tsar but to give orders for general mobilization.

The Tsar was silent. Then he said to me, in a voice full of deep feeling: "This would mean sending hundreds of thousands of Russian people to their death. How can one help hesitating to take such a step?"

I answered that the responsibility for the precious lives carried away by the war would not fall upon him. Neither he nor his Government desired the war. Both he and they had done everything humanly possible to avoid it and were prepared to sacrifice a great deal of our national pride. He could say to himself, with a full conviction of being right, that his conscience was clear and that he would not have to answer either before God or his own conscience or the Russian people for the bloodshed of the terrible war, thrust upon Russia and Europe by the ill-will of the enemy, determined to increase their power by enslaving our natural Allies in the Balkans, destroying our influence there and reducing Russia to a pitiful dependence upon the arbitrary will of the Central Powers. She could only succeed in freeing herself from that condition at the cost of unspeakable efforts and sacrifices, utterly isolated from other Powers and having nothing but her own resources to trust to.

I had nothing further to add and sat opposite the Tsar, watching him intently. He was pale and his expression betrayed a terrible inner struggle. I was almost as agitated as he. The fate of Russia and of the Russian people depended upon his decision. Everything had been done, all means had been tried to avert the approaching catastrophe, and it all proved of no avail. We had either to unsheath the sword for the defence of our vital interests and to wait, fully armed, for the enemy's attack which had, during the last few days, become for us almost a palpable fact, or to refuse to fight, surrender to the enemy's mercy and perish in the end covering ourselves with everlasting shame. We were in an impasse. Our French Allies, who wished for war as little as we did, were in the same position, and so were our Balkan friends. Both knew that no choice had been left them and decided, with a heavy heart, to accept the challenge. All these thoughts flitted through my mind during the painful moments of waiting for the Tsar's answer to what my reason and my conscience had prompted me to tell him. General Tatishtchev was sitting next to me; he had not uttered a word, but was, like me, in a condition of unbearable moral tension.

At last the Tsar said, speaking as it were with difficulty: "You are right. There is nothing left us but to get ready for an attack upon us. Give then the Chief of the General Staff my order for mobilization." I went downstairs where the telephone was and rang up General Yanushkevich to tell him of the Tsar's order. In answer Yanushkevich told me that his telephone was out of order. I understood the meaning of that phrase. He was afraid to receive by telephone an order countermanding the mobilization. His fears, however, were unfounded and the order was not countermanded either by telephone or in any other way. The Tsar had overcome the distressing doubts in his mind and his decision was irrevocable.

42

Program of the Progressive Bloc, September 1915

The Russian government's entry into World War I was supported by the Russian people, who believed that the war was one of national defense against unprovoked Austro-German aggression and they were jubilant over the initial successes of the Russian armies against the enemy. Then a series of military disasters (Tannenberg, the Masurian Lakes, Gorlice) on the German front, which inflicted heavy casualties, greatly affected Russian morale. These were caused by inept leadership, by military and economic unpreparedness, and by the superior organization of the enemy. The effectiveness of the German blockade left France and England, Russia's allies, unable to aid her, and she was forced to rely on her own inadequately developed resources. This was responsible for further deterioration of morale. The government's unwillingness and inability to correct some of its policies increased existing tensions and led in September 1915 to the formal establishment within the Duma of the opposition known as the Progressive Bloc. Its leaders, deputies of six of the leading parties in the Duma, sought to eliminate "the distrust of public initiative," advocated the curtailment of interference of the military in nonmilitary matters, pleaded for amnesty to persons convicted or deported without trials, and demanded an end to discrimination against national and religious minorities. The government responded to this appeal in its usual manner—it prorogued the meeting of the Duma. This action, in turn, brought imperial Russia to the brink of a new revolution.

From *Riech* [Talk], No. 234 (3257) September 8, 1915, p. 6. Translation mine. Items in brackets are mine.

The undersigned representatives of factions and groups of the State Council and of the State Duma, convinced that only a strong, firm, and active authority can lead the fatherland to victory, and that such an authority can be only that which rests upon popular confidence and is capable of organizing the active cooperation of all citizens, have arrived at the unanimous conclusion that the most important and essential task, that of creating such an authority, cannot be realized without the fulfillment of the following conditions:

1. The formation of a united government, composed of individuals who enjoy the confidence of the country and who have agreed with the legislative institutions upon the fulfillment, at the earliest possible time, of a definite program.

2. Decisive change in the methods of administration employed thus far, which have been based upon a distrust of public initiative. In particular:

(a) Strict observance of the principles of legality in administration.

(b) Abolition of the dual authority of civil and military power in problems which have no direct relation to the conduct of war.

(c) Re-establishment of local administrations.

(d) A sensible and consistent policy aimed at the maintenance of internal peace and the removal of differences between nationalities and classes.

For the realization of such a policy the following measures must be adopted, by means of administration as well as legislation:

1. By means of Imperial clemency, a termination of cases initiated on charges of purely political and religious transgressions not aggravated by transgressions of a generally felonious nature; the release from punishment and the restoration of rights, including the right of participation in elections to the State Duma, zemstvo, city institutions, and so forth, of persons convicted of such crimes; and the amelioration of the condition of others sentenced for political and religious crimes with the exception of spies and traitors.

2. The return of those who were exiled by administrative decree for matters of a political and religious nature.

3. Complete and decisive cessation of persecution on religious grounds, under any pretext whatsoever, and repeal of circulars aimed at limitation and perversion of the *ukaz* of April 30, 1905.

4. Solution of the Russo-Polish problem; namely, removal of limitations of the rights of Poles throughout Russia; the immediate drafting and presentation to the legislative institutions of a bill for autonomy of the Kingdom of Poland, and a simultaneous review of the laws concerning Polish land ownership.

5. Inauguration of a program aimed at abolition of restrictions upon the rights of Jews; in particular, further steps towards the abolition of

the Pale of Settlement, facilitation of admission to educational institutions, removal of obstacles to choosing professions, and restoration of the Jewish press.

6. A policy of conciliation regarding the Finnish question; in particular, changes in the composition of the administration and Senate, and cessation of persecution of officials.

7. Restoration of the Little Russian [Ukrainian] press; immediate disposition of cases of confined or exiled inhabitants of Galicia, and the release of those wrongfully subjected to persecution.

8. Restoration of activity of trade unions and termination of persecution of hospital workers' representatives on suspicion of membership in an illegal party. Restoration of the labor press.

9. Agreement between the government and the legislative institutions regarding early introduction of:

(a) All bills related to national defense, the supply of the army, welfare of the wounded, care of refugees, and other problems directly related to the war.

(b) The following legislative program aimed at the organization of the country to realize victory and maintain internal peace:

Equalization of peasants' rights with those of other classes.

Establishment of volost zemstvo.

Repeal of the land statute of 1890.

Repeal of the municipal statute of 1892.

Establishment of zemstvo institutions in the border regions, such as Siberia, Archangel Gubernia, Don *Oblast*, the Caucasus, etc.

Legislation concerning the cooperative societies.

Legislation concerning rest for business employees.

Improvement of the material condition of the post and telegraph employees.

Confirmation of temperance for all time.

[Legislation] concerning land and city congresses and unions.

Statutes concerning census.

Introduction of Justices of the Peace in those *gubernias* where their establishment was prevented by financial considerations.

Inauguration of legislative measures that may be indispensable to the administrative execution of the above outlined program of action.

For the progressive group of Nationalists, Count V. Bobrinskii.
For the faction of the Center, V. Lvov.
For the faction of Zemstvo-Octobrists, I. Dmitriukov.
For the group of the Union of October 17th, S. Shidlovskii.
For the faction of Progressivists, I. Efremov.
For the faction of Popular Freedom, P. Miliukov.

43

Russia and Japan
on the Division of China,
1907–1916

Between the Treaty of Nerchinsk in 1689 and about
1850, imperial Russia's policy in the Far East had
been generally peaceful. After 1850, however, she
assumed an aggressive attitude. Two basic facts seem
to have contributed to this change. The first was the
defeat, humiliation, and partial territorial dismem-
berment of China by West European powers in a
series of wars beginning with the Opium War
(1839–1842) and ending with the Boxer Rebellion
in 1900. The second was the sudden rise of Japanese
power and ambitions in the Far East. To remove
Russia's opposition to the Japanese advance into
Korea and Manchuria, Japanese forces attacked Russia early in 1904 and in a series of spectacular moves
inflicted a humiliating defeat.

The war was formally ended by the Treaty of
Portsmouth on September 5, 1905, but the terms of
the treaty were unpopular with both sides. Between
1907 and 1916, however, the two former adversaries,
through a series of secret agreements, divided Manchuria and northern China between themselves and
pledged to cooperate fully to prevent any third power
from seeking a "sphere of influence" at China's
expense. The overthrow of the tsarist government in
the March 1917 Revolution prevented realization
of these ambitious schemes.

Reprinted with the permission of The Johns Hopkins University Press from
Ernest B. Price, *The Russo-Japanese Treaties of 1907–1916 Concerning Manchuria and Mongolia* (Baltimore: The Johns Hopkins University Press, 1933),
pp. 107–108, 113–114, 117, 121–122.

Secret Convention of July 30, 1907

The Government of His Majesty the Emperor of All the Russias and the Government of His Majesty the Emperor of Japan, desiring to obviate for the future all causes of friction or misunderstanding with respect to certain questions relating to Manchuria, Korea and Mongolia, have agreed upon the following provisions:

Article 1

Having in view the natural gravitation of interests and of political and economic activity in Manchuria, and desiring to avoid all complications which might arise from competition, Japan undertakes not to seek to obtain on its own account, or for the benefit of Japanese or other subjects, any concession in the way of railways or telegraphs in Manchuria to the north of a line defined in the Additional Article of the present Convention, and not to obstruct, either directly or indirectly, any initiatives supported by the Russian Government with a view to concessions of that sort in those regions; and Russia, on its part, inspired by the same pacific motive, undertakes not to seek to obtain on its own account, or for the benefit of Russian or other subjects, any concession in the way of railways or telegraphs in Manchuria to the south of the above-mentioned line, and not to obstruct, either directly or indirectly, any initiatives supported by the Japanese Government with a view to concessions of that sort in those regions.

It is fully understood that all the rights and privileges belonging to the Chinese Eastern Railway Company by virtue of the contracts for the construction of this railway, dated August 28, 1896, and June 25, 1898, will remain in force on the section of the railway lying to the south of the line of demarcation defined in the Additional Article.

Article 2

Russia, recognizing the relations of political solidarity between Japan and Korea resulting from the conventions and arrangements at present in force between them, copies of which have been communicated to the Russian Government by the Japanese Government, undertakes not to interfere with nor to place any obstacle in the way of the further development of those relations; and Japan, on its part, undertakes to extend in all respects most-favored-nation treatment to the Russian Government, consular officers, subjects, commerce, industry and navigation in Korea, pending the conclusion of a definitive treaty.

Article 3

The Imperial Government of Japan, recognizing the special interests of Russia in Outer Mongolia, undertakes to refrain from any interference which might prejudice those interests.

Article 4

The present Convention shall be strictly confidential between the two High Contracting Parties.

In faith of which, the undersigned, duly authorized by their respective Governments, have signed this Convention and have affixed their seals thereto.

Done at St. Petersburg, July 30, 1907, corresponding to the thirtieth day of the seventh month of the fortieth year of Meiji.

Motono
Iswolsky

Additional Article

The line of demarcation between North Manchuria and South Manchuria mentioned in Article I of the present convention is established as follows:

Starting from the northwestern point of the Russo-Korean frontier, and forming a succession of straight lines, the line runs, by way of Hunchun and the northern extremity of Lake Pirteng, to Hsiushuichan; thence it follows the Sungari to the mouth of the Nunkiang, thereupon ascending the course of that river to the confluence of the Tola River. From that point, the line follows the course of that river to its intersection with Meridian 122° East of Greenwich.

Motono
Iswolsky

Secret Convention of July 4, 1910

The Imperial Government of Russia and the Imperial Government of Japan, desiring to consolidate and develop the provisions of the secret Convention signed at St. Petersburg July 30, 1907, have agreed upon the following:

Article 1

Russia and Japan recognize the line of demarcation fixed by the Additional Article of the secret Convention of 1907 as delimiting the respective spheres of their special interests in Manchuria.

…e Governments, have signed this Convention and have
…als thereto.

…Petersburg, July 8, 1912, corresponding to the eighth day
…month of the forty-fifth year of Meiji.

Motono
Sazonow

Secret Convention of July 3, 1916

…Government of Russia and the Imperial Government of
…g to consolidate the sincerely friendly relations established
…t Conventions of July 30, 1907, July 4, 1910, and July 8,
…greed on the following clauses designed to complete the
…ned agreements:

Article 1

…gh Contracting Parties, recognizing that their vital interests
…China should not fall under the political domination of any
…hostile to Russia or Japan, will frankly and loyally enter into
…on whenever circumstances may demand, and will agree
…asures to be taken to prevent such a situation being brought

Article 2

…that, in consequence of the measures taken by mutual agree-
…vided in the preceding article, war should be declared between
…Contracting Parties and one of the third Powers contemplated
…eding article, the other Contracting Party will, upon the
…its ally, come to its aid, and in that case each of the High
…Parties undertakes not to make peace without a previous
…ith the other Contracting Party.

Article 3

…ons in which each of the High Contracting Parties w…
…cooperation to the other Contracting Party, as stipulat…
…rticle, and the means by which this cooperation …
…be established by the competent authorities of t'…
…Parties.

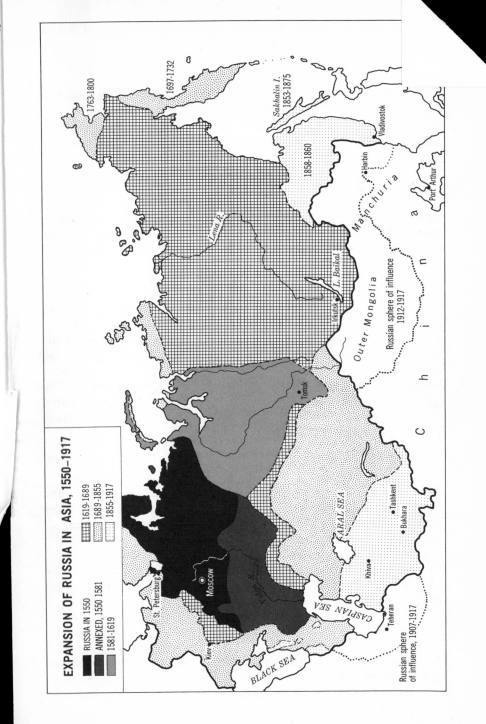

EXPANSION OF RUSSIA IN ASIA, 1550–1917

RUSSIA IN 1550
ANNEXED, 1550 1581
1581–1619
1619–1689
1689–1855
1855–1917

Russian sphere of influence, 1912–1917
Russian sphere of influence, 1907–1917

Article 2

The two High Contracting Parties undertake to respect reciprocally their special interests in the spheres above indicated. They consequently recognize the right of each, within its own sphere, freely to take all measures necessary for the safeguarding and the defense of those interests.

Article 3

Each of the two High Contracting Parties undertakes not to hinder in any way the consolidation and further development of the special interests of the other Party within the limits of the above-mentioned spheres.

Article 4

Each of the two High Contracting Parties undertakes to refrain from all political activity within the sphere of special interests of the other in Manchuria. It is furthermore understood that Russia will not seek in the Japanese sphere—and Japan will not seek in the Russian sphere—any privilege or any concession of a nature to prejudice their reciprocal special interests, and that both the Russian and Japanese Governments will respect all the rights acquired by each of them within its sphere by virtue of the treaties, conventions or other arrangements mentioned in Article 2 of the public Convention of today's date.

Article 5

In order to insure the good working of their reciprocal engagements, the two High Contracting Parties will at all times frankly and loyally enter into communication with regard to anything that concerns matters affecting in common their special interests in Manchuria.

In the event that these special interests should come to be threatened, the two High Contracting Parties will agree upon the measures to be taken with a view to common action or to the support to be accorded for the safeguarding and the defense of those interests.

Article 6

The present Convention shall be strictly confidential between the two High Contracting Parties.

In faith of which, the undersigned, duly authorized by their respective

Governments, have signed this
thereto.

Done at St. Petersburg, July 4,
of the seventh month of the forty

Secret Conven

The Imperial Government of Ru
Japan, desirous of making precise
secret Conventions concluded bet
1910, in order to avoid all cause
special interests in Manchuria and
the line of demarcation fixed by th
Convention of July 30, 1907, an
interests in Inner Mongolia, and ha

Art

Starting from the point of intersect
122° East of Greenwich, the above-n
the course of the Oulountchourh R
the line of the watershed between th
River; thence it follows the frontier li
kiang and Inner Mongolia until r
frontier between Inner Mongolia and

Artic

Inner Mongolia is divided into two pa
to the East, of the meridian of Pekin
The Imperial Government of Russ
respect the Japanese special interests
the East of the meridian above indica
of Japan undertakes to recognize and
terests in the part of Inner Mongolia t

Article

The present Convention shall be stric
igh Contracting Parties.
n faith of which, the undersigned, d

their respectiv
affixed their se
Done at St
of the seventh

The Imperial
Japan, desirir
by their secr
1912, have a
above-mentio

The two Hig
demand that
third Power
communicati
upon the me
about.

In the event
ment as prov
one of the C
by the pred
demand of
Contracting
agreement

The condit
its armed c
preceding a
fected, will
Contracting

Article 4

It is fully understood, however, that neither of the High Contracting Parties will be bound to lend its ally the armed assistance contemplated by Article 2 of the present Convention unless it has assured itself of cooperation, on the part of its allies, corresponding to the gravity of the impending conflict.

Article 5

The present Convention will come into force immediately after the date of signature, and will continue in effect until July 14, 1921.

In case neither of the High Contracting Parties should have given notice, twelve months prior to the expiration of that period, of its intention to bring the effectiveness of the Convention to an end, it will continue in force until the expiration of one year from the date on which one or the other of the High Contracting Parties shall have denounced it.

Article 6

The present Convention shall remain strictly confidential between the two High Contracting Parties.

In faith of which, the undersigned, duly authorized by their respective Governments, have signed this Convention and have affixed their seals thereto.

Done at Petrograd, July 3, 1916, corresponding to the third day of the seventh month of the fifth year of Taisho.

Motono
Sazonow

44

Abdication of the Romanovs, March 1917

Imperial Russia came to an abrupt end on March 12, 1917, when the old government, overrun by a revolutionary civilian mob and defiant soldiers, ceased to function. The remarkable ease with which the monarchy collapsed, first in the capital and then throughout the country, stunned everyone. Immediately two revolutionary institutions emerged to deal with the resulting confusion: the *soviets*, or self-appointed committees representing the victorious revolutionary mob; and the *Provisional Government*, whose members represented a solid cross section of the educated public.

Technically, between March 12 and 16, Russia still had a tsar. Nicholas II stayed at the General Headquarters at Mogilev until March 13, when he left for Petrograd. His train never reached its destination, for it was rerouted to Pskov, the Headquarters of the Northern Front. All military leaders the tsar consulted, including his uncle the Grand Duke Nicholas, urged him to abdicate in favor of his son Alexei with the tsar's brother Grand Duke Michael acting as regent. In the afternoon of March 15, Nicholas II signed documents to this effect. In the evening, pleading inability to part with his "beloved son," he changed his mind and abdicated in favor of his brother. Michael was willing to accept "only if and when our great people, having elected by universal suffrage a Constituent Assembly to determine the form of government and lay down the fundamental law of the new Russian State, invest me with such a power." The Russian people had no desire to make such an offer. The three-hundred-year-old Romanov dynasty, which had been founded by a Michael, technically expired with another Michael.

From *London Times*, March 19, 1917, p. 10, col. 4.

Abdication of Nicholas II, March 15, 1917

By the Grace of God, We, Nicholas II, Emperor of All the Russias, Czar of Poland, Grand Duke of Finland, etc., to all our faithful subjects be it known:

In the days of a great struggle against a foreign enemy who has been endeavoring for three years to enslave our country, it pleased God to send Russia a further painful trial.

Internal troubles threatened to have a fatal effect on the further progress of this obstinate war. The destinies of Russia, the honor of her heroic Army, the happiness of the people and the whole future of our beloved country demand that the war should be conducted at all costs to a victorious end.

The cruel enemy is making his last efforts and the moment is near when our valiant Army, in concert with our glorious Allies, will finally overthrow the enemy.

In these decisive days in the life of Russia we have thought that we owed to our people the close union and organization of all its forces for the realization of a rapid victory; for which reason, in agreement with the Imperial Duma, we have recognized that it is for the good of the country that we should abdicate the Crown of the Russian State and lay down the Supreme Power.

Not wishing to separate ourself from our beloved son, we bequeath our heritage to our brother, the Grand Duke Michael Alexandrovitch, with our blessing for the future of the Throne of the Russian State.

We bequeath it to our brother to govern in full union with the national representatives sitting in the Legislative Institutions, and to take his inviolable oath to them in the name of our well-beloved country.

We call upon all faithful sons of our native land to fulfil their sacred and patriotic duty of obeying the Czar at the painful moment of national trials and to aid him, together with the representatives of the nation, to conduct the Russian State in the way of prosperity and glory.

May God help Russia.

Declaration from the Throne by Grand Duke Michael, March 16, 1917

A heavy task has been intrusted to me by the will of my brother, who has given me the Imperial Throne at a time of unprecedented war and domestic strife.

Animated by the same feelings as the entire nation—namely, that the welfare of the country overshadows all other interests—I am firmly resolved to accept the Supreme Power only if this should be the desire of our great people, who must, by means of a plebiscite, through their representatives in the Constituent Assembly, establish the form of government and the new fundamental laws of the Russian State.

Invoking God's blessing, I therefore request all citizens of Russia to obey the Provisional Government, set up on the initiative of the Duma and invested with plenary powers, until, within as short a time as possible, the Constituent Assembly, elected on a basis of universal, equal and secret suffrage, shall express the will of the nation regarding the form of government to be adopted.

CHRONOLOGICAL TABLE

1689–1725   Reign of Peter I, the Great (sole ruler after the death of Ivan V in 1696).

1695–1696   Azov campaigns of Peter the Great and the seizure of the town of Azov.

1695–1697   Russian conquest of Kamchatka.

1697–1698   Peter the Great's first journey abroad (Prussia, Holland, England, and Poland).

1698   Revolt of the *streltsi* crushed; Peter the Great begins modernization of Russia by ordering the shaving of beards and wearing of Western clothes.

1700   Peter the Great adopts the Julian Calendar for Russia and suspends the patriarchate.

1700–1721   Northern War between Russia and Sweden over control of the Baltic ends in Treaty of Nystadt, giving Russia a "Window to the West," the Baltic region.

1703   Founding of St. Petersburg; the first Russian newspaper, *Vedomosti* (News) appears in Moscow.

1704   Reform of the alphabet.

1705   Beard tax introduced.

1705–1708   Revolts against Peter the Great's policies in Astrakhan, Bashkiria, and the Don region.

1708   Local government reforms; eight *gubernias* organized.

1709   Russian victory over Charles XII and *Hetman* Mazepa at Poltava; Ukraine loses its autonomy.

1710   Population census.

1711   Pruth campaign against the Turks; Russia loses Azov; monetary reform; establishment of the Senate to supervise administration.

1713   Capital of Russia transferred from Moscow to St. Petersburg.

1714   Decrees on primogeniture and education of nobles.

1715   Naval Academy founded in St. Petersburg.

1715–1717   Russian expedition to Central Asia.

1716–1717   Peter the Great's second visit to Western Europe (Holland and France).

1718   Trial and death of Tsarevich Alexei; establishment of the collegium system of central administration.

1719   Construction of the Ladoga Canal begun (completed in 1731).

1721	Peter the Great assumes the title of Emperor; Holy Synod established.
1721–1723	Russo-Persian War.
1722	Table of Ranks introduced; law on imperial succession.
1724	Russian Academy of Sciences chartered; Pososhkov completes *A Book on Poverty and Wealth.*
1725	Death of Peter the Great.
1725–1727	Reign of Catherine I.
1725–1729	First expedition of Captain Bering to find the limits of America (second expedition from 1732–1741).
1727–1730	Reign of Peter II (grandson of Peter the Great).
1730–1740	Reign of Anna (daughter of Ivan V) and her favorite, Biron (Bühren).
1733–1743	Kamchatka scientific expedition headed by G. F. Müller, J. G. Gmelin, S. P. Krasheninnikov, and others.
1736–1739	War with Turkey ending in Treaty of Belgrade; Russia regains Azov.
1736	Term of military service for nobles reduced to twenty-five years.
1740–1741	Reign of the infant emperor, Ivan VI.
1741–1761	Reign of Elizabeth, youngest daughter of Peter the Great.
1741–1743	War with Sweden; Treaty of Abö gives Russia a portion of Finland.
1744	Death penalty abolished in Russia.
1747–1762	Architect Rastrelli beautifies St. Petersburg with such structures as Winter Palace, Smolny Convent, and Peterhof Palace.
1753	Abolition of internal customs.
1755	University of Moscow chartered.
1756–1762	Russia's participation in the Seven Years' War.
1760	Nobles granted the right to exile their serfs to Siberia; Russian forces invade Berlin.
1761–1762	Reign of Peter III.
1762	Nobles freed from obligatory state service.
1762–1796	Reign of Catherine II, the Great.
1764	Final secularization of church lands; church lands placed under management of the Economic Collegium; Russo-Prussian alliance and secret convention concerning Poland; abolition of the office of *hetman* in the Ukraine.
1765	The Free Economic Society founded in St. Petersburg; nobles granted the right to exile their serfs to hard labor.
1766	Annexation of the Aleutian Islands.

1767–1768	Legislative Commission works unsuccessfully to prepare a new code of laws.
1768–1774	War with Turkey ends in Treaty of Kutchuk-Kainardzhi ceding Black Sea steppes to Russia.
1772	First partition of Poland by Russia, Prussia, and Austria; uprising of the Iaik or Ural cossacks.
1773–1775	Peasants revolt led by Pugachev engulfs the Volga region and the Don basin.
1775	*Gubernia* reforms; breakup of the Zaporozhian or Ukrainian cossacks.
1781–1786	Absorption of the Ukraine and the Crimea into the Russian Empire.
1782–1785	Architect Quarenghi builds the Hermitage.
1783–1784	Architect Starov builds the Taurida Palace.
1785	Charter to the Nobility and Charter to the Towns issued.
1787–1792	War with Turkey; Treaty of Jassy.
1790	Radishchev sentenced to death for writing *A Journey from St. Petersburg to Moscow*, then exiled for life to Siberia instead.
1793	Second partition of Poland by Russia and Prussia.
1795	Third partition of Poland by Russia, Prussia, and Austria.
1796–1801	Reign of Paul.
1797	Law issued on succession to the throne according to genealogical seniority.
1798	Russia joins the Second Coalition against France.
1799	Russian forces under Suvorov campaign in North Italy and Switzerland; Russian-American Company chartered (liquidated in 1862).
1800	Paul allies with Napoleon against England; import of foreign books into Russia prohibited.
1801	Paul assassinated; Georgia annexed by Russia.
1801–1825	Reign of Alexander I.
1801–1804	Internal reforms.
1802	Reorganization of Senate; establishment of Ministries and Committee of Ministers.
1804	University Code granted; Universities of Kazan and Kharkov chartered.
1805	Russia joins the Third Coalition against France; defeat at Austerlitz.
1806–1812	War with Turkey ends in Treaty of Bucharest and annexation of Bessarabia.
1807	Treaty of Tilsit with Napoleon; Russia joins the Continental System.
1807–1811	Reforms of Speranskii.

1809   Russian conquest of Finland.
1812   Napoleon's invasion of and retreat from Russia.
1814   Alexander I enters Paris in triumph.
1814–1815   Congress of Vienna.
1815   Holy Alliance and Quadruple Alliance conceived; Russia
            acquires the Duchy of Warsaw.
1816–1819   Serfdom abolished in Baltic provinces (landless emancipa-
            tion).
1816   Union of Salvation, the first Decembrist Society, organized.
1817   Union of Welfare, the second Decembrist Society, or-
            ganized.
1819   University of St. Petersburg chartered.
1821   Division of Decembrist Societies into Northern and South-
            ern Branches.
1822   Reforms of Speranskii in Siberia.
1825   Death of Alexander I; Decembrist Revolt.
1825–1855   Reign of Nicholas I.
1826   Trial and punishment of the Decembrist leaders.
1826–1828   War with Persia ends in Treaty of Turkmanchai and an-
            nexation of Armenia.
1828–1829   War with Turkey ends in Treaty of Adrianople and Greek
            independence.
1830–1831   Polish uprising against Russian rule.
1832   Uvarov enunciates the three principles of autocracy, Ortho-
            doxy, and nationality; duchy of Warsaw incorporated
            into Russia.
1833   Publication of the *Polnoe Sobranie Zakonov* (Complete
            Collection of the Laws).
1834   Kiev University founded.
1835–1844   216 peasant uprisings recorded.
1836   Gogol's *Inspector General* and Chadaev's *Philosophical
            Letters* appear.
1837   Pushkin fatally wounded in duel; first railway opened in
            Russia, linking St. Petersburg and Tsarskoe Selo.
1837–1841   Kiselev introduces reforms affecting state peasants.
1842   Gogol's *Dead Souls* appears.
1845   Russian Geographic Society founded.
1847   Herzen exiles himself permanently from Russia; arrest and
            trial of members of the Society of Sts. Cyril and Metho-
            dious; Belinskii writes *Letter to Gogol*.
1849   Dostoevskii sentenced to forced labor in Siberia; Russian
            forces intervene in Hungary.
1851   Herzen's letter to Michelet, *Russia and Socialism*.

1853–1856	Crimean War ends in Treaty of Paris and diplomatic humiliation of Russia.
1855–1881	Reign of Alexander II.
1857	Alexander appoints Secret Committee to plan steps toward abolishment of serfdom.
1858	Russia annexes the Amur Basin and Maritime Provinces by terms of the Treaty of Aigun.
1860	Treaty of Peking confirms Russia's gains; city of Vladivostok founded; State Bank chartered.
1861	Manifesto on emancipation of serfs published; re-establishment of local government in Polish provinces.
1861–1862	Peasant unrest and student revolutionary agitation.
1861–1863	Activity of the secret revolutionary organization *Zemlia i Volia* (Land and Freedom).
1861–1876	Activity of Bakunin in Western Europe.
1862	Turgeniev's *Fathers and Sons* published; Rumiantsev Public Library (now Lenin State Public Library) opened in Moscow; arrest of Chernyshevskii and Pisarev; closing of Sunday Schools.
1863	Uprising in Poland, Lithunia, and Belorussia against Russian rule; new University Statute promulgated.
1864	Judicial reform; *Zemstvo* Statute; Dostoevskii's *Memoirs from Underground.*
1865–1885	Russian conquest of Central Asia.
1865	Censorship relaxed; University of Odessa chartered.
1866	Attempt on Alexander II's life by Karakozov.
1867	Alaska and the Aleutian Islands sold to the United States; meeting of a Panslav Congress in Moscow; Katkov turns to Russification.
1869	Tolstoy's *War and Peace*; University of Warsaw chartered; Bakunin and Nechaev write *Catechism of the Revolutionary.*
1870	Municipal reforms; repudiation of Black Sea clauses of the Treaty of Paris of 1856; Lenin (Ulianov) born in Simbirsk.
1871	Danilevskii's *Russia and Europe* published; London Convention on the Straits.
1872	Translation of Marx's *Das Kapital* published in Russia.
1873	Three Emperors' League formed.
1874	Military reform; compulsory military service introduced; Mussorgskii's *Boris Godunov* produced.
1876	"Land and Freedom," populist secret society organized.
1877–1878	Russo-Turkish War.

1878	Treaty of San Stefano; Congress of Berlin; Tolstoy's *Anna Karenina*.
1879	"Land and Freedom" split into "People's Will" and "Black Partition"; Stalin (Dzhugashvili) born.
1880	Dostoevskii's *Brothers Karamazov*; Plekhanov, father of Russian Marxism, flees to Western Europe.
1881	Alexander II assassinated; Three Emperors' League revived (renewed in 1884 for three years).
1881–1894	Reign of Alexander III.
1882	Foundation of the Peasant Bank; reduction of peasant redemption payments; establishment of factory inspection.
1883	Plekhanov organizes first Russian Marxist group, "The Emancipation of Labor," in Geneva.
1884	Reactionary regulations for universities.
1885	Land Bank for the Nobility founded.
1886	Abolition of soul tax throughout the Empire (except Siberia).
1887	Reinsurance Treaty between Russia and Germany signed; attempted assassination of Alexander III by Lenin's brother.
1888	University of Tomsk chartered.
1891–1905	Construction of Trans-Siberian Railway.
1891–1892	The great famine in Russian agricultural regions.
1892	Secret Franco-Russian military convention against the Triple Alliance concluded.
1892–1903	Witte serves as Minister of Communication, Finance, and Commerce.
1894–1917	Reign of Nicholas II.
1896	Russo-Chinese alliance against Japan signed.
1897	First general population census in Russia; working day limited to eleven and one-half hours; Russia adopts gold standard; Lenin exiled to Siberia.
1898	First conference of the Russian Social Democratic party in Minsk; Nicholas II launches a drive for world peace and disarmament; Russians lease Port Arthur from the Chinese.
1900	Boxer Rebellion in China against foreign influence; Russian forces occupy Manchuria.
1902	Socialist Revolutionary party is formed to protect peasant interests; wave of peasant unrest; Lenin's *What Is to Be Done?* and Gorky's *Lower Depths* appear.
1903	Wave of industrial strikes hits Russia; Russian Social Democratic party splits into *Bolshevik* and *Menshevik* factions.
1904	Japan attacks Russian forces at Port Arthur without declara-

tion of war; Plehve assassinated; Baltic fleet sails for Far East and meets disaster at Tsushima Strait.

1905　　Surrender of Port Arthur; outbreak of general strike in St. Petersburg; "Bloody Sunday"; formation of first Soviet of Workers; mutiny on battleship *Potemkin;* Treaty of Portsmouth signed; October Manifesto promises a Duma for Russia and extends suffrage rights, freedom of speech, press, and assembly; Moscow uprising; cancellation of peasant redemption payments.

1905–1906　Witte's Prime Ministership.

1906　　France grants Russia a loan of two and one-half billion francs; First Duma opened and dissolved; Witte dismissed; Stolypin forms Cabinet; Vyborg Manifesto; beginning of the Stolypin agrarian reforms.

1907　　Meeting and dissolution of Second Duma; new electoral law published; Anglo-Russian Entente divides spheres of influence in Persia, Afghanistan and Tibet; meeting of the Third Duma.

1908　　Bosnian Crisis.

1910　　Death of Tolstoy.

1911　　Stolypin assassinated in Kiev.

1912　　Bolshevik newspaper *Pravda* makes first appearance; election of Fourth Duma.

1912–1913　Balkan Wars.

1914　　Outbreak of World War I; military disaster at the Mazurian Lakes; victory in Galicia; arrest of Bolshevik deputies of the Duma.

1915　　Retreat of Russian forces from Galicia; formation of the "Progressive bloc" in the Duma.

1916　　Rasputin murdered.

1917　　General strike and uprising in Petrograd; Romanov dynasty toppled; Nicholas II abdicates; imperial period of Russian history ends; Soviet period begins.

SELECTED BIBLIOGRAPHY

There is an impressive amount of literature in English on the history of imperial Russia. Some of this material (and in many ways the best of it) has been written by American and English scholars, while some has been made available to English-speaking readers through translations. The items listed below are representative of the many fine works that deal with the complexities of Russia's past. They have been selected not because I necessarily agree with their views, but because they might provide the reader with valuable keys to a fair and accurate understanding of problems that have been either touched on in this collection, or treated in more basic texts. The selected literature is divided into three parts: (1) General works and basic texts that are currently in use or were in use in the recent past; (2) Monographic literature (except works cited in the present collection); and (3) Periodical literature. The growing number of doctoral dissertations that have been completed in American universities since the end of World War II, and works in foreign languages have not been listed.

General Works and Basic Texts

Billington, James H. *The Icon and the Axe: An Interpretative History of Russian Culture,* New York: Knopf, 1965.

Blum, Jerome, *Lord and Peasant in Russia from the Ninth to the Nineteenth Century,* Princeton: Princeton University Press, 1961.

Clarkson, Jesse D., *A History of Russia,* New York: Random House, 1961.

Dvornik, Francis, *The Slavs in European History and Civilization,* New Brunswick: Rutgers University Press, 1962.

Ellison, Herbert J., *History of Russia,* New York: Holt, Rinehart and Winston, Inc., 1964.

Florinsky, Michael T., *Russia: A History and an Interpretation,* New York: Macmillan, 1953, 2 vols.

——, *Russia: A Short History,* New York: Macmillan, 1964.

Harcave, Sidney S., *Readings in Russian History,* New York: Crowell, 1962. 2 vols.

——, *Russia: A History,* 5th ed. Philadelphia: Lippincott, 1964.

Johnson, W. H. E., *Russia's Educational Heritage,* Pittsburg: Carnegie Press, 1950.

Kerner, Robert J., *The Urge to the Sea: The Course of Russian History*, Berkeley: University of California Press, 1942.

Kirchner, Walther, *A History of Russia*, New York: Barnes & Noble, 1959.

Kliuchevskii, Vasili O., *A History of Russia*, New York: Russell & Russell, 1960. 5 vols.

Lawrence, John, *A History of Russia*, New York: Farrar, Straus & Giroux, 1960.

Lerroy-Beaulieu, A., *The Empire of the Tsars*, New York: Putnam, 1893–1896. 3 vols.

Letiche, John M., ed., *A History of Russian Economic Thought: Ninth through the Eighteenth Centuries*. Translated with the collaboration of Basil Dmytryshyn and Richard A. Pierce. Berkeley: University of California Press, 1964.

Lossky, N. O., *History of Russian Philosophy*, New York: International Universities Press, 1952.

Lyashchenko, P. I., *History of the National Economy of Russia to the 1917 Revolution*, New York: Macmillan, 1949.

Masaryk, Thomas G., *The Spirit of Russia. Studies in History, Literature and Philosophy*, 2d ed. New York: Macmillan, 1955. 2 vols.

Mavor, James, *An Economic History of Russia*, New York: Dutton, 1925. 2 vols.

Mazour, Anatole, G., *Russia: Tsarist and Communist*, New York: Van Nostrand, 1961.

Miliukov, P., *Outlines of Russian Culture*, Philadelphia: University of Pennsylvania Press, 1942. 3 vols.

Mirskii, Dmitrii P., *A History of Russian Literature*, edited and abridged by Francis J. Whitfield. New York: Knopf, 1949.

———, *Russia: A Social History*, London: Cressent Press, 1931.

Pares, Sir Bernard, *A History of Russia*, definitive edition. New York: Knopf, 1953.

Platonov, Sergei F., *History of Russia*, New York: Macmillan, 1925.

Pokrovskii, Mikhail N., *History of Russia From the Earliest Times to the Rise of Commercial Capitalism*, New York: International Publishers, 1931.

Rambaud, A. N., *History of Russia From the Earliest Times to 1877*, New York: Collier, 1900. 2 vols.

Riasanovsky, Nicholas V., *A History of Russia*, New York: Oxford University Press, 1963.

Rice, Tamara T., *A Concise History of Russian Art*, New York: Praeger, 1963.

Riha, Thomas, ed. *Readings in Russian Civilization*, Chicago: University of Chicago Press, 1964. 3 vols.

Spector, Ivar, *An Introduction to Russian History and Culture*, New York: Van Nostrand, 1961.

Strakhovsky, Leonid I., ed., *A Handbook of Slavic Studies*, Cambridge, Mass.: Harvard University Press, 1949.

Sumner, Benedict H., *A Short History of Russia*, New York: Reynal & Hitchcock, 1943.

Tompkins, Stuart R., *Russia Through the Ages, From the Scythians to the Soviets*, Englewood Cliffs, New Jersey: Prentice-Hall, 1940.

Vernadsky, George, *A History of Russia*, 9th ed., New Haven: Yale University Press, 1961.

————, Political and Diplomatic History of Russia, Boston: Little, Brown & Co., 1936.

Vucinich, Alexander, Science in Russian Culture: A History to 1860, Stanford: Stanford University Press, 1963.

Wallace, D. M., Russia, New York: Holt, Rinehart and Winston, Inc., 1905.

Walsh, Warren B., ed. Readings in Russian History, 4th ed., Syracuse, New York: Syracuse University Press, 1963. 3 vols.

————, Russia and the Soviet Union: A Modern History, Ann Arbor: University of Michigan Press, 1958.

Wren, Melvin C., The Course of Russian History, 2d ed. New York: Macmillan, 1962.

Monographic Literature

Allen, W. E. D. and Muratoff, Paul, Caucasian Battlefields: A History of the Wars on the Turco-Caucasian Border, 1821–1921, New York: Cambridge University Press, 1953.

Almendingen, E. M., The Emperor Alexander II, London: Lane, 1962.

Anderson, Thornton, ed., Masters of Russian Marxism, New York: Appleton-Century-Crofts, 1963.

Anthony, K., The Memoirs of Catherine II, New York: Knopf, 1927.

Bain, R. N., The Daughter of Peter the Great, London: Constable, 1899.

————, Peter III, Emperor of Russia, London: Constable, 1902.

Baron, Samuel H., Plekhanov: The Father of Russian Marxism, Stanford: Stanford University Press, 1963.

Billington, James H., Mikhailovsky and Russian Populism, Oxford: Oxford University Press, 1958.

Black, Cyril, ed., Transformation of Russian Society: Aspects of Social Change Since 1861, Cambridge, Mass.: Harvard University Press, 1960.

Bowman, H. E., Vissarion Belinski: A Study in the Origin of Social Criticism in Russia, Cambridge, Mass.: Harvard University Press, 1954.

Carr, E. H., Michael Bakunin, New York: Macmillan, 1937.

de Caulaincourt, General, Duke of Vicenza, With Napoleon in Russia: Memoirs, New York: Morrow, 1935.

Chernyshevsky, N. G., Selected Philosophical Essays, Moscow: Foreign Languages Publishing House, 1953.

Christoff, Peter K., An Introduction to Nineteenth-Century Russian Slavophilism: A Study in Ideas of A. S. Khomiakov, The Hague: Mouton, 1961.

Churchill, R. P., The Anglo-Russian Convention of 1907, Cedar Rapids, Iowa: Torch Press, 1939.

Curtiss, John S., Church and State in Russia: The Last Years of the Empire, 1900–1917, New York: Columbia University Press, 1940.

————, The Russian Army Under Nicholas I (1825–1855), Durham, N.C.: Duke University Press, 1965.

Custine, Astolphe L. L., The Empire of the Czar . . . , London: Longmans, 1843.

Dobroliubov, N. A., Selected Philosophical Essays, Moscow: Foreign Languages Publishing House, 1956.

Fischer, George, *Russian Liberalism: From Gentry to Intelligentsia*, Cambridge: Harvard University Press, 1958.

Florinsky, Michael T., *The End of the Russian Empire*, New Haven: Yale University Press, 1931.

Footman, David, *Red Prelude: The Life of the Russian Terrorist Zhelyabov*, New Haven: Yale University Press, 1945.

Gibbs, Peter, *Crimean Blunder*, New York: Holt, Rinehart and Winston, Inc., 1960.

Gleason, John H., *The Genesis of Russophobia in Great Britain*, Cambridge: Harvard University Press, 1950.

Golder, Frank A., ed., *Documents of Russian History, 1914–1917*, New York: Appleton-Century-Crofts, 1927.

——, *Russian Expansion on the Pacific, 1641–1850*, London: Clark, 1914.

Gooch, George P., *Catherine the Great and Other Studies*, New York: Longmans, 1954.

Graham, Stephen, *The Life of Alexander II, Tsar of Russia*, New Haven: Yale University Press, 1935.

——, *Peter the Great*, London: Benn, 1929.

Grey, Ian, *Catherine the Great*, Philadelphia: Lippincott, 1962.

——, *Peter the Great*, Philadelphia: Lippincott, 1960.

Grunwald, Constantine, *Peter the Great*, Philadelphia: Saunders, 1956.

——, *Tsar Nicholas I.*, New York: Macmillan, 1955.

Gurko, V. I., *Features and Figures of the Past: Government and Opinion in the Reign of Nicholas II*, Stanford: Stanford University Press, 1939.

Haimson, Leopold H., *The Russian Marxists and the Origins of Bolshevism*, Cambridge: Harvard University Press, 1955.

Hans, N. A., *History of Russian Educational Policy, 1701–1917*, London: King, 1931.

Harcave, Sidney, *First Blood*, New York: Macmillan, 1964.

Hare, Richard, *Pioneers of Russian Social Thought*, 2d ed., New York: Random House, 1964.

——, *Portraits of Russian Personalities Between Reform and Revolution*, New York: Oxford University Press, 1959.

Harper, Samuel H., *The New Electoral Law for the Russian Duma*, Chicago: University of Chicago Press, 1908.

Haxthausen-Abbenburg, August F., *The Russian Empire, Its People, Institutions and Resources*, London: Chapman & Hall, 1856.

Hecht, D. *Russian Radicals Look to America, 1825–1894.* Cambridge, Mass.: Harvard University Press, 1947.

Helmreich, Ernst C., *The Diplomacy of the Balkan Wars, 1912–1913*, Cambridge: Harvard University Press, 1938.

Herzen, Alexander, *My Past and Thoughts: Memoirs*, London: Chatto & Winous, 1924–1927. 6 vols.

Hodgetts, Edward A. B., *The Life of Catherine the Great of Russia*, London: Methuen, 1914.

Hough, Richard, *The Potemkin Mutiny*, Englewood Cliffs, New Jersey: Prentice-Hall, 1960.

Izvolsky, A. P., *Recollections of a Foreign Minister*, Garden City, N.Y.: Doubleday, 1921.
Jackson, W. A. Douglas, *Russo-Chinese Borderlands*, New York: Van Nostrand, 1962.
Jelavich, Barbara, *A Century of Russian Foreign Policy, 1814–1914*, Philadelphia: Lippincott, 1964.
———, *Russia and the Rumanian National Cause, 1858–1859*, Bloomington, Ind.: Indiana University Press, 1959.
Jelavich, Charles, *Tsarist Russia and Balkan Nationalism: Russian Influence in the Internal Affairs of Bulgaria and Serbia, 1879–1886*, Berkeley: University of California Press, 1958.
Kaplan, Herbert H., *The First Partition of Poland*, New York: Columbia University Press, 1962.
Karamzin, A. M., *Letters of a Russian Traveler, 1789–1790*, ed. by F. Jonas, New York: Columbia University Press, 1957.
Karpovich, Michael, *Imperial Russia, 1801–1917*, New York: Holt, Rinehart and Winston, Inc., 1932.
Katz, Martin, *Mikhail N. Katkov, 1818–1887: A Political Biography*, The Hague: Mouton, 1966.
Kliuchevsky, V. O., *Peter the Great*, New York: St. Martin's, 1958.
Kohn, Hans, *The Mind of Modern Russia*, New Brunswick, New Jersey: Rutgers University Press, 1955.
———, *Pan-Slavism*, South Bend, Ind.: University of Notre Dame Press, 1953.
Kokovtsev, V. N., *Out of My Past: The Memoirs of Count Kokovtsev*, Stanford: Stanford University Press, 1935.
Kononenko, Konstantyn, *Ukraine and Russia: A History of the Economic Relations . . . 1654–1917*, Marquette, Wisconsin: Marquette University Press, 1958.
Korff, Baron S. A., *Russia's Foreign Relations During the Last Half Century*, New York: Macmillan, 1922.
Kornilov, Alexander, *Modern Russian History*, New York: Knopf, 1952. 2 vols.
Kropotkin, P., *Memoirs of a Revolutionist*, Boston: Houghton-Mifflin, 1930.
Kucherov, Samuel, *Courts, Lawyers and Trials Under the Last Three Tsars*, New York: Praeger, 1953.
Lampert, E., *Studies in Rebellion*, New York: Praeger, 1957.
Lang, David M., *The First Russian Radical: Alexander Radishchev, 1749–1802*, London: G. Allen, 1959.
Langer, William L., *The Franco-Russian Alliance, 1890–1894*, Cambridge: Harvard University Press, 1929.
Laserson, Max M., *The American Impact on Russia: Diplomatic and Ideological, 1784–1917*, New York: Macmillan, 1950.
Lederer, Ivo J., ed., *Russian Foreign Policy: Essays in Historical Perspective*, New Haven: Yale University Press, 1962.
Lensen, George A., *The Russian Push Toward Japan: Russo-Japanese Relations, 1697–1875*, Princeton: Princeton University Press, 1959.
Leslie, R. F., *Reform and Insurrection in Russian Poland, 1856–1865*, London: University of London Press, 1963.
Levin, Alfred, *The Second Duma: A Study of the Social Democratic Party and*

the Russian Constitutional Experiment, New Haven: Yale University Press, 1940.

Levitsky, Serge L., *The Russian Duma: Studies in Parliamentary Procedure, 1906–1917*, New York: Fordham, 1958.

Lobanov-Rostovsky, Andrei, *Russia and Europe, 1789–1825*, Durham, North Carolina: Duke University Press, 1947.

——, *Russia and Europe, 1825–1878*, Ann Arbor, Mich.: Wahr, 1954.

Lord, Robert H., *Second Partition of Poland: A Study in Diplomatic History*, Cambridge, Mass: Harvard University Press, 1915.

de Madariaga, Isabel, *Britain, Russia and the Armed Neutrality of 1780*, New Haven, Conn.: Yale University Press, 1962.

Malia, Martin E., *Alexander Herzen and the Birth of Russian Socialism*, Cambridge, Mass.: Harvard University Press, 1961.

Malozemoff, Andrew, *Russian Far Eastern Policy, 1881–1904*, Berkeley: University of California Press, 1958.

Marriott, John A., *The Eastern Question: An Historical Study in European Diplomacy*, Oxford: Clarendon, 1940.

Mathewson, R. W. Jr., *The Positive Hero in Russian Literature*, New York: Columbia University Press, 1958.

Maynard, Sir John, *Russia in Flux*, New York: Collier, 1962.

Mazour, Anatole G., *The First Russian Revolution, 1825*, Berkeley: University of California Press, 1937.

Mendel, Arthur P., *Dilemmas of Progress in Tsarist Russia: Legal Marxism and Legal Populism*, Cambridge, Mass.: Harvard University Press, 1961.

Menshutkin, B. N., *Russia's Lomonosov: Chemist, Courtier, Physicist, Poet*, Princeton: Princeton University Press, 1952.

Meyer, Alfred G., *Leninism*, Cambridge, Mass.: Harvard University Press, 1957.

Miliukov, Pavel N., *Russia and Its Crisis*, Chicago: Chicago University Press, 1906.

Miller, Margaret S., *The Economic Development of Russia, 1905–1914*. London: King, 1926.

Mirsky, Dimitrii S., *Contemporary Russian Literature, 1881–1925*, New York: Knopf, 1926.

von Mohrenschildt, Dimitri, *Russia in the Intellectual Life of the Eighteenth-Century France*, New York: Columbia University Press, 1936.

Monas, Sidney, *The Third Section: Police and Society in Russia Under Nicholas I*, Cambridge, Mass.: Harvard University Press, 1961.

Mosely, Philip E., *Russian Diplomacy and the Opening of the Eastern Question in 1838 and 1839*, Cambridge, Mass.: Harvard University Press, 1934.

Mosse, Werner E., *Alexander II and the Modernization of Russia*, New York: Macmillan, 1958.

Nechkina, M. V., ed., *Russia in the Nineteenth Century*, Ann Arbor, Mich.: Edwards, 1953.

O'Brien, C. Brickford, *Russia Under Two Tsars, 1682–1689*, Berkeley: University of California Press, 1952.

Okun, S. B., *The Russian-American Company*, Cambridge, Mass.: Harvard University Press, 1951.

Oliva, Lawrence Jay, *Misalliance: A Study of French Policy in Russia during the*

Seven Years' War, New York: New York University Press, 1964.

———, ed., *Russia and the West From Peter to Khrushchev*, Boston: Heath, 1965.

Owen, Launcelot A., *The Russian Peasant Movement, 1906–1917*, London: King, 1937.

Page, Stanley W., ed., *Russia in Revolution*, New York: Van Nostrand, 1965.

Paleologue, Georges M., *The Enigmatic Czar: The Life of Alexander I of Russia*, New York: Harper, 1938.

Pares, Sir Bernard, *The Fall of the Russian Monarchy*, New York: Knopf, 1939.

———, *Russia and Reform*, London: Constable, 1907.

Pasvolsky, Leo, *Russia in the Far East*, New York: Macmillan, 1922.

———, *Agricultural Russia on the Eve of the Revolution*, London: Routledge, 1930.

Petrovich, Michael B., *The Emergence of Russian Panslavism, 1856–1870*, New York: Columbia University Press, 1956.

Pierce, Richard A., *Russian Central Asia, 1867–1917*, Berkeley: University of California Press, 1960.

Pipes, Richard, ed., *Karamzin's Memoir on Ancient and Modern Russia*, Cambridge, Mass.: Harvard University Press, 1959.

———, ed., *The Russian Intelligentsia*, New York: Columbia University Press, 1961.

———, *Social Democracy and the St. Petersburg Labor Movement, 1885–1897*, Cambridge, Mass.: Harvard University Press, 1963.

Pisarev, Dmitry, *Selected Philosophical, Social and Political Essays*, Moscow: Foreign Languages Publishing House, 1958.

Prawdin, Michael, *The Unmentionable Nechaev: A Key to Bolshevism*, London: Roy, 1961.

Puryear, Vernon J., *England, Russia and the Straits Question, 1844–1856*, Berkeley: University of California Press, 1931.

Pushkarev, Sergei, *The Emergence of Modern Russia, 1801–1917*, New York: Holt, Rinehart and Winston, Inc., 1963.

Putnam, P., ed., *Seven Britons in Imperial Russia, 1698–1812*, Princeton: Princeton University Press, 1952.

Pyziur, Eugene, *The Doctrine of Anarchism of Michael A. Bakunin*, Milwaukee, Wisc.: Marquette University Press, 1955.

Radkey, Oliver H., *The Agrarian Foes of Bolshevism*, New York: New York: Columbia University Press, 1958.

Raeff, Marc, ed., *The Decembrist Movement*, Englewood Cliffs, New Jersey: Prentice-Hall, 1965.

———, *Michael Speransky: Statesman of Imperial Russia*, The Hague: Nijhoff, 1957.

———, ed., *Plans for Political Reform in Imperial Russia, 1730–1905*. Englewood Cliffs, New Yersey: Prentice-Hall, 1965.

———, *Siberia and the Reforms of 1822*, Seattle: University of Washington Press, 1956.

Reading, D. K., *The Anglo-Russian Commercial Treaty of 1734*, New Haven: Yale University Press, 1938.

Reddaway, W. F., ed., *Documents on Catherine the Great*, Cambridge, Eng.: Cambridge University Press, 1931.

Riasanovsky, N. V., *Nicholas I and Official Nationality in Russia, 1825–1855*, Berkeley: University of California Press, 1959.

———, *Russia and the West in the Teachings of the Slavophiles*, Cambridge, Mass.: Harvard University Press, 1952.

Robinson, Geroid T., *Rural Russia Under the Old Regime*, London: Longman's, 1932.

Rogger, Hans, *National Consciousness in Eighteenth-Century Russia*, Cambridge, Mass.: Harvard University Press, 1960.

Romanov, Boris A., *Russia in Manchuria, 1892–1906*, Ann Arbor, Mich.: Edwards, 1952.

Rosen, Baron R. R., *Forty Years of Diplomacy*, New York: Knopf, 1922. 2 vols.

Schuyler, E., *Peter the Great*, New York: Scribners, 1884. 2 vols.

Segur, Count Philippe-Raul de, *Napoleon's Russian Campaign*, Boston: Houghton Mifflin, 1958.

Seton-Watson, Hugh, *The Decline of Imperial Russia, 1855–1914*, New York: Praeger, 1952.

Skrine, Francis H., *The Expansion of Russia*, 3d ed., Cambridge, Mass.: Cambridge University Press, 1915.

Slonim, Marc, *The Epic of Russian Literature*, New York: Oxford University Press, 1964.

Soloveychik, George, *Potemkin: A Picture of Catherine's Russia*, London: Butterworth, 1939.

Spector, Ivar, *The First Russian Revolution: Its Impact on Asia*, Englewood Cliffs, New Jersey: Prentice-Hall, 1962.

Stavrou, Theofanis G. *Russian Interests in Palestine, 1882–1914*. Thessaloniki: Institute for the Balkan Studies, 1963.

Stepniak, S. M., *Underground Russia*, New York: Scribners, 1883.

Strakhovsky, L. I., *Alexander I of Russia*, New York: Norton, 1947.

Sumner, B. H., *Peter the Great and the Ottoman Empire*, Oxford: Blackwell, 1949.

———, *Peter the Great and the Emergence of Russia*, New York: Macmillan, 1951.

———, *Russia and the Balkans, 1870–1880*, Oxford: Clarendon, 1937.

Tarle, Evgenii V., *Napoleon's Invasion of Russia in 1812*, New York: Oxford University Press, 1942.

Thaden, Edward C., *Conservative Nationalism in Nineteenth Century Russia*, Seattle: University of Washington Press, 1964.

Thomas, B. P., *Russo-American Relations, 1815–1876*, Baltimore: The Johns Hopkins Press, 1930.

Thompson, G. S., *Catherine II and the Expansion of Russia*, New York: Macmillan, 1950.

Tompkins, Stuart R., *The Russian Intelligentsia: Makers of the Revolutionary State*, Norman, Okla.: University of Oklahoma Press, 1957.

———, *The Russian Mind: From Peter the Great Through the Enlightment*, Norman, Okla.: University of Oklahoma Press, 1957.

Treadgold, Donald W., *The Great Siberian Migration: Government and*

Peasant in Resettlement From Emancipation to the First World War,
Princeton: Princeton University Press, 1959.

——, *Lenin and His Rivals: The Struggle for Russia's Future, 1898–1906,*
New York: Praeger, 1955.

Ular, Alexander, *A Russo-Chinese Empire,* Westmister: Constable, 1904.

Vassilyev, A. T., *The Okhrana: The Russian Secret Police,* Philadelphia: Lippincott, 1930.

Venturi, Franco, *Roots of Revolution,* New York: Knopf, 1960.

Vinogradoff, Sir Paul, *Self-Government in Russia,* London: Constable, 1915.

Von Laue, Theodore H., *Sergei Witte and the Industrialization of Russia,* New
York: Columbia University Press, 1963.

Waliszewski, Kazimierz, *Paul the First of Russia, the Son of Catherine the
Great,* London: Heinemann, 1913.

——, *Peter the Great,* London: Heinemann, 1898.

——, *The Story of a Throne (Catherine II of Russia),* London: Heinemann,
1895.

Walkin, Jacob, *The Rise of Democracy in Pre-Revolutionary Russia: Political and
Social Institutions Under the Last Three Czars,* New York: Praeger, 1962.

Walsh, Edmund A., *The Fall of the Russian Empire,* New York: Blue Ribbon
Books, 1931.

White, John A., *The Diplomacy of the Russo-Japanese War,* Princeton: Princeton University Press, 1964.

Wiener, Leo., ed., *Anthology of Russian Literature From the Earliest Period to
the Present Time: The Nineteenth Century,* New York: Putnam, 1903.
Vol. 2.

Wolfe, Bertram, *Three Who Made a Revolution: Lenin, Trotsky, Stalin,* New
York: Dial, 1948.

Yarmolinsky, Avrahm, *Road to Revolution: A Century of Russian Radicalism,*
London: Cassell, 1957.

Zabriskie, Edward H., *American-Russian Rivalry in the Far East,* Philadelphia;
University of Pennsylvania Press, 1946.

Zernov, N., *The Russian Prophets: Khomiakov, Dostoevsky, Soloviev,* London:
Macmillan, 1944.

Zetlin, Mikhail O., *The Decembrists,* New York: International Universities Press,
1958.

Zilliacus, Konni, *The Russian Revolutionary Movement,* London: Rivers, 1905.

Periodical Literature

Adamov, E. A., "Documents Relating to Russian Policy During the American
Civil War," *Journal of Modern History,* vol. 2, no. 4 (December 1930),
pp. 603–611.

——, "Russia and the United States at the Time of the Civil War," *Journal
of Modern History,* vol. 2, no. 4 (December 1930), pp. 586–602.

Adams, Arthur E., "The Character of Pestel's Thought," *The American Slavic
and East European Review,* vol. 12, no. 2, (April 1953), pp. 153–161.

——, "Pobedonostsev and the Rule of Firmness," *Slavonic Review,* vol. 32,
no. 78 (December 1953), pp. 132–139.

Aldanov, Mark., "Count Witte," *Russian Review*, vol. I, no. 1 (November 1941), pp. 56–64.

———, "P. N. Durnovo—Prophet of War and Revolution," *Russian Review*, vol. 2, no. 1 (Autumn 1942), pp. 31–45.

Anderson, M. S., "English Views of Russia in the Age of Peter the Great," *The American Slavic and East European Review*, vol. 13, no. 2 (April 1954), pp. 200–214.

———. "Great Britain and the Russian Fleet, 1769–1770," *Slavonic Review*, vol. 31, no. 76 (December 1952), pp. 148–163.

———. "The Great Powers and the Russian Annexation of the Crimea, 1783–1784," *Slavonic Review*, vol. 38, no. 88 (December 1958), pp. 17–41.

———. "Samuel Bentham in Russia, 1779–1791," *The American Slavic and East European Review*, vol. 15, no. 2 (April 1956), pp. 157–172.

Askew, William C., "Russian Military Strength on the Eve of the Franco-Prussian War," *Slavonic Review*, vol. 30, no. 74 (December 1951), pp. 185–205.

Balmuth, Daniel, "The Origins of the Tsarist Epoch of Censorship Terror." *The American Slavic and East European Review*, vol. 19, no. 4 (December 1960), pp. 497–520.

Barghoorn, Frederick C., "The Philosophic Outlook of Chernyshevski: Materialism and Utilitarianism," *The American Slavic and East European Review*, vol. 6, no. 18–19 (December 1947), pp. 42–56.

———, "The Russian Radicals of the 1860s and the Problem of the Industrial Proletariat," *The American Slavic and East European Review*, vol. 2, no. 1 (March 1943), pp. 57–69.

Baron, Samuel H., "Legal Marxism and the Fate of Capitalism in Russia," *The American Slavic and East European Review*, vol. 16, no. 2 (April 1957), pp. 113–126.

———, "Plekhanov and the Origins of Russian Marxism," *Russian Review*, vol. 13, no. 1 (January 1954), pp. 38–51.

Baykalov, A., "A Brief Outline of the Russian Co-operative Movement," *Slavonic Review*, vol. 1, no. 1 (June, 1922), pp. 130–143.

Berlin, Isaiah, "Russia and 1848." *Slavonic Review*, vol. 26, no. 67 (April 1948), pp. 341–360.

Billington, James H., "The Intelligentsia and the Religion of Humanity," *American Historical Review*, vol. 65, no. 4 (July 1960), pp. 807–821.

Black, Cyril E., "The Nature of Imperial Russian Society," *Slavic Review*, vol. 20, no. 4 (December 1961), pp. 565–582.

Blumberg, Arnold, "Russian Policy and the Franco-Russian War of 1859," *Journal of Modern History*, vol. 26, no. 2 (June 1954), pp. 137–153.

Bolsover, G. H., "Nicholas I and the Partition of Turkey," *Slavonic Review*, vol. 27, no. 68 (December 1948), pp. 115–145.

Bowman, Herbert E., "Revolutionary Elitism in Černyševskij," *The American Slavic and East European Review*, vol. 13, no. 2 (April 1954), pp. 185–199.

Brown, Edward J., "The Circle of Stankevich," *The American Slavic and East European Review*, vol. 16, no. 3 (October 1957), pp. 349–368.

Bruce, Maurice W., "The Jacobites and Peter the Great (1721–1725)," *Slavonic Review*, vol. 14, no. 41 (January 1936), pp. 343–362.

Burgess, M., "Fairs and Entertainers in 18th Century Russia," *Slavonic Review*, vol. 38, no. 90 (December 1959), pp. 95–113.

Burtsev, Vladimir, "Police Provocation in Russia," *Slavonic Review*, vol. 6, no. 17 (December 1927), pp. 247–267.

Cheshire, Harold T., "The Radicals of the Sixties and their Leaders," *Slavonic Review*, vol. 1, no. 1 (June 1922), pp. 110–120.

Clark, Chester W., "Prince Gorchakov and the Black Sea Question," *American Historical Review*, vol. 48, no. 1 (October 1942), pp. 52–60.

Cloutier, H. Handley, "Belinsky—Advocate of Liberty," *Russian Review*, vol. 8, no. 1 (January 1949), pp. 20–33.

Cox, F. J., "Khedive Ismail and Pan-Slavism," *Slavonic Review*, vol. 32, no. 78 (December 1953), pp. 151–167.

Crisp, Olga, "Some Problems of French Investment in Russian Joint-stock Companies," *Slavonic Review*, vol. 35, no. 84 (December 1956), pp. 223–240.

———, "The State Peasants Under Nicholas I," *Slavonic Review*, vol. 37, no. 89 (June 1959), pp. 387–412.

Curtiss, John Shelton, "The Army of Nicholas I: It's Role and Character," *American Historical Review*, vol. 63, no. 4 (July 1958), pp. 880–889.

Dailey, Kenneth I., "Alexander Isvolsky and the Buchlau Conference," *Russian Review*, vol. 10, no. 1 (January 1951), pp. 55–63.

Dmytryshyn, Basil, "The Economic Content of the 1767 Nakaz of Catherine II," *The American Slavic and East European Review*, vol. 14, no. 1 (February 1960), pp. 1–9.

Dorpalen, Andreas, "Tsar Alexander III and the Boulanger Crisis in France," *Journal of Modern History*, vol. 23, no. 2 (June 1951), pp. 122–136.

Dvoichenko-Markov, Eufrosina, "Jefferson and the Decembrists," *The American Slavic and East European Review*, vol. 9, no. 3 (October 1950), pp. 162–168.

Dziewanowski, M. K., "Herzen, Bakunin, and the Polish Insurrection of 1863," *Journal of Central European Affairs*, vol. 8, no. 1 (April 1948), pp. 58–78.

Fay, Sidney B., "The Kaiser's Secret Negotiations with the Tsar, 1904–1905," *American Historical Review*, vol. 24, no. 1 (October 1918), pp. 48–72.

Fedotov, G. P., "The Religious Sources of Russian Populism," *Russian Review*, vol. 1, no. 2 (April 1942), pp. 27–39.

Florescu, Radu R., "British Reactions to the Russian Regime in the Danubian Principalities, 1828–1834," *Journal of Central European Affairs*, vol. 22, no. 1 (April 1962), pp. 27–42.

Florinsky, Michael, "Russian Social and Political Thought, 1825–1855," *Russian Review*, vol. 6, no. 2 (Spring 1947), pp. 77–85.

Frankel, Jonathan, "Economism: A Heresy Exploited," *Slavic Review*, vol. 22, no. 2 (June 1963), pp. 263–284.

Frederiksen, O. J., "Alexander I and his League to End Wars," *Russian Review*, vol. 3, no. 1 (Autumn 1943), pp. 10–22.

Godwin, Robert, "Russia and the Portsmouth Peace Conference," *The American Slavic and East European Review*, vol. 9, no. 4 (December 1950), pp. 279–291.

Golder, Frank A., "Catherine II and the American Revolution," *American Historical Review*, vol. 21, no. 1 (October 1915), pp. 92–96.

———, "The Purchase of Alaska," *American Historical Review*, vol. 25, no. 3 (April 1920), pp. 411–425.

———, "Russian-American Relations During the Crimean War," *American Historical Review*, vol. 31, no. 3 (April 1926), pp. 462–476.

———, "The Russian Fleet and the Civil War," *American Historical Review*, vol. 20, no. 4 (July 1915), pp. 801–812.

Goriainov, Serge, "The End of the Alliance of the Emperors," *American Historical Review*, vol. 23, no. 2 (January 1918), pp. 324–349.

Hammer, Oscar J., "Free Europe Versus Russia, 1830–1854," *The American Slavic and East European Review*, vol. 11, no. 1 (February 1952), pp. 27–41.

Hans, N., "Polish Schools in Russia, 1772–1831," *Slavonic Review*, vol. 38, no. 91 (June 1960), pp. 394–414.

Harcave, Sidney, "The Jews and the First Russian National Election," *The American Slavic and East European Review*, vol. 9, no. 1 (February 1950), pp. 33–41).

Hecht, David, "Lavrov, Chaikovski, and the United States," *The American Slavic and East European Review*, vol. 5, no. 1–2 (May 1946), pp. 138–161.

———, "Plekhanov and American Socialism," *Russian Review*, vol. 9, no. 2 (April 1950), pp. 112–123.

Heilbronner, Hans, "Alexander III and the Reform Plan of Loris-Melikov," *Journal of Modern History*, vol. 33, no. 4 (December 1961), pp. 384–397.

———, "The Russian Plague of 1878–79," *Slavic Review*, vol. 21, no. 1 (March 1962), pp. 89–112.

Hodgson, John H. "Finland's Position in the Russian Empire, 1905–1910," *Journal of Central European Affairs*, vol. 20, no. 2 (July 1960), pp. 158–173.

Horvath, Eugene, "Russia and the Hungarian Revolution (1848–1849)," *Slavonic Review*, vol. 12, no. 36 (April 1934), pp. 628–643.

Jelavich, Charles and Barbara, "Jomini and the Revival of the Dreikaiserbund, 1879–1880," *Slavonic Review*, vol. 35, no. 85 (June 1957), pp. 523–550.

Jelavich, Charles, "Russo-Bulgarian Relations, 1892–1896: with Particular Reference to the Problem of the Bulgarian Succession," *Journal of Modern History*, vol. 24, no. 4 (December 1952), pp. 341–351.

Kadic, Ante, "Vladimir Soloviev and Bishop Strossmayer," *The American Slavic and East European Review*, vol. 20, no. 2 (April 1961), pp. 163–188.

Kahan, Arcadius, "The Costs of "Westernization" in Russia: The Gentry and the Economy in the Eighteenth Century," *Slavic Review*, vol. 25, no. 1, (March 1966), pp. 40–66.

Kaplan, Frederick I, "Russian Fourierism of the 1840's: A Contrast to Herzen's Westernism," *The American Slavic and East European Review*, vol. 17, no. 2 (April, 1958), pp. 161–172.

Kazemzadeh, F., "The Origin and Development of the Persian Cossack Brigade," *The American Slavic and East European Review*, vol. 15, no. 3 (October 1956), pp. 351–363.

Keep, J. L. H., "Russian Social Democracy and the First State Duma," *Slavonic Review*, vol. 34, no. 82 (December 1955), pp. 180–199.

Kerensky, Alexander, "Russia on the Eve of World War I," *Russian Review*, vol. 5, no. 1 (Autumn 1945), pp. 10–30.

Kimball, Stanley B., "The Prague 'Slav Congress' of 1848," *Journal of Central European Affairs*, vol. 22, no. 2 (July 1962), pp. 174–199.

King, Vladimir, "The Liberal Movement in Russia, 1904–1905," *Slavonic Review*, vol. 14, no. 40 (July 1935), pp. 124–137.

Kirchner, Walther "The Death of Catherine I of Russia," *American Historical Review*, vol. 51, no. 2 (January 1946), pp. 254–261.

————, "Emigration to Russia," *American Historical Review*, vol. 55, no. 3 (April 1950), pp. 552–561.

Koyre, A., "Russia's Place in the World: Peter Chaadayev and the Slavophiles," *Slavonic Review*, vol. 5, no. 15 (March 1927), pp. 594–608.

Kucherov, Samuel, "The Jury as Part of the Russian Judicial Reform of 1864," *The American Slavic and East European Review*, vol. 9, no. 2 (April 1950), pp. 77–90.

————, "Administration of Justice under Nicholas I of Russia," *The American Slavic and East European Review*, vol. 7, no. 2 (April 1948), pp. 125–138.

Lang, David M., "Radishchev and the Legislative Commission of Alexander I," *The American Slavic and East European Review*, vol. 6, no. 18–19 (December 1947), pp. 11–24.

Langer, William L., "The Franco-Russian Alliance," *Slavonic Review*, vol. 3, no. 9 (March 1925), pp. 554–575; vol. 4, no. 10 (June 1925), pp. 83–100.

Lanz, Henry, "The Philosophy of Ivan Kireyevsky," *Slavonic Review*, vol. 4, no. 12 (March 1926), pp. 594–604.

Laserson, Max M., "Alexander Radishchev—An Early Admirer of America," *Russian Review*, vol. 9, no. 3 (July 1950), pp. 179–186.

Lavrin, Janko, "Chaadayev and the West," *Russian Rievew*, vol. 22, no. 3 (July 1963), pp. 274–288.

————, "Khomyakov and the Slavs," *Russian Review*, vol. 23, no. 1 (January 1964), pp. 36–48.

————, "Kireevsky and the Problem of Culture," *Russian Review*, vol. 20, no. 2 (April 1961), pp. 110–120.

————, "Populists and Slavophiles," *Russian Review*, vol. 21, no. 4 (October 1962), pp. 307–317.

————, "Vladimir Soloviev and Slavophilism," *Russian Review*, vol. 20, no. 1 (January 1961), pp. 11–18.

Lednicki, W., "Pushkin, Tyutchev, Mickiewicz and the Decembrists: Legend and Facts," *Slavonic Review*, Vol. 29, no. 73, (June 1951), pp. 375–401.

Lehovich, Dimitry, "The Testament of Peter the Great," *The American Slavic and East European Review*, vol. 7, no. 2 (April 1948), pp. 111–124.

Lensen, George Alexander, "Russians in Japan, 1858–1859," *Journal of Modern History*. vol. 26, no. 2 (June 1954), pp. 162–173.

Levin, Alfred, "The Russian Voter in the Elections to the Third Duma," *Slavic Review*, vol. 21, no. 4 (December 1962), pp. 660–677.

Lewitter, L. R., "Peter the Great and the Polish Dissenters," *Slavonic Review*, vol. 33, no. 80 (December 1954), pp. 75–101.

Lipski, Alexander, "A Re-examination of the 'Dark Era' of Anna Ioannovna," *The American Slavic and East European Review*, vol. 15, no. 4 (December 1956), pp. 477–488.

Loewenson, L., "The Death of Paul I and the Memoirs of Benningsen," *Slavonic Review*, vol. 29, no. 72 (December 1950), pp. 212–232.

————, "People Peter the Great Met in England, Mesrs Stringer, Chymist and Physician," *Slavonic Review*, vol. 37, no. 89 (June 1959), pp. 459–468.

Lord, Robert H., "Bismarck and Russia in 1863," *American Historical Review*, vol. 29, no. 1 (October 1923), pp. 24–48.

Luthin, Reinhard H., "The Sale of Alaska," *Slavonic Review*, vol. 16, no. 46 (July 1937), pp. 168–182.

MacKenzie, David, "Pan-Slavism in Practice: Cherniaev in Serbia (1876)," *Journal of Modern History*, vol. 36, no. 3 (September 1964), pp. 279–297.

MacMaster, Robert E., "Danilevsky and Spengler: A New Interpretation," *Journal of Modern History*, vol. 26, no. 2 (June 1954), pp. 154–161.

de Madariaga, Isabel, "The Secret Austro-Russian Treaty of 1781," *Slavonic Review*, vol. 38, no. 90 (December 1959), pp. 114–145.

Maklakov, V., "The Agrarian Problem in Russia before the Revolution," *Russian Review*, vol. 9, no. 1 (January 1950), 3–15.

Mazour, Anatole G., "Modern Russian Historiography," *Journal of Modern History*, vol. 9, no. 2 (June 1937), pp. 169–202.

————, "Russia and Prussia during the Schleswig-Holstein Crisis," *Journal of Central European Affairs*, vol. 1, no. 3 (October 1941), pp. 275–287.

McConnell, Allen, "Abbe Raynal and a Russian Philosophe," *Jahrbücher Für Geschichte Osteuropas*, New Series, vol. 12, no. 4 (February 1965), pp. 499–512.

————, "The Empress and her Protége: Catherine II and Radishchev," *Journal of Modern History*, vol. 36, no. 1 (March 1964), pp. 14–27.

————, "Radishchev's Political Thought," *The American Slavic and East European Review*, vol. 17, no. 4 (December 1958), pp. 439–453.

McNally, Raymond T., "Chaadaev's Evaluation of Peter the Great," *Slavic Review*, vol. 23, no. 1 (March 1964), pp. 31–44.

————, "The Origins of Russophobia in France: 1812–1830," *The American Slavic and East European Review*, vol. 17, no. 2 (April 1958), pp. 173–189.

Miller, Hunter, "Russian Opinion on the Cession of Alaska," *American Historical Review*, vol. 48, no. 3 (April 1943), pp. 521–531.

Milyukov, Paul, "The Influence of English Political Thought in Russia," *Slavonic Review*, vol. 5, no. 14 (December 1926), pp. 258–270.

Mirsky, Prince D. S., "The Decembrists," *Slavonic Review*, vol. 4, no. 11 (December 1925), pp. 400–424.

Morley, Charles, "Alexander I and Czartoryski," *Slavonic Review*, vol. 25, no. 65 (April 1947), pp. 405–426.

Mosley, Philip E., "Russian Policy in Asia (1838–1839)," *Slavonic Review*, vol. 14, no. 42 (April 1936), pp. 670–681.

Moser, Charles A., "A Nihilist's Career: S. M. Stepniak-Kravchinskij," *The American Slavic and East European Review*, vol. 20, no. 1 (February 1961), pp. 55–71.

Mosse, W. E., "The Russians at Villafranca," *Slavonic Review*, vol. 30, no. 75 (June 1952), pp. 425–443.

Nagengast, William E., "The Visit of the Russian Fleet to the United States: Were Americans Deceived?," *Russian Review*, vol. 8, no. 1 (January 1949), pp. 46–55.

O'Brien, C. Bickford, "Ivan Pososhkov: Russian Critic of Mercantilist Principles," *The American Slavic and East European Review*, vol. 14, no. 4 (December 1955), pp. 503–511.

Packard, Laurence B., "Russia and the Dual Alliance," *American Historical Review*, vol. 25, no. 3 (April 1920), pp. 391–410.

Papmehl, K. A., "The Problem of Civil Liberties in the Records of the Great Commission," *Slavonic Review*, vol. 42, no. 99 (June 1964), pp. 274–291.

Parry, Albert, "Yankee Whalers in Siberia," *Russian Review*, vol. 5, no. 2 (Spring 1946), pp. 36–49.

Patridge, Monica, "Alexander Herzen and the English Press," *Slavonic Review*, vol. 36, no. 87 (June 1958), pp. 453–470.

Pedler, Anne, "Going to the People: The Narodniki of the Seventies," *Slavonic Review*, vol. 6, no. 16 (June 1927), pp. 130–141.

Perkins, Dexter, "Russia and the Spanish Colonies, 1817–1818," *American Historical Review*, vol. 28, no. 4 (July 1923), pp. 656–672.

Petrovich, Michael B., "Juraj Križanič: A Precursor of Pan-Slavism," *The American Slavic and East European Review*, vol. 6, no. 18–19 (December 1957), pp. 75–92.

———, "Ludovit Štur and Russian Pan-Slavism," *Journal of Central European Affairs*, vol. 12, no. 1 (April 1952), pp. 1–19.

Pipes, Richard, "Narodnichestvo: A Semantic Inquiry," *Slavic Review*, vol. 23, no. 3 (September 1964), pp. 441–458.

———, "Russian Marxism and its Populist Background: The Late Nineteenth Century," *Russian Review*, vol. 19, no. 4 (October 1960), pp. 316–337.

———, "The Russian Military Colonies, 1810–1831," *Journal of Modern History*, vol. 22, no. 3 (September 1950), pp. 205–219.

Puryear, Vernon J., "New Light on the Origins of the Crimean War," *Journal of Modern History*, vol. 3, no. 2 (June 1931), pp. 219–234.

Radkey, Oliver H., "An Alternative to Bolshevism: The Program of Russian Social Revolutionism," *Journal of Modern History*, vol. 25, no. 1 (March 1953), pp. 25–39.

Raeff, Marc, "The Political Philosophy of Speranskij," *The American Slavic and East European Review*, vol. 12, no. 1 (February 1953), pp. 1–21.

———, "A Reactionary Liberal: M. N. Katkov," *Russian Review*, vol. 11, no. 3 (July 1952), pp. 157–167.

———, "State and Nobility in the Ideology of M. M. Shcherbatov," *The American Slavic and East European Review*, vol. 19, no. 3 (October 1960), pp. 363–379.

Riasanovsky, Nicholas V., "Fourierism in Russia: An Estimate of the Petraševcy," *The American Slavic and East European Review*, vol. 12, no. 3 (October 1953), pp. 289–302.

Rodichev, Fedor, "The Liberal Movement in Russia (1855–1917)," *Slavonic*

Review, vol. 2, no. 4 (June 1923), pp. 1–13, no. 5 (December 1923), pp. 249–262.

———, "The Veteran of Russian Liberalism: Ivan Petrunkevich," *Slavonic Review*, vol. 7, no. 20 (January 1929), pp. 316–326.

Schmidt, Hans A., "1812: Stein, Alexander I and the Crusade Against Napoleon," *Journal of Modern History*, vol. 31, no. 4 (December 1959), pp. 325–338.

Schmitt, Bernadotte E., "The Diplomatic Preliminaries of the Crimean War," *American Historical Review*, vol. 25, no. 1 (October 1919), pp. 36–67.

Serech, J., "Stefan Yavorsky and the Conflict of Ideologies in the Age of Peter the Great," *Slavonic Review*, vol. 30, no. 74 (December 1951), pp. 40–62.

Seton-Watson, R. W., "Russian Commitments in the Bosnian Question and an Early Project of Annexation," *Slavonic Review*, vol. 8, no. 24 (March 1930), pp. 578–587.

Sokol, A. E., "Russian Expansion and Exploration in the Pacific," *The American Slavic and East European Review*, vol. 11, no. 2 (April 1952), pp. 85–105.

Stojanovic, J. D., "Russian Slavophil Philosophy: Homyakov and Kireyevsky," *Slavonic Review*, vol. 6, no. 18 (March 1928), pp. 560–578.

Strakhovsky, L. I., "Count N. P. Ignat'yev, Reformer of Russian Education," *Slavonic Review*, vol. 36, no. 86 (December 1957), pp. 1–26.

———, "General Count N. P. Ignatiev and the Pan-Slav Movement," *Journal of Central European Affairs*, vol. 17, no. 3 (October 1957), pp. 223–235.

———, "The Statesmanship of Peter Stolypin: A Reappraisal," *Slavonic Review*, vol. 37, no. 89 (June 1959), pp. 348–370.

Tompkins, Stuart R., "The Russian Bible Society," *The American Slavic and East European Review*, vol. 7, no. 3 (October 1948), pp. 251–268.

Treadgold, Donald W., "The Constitutional Democrats and the Russian Liberal Tradition," *The American Slavic and East European Review*, vol. 10, no. 2 (April 1951), pp. 85–94.

———, "Was Stolypin in Favor of the Kulaks," *The American Slavic and East European Review*, vol. 14, no. 1 (February 1955), pp. 1–14.

Tyrkova-Williams, A., "The Cadet Party," *Russian Review*, vol. 12, no. 3 (July 1953·), pp. 173–186.

Von Laue, Theodore H., "Count Witte and the Russian Revolution of 1905," *The American Slavic and East European Review*, vol. 17, no. 1 (February 1958), pp. 25–46.

———, "The Industrialization of Russia in the Writings of Sergej Witte," *The American Slavic and East European Review*, vol. 10, no. 3 (October 1951), 177–190.

———, "Tsarist Labor Policy, 1895–1903," *Journal of Modern History*, vol. 34, no. 2 (June, 1962), 135–145.

———, "The Vitte System in Mid-passage, 1896–1899," *Jahrbücher Für Geschichte Osteuropas*, New Series, vol. 8, no. 2 (July 1960), pp. 195–229.

Yaney, George L., "The Concept of the Stolypin Land Reform," *Slavic Review*, vol. 23, no. 2 (June 1964), pp. 275–293.

Zyzniewski, Stanley J., "The Futile Compromise Reconsidered: Wielopolski and Russian Policy in the Congress Kingdom, 1861–1863," *American Historical Review*, vol. 70, no. 2 (January 1965), pp. 395–412.